Private Equity

A Transactional Analysis, Third Edition
Consulting Editor **Chris Hale**

Consulting editor
Chris Hale

Managing director
Sian O'Neill

Editorial services director
Carolyn Boyle

Production manager
Neal Honney

Group publishing director
Tony Harriss

Private Equity: A Transactional Analysis, Third Edition
is published by
Globe Law and Business
Globe Business Publishing Ltd
New Hibernia House
Winchester Walk
London SE1 9AG
United Kingdom
Tel +44 20 7234 0606
Fax +44 20 7234 0808
www.globelawandbusiness.com

Print and bound by CPI Group (UK) Ltd, Croydon, CR0 4YY

ISBN 9781909416215

Private Equity: A Transactional Analysis, Third Edition
© 2015 Globe Business Publishing Ltd

All rights reserved. No part of this publication may be reproduced in any material form (including photocopying, storing in any medium by electronic means or transmitting) without the written permission of the copyright owner, except in accordance with the provisions of the Copyright, Designs and Patents Act 1988 or under terms of a licence issued by the Copyright Licensing Agency Ltd, 6-10 Kirby Street, London EC1N 8TS, United Kingdom (www.cla.co.uk, email: licence@cla.co.uk). Applications for the copyright owner's written permission to reproduce any part of this publication should be addressed to the publisher.

DISCLAIMER
This publication is intended as a general guide only. The information and opinions which it contains are not intended to be a comprehensive study or to provide legal or financial advice, and should not be treated as a substitute for legal or financial advice concerning particular situations. Legal or financial advice should always be sought before taking any action based on the information provided. The publishers bear no responsibility for any errors or omissions contained herein.

Table of contents

Introduction —— 5
    Chris Hale
    Travers Smith

Private equity restructuring —— 11
    Justin Bickle
    Oaktree

The place of private equity —— 21
in corporate finance and
mergers and acquisitions
    Justin Bickle
    Oaktree

Private equity fund —— 31
structures – the limited
partnership
    Jonathan Blake
    Lorraine Robinson
    King & Wood Mallesons LLP
    (formerly SJ Berwin LLP)

Equity finance —— 53
    Helen Croke
    Travers Smith

Debt finance —— 73
    Kirstie Hutchinson
    Christopher Lawrence
    Macfarlanes LLP

Acquisition documentation —— 107
    Richard Lever
    Lorraine Robinson
    King & Wood Mallesons LLP
    (formerly SJ Berwin LLP)

Due diligence —— 137
    Tom Evans
    Benedict Nwaeke
    David Walker
    Latham & Watkins

Performance of private —— 169
equity
    Barry Griffiths
    Landmark Partners LLC
    Rüdiger Stucke
    Warburg Pincus LLC

Regulation —— 185
    Amy Mahon
    Clifford Chance LLP

Tax structuring and —— 195
management
    Kathleen Russ
    Travers Smith

Public-to-privates —— 221
    Graham Gibb
    Charles Martin
    Macfarlanes LLP

Benelux —— 259
    Gaike Dalenoord
    Elke Janssens
    Margaretha Wilkenhuysen
    NautaDutilh

France ———————————— 287
    Maud Manon
    Xavier Norlain
    Jeremy Scemama
    Guillaume Valois
    DLA Piper

Germany ———————————— 309
    Georg Schneider
    Noerr LLP

Italy ———————————— 335
    Raimondo Premonte
    Donato Romano
    Gianni Origoni Grippo Cappelli
    & Partners

Spain ———————————— 351
    Fernando de las Cuevas
    Pío García-Escudero
    Gomez-Acebo & Pombo

Sweden ———————————— 363
    Jens Bengtsson
    Malin Leffler
    Roschier

Private equity deals in ———— 375
the United States: separated
from the United Kingdom by
a common language?
    Lilian Lardy
    Howard Sobel
    Huw Thomas
    David Walker
    Latham & Watkins

About the authors ———————— 393

Introduction

Chris Hale
Travers Smith LLP

1. **Background**

Fifteen years ago, private equity was known as venture capital and operated at the fringes of corporate finance and corporate activity. By 2007 it had taken centre stage, with many household names and some large companies becoming private equity-owned. The post-Lehman financial crisis posed tough challenges for private equity but it emerged from that crisis in much better shape than many had predicted. So what is private equity, and why did it become so successful that it was viewed in some western economies as central to corporate finance and mergers and acquisitions activity?

In the United Kingdom, continental Europe and much of the rest of the world, 'private equity' means the equity financing of unquoted companies at many stages in their lifecycle, from start-up to expansion to management buyouts and buy-ins of established companies. 'Venture capital' is seen, in the United Kingdom at least, as a subset of private equity, covering the seed to expansion stages of investments.

The key elements of private equity are:
- investments in unquoted companies;
- equity capital by nature;
- medium- to long-term investments; and
- targeted at companies with growth potential.

Private equity is invested in exchange for a stake in a company; as shareholders, the investors' returns are dependent on the cash flows, growth and profitability of the business. Private equity emerged on the UK landscape in the post-war period, and saw its key period of growth from the late 1980s and in particular from the late 1990s. In 1981 there were just 44 private equity firms active in the United Kingdom, according to the British Private Equity & Venture Capital Association (BVCA). The BVCA now has some 200 private equity house members.

The Centre for Management Buyout Research (CMBOR) reported that in 1986 there were 370 buyouts in the United Kingdom, in which £1.4 billion was invested. By 1996 the number had risen to 647 and the amount invested to £7.7 billion. In 2007 – the high-water year in terms of value – there were 630 buyouts, in which £46.5 billion was invested. The consequences of the recent financial crisis can be seen in the statistics for 2009: only 370 deals were recorded by CMBOR, and just £5.5 billion was invested in these transactions. By 2013 the value of buyouts had shown considerably recovery, to £15.8 billion for that year according to CMBOR. Volumes, though, had not, 367 being recorded for 2013.[1]

Introduction

2. **How important is private equity?**

Each year, for nine years up to February 2008, the BVCA commissioned research from IE Consulting on the economic impact of private equity. The February 2008 report indicated as follows:

- Companies that have received private equity backing account for the employment of around 3 million people in the United Kingdom, equivalent to 21% of the UK private sector workforce. Approximately 1.1 million people were employed at the time of the report by companies then backed by private equity, equivalent to 8% of UK private sector employees;
- Private equity-backed companies generated total sales of £310 billion and contributed more than £35 billion in taxes; and
- Over the five years to 2006/2007, employment rates and sales all grew faster in private equity-backed companies than in FTSE 100 and FTSE Mid-250 companies.

This research also showed that during the five-year period to 2006/2007, UK private equity-backed companies increased their worldwide staff levels by an average of 8% per annum. This was significantly faster than the rate of growth of FTSE 100 and FTSE Mid-250 companies, at 0.4% and 3% respectively.

The effect of private equity on employment has in recent years been a particularly contentious issue. Research conducted by CMBOR on the employment effects of buyouts since 1985 broadly supports the IE Consulting findings, although there does seem to be a difference between management buyouts and management buy-ins, with the latter experiencing slower employment growth.

Private equity is even more important to those working in the mergers and acquisitions market. According to research published by CMBOR, buyouts accounted for 47% by number and 49% by value of total UK mergers and acquisitions in 2005, percentages sustained in the years leading up to the onset of the financial crisis. Reflecting the low level of UK mergers and acquisitions activity since 2008, these proportions have risen in recent years with buyouts accounting for 60% of UK mergers and acquisitions volume in 2013 and 67% of value.

In each of the three years up to 2008, record amounts were raised by private equity fund managers; $10 billion-plus funds became almost common. It is in part a result of this sheer weight of money that private equity pushed into ever-larger deal territory, in 2007 in particular. That year saw the first, and so far only, take-private of a FTSE 100 company: Alliance Boots.

The financial crisis caused private equity fund raising to slump but by 2013, according to research group Preqin, it had recovered to levels approaching those seen before the financial crisis. Indeed Preqin reported that at the end of September 2014 a record high of $1.19 trillion was available to private equity fund managers for investment globally. Funds of $10 billion or more disappeared from the landscape for

---

1   The CMBOR statistics cover both private equity-backed and other buyouts. Recently CMBOR has started recording separate figures for private equity. In 2007 CMBOR reports there were 324 private equity backed buyouts with a value of £44.1 billion. In 2009 it was 118 buyouts with a value of £4.9 billion, and in 2013 193 buyouts with a value of £15.1 billion.

a few years but in 2013 and 2014 began to return with, for example, Carlyle and Hellman & Freidman raising funds of this scale. Multi-billion dollar buyouts have also returned in the United States: the $24.9 billion Dell buyout of 2013 showing that in spectacular fashion. Such huge buyouts have yet, though, to return to the United Kingdom.

3. **The geography of private equity**
As Justin Bickle reveals in his chapter "The place of private equity in corporate finance and mergers and acquisitions", the United States has been the main driving force of the growth of private equity. Indeed, private equity is still heavily concentrated there and in the United Kingdom. According to a report published by Apax Partners in 2006, entitled *Unlocking global value – future trends in private equity Investment worldwide*, in the first 10 months of 2005 North America (including Canada) accounted for 50% of all new private equity funds raised globally. In the same period, 75% of all private equity investment (including venture capital) was made in the United States. Europe was then responsible for the vast bulk of the world's remaining private equity transactions, with the United Kingdom being by some way the largest European market. This Apax report attempted to rank 33 countries by how congenial their private equity environment was, measured by various criteria. The bottom two countries in this table were those carrying the greatest expectation of private equity development for the future: India and China. Since 2006, private equity investment has picked up considerably in Asia in particular, but there is a long way to go before private equity activity even in China, let alone parts of the world such as South America and Africa, comes to rival activity in the United States, the United Kingdom and other parts of western Europe.

4. **What about private equity performance?**
A study published by CMBOR in 2005 revealed that, for institutional investors, "[t]he most important reasons for investing in private equity are to achieve a greater return relative to other asset classes, to diversify the portfolio and to obtain a positive annual return". Is it right that private equity fund managers have indeed produced superior returns in this way? Regrettably, this has been one of the most difficult issues on which to obtain reliable information. Those with such information – investors in private equity funds and the fund managers – tended to keep it to themselves. Data sets of information are now appearing though. Perhaps the most complete are the Burgiss statistics, which have been used by Barry Griffiths and Rudiger Stucke who have written a new chapter for this edition on "The performance of private equity". They articulate some of the difficulties in assessing private equity returns, and look at the most common measures being used now to analyse those returns. As they point out, while classes of private equity have often, perhaps usually, beaten the Standard & Poor's 500 Total Return Index, on a risk-adjusted basis, they should do so materially.

What can be said is that it is highly likely that top quartile funds probably do beat public company indices materially. It is also the case, as Preqin surveys regularly show, that investors in private equity funds are overwhelmingly happy with the returns they obtain and are keen to continue investing in the asset class.

5. **Why have at least upper-quartile private equity funds outperformed listed investments?**

The reasons for upper-quartile funds at least materially outperforming listed assets are no doubt complex. It has been said that private equity made its money by leverage in the 1980s, by price/earnings multiple arbitrage in the 1990s and since then by genuinely changing companies. In fact, all three components have always played their part. Perhaps, though, one of the key reasons is the unique corporate governance structure of private equity, involving as it does active monitoring by private equity investors, high leverage and the concentration of equity under management control. This last element in particular creates a much more complete alignment of interest between a private equity fund manager and the senior executives that fund manager is backing to run a business than is the case in the listed company environment. As Paul Myners – who was a minister in the last Labour government, and who held senior positions at Gartmore and wrote a report at the request of Her Majesty's Treasury published in 2001 on institutional investment in the United Kingdom – said in a lecture given in Cambridge in May 2003:

> *Overly diversified portfolios with a significant number of underweight holdings mean there is little economic incentive for the fund manager (individually or organisationally) to adopt the mind-set of an owner and behave accordingly. If there is any sense of 'ownership' it applies to a portfolio as a whole and how individual securities interact to affect risk relative to benchmark – there is little focus on ownership responsibility towards individual companies. We thus have a critical vacuum in governance – no-one actually takes on the responsibility of ownership ...*
>
> *For the past year I have been chairing an unlisted company financed by private equity. I have been struck by the extent to which this ownership model leads to strong and effective governance focused on the aligned interest of owners and management. All are working to a common agenda, with shareholders fully engaged on strategic issues and in receipt of timely and complete management information going well beyond financial reporting. Contrast this with the situation for a public limited company where shareholder engagement on strategy is almost non-existent (reactive at best) and reporting is formulaic and limited in its inter-activity.*

6. **Private equity scrutiny and emergence from financial crisis**

As private equity moved in the first decade of this century to centre stage in some of the largest western economies, the authorities in those countries took a much greater interest in private equity and the way it operated. In November 2006 the Financial Services Authority (FSA), as it then was, published a paper entitled *Private equity: a discussion of risk and regulatory engagement*. While this, and the subsequent feedback paper which appeared in June 2007, gave private equity a qualified bill of health, the industry has had to become accustomed to much greater attention from regulators.

At the time the FSA was publishing these papers, private equity was the subject of a sustained attack by the GMB trades union and others. They charged that the industry made its money by loading acquisitions with debt, stripping assets, cutting jobs and using the extra cash flow from investee companies to pay itself huge dividends and then dodging tax on the wealth it generated. Very little of this criticism stood up to serious scrutiny.

This type of regulatory and union attention was not assisted by the understandable desire of private equity fund managers to keep their activities private. When private equity is analysed from a government perspective, it by and large comes out well. All surveys indicate that limited partners and fund investors are satisfied with the level of detail and information they receive from the private equity fund managers they back. The governance model between the private equity fund managers and the companies in which they work could be said to be superior to that of other comparators. The difficulty was that private equity fund managers in the years leading up to the financial crisis invested in very large companies in which a substantial wider community felt it had a stake. The stakeholders took the view that they were entitled to information about the companies in which their stake existed. The private equity world was slow to respond, not least because it had never had to grapple with these types of comments and criticisms before.

The response in the United Kingdom was the Walker Guidelines on disclosure and transparency. Because these guidelines apply only to larger companies, and even then only to companies that generate 50% of their revenues in the United Kingdom, their effects are relatively limited. They are designed to ensure greater disclosure on the part of companies that satisfy the criteria and greater disclosure on the part of private equity firms investing in those companies. The portfolio companies that are required to comply with the guidelines amounted to just 71 in total as of December 2014. A Guidelines Monitoring Group was established to monitor conformity with the guidelines and each December it publishes an annual report. The benchmark against which the group measures compliance is the FTSE 350, and on the whole the December 2014 report gives those companies subject to the guidelines and their private equity backers good marks.

Voluntary measures such as these turned out not to be enough, however. The private equity and hedge fund industries came under heavy attack in late 2008 from certain European Parliament members. This criticism gathered momentum and resulted in the publication by the European Commission in April 2009 of a draft directive, the Alternative Investment Fund Managers Directive (AIFMD). After intense debate and lobbying the directive was passed and is now in force in the European Union. It covers both hedge and private equity fund managers, and covers an enormous range, including the marketing of alternative investment funds, their authorisation, conflicts of interest and risk management, the need for independent valuers and independent depositories, and sweeping disclosure requirements. Amy Mahon in another chapter new to this edition, on regulation, discusses the asset stripping provisions of the AIFMD. The AIFMD has and will add substantially to the compliance burdens of private equity. Whether the costs associated with these burdens will produce benefits that justify them remains to be seen. The private equity industry is sceptical, but it will cope and adjust to the AIFMD as it will to the tide of other regulations which will continue to flow as a reaction to the financial crisis.

In the dark days following the collapse of Lehman, pessimistic commentators predicted that as many as a third of private equity fund managers then operating would go out of business and that many investee companies overburdened by debt would go bust or end up in the hands of banks. There was much talk of an approaching tsunami of debt maturity. These worst fears have not been realised. While a few private equity fund managers have not been able to raise new funds and may disappear (it takes a long time to kill off a private equity house because of the need to manage out investments already made), the vast majority have raised, or are likely to raise, new money. There have indeed been a number of new entrants to the private equity world since 2008.

Nor did the tsunami of debt defaults emerge. While conventional banks have to a greater or lesser degree retreated from leveraged buyouts, private debt funds, unitranche providers, a revived high-yield market and other sources of debt including new collateralised loan obligation funds have more than filled the gap. All this has provided enough liquidity to refinance much of the debt raised before 2008. 2014 has also been an exceptionally strong year for private equity exits – which has also helped cope with the pre-2008 debt issue.

Indeed 2014 saw debt pricing fall, covenant-light terms reappear and debt multiples increase. The challenge for private equity fund managers has not been either debt or equity availability – both are now plentiful – but the availability of good quality assets in which to invest.

The private equity industry has been through difficult periods before and will do so again. It has developed in waves. It has now emerged in good health from what appears to be (although this is still a tentative judgement) the worst of the financial crisis. Private equity is now an established part of institutional investors' portfolios and is likely to remain a significant part of corporate finance into the distant future.

7. **This book**

This book is intended to put private equity into context, to give some idea of its significance and, above all, to examine the nuts and bolts of private equity funds and the myriad issues associated with private equity deals. The principal focus – and indeed the assumption underlying much of what is in it – is that private equity equates to buyouts. While this is not the case in the United Kingdom, much of what is said here is of relevance to venture capital. The chapters in this book have been written by some of the leading practitioners in Europe. This third edition has not just been updated but substantially expanded, with new chapters on private equity performance and regulation, most western European jurisdictions and on the key differences between the terms of private equity deals in the United States and those in the United Kingdom. The book attempts to provide an introduction to those familiar with the mergers and acquisitions landscape, but not particularly with private equity, while also highlighting points of interest and guidance to more seasoned private equity practitioners.

Private equity restructuring

Justin Bickle
Oaktree

The onset of the summer 2007 financial crisis caused immediate and far-reaching shocks for the European private equity industry. This chapter explores private equity's approach to restructuring portfolio businesses and considers the tools that are available to financial sponsors when their underlying investments get into trouble.

1. **Why was private equity so exposed when the market turned?**
With the benefit of hindsight, before the onset of the financial crisis in August 2007, companies acquired by European private equity firms were much more highly levered and acquired at significantly higher acquisition multiples than equivalent buyouts undertaken by US private equity firms during 2006 and 2007. The glut of cheap debt financing, together with business plans that left room for little or no margin of error, meant that when the market correction came, coping with the downturn in Europe was destined to be prolonged and bloody for the majority of financial sponsors.

2. **Reaction of private equity to the financial crisis**
For the first 12 months of the credit crunch, most European mid-market private equity firms struggled to come to terms with the changed market and appeared not to know how to operate in such an alien environment. The market informally divided between:
- those with significant committed but unspent capital, which therefore fared relatively well;
- those whose problems were exacerbated by their reliance, in whole or part, on publicly listed funded vehicles; and
- those firms with no new funds, little operational know-how and limited experience in dealing with distressed portfolio businesses.

Therefore, 2008 was characterised, depending on the financial sponsor involved, as a time of either intense portfolio firefighting or of inactivity on the deal front as firms sought to hunker down, protect their existing investments and attempt to weather the economic storm.

By way of illustration, it has been suggested that during the 12 months up to August 2007, when the deal market changed, the top 10 private equity firms globally deployed around $120 billion in equity capital; in the 12 months following the collapse of Lehman Brothers in September 2008, those same top 10 firms deployed less than one-tenth of that amount. The lack of third-party debt financing meant that many transactions reached only preliminary stages at best and were seldom consummated. Fear and inertia won out over greed and deal making.

For most, the financial restructuring of portfolio companies became the new focus. The tools available to and most commonly deployed by financial sponsors are the subject of this chapter.

3. Considerations prior to financial restructuring

Each financial sponsor considered different factors when determining how and when to support its troubled portfolio companies. The most relevant factors fall into two broad categories: those relating to the portfolio as a whole and its reputation, and those relating to individual companies within the portfolio.

The questions arising with regard to portfolio/reputational issues included the following:

- How many portfolio companies were actually troubled in terms of being likely to default on their third-party debt facilities or requiring the injection of new money?
- For those companies that would default, what amount of equity would be required to avoid further defaults and/or cure the problem, either for the next 12 months or for the lifetime of the debt facilities?
- Did the financial sponsor have the funds available to make the necessary equity injection(s)?
- How would its limited partners react to multiple equity injections across its portfolios?
- Would injecting equity cause any issues between either different vintages of private equity funds or different limited partners across numerous fund vehicles?
- What would be the consequences for the sponsor if it did not financially restructure the portfolio company, aside from the loss of all or part of its original equity investment?
- Could the sponsor simply afford to walk away from its investment and would it be economically rational to do so?
- Had the sponsor already taken its equity out of the investment (known as a 'dividend recapitalisation') or made a return on its original investment during the bull market?
- Did the syndicate comprise financial institutions – whether banks, credit funds or collateralised loan obligations (CLOs)[1] – that had cross-exposure to a number of different portfolio companies of the financial sponsor, and therefore were important for relationship purposes in terms of these current investments or future investments by the sponsor when primary credit markets returned?

---

1   CLOs are structured investment vehicles which exist to make a return on an underlying pool of around 70 leveraged loans in different portfolio companies. Many of these specialist credit investors had significant exposure to the same troubled credits during the downturn and often found themselves opposite the same financial sponsors and their advisers in restructuring negotiations.

- Had the original deal team remained with the sponsor, been replaced or moved on?
- Would the sponsor's credibility and financial resources survive a contested battle with a bank syndicate that might wish to take control of the company and not permit the sponsor to be a significant shareholder in the business going forward?

The considerations with regard to individual companies included the following:
- Was the problem simply one of 'good company, bad balance sheet' (ie, the business itself was sound, but was hampered by too much leverage having been borrowed to fund the original acquisition), or had the downturn in fact exposed structural weaknesses in the underlying investment, which was unlikely to be profitable after all or to generate the originally anticipated investment rate of return?
- Was the business simply unduly cyclical and/or volatile, but likely to return to profitability once markets normalised?
- Was there any prospect of the sponsor's equity investment being 'in the money' in future if its product market recovered, even if at the present time the equity was wholly or partly impaired?
- If new money was required to be injected, would it be possible to make an appropriate return on equity employed so as to justify that incremental investment to the sponsor's limited partners?
- Would it be possible to keep equity control of the company irrespective of any new money offered up by the sponsor?

Although each sponsor weighted these factors according to its own financial strength, survival instincts and know-how at the time, the experience of the downturn was that the most successful sponsors were those that took proactive steps to address the financial issues relating to their portfolio businesses early, and coupled balance-sheet restructuring efforts with operational improvements. It is also noteworthy in the European context that the private equity mega-firms had relatively fewer problem portfolio companies than their peers in the European mid-market.

4. Financial restructuring: the process

For the first 12 months of the financial crisis, most sponsors underwent a significant learning process in understanding which restructuring tools were available to them, how these could be implemented and which advisers had experience to navigate them through the financial restructuring process itself.

In truth, financial restructuring techniques across Europe are still relatively unsophisticated compared to those in the United States, where Chapter 11 workout techniques have a long-established and reassuring track record in terms of timing and outcomes. Since the development of high-yield financing techniques in Europe in the 1990s, Europe had faced only one significant downturn before the 2007 crisis. This was in 2001 to 2003, when the defaulting companies had principally issued public bonds rather than private bank debt and were limited to the telecommunications, cable and energy sectors, which were not predominantly owned by private equity. As a result, many of the multi-tiered leveraged buy-out capital structures, often of a cross-border nature and featuring complex and detailed Luxembourg or Dutch tax vehicles, had not been the subject of previous workouts, leaving many of the basic principles unsettled, particularly in continental Europe, where earlier insolvency reforms were also not battle-tested. For financial sponsors and their restructuring advisers, this proved a frustrating education, with experienced advisers overworked, in short supply and commanding premium fee rates.

As a hedge against many of the documentary shortcomings exposed by the financial crisis, before commencing restructuring discussions with their lenders, most sponsors supplemented or replaced their original legal teams who had authored the original buyouts with specialist restructuring lawyers and bankers, paid for by the companies that were themselves troubled. Due to market convention, each stakeholder in the capital structure usually retained its own financial and legal advisers paid for by the portfolio company, making each financial restructuring process protracted, complex and very expensive in terms of professional fees.

As a first step, sponsors usually asked the company's restructuring lawyers (often the same firm advising the sponsor):

- to prepare advice on the company's corporate structure, where the financial debt resided and the respective rights and remedies available to the financial creditors and other stakeholders;
- to produce a roadmap as to how a consensual restructuring would be undertaken, either in or out of court; and
- to consider the options open to the company and the sponsor if a consensual restructuring could not be achieved.

Often this legal analysis was the sponsor's early warning system against the potential leverage of difficult or unwieldy creditor groups, and usually provided at least an understanding of the tools that the sponsor might deploy to retain economic control, assuming that the sponsor wished to preserve its ownership option.

5. Financial restructuring: the tools

Although each balance-sheet restructuring is fact-specific, the following paragraphs outline the most common tools used by sponsors in the last downturn to restructure their underlying portfolio companies in circumstances of distress or anticipated default.

5.1 Equity cures

Often the first tool considered or used by the financial sponsor was injecting new money into the troubled company by means of an equity cure.

Equity cures were permitted by some of the less restrictive leveraged finance documents prepared during the bull market prior to August 2007, depending on the relative bargaining position of the underwriting banks, the relative aggressiveness and track record of the financial sponsor and the size of the debt finance involved. Equity cures were typically either earnings before interest, taxation, depreciation and amortisation (EBITDA)[2] cures or, less frequently, cashflow cures, depending on the terms of the financing documents, which were typically governed by English law.

EBITDA equity cures were more useful to sponsors than cashflow cures as every £1 of new equity injected by a sponsor, either ahead of or in response to a financial covenant default, counted as £1 towards the company's earnings (or EBITDA), typically for a 12-month period that covered four quarters for financial covenant calculation purposes. For most sponsors the EBITDA equity cure, if available, was a tempting first weapon in the restructuring toolbox insofar as a relatively small equity investment by the sponsor might not only restore the financial documents to full covenant compliance and pacify the lending syndicate, but also preserve the sponsor's optionality while it waited for markets to recover and for its equity value to return.

The reaction by bank syndicates to the use of EBITDA equity cures was generally positive, as the sponsor's conduct was viewed as supportive of the credit and a reaffirmation of its original investment thesis; moreover, the syndicate was spared any provision of its loans as being impaired or constituting bad debt if covenants were brought back into compliance and the injection of new money by the sponsor had an overall de-levering effect.

However, with hindsight, many of the EBITDA equity cures utilised by sponsors in the first year or so of the financial crisis amounted to only the first in a series of sticking plasters that gave temporary relief to the symptoms of financial distress, but did not address the root cause of the problem, which was the inherently over-levered nature of the portfolio company. Many of these cures were applied to companies with no actual ongoing equity value for sponsors, and led some limited partners to question why more of their funds were being used to prop up investments that were no longer capable of generating economic return for either the limited partners or the private equity firm in terms of carried interest.

5.2 Debt buy-backs

The second weapon in the sponsor's restructuring toolbox was buying back debt in its portfolio companies, often at a significant discount to its par value in the secondary trading market.

The first debt buy-backs in Spring 2008 caused considerable consternation among leveraged finance lawyers and banks that were significant participants in the European loan markets. Conceptually, the idea of buying back debt without triggering mandatory pre-payment provisions or requirements to treat all lenders rateably was anathema to most legal practitioners, save for those who typically advised private equity sponsors. Despite a vigorous debate in legal circles as to whether such buy-backs were appropriate or available, most London Market Association standard leveraged loan documents either did not expressly prohibit such buy-backs or gave the benefit of any documentary ambiguity to the sponsor.

The methods of navigating these loan document provisions were usually fairly innovative, and they sometimes crossed the line as to what was credible or logical.

---

[2] EBITDA is a common valuation tool used in private equity investments.

Although the conduct of debt buy-backs is a detailed and specialist topic outside the scope of this chapter, suffice it to say that the principal considerations when attempting any plan of debt purchases included the following:

- Was the debt buy-back permitted as a matter of law or with respect to the actual financing documents governed the loan?
- If it was permissible, what were the tax implications?[3]
- Was it preferable or necessary for the company itself to repurchase the debt or should the sponsor do so, usually via a special purpose entity incorporated for that purpose?
- What part of the debt repurchased would count against relevant covenant calculations and for what duration?
- What would be the implications, if any, for the company or the sponsor if the debt buy-back were undertaken, but the portfolio company then filed for insolvency in any jurisdiction?[4]
- How would the lending syndicate react to the buy-back? Should it be done in a transparent and uniform fashion with prior notification of the sponsor's intention, or should the syndicate be formally notified after the buy-back had already occurred?[5]

Again, with hindsight, the sponsor debt buy-backs that occurred during 2008 and 2009 had a mixed track record in practice. The principal criticism made was not that this was a wholly unmeritorious use of limited partners' moneys by sponsors without the necessary credit skills, but that in a number of instances the wrong debt tranche was repurchased by the sponsor or the company, usually on the basis that its secondary trading price was excessively cheap compared to other more senior debt tranches. Although the subsequent rally in secondary market prices throughout 2009 and 2010 vindicated the actions of some sponsors to repurchase second-lien or mezzanine debt at very low prices in 2008, certain sponsors came to rue the fact that they had exhausted limited partners' funds in acquiring debt securities that then turned out to have no economic interest in restructuring negotiations, and that there would have been more strategic and practical benefit in purchasing the first-lien debt in the secondary market so as to best position themselves for a successful negotiation with their syndicate banks or to best preserve their equity option.[6]

---

3 In late 2009, in the United Kingdom, Her Majesties Revenue and Customs tightened the loophole affecting debt buy-backs, as it was said that the favourable tax treatment on such buy-backs made them too attractive from a tax perspective.
4 Certain European jurisdictions (eg, Germany and Spain) have doctrines of equitable subordination, meaning that in certain circumstances a party holding equity and debt on the insolvency of a company can find that its debt interests are treated as equity too.
5 Some sponsors sought to effect buy-backs using special purpose vehicles without fanfare in the secondary market and announced this fact to lenders only after the event, sometimes attributing novel accounting treatments to the debt that had been repurchased for covenant calculation purposes. Other sponsors announced their intentions to buy back debt at specific prices through formal tender offers or Dutch auctions organised by investment banks on their behalf.
6 It became clear after the event that certain sponsors had also purchased debt directly from their original underwriting banks at levels below or close to par in circumstances where the underwriting banks were stuck with significant debt that they had been unable to syndicate prior to the onset of the financial crisis. This allowed sponsors to de-lever the balance sheet without any risk of losing control, although it did also represent a significant doubling down on their original investment.

5.3 Covenant re-sets

As it became clear to sponsors that the financial crisis would be protracted, equity cures and debt buy-backs were supplemented by more formal requests from sponsors for covenant relief, often for prolonged periods. These requests, informally known as 'covenant re-sets', usually involved the financial sponsors agreeing to allow the company to retain one of the Big Four accountancy firms or other specialised restructuring consultants to undertake an independent review of the business with a legal duty of care owed to the lenders. This report would give an update on the performance of the business in question, provide some commentary as to its market position and business plan and give general views on its debt capacity and the types of covenant (financial and non-financial) that ought to govern the loan in future years.

The independent business review was then used as the backdrop against which the sponsor and the company would negotiate with its lending group. Over time, certain market principles developed: if the sponsor wanted a smooth passage for its covenant amendment request, it was expected to increase the interest rate or margin payable on the respective debt, pay a work fee to the syndicate in return for its support, pay the professional fees of the lenders' financial and legal advisers and/or inject new equity in return for obtaining a lengthy period during which covenants would not be tested or would be removed in their entirety.

At the outset of the crisis these covenant holidays were resisted by lenders but then became more attractive to the traditional European banks, credit funds or CLOs that had purchased the debt at par as such relief granted to the company and the sponsor avoided the need for those lenders to provide against or write down their debt obligations. This was helpful to them, given the significant number of their credits that were stressed, distressed or in default.

5.4 Liquidity-driven restructurings

These covenant-driven negotiations were not balance-sheet restructurings in the traditional sense, but were more akin to bespoke refinancings that gave the portfolio companies and their sponsors temporary respite and allowed lenders to avoid taking costly or embarrassing write-downs. In a number of cases during the financial crisis, such refinancings were sufficient to keep the patient company alive long enough to see whether economic conditions would improve, but did nothing to address the fundamental fact that too many private equity-owned companies were operating under mountains of third-party leveraged debt that they could not service or repay at maturity.

However, such refinancings did not work where the business in question faced a near-term liquidity crunch or was simply unable to service principal or interest payments on its bank or bond debts when they fell due. These liquidity-driven restructurings unveiled a new dynamic to establish who, either within the capital structure or outside, was willing and able to provide the cash to fill the funding hole. These so-called 'white knight new money' cases were relatively infrequent in the European market during the downturn, but where they did arise they meant that the party providing the new injection of funds was in a strong negotiating position to dictate the terms of the new investment and to take a significant portion of the equity upside.

For some financial sponsors, these liquidity-driven restructurings allowed them to take advantage of the passivity or economic weakness of their lending syndicates and effectively to buy the company for a second time under a wholly reconstituted capital structure. Depending on how much money the company needed, financial sponsors were able to wring substantial write-downs from lenders if the lenders were in no position to provide the cash themselves and the alternative was a free-fall insolvency process where both lenders and shareholders would lose.

Despite the financial distress of the underlying credit and its urgent need for new funds to avoid insolvency, certain lenders – whether European banks, credit funds or CLOs – were not prepared to take excessive write-downs of their debt, but were also not prepared or able to take equity in the business if this was offered. Therefore, those lenders expected the sponsor to support the business financially, but not on terms that would otherwise be considered economically rational. In some cases sponsors were prepared to inject fresh cash into the business as equity, but obviously, from the sponsor's perspective, were prepared to do that only where the balance sheet was properly right-sized and the business going forward was carrying an amount of debt commensurate with its business plan and ability to repay the debt at maturity. Where the lenders were not prepared to take the necessary write-offs, the debate shifted not to whether the new money was required – the consensus was that it was definitely needed – but rather to the terms of the new money and where in the capital structure it should be injected.

5.5 Super-senior new money deals

This led to certain instances of sponsors injecting very significant sums into their portfolio companies – often in the region of €100 million – as super-senior new money in consideration of only a partial write-down from lenders. The rationale for the sponsor was that this money was relatively secure in terms of downside protection, as it was the first to be repaid on any liquidation of the business, and that some economic return would be made on the new money while equity control was retained at the bottom of the capital structure. For the lenders, the attraction was that the business received the required capital injection without the lenders themselves having to pay out or write off as much of their debt as they had once feared. However, in most instances this type of refinancing, again falling short of a proper balance-sheet restructuring or debt-for-equity swap, perpetuated the spiral of over-leverage, leading to the 'zombie' phenomenon where companies continued to be owned by the same private equity sponsor but without the debt reduction that the business would require either to service its debt on an ongoing basis or to be able to repay all the debt at maturity.[7]

---

[7] The common interest of sponsors wanting to preserve their ownership option and lenders not wishing to provide against losses or take write-downs led to collective conduct that was first characterised by market participants as 'amend and extend' and then, somewhat cynically, as 'amend and pretend'. In truth there were more amend and extend deals undertaken during the downturn in Europe than full-blown balance-sheet restructurings.

6. **Presence of distressed debt investors**

   The wild card in each of these instances was the actual or potential presence of specialist secondary debt investors in the lending syndicate. These funds were established to purchase debt securities, whether bank or bond debt, in the secondary trading market, with a view either to having a significant influence over restructuring discussions or to being in a position to take control of a troubled credit upon an equitisation where economic ownership transferred to the lenders or new money was required, but neither the sponsor nor the par lenders were in a position to, or were prepared to, provide it.

   In circumstances where sponsors discovered that distressed investors had purchased significant amounts of their portfolio companies' debt in the secondary market, the sponsors saw this either as an immediate threat to the sponsor continuing to be the majority equity owner of the business, or as an opportunity to partner with that specialist debt investor to perfect a full-scale balance-sheet restructuring of the business for their mutual benefit. Depending on the entry price they paid for the debt, distressed investors – particularly those with a 'loan to own' philosophy at the heart of their investment thesis – stood to make an equity-like return on their debt positions if they did not take corporate control, or could end up owning the business if the sponsors or the other lenders were unable to support the business through the downturn. In truth, very few of these firms were established in Europe before the onset of the financial crisis, and even fewer with an established track record, long-term committed capital and operational and financial restructuring expertise.

7. **Sponsors retaining control of their portfolio companies**

   From the sponsors' perspective, in addition to the use of such tools as equity cures and debt buy-backs highlighted above, a number of other factors contributed to their being able to keep control of their portfolio companies during the financial crisis.

   First, the severe financial dislocation suffered by the vast majority of European banks, credit funds and CLOs was such that they were simply unwilling or unable to take the keys to private-equity-backed businesses even if an ownership situation arose. Those institutions did not usually have the resources, skills or investment mandate to own or control businesses and so preferred the incumbent sponsor to remain in place, particularly if, in the absence of a liquidity need by the portfolio company, there was no need to write down or sell their debt either.

   Secondly, this inertia and financial weakness on the part of traditional lenders meant that the secondary trading market for debt in Europe remained highly illiquid, since much less debt traded into the hands of distressed investors given the dearth of forced sellers. There were therefore relatively few opportunities for distressed investors to seek to take control of sponsor-backed portfolio companies by stake-building significant debt positions.

   Thirdly, the periodic re-opening of the European high yield market from time to time also allowed over-leveraged companies to refinance their debts at cheap levels and to extend their maturities, given the almost insatiable thirst for yield by those credit investors in a low interest rate environment.

Finally, as the recession in the Eurozone receded, sponsors were also assisted by the entry into the European market of specialist credit solutions funds who were not seeking corporate control, but who were prepared to refinance out most of the existing capital structure so that they could lend significant sums to stressed corporates.[8] This was attractive for certain sponsors who wished to retain control of their portfolio companies for franchise purposes, even if their ability to generate an equity return from their original investment was unlikely.

The views expressed herein are personal to the author and do not necessarily reflect those of Oaktree Capital Management (UK) LLP and its affiliates.

---

8   Examples would be Uralita and Hilding Anders where funds advanced by the special situations division of KKR were used to refinance significant debt obligations of sponsor-backed portfolio companies, allowing those sponsors to retain control.

The place of private equity in corporate finance and mergers and acquisitions

Justin Bickle
Oaktree

1. Introduction

The world has changed for private equity since summer 2007.

The global financial crisis highlighted a number of inherent flaws in the traditional buy-out model and caused a crisis of identity among private equity firms and their investment professionals. The economic downturn confirmed that, like other forms of economic behaviour, private equity is not immune from the ravages of the market and the booms and busts of the economic cycle, and does not and never did represent a risk-free form of financial alchemy. As the world emerges from the financial crisis the question facing the private equity industry is whether it has truly learnt any lessons from the downturn and what steps (if any) will it take to mitigate the use of leverage to generate its economic returns in the future.

Before the onset of the economic slowdown in 2007, private equity was at the centre of corporate finance and merger and acquisition (M&A) activity, and comprised approximately a quarter of such activity worldwide. What had been perceived in the early 2000s as an alternative asset class on the fringes of unrestrained financial capitalism had become a mainstream and accepted investment activity, attracting the best investment professionals, the highest-calibre operational managers, world-class executive managers and waves of institutional money.

At its core, and at its best, private equity still represents one of the most potent means of creating corporate value yet devised. Before the credit crunch, industry participants proclaimed a golden age for the industry and speculated that the first $100 billion buy-out could be within reach.[1] Although confidence returned to some parts of the industry with particular speed given the troughs experienced in the downturn, even a $5 billion buy-out deal is considered particularly noteworthy these days, and club deals are still infrequent and relatively unusual.

So, how did private equity rise and fall over its first 40 years, and do history and prior market corrections hold clues as to how the asset class may best mitigate its flaws during the next decade? As Mark Twain is often (erroneously) credited with observing: "History does not repeat itself but it does rhyme." Will private equity heed that advice?

---

1 Attributed to Carlyle co-founder David Rubenstein during early 2007.

2. **The development of private equity**

The growth of private equity is typically traced back to the founding of buy-out firm Kohlberg Kravis Roberts & Co (KKR) in the United States in the mid-1970s and the development of the leveraged buy-out model.[2]

However, in many ways the development of private equity is just another milestone in the growth of entrepreneurship that has been ongoing since the industrial revolution. The pursuit of profit and wealth is not a new concept, however well developed current methods of financial engineering may seem compared to earlier methods to try to get rich quick.[3]

Private equity developed in the United States for a number of reasons.[4] First, antitrust laws in the early part of the last century made it increasingly difficult for rapacious entrepreneurs to continue to exercise dominance over large parts of US society, including key sectors such as oil and steel. Second, and following the Wall Street Crash and the survival of the US economy after the Great Depression, by the 1960s it had become clear that the wave of mergers and acquisitions in corporate America could not continue and that the conglomerate was an outdated business model. The short-termism of earnings per share goals and beating analysts' expectations each quarter left many of the brightest and best corporate managers feeling unfulfilled. Third, the arrival of hostile takeovers meant that corporate norms were jettisoned in favour of a more aggressive, and unrestrained, form of economic behaviour. Fourth – and perhaps most importantly, given the importance of the leveraged buy-out model to private equity in the early years – was the rise of high-yield or 'junk' bonds from the early 1980s in the United States, at the same time as financial investors such as KKR first began to emerge.[5] In essence, junk bonds provided private equity with a highly liquid market for available debt below investment grade, meaning that larger corporations were no longer beyond the reach of private equity players or ambitious managers who saw the attractions of selling out to private equity investors and making large personal returns for themselves.

3. **The leveraged buy-out model**

In essence, the leveraged buy-out model involves buying a business through borrowing money from a third-party bank or other financial institution. The company's cash flows are used to make the loan repayments and, together with the company's assets, provide security to the lenders until the debt is repaid.[6]

In the early days of private equity, and indeed for the majority of today's financial sponsors, the driver for returns in the classic leveraged buy-out model was to buy the greatest amount of assets with the least amount of personal (or equity)

---

2   For the definitive commentary see George P Baker and George David Smith, *The New Financial Capitalists: Kohlberg Kravis Roberts and the Creation of Corporate Value* (Cambridge University Press, 2005).
3   For interesting accounts of the decline of the robber barons see Ron Chernow, *The House of Morgan: An American Banking Dynasty and the Rise of Modern Finance* (Atlantic Books, 2003) and Ron Chernow, *Titan: The Life of John D Rockefeller, Snr* (Vintage Books, 2004).
4   For more see Bruce Wasserstein, *Big Deal* (Warner Books, 1998).
5   For the definitive account of the rise of the US high-yield market and the influence of junk bonds on M&A activity from the mid-1980s, see Connie Bruck, *The Predators' Ball: The Inside Story of Drexel Burnham and the Rise of the Junk Bond Raiders* (Penguin, 1998).
6   See *Big Deal* referred to above.

investment. In short, a company's future was mortgaged in favour of being able to service debt from the company's existing cash flows. There was often little margin for error, so usually the companies that found themselves attractive to private equity firms were mature businesses enjoying leading market positions in their sectors and stable cash generation without any seasonal swings or need for high capital expenditure.

Over time, and as the private equity space became more crowded given the personal financial rewards on offer, other variants on the classic leveraged buy-out model emerged. There were 'break-up' leveraged buyouts, where asset sales were seen as the main means of repaying acquisition debt (being either traditional bank loans or junk bonds), since existing cash flows would be insufficient to service the company's debt pile, and also 'strategic' leveraged buyouts, where fragmented industries would be targeted by the private equity investors so that a number of unglamorous (sometimes loss-making) single entities could be consolidated or rolled up into a more attractive whole before being offered for sale on the public markets by way of an initial public offering.

4. The growth of buy-out firms

By the late 1980s a number of leading buy-out firms had been established in the United States. These were able to tap into the increased demand for private equity product among US state pension funds, which had been disappointed by relatively unexciting performances of their investments in the US stock and bond markets during the previous decade and which had turned instead to alternative investments such as private equity to prop up ailing returns. These twin drivers – more and more capital available for investment and more and more specialist firms prepared to invest it – meant that by 1988 there were said to be over 200 buy-out firms controlling an estimated $200 billion for acquisitions worldwide once leverage was taken into account.

5. The end of the first golden age: private equity grows up

With hindsight, KKR's $31 billion hostile takeover of the US listed foods and tobacco giant RJR Nabisco/Borden in 1989 still represents the high-water mark for private equity investing, and continues to be the single deal most associated with private equity as an asset class in the educated public's consciousness, even if the returns for KKR on that deal were considerably less than those for some of its other investments. It is worth mentioning in passing now not only for its historical significance, but also for the fact that until early 2007 it remained the largest private equity buy-out ever consummated, and before the credit crunch it symbolised the type of transaction that private equity mega-funds coveted using their ever-increasing pools of capital. Even with the re-emergence of the capital markets in the US during the past two years it is difficult to imagine exactly when the next $30 billion private equity buy-out will occur.

The heady days and hubris of the late 1980s inevitably led to a correction and more sober attitudes in the private equity industry during the following decade. To that extent, private equity's recent problems can be seen as another swing of the pendulum for those (old-fashioned) investors willing to place recent history's trials and tribulations in their proper historical context. The collapse of Drexel Burnham Lambert, the main underwriter and arranger of junk bond issues, amid recrimination and scandal in 1990, and the consequent drying up of junk bond easy money to finance LBOs meant that private equity had to face up to the fundamentals of its investment approach, rather than relying on financial alchemy to deliver returns. Would the business being evaluated perform well, with or without leverage? How competent or skilled were the management team? How could their skills be supplemented? How could cost discipline be introduced into the business? Assuming that an investment was made and all went well, what were the means of exit for the private equity firm among the public or private markets?

The tightening of economic conditions at the beginning of the 1990s and the consequent slowdown in M&A activity inevitably led some commentators to question private equity as a viable investment class and to focus attention on trying to grow the equity of an acquired business, rather than on applying more debt via the highly leveraged model. The lessons of the 1990s are equally applicable today; private equity investors would be well served in remembering what recent history teaches us.

6. New players and strategies

During the 1990s private equity firms continued to expand their own operational capabilities and portfolio management skillsets to cope with the change in the economy and more difficult conditions in which to find and produce superior returns. 'Turnaround' private equity firms emerged, where the ability to run businesses for cash and to restructure their operations became even more important than a consideration of which financing multiples could be applied to the company. Often these private equity firms would hire key senior personnel or distinguished chief executive officers from established blue-chip corporations, whom they would then parachute into an existing portfolio business, either to supplement the skills of the existing managers or to replace them entirely. In these firms, managing each portfolio business post-acquisition and extracting value became at least as important as, or sometimes more important than, acquiring the business in the first instance.

Additionally, as the technology boom and rise of the Internet fuelled the dotcom bubble of easy lending and rising stock markets globally, at the end of the 1990s a number of venture capital firms emerged, particularly in the United States, dedicated to investing funds in start-up companies with limited profitability or management track records, but with more upside than less glamorous, but stable, cash-generative companies. Some of these investments, particularly in Silicon Valley, were spectacular while they lasted, but resulted in non-existent returns or significant losses for investors when the financial markets finally corrected and indeed collapsed in 2000/2001. As before, history has proved that it is relatively easy to make money when debt is cheap and economic conditions benign, and even easier to lose all those gains and post a nil return when the cycle turns.

7. The effects of September 11 2001 and increased public regulation of financial markets

By the time the events of September 11 2001 occurred and highlighted the systemic deficiencies in the world economy caused by a decade or more of low interest rates and a consumption-led consumer boom, private equity was a global business, intrinsically linked with, and therefore a prisoner of, the twin global worlds of corporate finance and M&A. Therefore, it is not surprising that private equity, as with M&A, remained relatively quiet as the world economy went through a sustained recession from late 2001 onwards.

In Europe, private equity players were relatively unscathed by the ravages of the 2001 to 2004 collapse of the nascent European high-yield market and energy space (caused by deregulation). Although some leveraged buyouts had been conducted in the telecommunications and cable sectors generally, European private equity had largely invested elsewhere, meaning that while there were one or two examples of portfolio firms defaulting on their loans during this contraction of economic activity, the asset class was less troubled than some doomsayers predicted at the time.

However, the collapse of Enron and WorldCom and a number of other fraud-related cases in the United States did result in increased financial regulation of public corporations, not least via the introduction of the Sarbanes-Oxley Act, the US legislature's reaction to malfeasance in corporate America. Again with hindsight, this led to a sense among some US corporate managers that the extra regulatory burden imposed by the Sarbanes-Oxley Act meant that the opportunities afforded by private equity ownership were a panacea for their problems going forward and ensured that private equity was once again in vogue in corporate America.

8. The re-emergence of M&A and private equity activity

Following the recovery of the world economy in the years leading up to late 2007, M&A and private equity transactions stood at record highs, with both leverage and acquisition multiples smashing all previous records. The potent cocktail of low interest rates, plentiful and cheap third-party debt and rising valuations for private equity firms and their portfolio companies was not destined to last forever. Some market participants proclaimed that private equity had consigned the credit cycle to history and had eradicated future slumps. Others, not prepared to join the traditional madness of crowds that precedes every major economic correction, were derided as risk-averse and out of touch with the times.

9. The rise of the mega-funds

Before summer 2007 the availability of unparalleled amounts of third-party leverage and huge investor appetite for exposure to the asset class meant that the private equity industry divided into the (traditional) mid-market on the one side, and the mega-funds on the other.[7] These latter players seemed capable of raising new investment funds in the $10 billion to $20 billion range with ease, when merely a few years previously a $3 billion fund would have been one of the 10 biggest private

---

7   Traditionally, in the United Kingdom, transactions of £500 million or less are mid-market.

equity investment vehicles of all time. The global reach of the mega-funds meant that ever-greater targets now seemed within their grasp, with their strategies and market behaviour polarising the industry with each passing year.

10. Club deals

A side effect of the rise of the mega-funds was their propensity to form consortia to acquire some of the larger public and private companies in the United States and Europe, with the consequent complications in terms of legal structuring and competitive business behaviour that this entailed. Industry realists wondered what would happen if a high-profile consortium or club deal lost money or filed for bankruptcy, but these questions were deferred until the inevitable market correction took place. Looking back at this period now, it is interesting to consider how little thought was given to the consequences of restructuring or reversing these investment structures. In practice though, the number of club deals that slipped into bankruptcy were relatively few.

11. Private equity's impact on public corporations and their boards

As private equity continued its rise, its own models of corporate governance and compensation became so lauded that public corporations and boards began to feel under pressure to replicate those models in case the best managers were tempted to switch sides. Equally, certain public boards were sceptical of accepting private equity overtures in case, post-acquisition, the newly owned private entity generated abnormal profits to the benefit of the private equity sponsor and their investors by applying private sector governance to the formerly publicly owned asset. With hindsight, those independent boards served their shareholders well as, although they did not sell out to private equity at the top of the market, they did at least spare those companies from an inevitable crash once the market correction exposed the flaws of borrowing too much cheap third-party debt to finance public-to-private transactions at ever-higher acquisition multiples.

12. Competition from hedge funds

As with other successful financial models, the emergence of private equity power meant that other entities were anxious to enter the same space in an attempt to achieve the same rewards. The expansion of hedge funds[8] globally meant that they increasingly tried to chase the same targets as traditional buy-out firms to such an extent that discussion of convergence between the two asset classes was common in mid-2007, with some commentators expecting that the 'private equity' and 'hedge fund' labels would be meaningless in 10 years' time as alternate asset managers offered the same products from a single platform worldwide.

Ironically, the forced investor redemptions of the fourth quarter of 2008 in the aftermath of the Lehman Brothers worldwide bankruptcy filings also exposed the inherent flaws in the hedge fund model. What has occurred, though, is that a

---

[8] Hedge funds are (or were until the passing of the Alternative Investment Fund Managers Directive) in essence unregulated (or lightly regulated) private pools of investment capital.

number of the major private equity firms have diversified their business models to include new credit and hedge fund strategies. Many now offer investors a range of returns from single digits for lower-risk products to mid to high teens returns for more traditional buy-out products, meaning that the hedge fund and private equity labels have become less meaningful.

13. The effects of the downturn: disaster and opportunity

Clearly, most buy-out firms seemed to miss the possibility of an imminent economic downturn before summer 2007. Although industry historians could have predicted that recessionary pressures would slow the pace of new investment and place some sponsors' own liquidity at risk (the increasing reliance on funding firm overheads through deal fees rather than annual management fees, as was traditional, was an accident waiting to happen), many firms were singularly unprepared for the downturn when it occurred and spent most of 2008 contemplating a different world in which they were no longer the soothsayers, but instead the followers of events beyond their comprehension or control.

Most European buy-out firms were frozen for the first 12 months of the downturn. The savvy among them began to focus not on new deals, but instead on their existing portfolio companies and how they would survive the economic storm when neither their business plans nor their capital structures had been designed for that purpose. The fortunate firms had raised large funds in 2006 and early 2007 and had existing limited partner commitments, which could be used to keep their investment professionals paid during the slowdown in new and prospective deals and to buy them time to rethink their investment strategies and risk criteria.

Aside from portfolio tinkering, which usually involved commissioning consultants to investigate cost reductions, working capital improvements and other defensive quick wins, sponsors' first reaction was to try to buy themselves more time to hunker down and ride out market conditions. This came in the form of 'equity cures', allowing sponsors the ability to drip money into their portfolio companies to avoid breaching covenants under their debt financing. Such conduct was welcomed by banks and other par holders of bank debt,[9] as it indicated that the sponsor was supportive, even if it did postpone the balance-sheet deleveraging that was necessary in most cases. This sponsor support, allied to bank groups' unwillingness to write down or write off their impaired debt, assisted the development of the 'zombie' phenomenon, where portfolio companies limped along under a heavy burden of debt, unable to invest in the capital expenditure or debt pay-downs that their business plans required, but also not technically in breach of any of their debt obligations and so therefore not requiring any balance-sheet restructuring.

Sponsors' second reaction, when equity cures either were unavailable under the financing documents or, more particularly, were unlikely to assist as the decline in operating performance was so great, was to seek to buy back their portfolio companies' own debt in the secondary trading market. These sponsor buy-backs were

---

9   Typically specialist leveraged loan funds and collateralised loan obligations (pools of leveraged loans managed by a single investment manager).

achieved via a variety of methods (either directly by the sponsors in acquiring the debt or by them funding the investee company to acquire the debt itself), and caused some market consternation as debt was being purchased and retired not at par, but instead at the deep discounts for which the debt could be acquired in the secondary market.

With hindsight, these sponsor buy-backs, which occurred for much of the downturn, were flawed in a number of ways. First, they demonstrated that most European mid-market buy-out firms were better at borrowing third-party debt than they were at knowing how to buy it. Second, sponsors erroneously saw certain subordinated tranches of debt as cheap and therefore bought and retired those, rather than focusing on the senior debt that could prove more useful to them in future balance-sheet restructuring discussions.

The effect of buying back often the wrong tranche of debt, only to see the portfolio companies' operating performance continue to decline as operating cash ran dry, was to diminish the credibility of the sponsor to tell its investors that it knew what it was doing in this alien environment, and meant that the capital allocated by the sponsor to prop up a single portfolio company was quickly diminished, leaving the sponsor with limited financial options and negotiating leverage in subsequent discussions with creditors. Sponsors began to walk away from those portfolio companies that they could not save, and dramatically reduced their own headcount and costs base as their own investment income and deal fees began to diminish.[10]

The market dislocation caused by the downturn resulted in opportunities for other investors. To some private equity firms, a recession or rise in corporate defaults is a time to harvest opportunities, rather than to retrench. For turnaround or distressed private equity funds, economic uncertainty followed by significant debt defaults is usually the best investment period. This 'distressed for control'[11] approach gained some traction in Europe during this period, although the number of sponsor-owned businesses which were taken over by distressed investors was relatively low given the preponderance of zombie behaviour by the banks and others.

14. Public listings

The other significant development that occurred during the downturn was that a number of major private equity firms listed themselves on the public markets.[12] Part

---

10 The exception would be private equity firm Apollo, which very successfully purchased significant debt of a number of its US portfolio companies during the financial crisis, often at huge discounts. As the markets recovered, Apollo was then able to refinance much of this debt, or to extend its maturities, thereby retaining control of most of its portfolio companies and making very large profits on its debt purchases: "Apollo Fuelled by $9.6 Billion Profit On Debt Beats Peers", Bloomberg.com, June 25 2013.

11 In the 'distressed for control' or 'loan to own' context, rather than purchasing a majority of the company's equity, the (distressed) private equity investor seeks to acquire a controlling position in the company's debt (whether bank debt, second lien, mezzanine or bonds, as the case may be) prior to a balance-sheet restructuring. Once a debt-for-equity swap has occurred, that investor retains its controlling (now equity) investment in the company and holds it on a long-term basis like any other private equity investor. This investment strategy has been common in the United States for a number of years. The first major example of a successful distressed for control transaction in Europe during the last downturn was the acquisition of Countrywide Plc (the United Kingdom's leading estate agent chain) by Oaktree and others in May 2009.

12 Examples would include The Blackstone Group which listed on the New York Stock Exchange in June 2007, KKR in July 2010 and Carlyle which listed on the NASDAQ exchange in October 2012.

of the reason was said to be their founders need for liquidity, although the ability to compensate senior investment professionals with stock-based compensation, in addition to cash and carried interest, was also useful to those firms.

15. The end of the financial crisis and the future for the asset class

Since the financial crisis, the private equity industry is more fragile than at any other stage of its history.

What the crisis demonstrated is that reliance can no longer be placed on cheap available debt to ensure outsized investment returns; investment skill can no longer be subservient to financial engineering or market timing. The least flamboyant investment skills are often the best: finding an unloved asset, acquiring it, improving it and selling it for a higher price than one paid for it. Although some private equity firms have always endeavoured to do that, irrespective of the economic cycle, those firms without that disciplined approach or skillset have diminished in importance, or ceased to invest.

Limited partners who also witnessed the financial crisis are now more demanding of their private equity general partners. Raising giant and general pools of private equity capital in closed-end funds may become less common than before, and limited partners will demand more industry specialisation, geographical focus, and operational expertise to underpin and drive returns. Private equity should become more about long-term investment track records and investment out-performance, which is probably the best single sign that the asset class has finally come of age.

The views expressed herein are personal to the author and do not necessarily reflect those of Oaktree Capital Management (UK) LLP and its affiliates.

Private equity fund structures – the limited partnership

Jonathan Blake
Lorraine Robinson
King & Wood Mallesons LLP (formerly SJ Berwin LLP)

1. **Introduction**

    Notwithstanding the recent global downturn, the private equity market has continued to benefit from the support of investors based in many jurisdictions. Over the last few years, fundraising levels have been recovering to those last seen in 2008. The difficult market conditions that have prevailed are easing, with fundraising recovering strongly. Traditional private equity investors have been joined by newer players in the market, such as sovereign wealth funds and development finance institutions, and this has all had an influence on fund terms, based on market conditions. While there is renewed investor appetite, fund managers are aware that investors are increasingly selective, and well-established managers are more likely to attract capital for investment. Private equity funds continue to be a significant source of funding for businesses in the United Kingdom and other European countries, and private equity is maintaining its role as an extremely important alternative asset class.

    In the early days of private equity, many private equity organisations were wholly owned subsidiaries of large financial institutions, known as 'captives'. Over time, many of these organisations have spun out from their parent institutions and have become independent, raising their funds for investment from external sources – mainly institutional investors such as pension funds and insurance companies. One of the primary motivations for these spin-outs relates to the fact that the private equity teams become entitled to the entire upside of their fund's performance rather than a certain percentage. Additionally, in the event of downturns in the market, many investment banks, for example, chose to focus on their key areas and their private equity divisions were dispensed with. In certain circumstances, former captives now also raise funds from external sources and are known as 'semi-captives'. In the United Kingdom, a sophisticated market has emerged with a range of management teams able to raise an array of funds, including:
    - generalist funds investing in both buyout and venture capital transactions;
    - specialist funds that invest in technology, healthcare or telecommunications, for example;
    - buyout funds;
    - debt funds and credit opportunity funds, which have shown huge growth;
    - secondary funds that acquire limited partnership interests in other funds, generally once the underlying fund has been operating for some time; and
    - funds of funds that invest themselves in other private equity funds.

Private equity fund structures – the limited partnership

One would expect that in such a developing market, structures and their relevant key terms and conditions would also emerge and develop as quickly. However, since May 1987, when Her Majesty's Revenue and Customs and the Department for Business, Innovation and Skills approved the guidelines that King & Wood Mallesons LLP drafted on behalf of the British Venture Capital Association, the English limited partnership has been established as the largely standard vehicle of choice in the United Kingdom and Europe and the favoured flexible vehicle for institutional investors (although Guernsey, Jersey, Scottish and Delaware limited partnerships are also used in certain circumstances). Before May 1987, a number of different structures were historically used by the British private equity industry for raising funds, including investment trusts, offshore companies, unit trusts and direct investment plans (simply comprising parallel management agreements). Although in certain circumstances these structures are still used, they have now been largely superseded in the institutional private equity environment. However, some of these structures are discussed in summary later in this chapter. Venture capital trusts, which are specifically for investment by individuals, are also discussed.

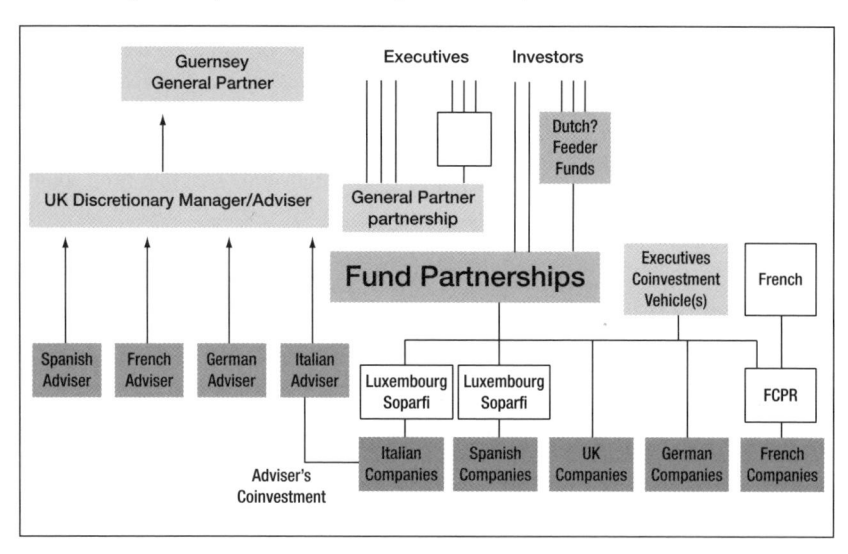

[Diagram: Fund Partnerships structure showing Guernsey General Partner, UK Discretionary Manager/Adviser, Spanish Adviser, French Adviser, German Adviser, Italian Adviser, Executives, Investors, General Partner partnership, Dutch? Feeder Funds, Fund Partnerships, Executives Coinvestment Vehicle(s), French, Luxembourg Soparfi, Luxembourg Soparfi, Italian Companies, Spanish Companies, UK Companies, German Companies, French Companies, FCPR, Adviser's Coinvestment]

The limited partnership has also proved attractive to pan-European fund management groups investing elsewhere in Europe, although often structures local to specific European countries may have to be used alongside a limited partnership for local reasons (eg, some foreign tax authorities, such as the French authorities, do not recognise a limited partnership as being tax transparent).

This chapter seeks to explain the limited partnership structure for international investors in UK investment funds, together with some of the additional issues encountered when applying the structure to funds investing in other European countries. Further, discussion is given to the current status of the terms and conditions of private equity funds and the primary negotiations between investors and their management teams.

An example of a typical European private equity limited partnership structure is shown above. The various overseas entities in this example are required for either tax or regulatory reasons, depending upon the jurisdiction in which investors and/or carried interest holders are present.

1.1 Limited partnership funds – background

The limited partnership structure has been adopted by the majority of private equity institutions in the United Kingdom, whose investors include not only the traditional UK pension funds, insurance companies and local authorities, but also US pension fund investors and large overseas and multinational corporates. Marketing limited partnerships to individuals in the United Kingdom, however, is highly regulated by the Financial Conduct Authority (FCA) and is very difficult to do in practice. Therefore, investment in private equity by private individuals, with the exception of investments made by sophisticated or high net worth individuals, is mainly through publicly listed vehicles such as investment trusts and venture capital trusts.

Private equity funds have a typical lifespan of approximately 10 years, within which time the aim of the fund's management team is to maximise the return to investors by investing in, and then realising successfully, a portfolio of primarily privately held companies. Realisations or 'exits' may take the form of flotations, trade sales or sales to other funds (secondary purchases). Commonly, investments are made in the first three to six years following closing, after which no further new investments may be made. Following the end of this investment period, drawdowns will be made from investors only to fund management charges, expenses or 'follow on' investments in existing portfolio companies.

In limited partnership funds, the partnership agreement is the primary document governing the relationship between the general partner (which manages the fund and has unlimited liability) and the limited partner investors (which specifically do not manage the fund and have limited liability). The track record of the management team is fundamental to an investor's decision to commit to a particular fund – a thriving fund manager may often see their successor funds oversubscribed on closing. As the investors in these funds are mostly financial institutions, the partnership agreement is negotiated by lawyers representing both sides. Once investors have agreed internally to make an investment, they typically seek to negotiate restrictions on the types of investment that may be made by the fund and the other activities of the fund management team – as well as management fees, carried interest (which remains stable in amount) and other economic and commercial terms.

2. Objectives

Traditionally there have been a number of key objectives in structuring private equity funds:
- In order to prevent double taxation, the fund must be exempt or transparent for the purposes of capital gains tax and income tax, so that tax is not suffered on the sale by the fund of its interests in portfolio companies and again on the distribution of those gains to investors.

- It is desirable for the expenses of management to be charged against income and gains arising within the fund, to prevent investors being liable to tax on income and gains without the benefit of a corresponding deduction.
- Management charges should be structured to eliminate or minimise value added tax.
- Withholding taxes on income, dividends and interest from portfolio companies should be minimised, and no tax should be chargeable on capital gains in the country of residence of the portfolio company.
- The fund should confer limited liability on investors.
- The fund should be capable of incorporating a suitable capital incentive for the management team, the 'carried interest', structured so as to minimise or defer income tax and capital gains tax.
- The fund should be suitable for all types of investor.
- The fund should be capable of being marketed to suitable investors under relevant securities legislation.
- The fund structure should be straightforward to operate.

3. Features of the structure

3.1 English limited partnership funds

Under English law, a limited partnership is a partnership comprising both general and limited partners and is established under the Limited Partnerships Act 1907. One or more persons are known as the 'general partners', which have responsibility for managing the business of the partnership and which are liable for all debts and obligations of the partnership. The general partner is usually itself structured as a limited liability entity.

Additionally, there are one or more 'limited partners' – the investors – which contribute capital to the partnership at the time of becoming a partner and whose liability for such debts and obligations is limited to the amount contributed, provided they do not participate in the management of the business of the limited partnership. Once a capital contribution has been made, the limited partner must not draw out or receive back any part of this contribution. If it does, the limited partner is liable for debts and obligations of the partnership up to the amount drawn out or received back. In practice, a limited partner contributes a commitment to a limited partnership by way of a very small amount of partnership capital (often 0.001%), together with a large percentage of non-interest bearing loan (99.999%). This is to ensure that any loan returned to investors (eg, upon realisation of an investment) does not fall within the remit of 'capital' and does not breach the prohibition on return of capital. This structuring should provide investors with confidence that such amounts returned cannot generally be drawn down again (subject to the terms of the limited partnership agreement). Once a limited partner has made a commitment to a fund, subject to the terms of the limited partnership agreement, it will generally not be entitled to withdraw from a fund or transfer its partnership interest.

Limited partners have no power to bind the partnership. If limited partners take part in the management of the business of the limited partnership, they effectively become a general partner and will be liable for all debts and obligations incurred while acting as a general partner. The loss of limited liability should be restricted to the period in which such contravention occurred and the partner does not become constituted as a general partner.

In order to be an English limited partnership, a partnership must be registered with the registrar of limited partnerships in England and Wales under the Limited Partnership Act 1907. On establishment, the general partner must have a principal place of business in England – that is, it must carry out some business in England or Wales; but it is not necessary for this to be maintained throughout the life of the limited partnership and, therefore, 'migration' by an English limited partnership to an offshore jurisdiction is possible.

The interests in a limited partnership may be quoted on stock exchanges in overseas jurisdictions. However, this is rarely seen because it is not a straightforward process and may not be commercially appropriate for a fund, but it may be something undertaken more frequently in the future.

3.2 Management

In practice, the fund will generally be managed by a separate vehicle to the general partner, the fund manager, which will usually be owned by the management team. The fund manager provides the limited partnership with an investment management strategy and makes investment decisions on behalf of the limited partnership, and is an entity regulated by the Financial Conduct Authority. By utilising this separate management structure, a private equity house will establish separate general partners for each successive private equity fund managed by that private equity house so that it needs only one vehicle, the fund manager, authorised by the Financial Conduct Authority, rather than requiring authorisation of the general partner company of each fund.

A management agreement will be entered into between the fund, acting through its general partner, and the manager; this sets out the terms of the management vehicle's appointment. Separately to the carried interest structure, the fund's management company will usually be paid a management fee by the general partner on a quarterly or semi-annual basis. This fee is required to cover the managers' salaries and ongoing fund operating costs. The management charge is usually an amount between 1% and 2.5% per annum of the total commitments to the fund during the period in which investments are made. These percentages have remained consistent for many years and continue to be so, with fees for larger funds generally lower than those for smaller funds. After the end of the investment period, this fee will often be reduced to a percentage of the commitments actually invested; additionally, in some cases the actual percentage rate itself is reduced. The amount of the management charge depends on the size of the fund, the strength and ability of the management team and the types of investment that the fund makes.

Under the terms of the limited partnership agreement, the general partner is entitled to a priority share of the profits of the partnership, which is usually utilised to pay the management fee. As there will be no profits initially, the general partner is entitled to draw down the required amount from the investors and to take a loan from the partnership's cash funds, with such amount being repaid by the general partner upon receipt of future proceeds of realisations.

Additionally, transaction fees paid to the manager by third parties, such as corporate finance fees, monitoring fees or underwriting fees, are frequently offset against the management charge either in whole or in part, depending on what is agreed in the limited partnership agreement for the fund.

3.3   **Tax transparency**
An English limited partnership permits limited partners from different countries with various financial requirements to invest alongside each other and be treated for tax purposes as if they owned the shares in portfolio companies directly. This is due to the fact that a limited partnership is regarded by Her Majesty's Revenue and Customs as fully tax transparent and, even if its manager or general manager is in the United Kingdom, it is not regarded as a permanent establishment in the United Kingdom for overseas investors other than those carrying on a financial trade, such as banks. As an English limited partnership is not a body corporate and does not have a legal personality separate from that of its partners, the limited partnership is often afforded similar treatment elsewhere. Most investors should therefore be treated in their home jurisdiction as receiving dividends, interest and capital gains as if they were the direct owner of the relevant shares in the portfolio company from which the profit is derived, and taxed as such. Additionally, there is no liability to tax when the limited partnership distributes assets *in specie* to its partners.

3.4   **Deductibility of management expenses**
A management fee is generally charged by a manager to the general partner in consideration of it being the manager of the partnership, and the general partner receives a priority fixed share of profit which is passed on to the manager as its fee. The general partner will discharge that expense out of its profit share and, as it is an investment company, it can deduct the management fee from its profit share as an expense of management. This avoids the limited partners having to pay a management charge out of post-tax profits (to the extent that they are taxpaying entities).

3.5   **Value added tax**
One of the principal difficulties with some structures is the payment of value added tax (VAT) on management fees. By taking the management charge as a share of profits the general partner does not suffer VAT, because it is outside the scope of the tax and there is no VAT on the payment of fees to the manager if it is in the same VAT group as the general partner or if the general partner carries on business outside the European Union. This may, however, lead to VAT recoverability issues arising within the general partner's group where the general partner is UK-resident.

3.6   **Limited liability**
Limited liability is available to investors in a duly registered limited partnership,

provided they do not participate in the management of the partnership business. The Limited Partnership Act 1907, which prohibits limited partner participation in management, provides no further guidance as to what constitutes participation in management and, under UK partnership law, limited liability is lost whether or not a third party is aware of a limited partner's participation in management. However, the receipt of financial information regarding the progress of the investments and normal exercise of voting rights should not amount to participation in management. It is hoped that reform of the Limited Partnerships Act 1907 will lead to a legal definition as to what may constitute 'participation in management', but it is unclear when this is likely to occur.

3.7 Incentives for managers

Carried interest structures, as they are known, may readily be incorporated in the English limited partnership structure. A carried interest is an interest in the profits of the fund that is payable to the management team after the investors have received back the money invested together with a predetermined return on their investment. Carried interest is calculated either by reference to returns from a particular portfolio company – deal-by-deal carried interest – or, more commonly, by reference to the overall profits made by the fund as a whole. In the latter case, the carried interest becomes payable only after the investors have received repayment of all amounts drawn down, together with any preferred rate of return or 'hurdle' on their investment. Importantly, carried interest should take the form of an allocation of capital gains so that a UK-based management team would be liable to capital gains tax on that allocation rather than it being taxed as an emolument of their employment. However, as a result of an employment-related securities regime introduced in 2003 (now contained in Part 7, Chapters 2 to 4 of the Income Tax (Earnings and Pensions) Act 2003), in certain cases (particularly if carried interest is reallocated when a member of the management team leaves), income tax and national insurance liabilities can arise in certain limited partnership structures. A memorandum of understanding agreed between the British Venture Capital Association and Her Majesty's Revenue and Customs clarifies, generally, the tax treatment of the receipt of carried interest. However, this is in respect of funds falling within the terms of the memorandum and, therefore, the treatment of carried interest for capital gains tax purposes under a particular structure needs careful review to determine whether the regime may apply.

The simplest structure entitles the management team, which receives an indirect partnership interest, to share in, usually, 20% of the profits of the fund after the investors have received repayment of their investment together with a hurdle rate of return, generally 8%. Investors are entitled between them to the other 80% of profits thereafter. Profits are allocated between the partners so as to ensure that the management team does not incur a tax liability until it receives a distribution of profits. The rate of 20% is near-universal for both buyouts and venture funds.

It is generally preferable for the individual members of the management team not to be direct limited partners in the fund partnership in order to receive their carried interest. In most cases, a Scottish limited partnership (because it has legal personality and is therefore able to invest in English limited partnerships) is used to hold the separate carried interest of the management team. Any movement in members of the management team to and from the entitlement to carried interest may, therefore, be dealt with more simply at the Scottish limited partnership level rather than at the level of the fund.

Where a Scottish limited partnership is used as the fund's carried interest vehicle, then the Scottish limited partnership agreement will contain provisions governing the rights and obligations of the individuals in the management team in respect of their proportions of the 20% carried interest. A considerable part of any carried interest agreement will govern what happens if one of the members of the management team leaves and/or a new person joins. As a matter of terminology, the carried interest agreement may alternatively be referred to as a leavers and joiners agreement.

In simple terms, the carried interest agreement invariably provides that if one of the members of the management team ceases to be, for example, a director of the management company, a member of a limited liability partnership (if such vehicle is used as the management vehicle) or an employee, then that member is required to give up all or part of his share of the carried interest. Normally, the member is entitled to retain some or all of his interest if he retires, dies or leaves because of ill health (a 'good leaver'), but will be entitled to retain little or nothing if he leaves, for example, because of gross misconduct (a 'bad leaver'). In many funds, an additional level of 'intermediate leaver' may also be included for situations where, for example, an executive leaves to join a competitor. In those circumstances and depending upon the length of service before the executive joins a competitor, it is likely that such a leaver would receive more carried interest than a bad leaver but probably significantly less than a good leaver.

A leaver's interest is then often apportioned to the remaining members of the management team or to the leaver's replacement. Usually there is provision that if the remaining management team members take part of the interest of a leaver, they may be required to give up that interest in the future to a new member (a 'joiner').

3.8 Ease of operation

Perhaps the greatest benefit of the limited partnership to UK private equity houses, and the overriding reason for use of this form, has been the ability to manage the fund in the United Kingdom without the seemingly artificial advisory structures frequently put in place with offshore unit trusts and offshore management company structures.

Additionally, a private equity fund may be established as a series of limited partnerships that make parallel co-investments. This method can be used to ensure a particular partnership meets the special requirements of particular investors – for example, US investors.

3.9 Non-UK investors

As a limited partnership is regarded as tax-transparent in the United Kingdom by Her Majesty's Revenue and Customs, non-UK resident investors can become partners without being subject to UK tax, other than in respect of UK source income, which is generally subject to withholding tax of 20%, and overseas financial traders. The United Kingdom does not generally charge non-residents to tax on chargeable gains unless the non-resident is carrying on a trade in the United Kingdom through a branch or agency in the United Kingdom. Where investments are made in the United Kingdom, relief from UK withholding tax on UK source interest should be available to non-resident investors from countries that have an appropriate double taxation treaty with the United Kingdom. For this purpose, the non-resident investor is not treated as carrying on business in the United Kingdom through a permanent establishment and is therefore able to enjoy the benefit of the usual dividend and interest articles in the UK double taxation treaty network. As mentioned, there are exceptions to the freedom from UK tax. Partners that hold their partnership interests as part of their financial trade, such as banks, will be treated as carrying on that part of their trade in the United Kingdom through a permanent establishment (for example the UK general partner or the UK manager), and will therefore be subject to UK tax on their share of partnership profits, for which the general partner or manager will have to make a retention. It is common for such banks to hold their investments through other companies in their group which clearly qualify as investment companies. The second example is where partners resident in countries without appropriate double taxation treaties with the United Kingdom are entitled to UK source income, such as interest on a loan to a UK borrower. Once again, this would be liable to UK tax and the general partner or manager will make an appropriate retention.

US tax requirements and the special regulatory requirements for US Employee Retirement Income Security Act of 1974 (ERISA) funds can also be accommodated within the structure, so as to ensure that the structure is attractive to US investors.

3.10 Regulatory matters

Regulatory issues arise in most countries as to the way in which an offering document can be marketed. This is most relevant in the United Kingdom, North America and Europe. In the United Kingdom, no major issues arise as long as:
- the manager or adviser of a limited partnership is properly authorised by the Financial Conduct Authority under the Financial Services and Markets Act 2000 (the limited partnership being an unregulated collective investment scheme); and
- the potential investors are large companies or other fund managers such as pension fund managers.

The fund cannot be marketed easily in the United Kingdom to individuals. The provision of management, advisory and arranging services to a fund or its investors in or from the United Kingdom constitutes a regulated activity, for the purposes of Section 19 of the Financial Services and Markets Act 2000 and the Financial Services and Markets Act 2000 (Regulated Activities) Order 2001, which may be carried out only by a person authorised under the Financial Services and Markets Act 2000. As part of the authorisation process for the management company, individual 'executives' within the company must themselves be approved by the Financial Services Authority and are required to satisfy the Financial Conduct Authority that they are 'fit and proper persons'. Those new to the industry or returning after a significant absence will also need to pass a Financial Conduct Authority approved examination. New European regulation has now been implemented into UK law – see point 6.2 below.

3.11 Disadvantages of limited partnerships

The limited partnership has the following disadvantages, although clearly these are outweighed by the above advantages:

- As the limited partnership is tax-transparent, its investors are liable to tax when gains or income are received by the partnership, so if the partnership reinvests these proceeds (or otherwise does not distribute them), investors will still be liable to tax without having actually received the proceeds.
- The limited partnership allows the management charge to be paid to the general partner as a share of profits, and therefore no VAT is chargeable, which would be irrecoverable by the partnership. However, this can lead to irrecoverable VAT arising elsewhere within the general partner's group if the general partner is based in the United Kingdom.
- Limited partnerships cannot directly be marketed under the Financial Services and Markets Act 2000 to most individual investors, as they are unregulated collective investment schemes.
- The interests in a limited partnership are not generally quoted on a stock exchange.

4. Special issues for pan-European funds

The principle of tax transparency means that an English limited partnership will qualify for the basic attributes needed for a successful fund – that is, freedom from tax in the United Kingdom and, generally, the absence of any form of withholding tax on distributions made by the fund to non-UK investors. It is sometimes important to have protection under double taxation treaties in such a fund; for example, some countries (eg, France, Germany and Spain) can, in certain circumstances, subject non-resident investors to local capital gains tax on the disposal of locally registered shares in the absence of treaty protection. The principle of transparency, where it applies, should mean that investors can take advantage of the double taxation treaty between the country in which they are resident and the country in which the portfolio company is resident – the treaty between the United Kingdom and the country in which the portfolio company is resident is irrelevant for non-UK investors where the other country recognises the transparency of the partnership.

Similar considerations arise in connection with claiming a reduced rate of withholding tax or an exemption from tax on dividends and interest paid by portfolio companies. Some countries (eg, Germany, the Netherlands, Belgium and Spain) recognise the transparency principle quite clearly and do not seek to rely on their respective treaties with the United Kingdom, other than in respect of UK investors – although local rulings may sometimes be required. Italy recognises the transparency principle if the wording in the relevant treaty is acceptable, as it is for US and UK investors, among others. France and the Netherlands treat partnerships as opaque in some circumstances and this can result in loss of investors' treaty protection. Her Majesty's Revenue and Customs itself adopts the principle of transparency unequivocally and has corresponded with other revenue authorities in Europe to this effect.

5. Terms and conditions of the fund

In most cases, a private equity fund is principally marketed in accordance with regulatory requirements to investors through the medium of an offering memorandum. This document generally includes a description of the purpose, investment strategy and size of the fund, together with a summary of the terms and conditions of the fund. Additionally, fundamental details of the management team's track record and background are included, along with details of any proposed management investment. Following the marketing process, investors are invited to review and negotiate the key legal document, the limited partnership agreement, which sets out the terms of the contractual relationship between the partners in the fund and details the internal governance of the fund. A limited partner's ability to negotiate and influence terms obviously depends on the leverage gained from the size of its commitment to the fund. A degree of standardisation is evident in relation to key terms such as rates of management fees and carried interest, subject to the individual circumstances of particular funds. Corporate governance and investor protection issues are currently seen to rate highly as part of investor requirements.

Set out below is a summary of the key provisions found in a limited partnership agreement, together with a discussion of market terms where relevant.

5.1 Management fees

As set out above, management fees range between 1% and 2.5%, with fees for larger funds generally lower than those for smaller funds. Currently, for most buyout funds, management fees appear to be between 1.5% and 2% compared to venture fund management fees, which are more likely to be between 2% and 2.5%. These percentages are usually based on the amount of total commitments for the initial period of investment and are reduced thereafter to a percentage of either the total amount drawn down from investors or the amount employed for making investments (the difference between the two amounts being the total amount drawn down to pay for the general partner's share and expenses or 'fees on fees'). Additionally, it is not unusual to see the percentage reduce at this stage of the life of a fund, as well as a change in the basis of calculation.

5.2 Transaction fees

In many cases the management company may be required to share with the fund any fees received in connection with a fund's investment activities; for example, investment-related fees (eg, directors' fees or monitoring fees) and underwriting fees. The sharing ratio varies from fund to fund, from 100% to limited partners to between

50% and 80%. In most cases, however, any investment-abort costs (ie, those costs incurred in identifying, evaluating, structuring and negotiating transactions that fail to complete) must be offset initially against the transaction fees received. In many cases 100% of any fees received are offset against the general partner's priority share of profits, which means that investors effectively benefit from the entire amount of such fees.

5.3 Carried interest

A rate of 20% of the profits of the fund is near-universal as the rate of carried interest for management of a private equity fund in both buyout and venture funds in Europe. Additionally, a preferred return or hurdle of 8% is generally consistent across these groups, although there are specific circumstances where no hurdle is included in a fund. The most common carried interest structure throughout Europe is that of fund as a whole, whereby an investor's total investment in the fund together with a preferred return must be repaid before any carried interest is payable to the management team. Clawbacks (ie, the return to the fund of carried interest already received by the management team) are becoming a more frequent feature for these funds. The deal-by-deal structure is more common in the United States, whereby carried interest is payable by reference to the performance of each separate investment, subject to losses on realised investments having been recouped, and a clawback from the management team in the event that subsequent investments under-perform. The deal-by-deal model is noticeably more general partner-friendly, as it allows the management teams to receive carried interest earlier than the fund-as-a-whole model.

5.4 Distributions

The timing and manner in which a private equity fund makes distributions to its partners is provided for in the limited partnership agreement. Often distributions are likely to be made to limited partners within a specified timeframe following the realisation of a portfolio company, subject to any required retention of funds for expenses of the fund. The 'waterfall' provisions, as distributions to partners are commonly referred to, operate to share profits between the investors and the management team so that the management team may earn a return disproportionate to its carried interest investment. Initially, the investors have their contributions returned to them together with the preferred return. Thereafter, profits are usually allocated between the investors and the management team, generally in an 80:20 split. Provision is frequently made for the management team to receive a 'catch-up' of the profits after the preferred return has been paid until, in aggregate, the carried interest percentage has been paid in respect of all profits of the fund and not just those in excess of the preferred return.

In most circumstances, distributions are made in cash. However, provision is usually made for distributions to be made *in specie* in certain circumstances, such as where a portfolio company's securities have been the subject of flotation.

At the end of the life of the fund, all remaining assets must be distributed in cash or *in specie*, in accordance with the distribution waterfall, subject to the payment of any fund expenses.

5.5 Key executive provisions

Investors go to significant effort and spend considerable time on management team due diligence. It is therefore unsurprising that investors are increasingly looking for assurances that their investment will actually be managed by those individuals in a management team who have been so carefully investigated. Many investors now expect management teams to have considered succession issues, and for there to be active and early debate about possible changes to the management team. Additionally, management companies need to show that their management teams have depth and can demonstrate that their success is not dependent solely on one or two individuals.

Consequently, key executive clauses have become present in almost all funds and the clauses themselves have become more detailed. In the past, an investor vote was usually needed to trigger a suspension of the fund's investment powers following a key executive departure. It is now usual for suspension of investment powers to be triggered automatically by such a departure, with an investor vote required to lift the suspension.

The trigger events themselves have also become more sophisticated, and a two-tier approach is often seen. Under this method, a key executive clause may be triggered if, for example, any one senior member of the management team ceases to be actively involved in the management of the fund or any three junior team members depart. This requires management teams not only to keep the headline names, but also to maintain a team of sufficient depth. As key executive clauses have grown in popularity, many advisory committees have taken on the role of approving new key executives as the composition of the management team changes over time.

5.6 No-fault divorce

Private equity funds have almost always allowed investors to remove management teams for acts of default, such as fraud, gross negligence or wilful disregard for their obligations to the fund. However, a majority of limited partnership agreements now also include 'no-fault divorce' clauses. These clauses permit investors, acting together, to remove a general partner where there is no identifiable fault (eg, where investors believe that a fund is under-performing), although the general partner is usually protected from removal for an initial period, perhaps two or three years. In the event of such removal, in Europe, it is standard for the management team to receive compensation, the amount generally being calculated by reference to the general partner's annual priority profit share (once or twice this amount is common).

5.7 Drawdowns

Capital contributions are payable by limited partners to the fund immediately on admission to the partnership. In contrast, the loan commitments to the fund are drawn down on an 'as needed' basis – on not less than, generally, 10 business days' notice – in order that the fund can make investments and pay expenses. This is because fund managers do not wish to have excess commitments on their hands, as they are not engaged to manage cash. Additionally, there would likely be a negative impact on a fund's internal rate of return if the fund were to hold cash for an extended period.

An investor's interest in a limited partnership will frequently not be assignable or transferable without the prior written consent of the management vehicle and/or the general partner, which may be given or withheld in their sole discretion. Exceptions to this may apply where transfers are made to an affiliate of the investor.

5.8 Advisory committees

Most funds have an advisory committee comprising a number of limited partner representatives who are usually selected by the management vehicle. The advisory committee's exact role varies from fund to fund, but importantly its role is curtailed by the prohibition on limited partner participation in the management of the fund. One of the main functions of the advisory committee is generally to review issues relating to conflicts of interest arising from time to time between the general partner or the management team and the fund or its investors, with the aim of ensuring that conflicts are resolved fairly. Additionally, advisory committees are commonly involved in reviewing investment valuations so that they are seen to accord with the fund's valuation guidelines. The advisory committee may also be used as a means for general consultation with the management team on a regular basis in accordance with the terms of the limited partnership agreement, specifically on the performance of the fund and its investments. Although investors will expect a management team to listen to and take account of the views of the advisory committee in relation to certain matters, all decisions ultimately rest with management. This is due to the restrictions on limited partners taking part in management of the fund – the management team are under no obligation to follow any advisory committee recommendations.

5.9 Management financial commitment/co-investment rights

Investors frequently expect to see the management team making a financial commitment to the fund alongside limited partners. This is usually in the region of 1% of total commitments to the fund, but this is very much dependent on the size of the specific fund and the number of funds that the fund manager has raised previously.

In certain circumstances, the management team may have a right to co-investment in target companies of the fund. It is usual that the management team would invest in all target companies *pro rata* rather than be able to cherry pick certain investments, which may lead to a conflict of interest.

These commitments or co-investments are generally either made through a vehicle that invests in the target companies alongside the partnership fund, or directly or indirectly into the limited partnership fund itself.

5.10 US Employee Retirement Income Security Act of 1974 (ERISA)

ERISA imposes significant obligations and fiduciary standards on any fund in the event that it receives money from US pension plans or other US employee benefit plans in circumstances where ERISA applies. Private equity fund managers will generally use one of the following ERISA exemptions to avoid the application of ERISA's fiduciary duty requirements:

- The insignificant interest exemption – this applies where benefit plan investors own less than 25% of the value of the fund, ignoring interests held by the general partner and its affiliates. This is a relatively easy test to meet, but limits the amount of capital a fund can raise from benefit plan investors.
- The venture capital operating company exemption – this applies if at least 50% of the investments of the relevant private equity fund, by cost, are in qualifying venture capital investments and where the fund has specific contractual rights substantially to participate in or influence the conduct of management of those entities ('management rights').

With respect to determining whether any specific right or package of rights qualifies as management rights, a fund should attempt to secure for itself with respect to a portfolio company investment, cumulative rights that provide significant opportunities for the fund to monitor and provide input, and otherwise influence to the management of that portfolio company. This is ideally influence comparable to that afforded by the right to a seat on the board of directors. Other rights that a fund may seek include:
- the right to have a representative attend meetings of a portfolio company's board of directors;
- the right to inspect a portfolio company's books and records and to inspect business premises and other properties;
- the right to receive financial statements, operating reports and budgets and other financial reports on a regular basis (at least quarterly) describing the portfolio company's financial performance, material developments or events and significant proposals; and
- the right to consult with and advise the management of the portfolio company on matters materially affecting the business and affairs of the portfolio company.

Due to the fact that US law prescribes no safe harbour as to management rights, the determination of whether any set of rights will constitute the requisite management rights in a particular circumstance must be determined on a case-by-case basis.

5.11 Investment purpose and restrictions

The limited partnership agreement almost universally sets out express limitations on the types of investment to be made by the fund, and often includes limitations on borrowing, restrictions on diversification requirements and limitations on investment in other funds or foreign investments, for example. It is possible that, due to a change in the economic environment, funds may need to consider amendment of their investment strategies, something that usually requires limited partner consent or advisory committee approval.

5.12 Excused investors

In some circumstances certain investors may be excused from making investments because, for example, such investments do not fall within their own investment restrictions, and therefore they are not subject to drawdowns at the time such an investment is made.

5.13 Defaulting investors

A limited partner that fails to provide a loan commitment to the limited partnership when requested is likely to create serious adverse consequences for the fund as a whole. Limited partnership agreements generally provide that in these circumstances a limited partner will be dealt with accordingly. It is often possible for the general partner to forfeit the whole of an investor's participation in the fund, with that investor retaining only a right, subject to cash being available in the limited partnership, to repayment of its drawn-down commitment at the end of the life of the fund after all other investors have received full repayment of their drawn-down commitments.

During the recent change in the economic environment, there were a few cases of funds where investors defaulted. The reasons for this included investors themselves being financially stressed or where they did not wish to invest further into a particular fund. Thankfully defaults are rare, and early communication between the fund managers and investors is crucial to resolve issues in this regard.

5.14 Restrictions on raising new funds

It is important for the investors to have confidence that the management team will focus on the management of the fund and that they will dedicate sufficient time to such a task. Provisions covering this issue are almost always included in limited partnership agreements, as are prohibitions on the closing of future similar funds until either the investment period has expired or the fund is, for example, 75% invested.

5.15 Indemnification

It is normal for a limited partnership agreement to include a wide-ranging indemnity and limitation of liability in favour of the management team, the general partner, the advisory committee and relevant individuals. However, this is subject to, and will not cover, circumstances where a person has, for example, been grossly negligent or acted in bad faith or, in the case of a UK authorised manager or adviser, where there is a breach of the Financial Services and Markets Act 2000.

5.16 Establishment costs

Establishment costs of the fund (plus any VAT) will usually be borne by the limited partnership, either up to a specified percentage of total commitments or up to a financial limit. In most cases, the management company will bear any establishment costs in excess of this amount. Placement fees are usually borne by the manager and not the fund.

5.17 Reporting

Funds are usually required to provide periodic financial, tax and other information to investors.

5.18 **Freedom of information**
Protecting the confidentiality of fund information and, in particular, portfolio company information is an area of huge importance to general partners. Generally speaking, general partners have an extremely open relationship with their investors. Limited partners typically undertake extensive due diligence before deciding to invest in a fund and, once invested, receive detailed reports from the general partner containing comprehensive performance information for both the fund and its portfolio companies. This transparency requires an understanding between general partners and limited partners that the information provided by the fund will be kept confidential. However, the open relationship between funds and their investors came under pressure from the introduction of freedom of information legislation entitling members of the public to require investors which are public bodies to disclose information they hold.

The entry into force of the United Kingdom's Freedom of Information Act 2000 in January 2005 put freedom of information issues firmly on the European agenda. Uncertainty over the application of freedom of information legislation led to a change in fund terms. General partners are more conscious of confidentiality issues, and this has resulted in a strengthening of the confidentiality provisions applicable to all investors. In addition, some funds whose investors are subject to freedom of information laws have introduced specific terms to combat the risk of disclosure of sensitive information. Although public bodies cannot contract out of the requirement to disclose, they can acknowledge that certain information is confidential and commercially sensitive and, therefore, likely to be exempt from disclosure.

In certain cases, public bodies will agree to receive less information from the fund than other investors, especially if the manager believes that the information may become subject to a valid disclosure request. Other protections include a requirement for the investor to inform the manager if a disclosure request is received and to consult with the fund before responding to it.

5.19 **Closing**
Following the finalisation of the terms of the limited partnership agreement, the management team will proceed to close the fund. At this stage, investors will be required to complete their application to become investors in the fund and to provide their small amount of capital in order to become registered limited partners under the Limited Partnerships Act 1907. Some investors may also require a side letter to be provided by the management vehicle that sets out additional investor-specific arrangements. It is now very common for certain limited partners to request a side letter with a 'most favoured nations' provision, which guarantees that limited partner the same rights as each other investor that receives a side letter. It makes sense for the management teams to include certain of these provisions in the limited partnership agreement as there can be a significant administrative burden on the fund managers if large numbers of side letters are entered into on the closing of a fund.

It is unusual for there to be a single 'first and final' closing of a private equity fund. The limited partnership agreement will provide that subsequent closings may be held after the initial closing when further limited partners are accepted into the partnership. This is subject to a cut-off date of, generally, between one year and 18 months following the first closure of the fund (because the investors require assurance that the management team is concentrating on following the fund's investment objectives rather than raising additional finance). When late investors are accepted into the fund, they are required to pay for an appropriate share of the investments already made and the expenses incurred by the fund to that date, together with a nominal level of interest payable to the earlier close investors.

6. Current issues affecting private equity funds

6.1 Going public

Private equity houses have made moves into the public markets. Significantly, in 2006 Kohlberg Kravis Roberts raised $5 billion for an investment vehicle on the Amsterdam Stock Exchange, following strong demand from investors. The benefits for such private equity groups include additional liquidity and the ability to issue new shares quickly to raise further funds and recycle proceeds of realisations, when compared to the traditional limited-life closed funds which require new funds to be raised periodically.

Kohlberg Kravis Roberts is not the first to enjoy an evergreen status and unlock new categories of investor, as 3i, Apax, Hg and Permira, for example, already access the public markets to varying degrees. The temptation for public listings may continue to grow as the private equity industry matures and the larger buyout groups look to exploit their brand names and to secure a permanent source of capital.

6.2 European regulation

After several years of discussion, the Alternative Investment Fund Managers Directive entered into force on July 21 2011, and was implemented by the United Kingdom in July 2013. It has introduced significant regulatory burdens on alternative investment fund managers (AIFMs) based in the European Union and managing, among other things, private equity funds. The directive is far-reaching and is having a huge impact on AIFMs who have need to consider the significant increase in capital requirements, the need to appoint a depositary, increased reporting and disclosure requirements, and their remuneration and internal organisational structures.

The directive imposes a mandatory authorisation requirement on AIFMs that:
- provide management services to one or more 'alternative investment fund'; or
- markets the shares or units in an alternative investment fund.

Under the new regime, AIFMs are subject to conduct of business, capital, organisational, transparency and marketing requirements.

The directive has been extremely controversial to the European private equity industry who described it as "deeply undesirable", "immensely damaging" and "anti-competitive". The substance of the directive was viewed as politically driven and much of the content disproportionate and unjustified, and there is a likelihood that a large number of the changes would not offer any real protection against any identified regulatory risks, let alone systemic ones.

Time will tell how this regulation will affect the private equity industry but certainly, in the short term, there will be disruption to fund raising for many European funds.

6.3 Limited Partnership Act reform

On October 1 2009, The Legislative Reform (Limited Partnerships) Order 2009 (LRO) came into force. The LRO makes two significant changes to the current legislation, the Limited Partnerships Act 1907:

- In order to register as a limited partnership, the name of the limited partnership will be required to end with the words "limited partnership", or the abbreviation "LP" (the suffix to be in either upper or lower case, or any combination, with or without punctuation), or the Welsh equivalent in the event that the principal place of business of the limited partnership is in Wales. This requirement will not, at this stage, be retrospective in its effect.
- On the registration of a limited partnership, the Registrar of Companies will issue a certificate of registration, and this will be "conclusive evidence that a limited partnership came into existence on the date of registration".

This reform is helpful in making it clear that administrative errors in the application process will not call into question the due registration of the limited partnership.

Further reform to the Limited Partnership Act 1907 has not transpired since then, but this would undeniably be welcome so as to provide more certainty on various other issues relating to UK limited partnerships or to reduce the administrative burden for fund managers; for example, specific provisions on actions that a limited partner may take without participating in management or a reduction in the level of information that is required to be held with the Register of Companies.

6.4 UK Partnerships (Accounts) Regulations 2008

Changes to the UK Partnerships (Accounts) Regulations 2008 have long been expected and they have now come into force and will subject many UK limited partnerships to similar accounting requirements to those which currently apply to limited companies. However, they have had a wider impact than anticipated because even qualifying partnerships that do not have a principal place of business in the United Kingdom will have to make arrangements to have their annual accounts available for inspection in the United Kingdom without charge during business hours.

The revised rules apply to accounting periods beginning on or after October 1 2013 and affect many private equity funds that are established as English or Scottish limited partnerships. The requirements only apply to qualifying partnerships, that is, English and Scottish limited partnerships each of whose general partners is a limited company (or an unlimited company, or a Scottish partnership or limited partnership each of whose members or general partners is a limited company) or a comparable undertaking established outside the United Kingdom.

A general partner of a qualifying partnership will have to prepare annual accounts, a director's report and an auditor's report within nine months of the partnership's year end. These accounts must be appended to the general partner's own accounts and filed at Companies House in the United Kingdom. If neither the partnership itself nor any of its members has a UK head office or principal place of business, the accounts must be made available instead at a UK address nominated by the general partner.

7. Other structures used in UK private equity

7.1 UK investment trust

UK investment trusts are companies that invest in securities and whose shares may be marketed by a prospectus and are quoted on the London Stock Exchange. The investment trust also needs to comply with Section 842 of the Income and Corporation Taxes Act 1988, which provides, among other things, that it is not permissible to distribute capital gain by dividend. Capital gains must therefore be obtained during the life of the investment trust by the investors selling shares at a quoted price, which is often at a significant discount to net asset value. Alternatively, capital gains can be distributed on liquidation. With respect to chargeable gains, an investment trust is exempt from corporation tax; however, as regards income, it is taxed like any other UK-resident company, although investment trusts are able to pay interest income out to investors in the form of tax deductible interest distributions, thereby eliminating tax on interest at the level of the investment trust. An investment trust would be UK-resident for the purposes of the UK double taxation treaties and therefore could benefit under them. An example of a private equity-focused investment trust is 3i.

Any management charges paid by an investment trust are deductible, and should now be VAT-exempt.

A carried interest may be incorporated through the issue of options or warrants, but investors in investment trusts usually expect the number of shares issued by this method to be very limited.

7.2 Venture capital trust

A venture capital trust is an adaptation of the investment trust structure providing income tax relief and tax-free income and capital gains to individual investors, but with restrictions on the types of company in which it can invest. From April 2011, venture capital trusts are companies admitted to trading on a regulated market, which provides an element of marketability. Individual investors resident in the United Kingdom will be entitled to income tax relief on the amount invested in the venture capital trust up to £200,000 a year provided that the shares are held for five years. They will also be exempt from UK tax on dividends received from the venture capital trust in respect of shares acquired within the permitted annual maximum for income tax relief, and on capital gains on disposal of shares in the trust when they are made (but there is no tax relief for capital losses).

Venture capital trusts are generally subject to the same tax regime as investment trusts, except that they are permitted to distribute capital profits. Throughout a relevant accounting period, at least 70% of a venture capital trust's assets must be invested in unlisted trading companies meeting certain requirements (qualifying holdings), and although investments in these companies may include both equity and debt, at least 70% of its qualifying holdings must be in the form of eligible shares. Eligible shares are ordinary shares carrying no preferential rights to dividends or the company's assets in a winding-up and no present or future rights to redemption. A venture capital trust must also derive its income wholly or mainly from shares or securities and must distribute at least 85% of its income from shares or securities. Among other things, the portfolio companies must have gross assets of no more than £15 million immediately prior to the investment and not more than £16 million thereafter. Not more than £5 million may be invested in any one company in any year. Additionally, not more than 15% of the assets of a venture capital trust at the time of making an investment may be in any one company or group of companies.

7.3 Unauthorised unit trust for exempt funds

For UK tax purposes, a unit trust, being any arrangement whereby assets are pooled and held on trust for the benefit of participants, is treated as a company and is therefore liable to UK corporation tax on chargeable gains unless it qualifies as an authorised unit trust. The exception to this is where every investor in the unit trust is itself exempt from tax on chargeable gains otherwise than by reason of residence. In such circumstances, chargeable gains made by the unit trust are not taxable. This is, therefore, a suitable structure for UK pension funds, charities and investment trusts.

The management charges payable by the trustees are not deductible for tax purposes. Generally, the trustees distribute the gross income to unit holders, with a contractual right to claw back the expenses from the unit holders, thereby maximising any tax credit in the hands of the unit holders. The management charge paid by the trustees is subject to VAT at the standard rate of 20% and there is no scope to avoid this by establishing a VAT group.

As the holders of the carried interest are not tax-exempt, they cannot be unit holders and the carried interest must therefore be structured as an addition to the management fee or through options. In either case, the benefit is likely to be subject to income tax rather than to capital gains tax.

7.4 Direct investment plans

This structure has been used for a few funds, and simply comprises a series of parallel management agreements, each between the private equity manager and a single investor, with a custodian or nominee company acting as nominee for all investments held. There is therefore no 'fund' at all and the arrangement is transparent for tax purposes. However, the main disadvantages are that the structure is difficult to operate and it is difficult to incorporate a suitable carried interest scheme. Carried interest can be provided only in the form of options, and these are subject to income tax and not taxed as capital gains. This structure is less flexible than, and offers no real advantage over, the limited partnership.

8. Conclusion

The limited partnership is a relatively simple and practical structure for UK private equity funds and its status as a standard onshore structure in the United Kingdom which has been specifically approved by Her Majesty's Revenue and Customs is likely to make it remain the most popular structure for raising UK private equity funds with international investors. Investors have the ability to negotiate, upfront, particular terms of the limited partnership agreement, which allows them greater influence and should provide them with sufficient protection for the duration of their investment in the fund.

As a result of the structure's versatility and tax efficiency, the limited partnership is also often used in the context of funds managed by non-UK groups targeting investments on a pan-European basis. However, matching the taxation requirements of different categories of investor (eg, pension funds, taxpaying companies, banks and insurance companies) from different countries with managers and portfolio companies that may also be in different countries cannot always be achieved through the use of a single structure. Such cross-border features are becoming increasingly common and it will not be until a single pan-European structure is available that this will be possible.

Equity finance

Helen Croke
Travers Smith

1. **Introduction**

   The 'equity' part of a private equity transaction deals with some of the key principles of private equity:
   - incentivising management to drive a financial return for the private equity fund by aligning the amount that the management team will receive with the return to the investor; and
   - creating the checks and balances that allow a private equity fund to be a back-seat financial investor while giving it significant protection against any change in the status quo.

   When a corporate buyer buys a company it acquires 100% of the shares and subsumes the company into its corporate group. The business becomes a wholly owned subsidiary of the buyer and, typically, its systems and operations are integrated into those of its parent. The management of the business will usually be employees. If the owner of the business chooses to reward the management for improved performance, it will usually do so through discretionary annual cash payments such as bonuses.

   A private equity fund adopts a different model when acquiring a business. The primary aim of a private equity fund is to increase the value of the business it acquires in order to make a profit when it exits. A profitable exit can be achieved in three main ways:
   - by paying down the business' debt so the equity becomes more valuable;
   - by exiting at a higher multiple than that paid on entry; or
   - by improving the operation of the underlying business to increase its value.

   The private equity investor will look to the business' management, in particular, to achieve the last of these.

   A fundamental principle of private equity is alignment of economic interest. The financial interests of the individuals who manage a private equity fund are aligned with those of the investors in the private equity fund through the carried interest structure. In a similar way, the private equity fund tries to align the financial interests of the management of the businesses in which it invests with those of the private equity fund. When a private equity investor acquires a business it expects management to invest in that business alongside it. Management's performance is rewarded not through increases in annual salaries or annual bonuses but through increases in the value of their and the private equity fund's investment in the business. By giving the management team equity in the business acquired, it is hoped that they will be incentivised to increase the return both the private equity fund and management receive on exit.

2. **Management buyout or leveraged buyout?**

The earliest private equity transactions were generally led by management teams. The management of an unloved division of a large conglomerate would approach its parent company and suggest that they be allowed to lead a management buyout and find a financial backer for the acquisition. The sale would generate cash for the parent and allow management to direct the future course of the business.

The management team would then approach private equity backers to see if they would provide financial support for the buyout. Originally, many private equity investments followed a similar strategy to current venture capitalist or development capital models. The investors would provide finance to businesses in return for a minority interest in the shares of the company. While venture and development capital funds still follow this model, many private equity managers have moved towards larger and more complex buyouts. As private equity has grown and developed, its acquisitions have become larger and more sophisticated, and are increasingly led by the private equity investor rather than management. While some management teams do still instigate buyouts, increasingly private equity transactions are put together by corporate finance advisers or the private equity funds themselves. The market has moved from small venture transactions, where investment was provided to help management to develop the business, to private equity funds using bank finance and large amounts of equity finance to buy substantial public companies. The high-water mark of the mergers and acquisitions boom in the mid-2000s was the first public-to-private of a FTSE100 company, Alliance Boots, backed by KKR, which was completed in the middle of 2007 as the global financial crisis took hold. Venture and development capital investments are still an important part of the market, but private equity has increasingly become synonymous with large leveraged buyouts of mature businesses.

In early private equity transactions, the private equity fund would typically be a minority shareholder, holding between 25% and 50% of the shares. The remainder of the shares were held by management. In contrast, it is now unusual for management to hold more than 25% of the shares in the investment vehicle. The larger the business acquired, the smaller management's equity stake tends to be. Whereas private equity funds were happy to take only, say, 30% of the shares on a £3 million investment, on a £1 billion acquisition using bank debt and large amounts of the private equity fund's money, the private equity fund will hold a much larger proportion of the equity. As the size and complexity of transactions have increased, power and control have shifted from management to the private equity fund.

Nonetheless, management are still a key part of any buyout, and the equity package is a fundamental part of any private equity transaction.

3. Structure of investment

Each time a private equity fund acquires a business, it sets up a new corporate group structure to effect the acquisition. A chain of newly incorporated companies are established which, following completion of the acquisition, are ultimately owned by the private equity fund and the management team. While it is common to refer to private equity funds 'buying' businesses, they do not buy businesses directly. The private equity fund invests in a corporate structure which then acquires the business. A diagram of a typical investment and acquisition structure is set out below. For simplicity, references to the 'buyer' in this chapter are to Topco, Midco 1, Midco 2 and Bidco together.

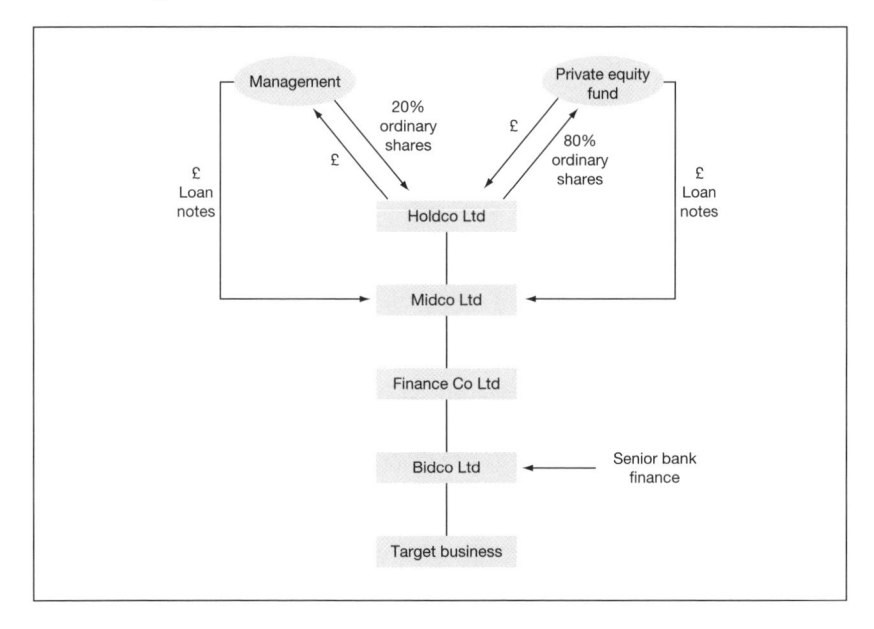

```
                    Management                    Private equity
                                                      fund
                              20%
                            ordinary       £
                             shares               80%
                                                ordinary
        £         £                              shares        £
       Loan                                                   Loan
       notes                                                  notes
                            Holdco Ltd

                             Midco Ltd

                           Finance Co Ltd

                             Bidco Ltd  ←——  Senior bank
                                              finance

                          Target business
```

The structure described above is typical for a UK investment and acquisition using English companies. Over the years, many variations of this structure have developed (eg, using companies incorporated in Luxembourg or using limited partnerships rather than companies), largely to address the internal structure of the private equity funds and to prevent unfunded tax charges from arising for the investors in the private equity fund during the life of the investment.

The newly incorporated companies obtain their funding to acquire the target business from a combination of debt finance from banks and equity finance from the private equity fund and management. The debt finance is used to pay part of the purchase price for the business and is lent by the banks to the acquiring company. Because the buyer is a new company established simply to buy the business and has no other assets, the debt finance is usually secured against the assets of the business being acquired if, as in the United Kingdom, the law allows this. Using a chain of three or four newly established companies to acquire the business is usually driven by the banks' requirement that their debt be structurally subordinated to the private equity fund's investment. By lending to Bidco, rather than Topco, the banks have direct rights against the company that owns the business and therefore the assets of the group. The private equity fund and management have no rights against Bidco. So, if the banks need to take action and enforce their security over the assets they can largely do so – in theory at least – without taking account of the private equity fund's or management's interests.

The private equity fund will usually make its investment through a combination of ordinary shares and a shareholder debt instrument. Depending on the internal structure of the private equity fund itself, the shareholder debt instrument may be structured as either preference shares or, more typically, loan notes.

The expression 'equity' usually means the ordinary shares in a company. However, in private equity transactions it is used loosely to refer to all monies invested in the structure by the private equity fund and management, whether in shares or shareholder debt instruments. The equity finance ranks behind all of the debt finance lent to the group by the banks. A private equity fund's investment in a business is a medium-term investment. The private equity fund does not expect to receive cash flow through dividends or interest payments during the life of its investment. Usually, the amount of equity finance provided and any interest or return on it can only be paid to the private equity fund once the debt finance has been repaid to the banks in full. The equity finance and any interest or return that has accrued on it will typically be received by the private equity fund and management only when the business is sold or floated on the stock exchange or the debt finance is refinanced with new banks (an 'exit event').

If preference shares are used, either a fixed annual dividend or occasionally a dividend that relates to the level of profits in the business each year will accrue on the preference shares and be payable on an exit event. Even if the business has cash available that could be distributed to its shareholders, the group's banks will usually not allow this to happen. Therefore, no dividend will actually be paid on the preference shares until an exit.

If loan notes are used, the private equity fund will lend money to the issuer, usually Midco 1. The amount lent will be repaid on a sale or listing or on a date, say, 10 years in the future. Interest will be payable on the loan notes. However, the private equity fund does not expect to receive yearly payments of interest from its investment. Interest will accrue on the loan note, but will roll up (or will be satisfied by the issue of further loan notes to the private equity fund, known as 'PIK' or 'payment-in-kind' notes) and will not be paid until the principal amount of the loan is repaid. Using loan notes has advantages over preference shares. Because loan notes are debt rather than shares, they can be repaid or the interest on them can be paid even if a company does not have profits available for distribution, which is a requirement before dividends can be paid on the preference shares or (unless the more cumbersome provisions enabling redemption out of capital are used) the preference shares can be redeemed. A further advantage in using loan notes is that, if structured correctly, the company may be able to claim a tax deduction each year for the interest due to be paid on the loan notes, whether the interest is paid or not. Loan notes are also often listed on a recognised stock exchange such as the Channel

Islands Securities Exchange or the Cayman Stock Exchange to take advantage of the quoted eurobond tax exemption, which enables interest to be paid to investors without the deduction of holding tax by the issuer.

Almost all of the private equity fund's money will be invested in loan notes or preference shares. A small amount will be invested in ordinary shares in Topco. Management will also invest their money in ordinary shares. Just as the equity finance is subordinated to the debt finance from the banks, some of the instruments that make up the equity finance rank above others. The loan notes or preference shares will be payable in priority to the ordinary shares. The loan notes or preference shares will only ever be entitled to a fixed return (the original amount invested plus the annual interest or accruing dividend on that amount). Once the debt provided by the banks and loan notes/preference shares plus accrued interest or dividend on them have been repaid, the ordinary shares will be entitled to all remaining value in the business. While the loan notes or preference shares get the private equity fund back the money it invested plus a healthy annual return, it is the ordinary shares that will hopefully increase substantially in value.

If this is the first time that the business has been acquired by a private equity fund – a 'primary buyout' – the management will not usually have shares to sell in the transaction and therefore will not receive any of the proceeds from the transaction. In these circumstances the management will acquire only ordinary shares in the buyer structure. This investment is known as 'sweet equity' because, due to the large amount being invested by the private equity fund in its debt instruments, the amount payable for the ordinary shares is relatively small – say, £100,000 for 20% of the ordinary shares. If management achieve the business plan and enhance the value of the business, their ordinary shares will entitle them to 20% of that value once the private equity fund has been repaid its loans plus a fixed return.

If the business is being sold by a private equity owner to another private equity investor – a 'secondary buyout' – management will be selling the shares they hold in the company. They will usually be required to reinvest some of their proceeds in the new vehicle. If so, management will acquire loan notes or preference shares alongside the private equity fund, as well as ordinary shares. For management, a tax-efficient way to do this may be to roll over their capital gain on the shares they are selling into the new investment. Mechanically, this is done by exchanging management's shares in the target for loan notes in Bidco, these are then exchanged for loan notes in Midco, and so on until the managers hold shares in Topco. Management's capital gains tax charge is then deferred until the disposal of the Topco shares.

The involvement of management is a key part of the private equity structure. In assessing the price to pay for a business, the private equity fund relies heavily on management's assessment of their business. Together, management and the private equity fund will develop a business plan that sets out the anticipated future strategy for the business and the anticipated growth in value of the private equity fund's investment over a timeframe of between three and five years. This projected growth is key to the fund's decision as to whether to make the investment and acquire the

Equity finance

business. The fact that management are investing their own money alongside the private equity fund gives some comfort that management believe both in the business being acquired and that the projected growth in value is achievable.

In backing a management team, a private equity fund will want to ensure that:
- the management team will run the business properly and will maximise value for its investors;
- the management team will remain involved in the business following the acquisition – the fact that the team have personal money locked into the business should incentivise them to stay involved and not leave for a competitor;
- the business's financial performance targets as predicted by management will be achieved;
- the private equity fund can protect its investment even if management have full day-to-day operational control of the business; and
- the private equity fund can realise its investment within a timeframe of between three and five years, with a particular level of return.

These principles underpin the private equity investor's approach to its investment and form the framework of the legal equity documentation that provides the structure to the equity relationship.

4. The acquisition

In principle, a private equity transaction is like any other private company acquisition. However, there are certain key distinguishing features relating to:
- the fact that management probably have a greater day-to-day knowledge of the business being sold than the seller;
- management's relationship with the proposed buyer of the business; and
- the fact that, following completion of the sale, management will own part of the business and, therefore, while working as the seller's employees, will also have a personal financial interest in the buyer which they want to protect.

These issues cut across the standard divide in a transaction process between the seller, the buyer and the business' employees.

As in any corporate acquisition, the vehicle acquiring the business, Bidco, will enter into sale documentation with the seller (sale and purchase agreement, tax indemnity etc). The documents will set out the terms on which the business is being acquired from the seller. The sale documentation will generally be very similar to other private mergers and acquisitions contracts.

However, the fact that management are a key component in the private equity structure and will be part-owners of the buyer gives the buyer and the seller both issues and advantages. A key part of the legal sale documentation is apportioning the risk for any liabilities that arise in the companies being sold. Risk is usually apportioned by the seller giving warranties and indemnities through which it will reimburse the buyer for any related loss that arises following the sale.

When negotiating warranties and indemnities (if any), the seller will often seek to argue that it is merely a shareholder of the business – all knowledge relating to the business rests with management. The seller will therefore want the private equity investor to look to the management team, rather than the seller, for comfort on the risks relating to the business. The seller will use this position to try to give only limited warranties and indemnities to the buyer in the sale documentation in order to minimise its liability for losses relating to its period of ownership. From a commercial perspective, a corporate or institutional seller may baulk at the idea of giving the buyer, which is partly owned by management, comfort on the way in which management have run the business.

However, the buyer will argue that the seller has received past profits from the business and therefore should take all liabilities relating to those profits – therefore reducing the buyer's exposure to such liabilities. The seller is also receiving all of the consideration payable for the business. A buyer will argue that as the seller is taking all the benefit, it therefore should take the risk. On a first-time sale, where management are receiving only an exit bonus, the seller will struggle to convince the buyer that management rather than the seller should take legal responsibility for all past liabilities.

If the sale is a secondary buyout, a private equity fund will be selling most of the shares and receiving most of the consideration. Private equity funds may be prohibited by the terms of their constitutional documents from giving warranties and indemnities. While this is commercially convenient, it also prevents contingent liabilities arising in the fund that would prevent it from being wound up at the end of its 10-year life span. As a consequence, only the management shareholders will give a buyer warranties on a secondary buyout. While management should be receiving some cash for the sale of the shares they hold, the amount will usually be small in comparison to the consideration payable to the private equity fund – perhaps just 25% of the total amount. As a result, a buyer in a secondary buyout must rely even more on the fact that management are investing alongside it in the acquisition, and will look to management to give it some level of contractual comfort about the business being acquired. In this situation buyers may also look to obtain warranty and indemnity insurance to provide additional protection and bridge the gap between the level of warranty protection they would ordinarily expect to receive and the level of protection available.

Managers have a potential conflict between their role as employees of the business being sold and as potential investors in the buyer. As the seller's employees, the management team have a duty under their service agreements to act in the best interests of their employer and, if applicable, as directors to act in the best interests of the company. In particular, the management team have an obligation to keep information about the business confidential. These obligations do not sit easily with their role as future part-owners of the business and the role the management would ideally wish to play in a management buyout: interacting with potential buyers and negotiating the terms of management's investment in the buyer.

Where management are being allowed to lead the buyout, they will usually obtain a waiver from their employer allowing them to discuss the business and its anticipated financial results with potential investors. This information is very useful to the private equity fund in deciding whether it wishes to acquire the business. However, it also helps the private equity investor determine whether the business is truly worth the price that the seller is demanding. Where the parent company is running the sale, it will want to keep the managers on a tight leash, restricting their access to potential buyers and limiting the information that they can disclose to potential buyers.

Regardless of the restrictions that the seller puts in place, at some point in the sale process management will cross the table, and their allegiance will shift from their employer to their new private equity backer. For example, a seller will want to maximise the price achieved on the sale. Management (as part buyers) will hopefully want to minimise the price paid for the business and obtain whatever protection possible from the seller for known liabilities. If the buyer overpays for the business, the value of management's investment in the buyer will be reduced and it will be more difficult for them to receive the expected return on an eventual exit. The involvement of management in the ownership of the buyer should create an alignment of interest between the private equity investor and management that can work to the seller's detriment. Therefore, the management team may want as much information as possible (both negative and positive) about the business provided to the buyer in the disclosure process. In contrast the seller will not want openly to raise issues that may cause the buyer to revaluate the business and reduce its price.

5. **The equity documents**

The ongoing relationship between the private equity fund and management as investors in the buyer is governed by the equity documents, which are usually a shareholders' agreement (sometimes called an investment agreement) and the articles of association of the company in which they hold shares, Topco.

The shareholders' agreement is a contract between the various shareholders in the company setting out what they can and cannot do in respect of their investment. If a shareholder breaches the terms of the agreement, another shareholder can sue it for breach of contract, claiming damages in respect of the loss it has suffered or, in certain circumstances, specific performance.

The articles are the constitution of the company; they set out how the company is to be operated and the rights that the shareholders have against the company. The shareholders are expected to enforce their rights by taking action against the company if an act is carried out in breach of their rights under the articles and is unconstitutional. However, it is difficult legally for a shareholder to enforce its rights under the articles directly against another shareholder that has breached the terms of the articles. This is why the shareholders' agreement is used in conjunction with the articles to create the necessary contractual obligations and remedies between the shareholders.

The shareholders' agreement and the articles are therefore used by private equity funds both to maximise their control over their investment and to protect their interests legally. This is particularly important because a private equity fund is not involved in the day-to-day operation of the business and it relies on management to a significant extent to run the business properly and to provide the investor with accurate information.

6. The shareholders' agreement

The shareholders' agreement fulfils two over-arching functions. It sets out:
- the basis on which the investee company is capitalised and how this 'equity finance' is to be used in completing the acquisition and/or for the business' general working capital; and
- the basis on which the shareholders in the investee company have agreed to regulate themselves after the initial investment has been made and during the life of that investment.

6.1 Investment mechanics

The mechanics of the investment will depend on its structure – for example:
- whether there are one or several new companies in the buyout structure;
- how many investors there are; and
- whether management are investing directly in Topco or whether they are rolling over all or part of an existing shareholding in the company being sold.

Regardless of the structure, the principles behind the investment mechanics remain the same:
- the private equity fund is obliged to invest money into the structure in return for being allocated ordinary shares and loan notes or preference shares; and
- the management team are contractually obliged to make their investment in return for the allotment of ordinary shares and possibly loan notes or preference shares.

The contractual obligations on the private equity fund and management to make their investment are particularly important where the buyer must prove that it will have the funds to complete the acquisition and pay the seller the consideration due. If a public company is being acquired, the buyer will need to demonstrate that the private equity fund is contractually obliged under the shareholders' agreement to invest in the buyer's structure, and that the private equity fund can call down the monies required from its investors. In large acquisitions of private companies, if there is a period of time between exchange and completion, sellers have increasingly asked for contractual comfort that the private equity fund will invest the monies to allow the buyer (which is only a newly established company with assets of, say, £2) to complete the acquisition and pay the seller the monies due. Without that comfort, the seller's only remedy would be to sue a shell company with no assets. This comfort takes the form of an equity commitment letter written by the private equity fund to the seller stating that on the satisfaction of certain conditions (including availability of the buyer's debt funding) the fund will invest cash into the buyer, as it is obliged to under the shareholders' agreement.

6.2 Investor protections

The shareholders' agreement will typically afford the forms of protection to the private equity investor that are set out next.

(a) **Restrictive covenants**

In recognition of the central importance of management to the private equity investor's decision to invest, management give covenants that will be activated if they cease to work for the business. These covenants typically restrict a manager for a specified period of time following his departure from the business, from:
- working for a business that competes with the business being acquired;
- engaging existing employees of the business; or
- dealing with or enticing away clients and customers of the business.

There is typically a debate as to how long this restriction should apply for and how extensive it should be. This debate operates against a broader legal framework relating to restrictive covenants. As a general principle, it can be fairly difficult for a business to enforce these provisions against ex-employees because it is deemed unfair to prevent someone from earning a living. However, these covenants relate to the employee's financial investment as a shareholder in the group rather than his role as an employee. Therefore, if correctly drafted, they should be more enforceable than similar restrictions in employment contracts.

(b) **Investor consents and veto rights**

The private equity investor is an institutional investor; looking for a financial return on its investment rather than acquiring a business in order to make a part of a larger trading group. As a result, the private equity investor will generally not want to be involved in the day-to-day management of the business. However, the fund will want to ensure that the business is run within pre-agreed parameters, so as to ensure that its investment is protected and that the business is run in the manner contemplated in the business plan that formed the basis for the private equity investor's original investment.

The private equity fund will hold investments in various businesses. Each business will be held separately, and there will be no sharing of resources by either the private equity fund or its other investments and the business it acquires. They will have entirely separate finance and accounting systems. The business will be run separately by the managers of the business, many of whom will also be shareholders in the business. As a result of its lack of day-to-day involvement, the private equity investor will try to protect its financial investment through certain contractual rights that are built into the shareholders' agreement and the articles. The shareholders' agreement will provide, among other things, covenants from the group companies and management that:
- the business will always be operated in a certain way unless the private equity investor agrees otherwise;
- certain steps will not be taken by the business unless the private equity investor agrees; and
- certain information about the business will be provided to the private equity fund.

A shareholder, even a majority shareholder, is only automatically legally entitled to limited information about the business in which it invests. Decisions about the day-to-day control and operation of the business are made by the company's board rather than its shareholders. A private equity investor usually only takes two or three seats on Topco's board of directors, generally putting it in the minority of directors and therefore unable to block any decision with which it disagrees. A private equity fund will usually ultimately have the right to appoint and dismiss directors as it decides, usually because of the size of its shareholding. However, even if the directors appointed by the private equity fund could block or force through board decisions, a director has fiduciary duties to the company, its shareholders and, in some circumstances, its creditors. He therefore cannot necessarily force the board to take a decision just because it suits the interests of one shareholder, even a majority shareholder. Therefore, the shareholders' agreement usually sets out a list of things that the companies in the group either must do or cannot do unless the private equity fund (in its role as shareholder) consents otherwise.

As a general principle, the investor's consent operates as a negative right: the private equity fund cannot direct the company to take a particular action, but may only veto an action being taken. The key exception to this is the annual budget, which is typically sent to the private equity fund for its approval.

The aim of the veto is to protect the private equity investor's financial investment and to maintain the structure of the investee company in the same form as when it was acquired and the investment decision was made. For example, an investment decision may have been made based on an assumed capital expenditure for a financial year. If the board decides to spend more than this, that may prejudice the value of the private equity fund's investment. The private equity fund does not control the board and is not involved in day-to-day management. It therefore needs to be asked about, and given the opportunity to veto, such matters in order to protect its investment. Veto rights may also be necessary to ensure that the company does not inadvertently cause the private equity investor to breach certain laws and regulations that are applicable to it.

These veto rights are contractual only. An investee company could still choose not to disclose a matter to its shareholders and to take action without obtaining the necessary consent. If this were to happen, the private equity fund would be left trying to sue for damages for any loss it may have suffered. In some circumstances there may be no loss; the business may be taking a direction with which the private equity fund does not agree, but that does not necessarily mean that the private equity fund has lost money on its investment.

Most private equity-backed companies will also have entered into extensive financing documents with their banks, which impose heavy restrictions on the manner in which the business can operate. The restrictive nature of these banking documents can make the investor's consent/veto irrelevant in practice, since the primary concern is always obtaining the bank's consent. The investor consent restrictions are explicitly subject to the terms of the banking documents.

(c) **The board of directors**
The articles and/or the shareholders' agreement will provide that the private equity

fund may appoint a prescribed number of directors to the boards of all companies in the group. The directors appointed by the private equity fund usually constitute the minority of directors on the board of a company. The majority of board members will typically be executive management, plus (sometimes) independent non-executive directors.

Generally, if the private equity fund holds sufficient shares in the investee company, it will also be able to appoint an unlimited number of directors to the board at any time by giving notice. In practice, this right, which is known as a 'flooding right', will be exercised only in extreme circumstances, because the private equity fund usually has no desire to take control of the business unless it feels it must.

In larger transactions and private equity transactions outside the United Kingdom, it is not unusual to find that all directors on the board of the top company in the group are appointed by the private equity investor or are non-executives.

The private equity fund usually encourages the board to appoint an independent chairman. The chairman can provide strategic oversight and create an independent bridge between the private equity fund and the management team.

(d) ***Communication rights***

The private equity investor will want to ensure that it receives regular information in relation to the business during the life of the investment in order to track its performance. As a shareholder, the private equity fund is legally automatically entitled to receive only limited financial information about the business. Instead, a direct contractual obligation on the group and management is required to send it the information it needs. The private equity investor devotes a significant amount of time to monitoring its investment. To enable this, management are required to produce detailed financial information on cash flow, profit and loss, balance-sheet liabilities and so on every month. The private equity investor analyses this information each month to determine whether the investment is performing in accordance with the business plan. Having regular access to this information allows the private equity investor to play a more active role and should help it to respond quickly if the business deviates from the business plan. In addition to financial information that will allow the private equity investor to monitor its investment, the private equity investor may also require information to enable it to comply with its own obligations under various laws and regulations that apply to it, such as the Alternative Investment Fund Managers Directive, the Carbon Reduction Commitment (CRC) Energy Efficiency Scheme and the Walker Guidelines on Disclosure and Transparency.

When the private equity investor is proposing to realise its investment in the group, it will want to ensure that it can pass on information, which would otherwise be confidential, as required to its advisers, potential investors in its fund structure, potential purchasers and the advisers to potential purchasers.

(e) ***Warranties***

For the managers, the most important aspect of the shareholders' agreement is often the warranty protection sought by the private equity investors from the management team. As discussed above, the buyer will seek warranty protection from the seller in the transaction documents. In addition to these warranties, the management team will be asked to give warranties in the shareholders' agreement directly to the private equity investor.

The warranties given by management in the shareholders' agreement are different from the usual warranties found in a sale and purchase agreement. The warranties in a sale and purchase agreement cover the various areas of the business being acquired and its assets and liabilities. The warranties in the shareholders' agreement tend to cover the information that assisted the private equity investor in making its investment decision (eg, how good the due diligence work is), and the relationship between the private equity investor and management. The warranties requested in the shareholders' agreement usually cover statements confirming that:

- the personal information that each manager has provided to the private equity fund in response to its questionnaire is complete and accurate;
- the managers have read the various financial, legal and commercial due diligence reports that the buyer (and, on some occasions, the seller) has had prepared, and that they agree with factual issues contained in the due diligence reports and the opinions expressed therein. Management are also often asked to warrant that there is nothing that is not contained in the due diligence reports (and vendor due diligence reports, if applicable) that the private equity fund should be aware of before investing; and
- the management have prepared the business plan properly, taking into account the relevant information and using reasonable assumptions, and have not since become aware of anything that materially alters the projections in the plan.

The private equity fund may also ask management to provide a 'sweeper' warranty that management are not aware of any breach of the warranties given by the seller in the sale documents. Any breach management feel they have to disclose against this warranty will be embarrassing for the seller, but this is also a useful way for the buyer to check that management have not been forced by the seller to suppress any information.

These warranties are not designed to allocate the financial responsibility between management and the private equity investor. The aim of the management warranties is to try to flush out anything that management know which could influence the private equity fund's decision to invest. For that reason, the drafting of the warranties is generally softer than acquisition warranties in sale and purchase agreements. The warranties are often subject to materiality thresholds or the subjective opinion of the managers. As with the seller's warranties, the managers will produce a disclosure letter that discloses any areas where the warranties would otherwise be breached.

The management will be personally liable for these warranties. If there is a successful claim for breach of warranty, they will have to pay the private equity fund damages from their own assets. Therefore the managers will want to cap their liability at as small an amount as possible and considerably less than the amount invested by the private equity fund. Management's liability will usually be capped at a multiple of their salary or as a proportion of the proceeds they are receiving from the sale. Each manager will also want to ensure that they are each liable only for their proportionate part of any loss suffered as a result of a breach of warranty. There will be a cap on the aggregate liability of each manager, and the percentage of each claim for which each manager can be liable will be capped. Although giving warranties can cause the managers concern, it is unusual for a private equity investor to bring a claim under these warranties given the relatively small amount that can usually be claimed under them, their subjective nature and an understandable reluctance on the part of private equity investors to sue their management teams.

7. The articles of association

Certain further protections are afforded to the private equity investor by means of the articles. There is a level of interplay between the provisions of the articles and the shareholders' agreement.

Like the shareholders' agreement, the key aim of many of the provisions in the articles is to protect the private equity investor's position. For that reason, the articles of a private equity-backed company are typically more complicated than the articles of a normal private or public company.

7.1 Permitted transfers

As discussed above:

- the identity of the management team is central to the private equity investor's decision to invest in a business;
- the managers' investment in the business alongside the private equity investor is a central feature of their incentivisation and the private equity model; and
- management should receive a return on their investment (or their money back) only when the private equity fund does.

Therefore, as a general principle, the managers' equity stake is not transferable. There are typically certain caveats to this general restriction on transfers. Managers are usually permitted to transfer their shares:

- to a trust established to benefit their family;
- to their immediate family members; and
- as part of their personal pension arrangements.

The extent of the restrictions on the transfer of shares will be a function of the degree of commercial leverage that the management team enjoys. However, it is certainly market standard for these provisions to be extremely restrictive. In addition, the articles will typically provide for a deemed transfer back of shares transferred to permitted transferees if the initial permitted transferee ceases to qualify as such.

In contrast, the private equity investor will want to have considerable flexibility to transfer its shareholding in the investee company to another member of its group, to an associate or investors in its funds or similar. In some circumstances the private equity investor can transfer its shares freely. It will want to ensure that it has maximum flexibility to facilitate any reorganisation of its fund structure or to move the shares to another fund managed or advised by the same manager or adviser. In addition, if syndication of its proposed investment is contemplated, the private equity investor will want to ensure that it can transfer its interest to a proposed syndicatee.

7.2 Leaver provisions

As a corollary to the fact that management hold their equity stake in the company in order to incentivise them and to drive their performance by allowing them to share in any value upside on an exit, if their employment with the business terminates the private equity investor will want to ensure that managers' shares are taken from them. It is a key principle that, other than in exceptional circumstances, management should benefit from the proceeds of an eventual exit only if they are working in the business pushing to achieve the value at the time of exit.

From management's perspective, this principle is open to abuse. A manager could work for three years driving value in the business for the investors, but if his employment is terminated for no good reason shortly before an exit, he will lose all the value he has helped to create.

Trying to reconcile these different commercial positions leads to much of the complexity in leaver provisions and the concepts of 'good' and 'bad' leavers.

(a) Classification of leavers

The leaver provisions are typically referred to as the 'compulsory transfer provisions'. They usually operate so as to permit Topco (very often only at the private equity investor's discretion) a period following the manager's departure within which to force the manager to sell his shares in Topco. In the meantime, the leaver's shares will usually become non-voting shares. The decision on whether to force the manager to sell his shares will most often be at the discretion of Topco. It does not give the departing manager a guaranteed right to have his investment returned to him. The provisions typically give Topco the discretion to decide whether the departing manager should transfer his shareholding to an incoming manager, to another existing manager, to an employee benefit trust or to the company, by means of a share buy-back.[1] The value the manager receives for his shares is usually a function of whether the manager is a 'good leaver' or a 'bad leaver'. These definitions will be carefully negotiated by the private equity investors and the management team. Generally, the private equity fund will want to prescribe narrowly the circumstances in which a leaver can count as a good leaver. Accordingly, the definition of good leaver will often be limited to certain circumstances (eg, death or permanent disability) and bad leaver will be defined as departure in any other

---

1   The tax treatment of a share buy-back is likely to be different for the departing manager. His proceeds will probably be taxed as a distribution.

circumstances. Conversely, management will want to prescribe narrowly the circumstances in which a leaver counts as a bad leaver. They will want to limit the definition of bad leaver to only certain serious circumstances where they are at fault (eg, termination for serious cause) and for good leaver to be defined as departure in any other circumstances.

The precise scope of these definitions will vary from investment to investment. Most private equity investors will have their standard preferred position. However, the strength of the management team's negotiating position will have an impact on this.

In circumstances where a leaver is a good leaver, he will most often receive fair market value for his shares. Conversely, where a leaver is a bad leaver, he will often receive the lower of cost and fair market value for his shares. An increasingly common position taken by private equity investors is to also introduce a concept of a 'very bad leaver', being a manager who has left the business and subsequently breaches his restrictive covenants by competing with the business, for example. In these circumstances, a good or bad leaver may be reclassified as a very bad leaver and more draconian consequences may apply.

If the interest on the bank debt in a private equity structure is rolling up and is not being paid in full each year, even where a business is doing well, the shares could be worth less during the first couple of years of the investment than the price they were originally acquired for. Conversely, a good leaver whose shares are acquired at the high point in an economic cycle could receive more money than his fellow managers on a later eventual exit. In circumstances where the parties are unable to agree on the fair market value of the shares, the matter will typically be referred to an accountant to act as an independent expert. There is a divergence of approach across the market as to whether the articles should set out the key reference points for the accountants in carrying out this process or whether it should be left to their discretion (it may also be the case that, even where the articles specify a valuation procedure, the valuer may in practice refuse to follow this). Calculating the fair market value of illiquid shares in a private company that is carrying a substantial amount of leverage is difficult. With no market for the shares, the valuers usually look to comparable public companies, if there are any, and adjust to take account of the bank debt, shareholder debt and limited market for the shares. The valuation process may also be costly and the articles will usually provide that the leaver must contribute to the cost of obtaining a valuation where the fair market value is disputed.

On a secondary buyout where managers have rolled over their proceeds from the sale of original shares in the company being sold into the new investee company, part of their equity interest may form part of the 'institutional strip'. The loan notes or preference shares and related ordinary shares that have been acquired by management were, in the past, not usually subject to the leaver provisions. Previously, the manager would usually continue to own these interests although the accruing interest rate on them may be reduced. However, practice on this is now changing, and it is not uncommon for leaver provisions to apply to both the managers' sweet equity and their institutional strip. The terms on which leaver provisions apply to institutional strip (both any loan notes or preference shares and related ordinary shares) tend to be heavily negotiated and may be more favourable than the leaver provisions applying to sweet equity.

(b) *Vesting*

The starting point on a primary buyout, as discussed above, is that a manager who leaves for whatever reason is likely to be forced to transfer all of his shares in the company. However, the articles may provide that either:
- the manager is entitled to retain a specific percentage of his shares (which is typically determined by reference to his period of ownership). This is known as 'ownership vesting' and is uncommon; or
- the compulsory seller may receive market value for a certain percentage of his shares and cost for the remainder. This is known as 'value vesting' and is common. It is often articulated in a third category of leaver, 'intermediate leavers', which can be used to resolve differences between management and the private equity investor on good and bad leaver terms, although increasingly value vesting may apply to good leavers where a wider definition of good leavers is used.

Ownership vesting and value vesting are negotiation points, and the result is often a function of a given manager's historic involvement with the company.

7.3 Drag-along and tag-along rights

(a) *Drag along*

The private equity investor's key focus will be to maximise the return on its investment within a particular timeframe. It is central to this goal that the private equity fund not be prevented from realising its investment, when it chooses to do so, without being constrained by management. A buyer will usually want to acquire only 100% of the shares in a company, even if it then chooses to give a certain percentage to management. Therefore, it would not be interested in acquiring a company in which a disgruntled management team held a minority stake.

If, say, more than 50% of the shares in the company are being sold, the sellers can usually invoke the drag-along provisions and compel the remaining shareholders to transfer their shares in the company to the proposed buyer of the shares. Whether or not the trigger sale will require the consent of certain of the management team will be a function of the respective negotiating positions of the parties at the time the articles are agreed, but usually it will not. While drag-along provisions are often a useful threat against difficult members of management, they are not typically used to transfer a company to a buyer. Historically, there were questions about the legal basis for operating a drag and, furthermore, it was recognised that a third-party purchaser might have little appetite to acquire a company where a significant percentage of the shares were being forcibly delivered.

That said, the general view is that, subject to strict compliance with the procedure contemplated in the drag-along provisions, if the shareholders against whom the drag-along provision is being operated acquired or subscribed for their shares at a point in time when those provisions were contained in the articles, then the provisions are enforceable and valid. However, it is clear that the question as to whether a third-party purchaser or its financing banks are prepared to acquire shares in this way, and without the benefit of any warranty on title, remains; albeit that in substance this is no different from a buyer of shares under the statutory squeeze-out provisions in a takeover. In practice, a third party's willingness to accept a sale on this basis will be determined by how keen it is to purchase the asset in question.

It would be very unusual for the management shareholders to be able to drag the private equity shareholders into a sale.

(b) *Tag along*

Tag-along rights go hand in hand with drag-along rights. Whereas drag-along provisions enable the private equity fund to deliver the entire issued share capital of the company to a third-party purchaser, tag-along provisions permit the management shareholders to participate in sale by the private equity fund of its shares. If the private equity fund proposes to sell a certain percentage of its shares to a third-party purchaser, the other shareholders will be entitled to participate in the sale process and to compel the purchaser to acquire their shares. Depending on the negotiating position of management, they will be entitled to sell either all of their shares or just the same percentage as the private equity fund.

7.4 Ratchet

An increasing number of transactions use ratchets, the drafting of which, in an English company structure, will be set out in the articles. Ratchets are used as a further incentive for management shareholders. A ratchet is a mechanism that permits holders of a particular class of shares in the capital of a company to be allocated a larger percentage of the share capital of the company on an exit by means of the operation of a conversion or other procedure contained in the articles.

Typically, a ratchet mechanism will be used to increase the percentage of the ordinary shares held by the management team on an exit by way of reward for the success of the investment. As the percentage of shares held increases, so too does their share of the exit proceeds allocated to those shares. At the start of an investment, management may hold 20% of the shares and the private equity investor 80%. It is agreed upfront under the articles that if the private equity investor receives on an exit, say, more than 2.5 times the amount it invested, management's shareholding will increase to 25% and the private equity fund will be entitled only to 75% of the proceeds attributable to the ordinary shares. Private equity investors often use ratchets when faced with a difference of opinion between themselves and the management team as to how the investment will perform and the return that management will receive on an exit. Notwithstanding the difference of opinion, the private equity investor may be prepared to allow a greater proportion of equity to be allocated to the managers on exit if the business performs beyond their expectations and if, despite having a lower share of the equity following the operation of the ratchet, the private equity investor is still in a position to realise its target return on its investment. These are typically referred to as 'positive ratchets'. Conversely, a ratchet mechanism can also be used to decrease the percentage of equity held by the managers if the targets are not met. For self-evident reasons, negative ratchets are not considered to be an effective motivational tool.

While the concept underpinning the principle of a ratchet mechanism is relatively straightforward, the specifics of particular ratchet mechanisms means that they are usually relatively bespoke.

Ratchets will typically operate by reference to a hurdle, which is either a target internal rate of return on the investor's investment or a target multiple of the investor's investment to be returned (or both). An exit multiple will typically be calculated by dividing the total cash outflows by the total cash inflows.

Debt finance

Kirstie Hutchinson
Christopher Lawrence
Macfarlanes LLP

1. Introduction

The use of debt finance in private equity transactions is a key tool for private equity sponsors to enhance the potential returns from their equity investments. Structuring the debt finance package and negotiating its terms are therefore a fundamental part of implementing most private equity transactions.

Historically, the majority of this debt finance was provided by the major commercial and investment banks, whose capacity to originate and distribute this debt finance during the years running up to the height of the leveraged finance market in 2007 was vastly increased by the liquidity provided by collateralised loan obligation and collateralised debt obligation investment vehicles (which are described in more detail below). However, the debt finance industry has matured and – following the global financial crisis and the actions taken in response to it by governments and business – evolved, such that funding is now available from a deeper and wider range of sources.

In the European debt markets, these sources now include European, US and global banks, institutional investors such as specialist investment funds and hedge funds (many of which operate solely in the secondary market),[1] insurers, pension funds, alternative lenders and high-yield bond investors.

These providers of debt finance have developed and expanded the range of debt instruments they offer, resulting in a variety of innovative debt finance structures being available to private equity sponsors, particularly in respect of junior (or subordinated) finance.

This chapter will look at typical debt finance structures used in the European debt markets to fund private equity sponsored leveraged acquisitions of private companies.

1.1 A typical newco structure

A new corporate vehicle (a 'newco'), or more commonly a series of newcos, will be incorporated to provide a tax-efficient holding company structure, and these newcos will be funded with a combination of equity, quasi-equity and debt finance to allow one or more of them to acquire the target group. Tax considerations may mean that the newcos are incorporated and tax-resident in jurisdictions that are not associated with either the private equity sponsor or the target company (or companies) to be acquired.

---

[1] The secondary market is the market for trading participations in funded loans.

The lawyers or the accountants acting for the sponsor will develop this acquisition structure, which will be specifically tailored for the transaction and the tax sensitivities of the funds advised or managed by the sponsor that is investing in it. These advisers will prepare a detailed tax structure memorandum for the sponsor, which will provide an in-depth analysis of the relevant laws of the tax regimes applicable to the acquisition. Central to this structure will be the ability to achieve an optimum level of deductibility of the interest costs that will be incurred in respect of the various debt instruments that will be introduced into the structure to finance the acquisition.

Key features of the structure that will be covered by the tax structure memorandum may include:
- the choice of the jurisdiction of incorporation and tax residence of the newcos and the type of corporate entities incorporated;
- the method of transferring funds down through the structure, ultimately to fund the acquisition (for example, by way of intercompany loan, loan notes, equity subscription or capital contribution);
- the taxes that will be incurred in creating the structure and completing the acquisition (for example, stamp or other transfer taxes, capital taxes, registration duties, notarial costs and the costs of incorporation of the newcos);
- strategies to maximise the corporation tax relief for transaction costs and the recovery of VAT on those costs;
- the required notifications, elections and rulings that will be required to be made to, or sought from, the relevant tax authorities;
- the taxes that may be incurred in extracting surplus cash to the investors or on an exit;
- the tax status and treatment of the investments held by the sponsor funds and the management team – for example, in a UK deal determining whether entrepreneurs' relief can be adopted by members of the management team.

A simplified example of a typical newco structure is shown in Diagram 1.

1.2 The total funding package

The total funding package that will be required to fund the cost of the acquisition of the target (the 'Sources' column of the 'Sources and Uses' table set out in Diagram 2) for a leveraged acquisition will comprise:
- one or more layers of debt finance lent into the newco structure, commonly known as senior and junior (or subordinated) debt. This debt finance will usually constitute the largest part of the total funding package, often around 50% of the total transaction value (the proportion constituting debt finance fell significantly following the global financial crisis, as debt finance providers required a greater proportion of sponsor equity investment, but it has crept back up more recently). The debt package will itself, for many mid- and upper-market transactions, comprise more than one type of debt instrument;

Diagram 1.

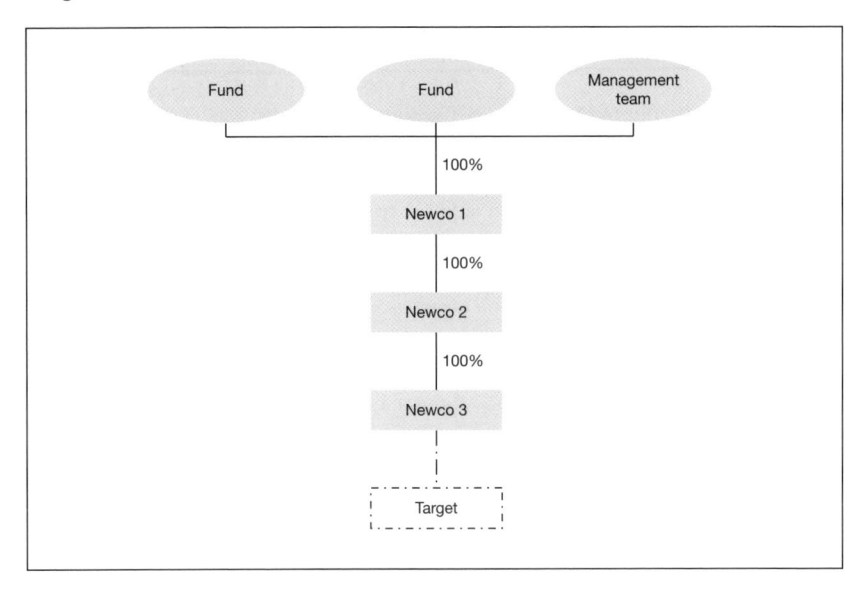

```
    Fund          Fund        Management
                                 team
      └────────────┬────────────┘
                 100%
                   │
               ┌───────┐
               │Newco 1│
               └───────┘
                 100%
                   │
               ┌───────┐
               │Newco 2│
               └───────┘
                 100%
                   │
               ┌───────┐
               │Newco 3│
               └───────┘
                   │
               ┌ ─ ─ ─ ┐
                Target
               └ ─ ─ ─ ┘
```

Diagram 2.

Sources	(£000s)	Uses	(£000s)
Equity contribution, comprising:		Cash consideration	[•]
		Refinancing existing	
Institutional equity	[•]	target debt	[•]
Management equity	[•]	Transaction costs	[•]
Institutional and		Transaction taxes	[•]
management loan notes	[•]		
Senior debt, comprising:			
Facility A	[•]	Cash over-funding (at completion)	[•]
Facility B	[•]	Working capital [•]	[•]
Facility C	[•]		
Revolving credit facility	[•]		
Second lien debt	[•]		
Mezzanine debt	[•]		
Total	[•]*	Total	[•]*

* These should equal one another.

- the equity investment made by the management team and the funds managed or advised by the sponsor, and by the management team. This funding will usually comprise true equity, in the form of share equity, and quasi-equity, in the form of redeemable preference shares, loan notes, discounted bonds or deeply subordinated debt.

The total funding requirement (the 'Uses' column of the 'Sources and Uses' table set out in Diagram 2) will be required to fund:
- the cash consideration payable to the sellers of the target;
- the refinancing of existing financial indebtedness, including bank and other third-party debt in the target group;
- the fees, costs, expenses and taxes incurred in connection with the acquisition, the refinancing of the target group and the preparation and execution of the sale-and-purchase, equity and finance documents relating to the acquisition.

In addition, the senior debt may include additional facilities to be made available to the target group on an ongoing basis (after completion of the acquisition) to:
- fund the target group's capital expenditure;
- fund future strategic and bolt-on acquisitions by the target group;
- fund working capital of the target group;
- provide ancillary facilities, such as overdrafts, letters of credit, bank guarantees and corporate credit lines.

A simplified example of a typical funding structure is shown in Diagram 3.

Diagram 3.

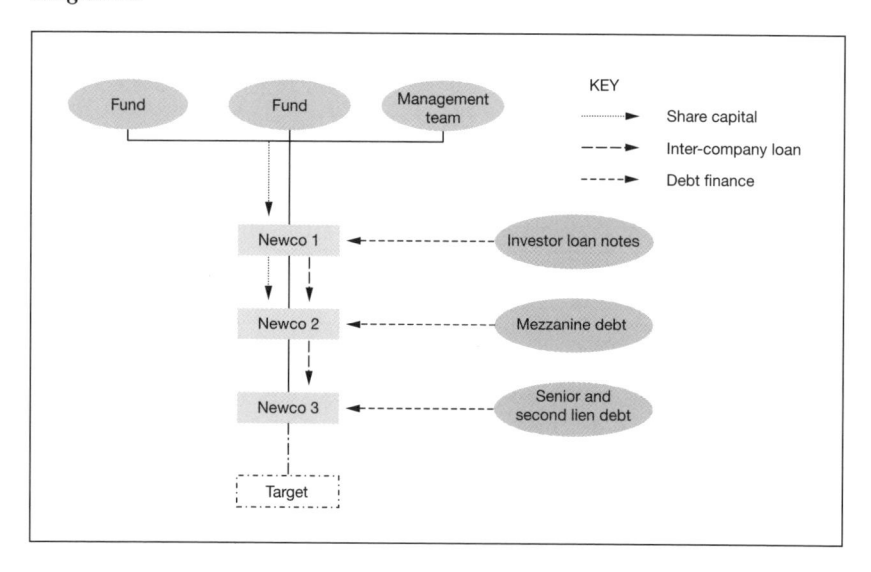

2. The debt finance package

2.1 Overview

The debt finance package for many mid-market and upper-market acquisition finance transactions will comprise two or more layers of debt. During the years running up to the height of the leveraged finance market in 2007, these were typically comprised of senior debt and mezzanine debt, and increasingly in the European lending markets, second lien debt. Larger or more complex acquisitions also sourced debt funds from the issuance of high-yield bonds or payment in kind notes, and the mezzanine debt may have been subdivided into senior mezzanine and junior mezzanine layers of debt.

While European bank debt liquidity recovered significantly in 2012 and 2013 from the severe constraints seen in the aftermath of the financial crisis, a key development over that period was the steady increase in the importance of European high-yield bonds as a major funding element of private equity acquisition financing transactions. This was particularly the case in larger deals requiring debt financing of over £100 million (due to the effective minimum economic size of a high-yield issuance), where high-yield debt has largely supplanted the use of mezzanine debt.

Where exits, whether through a flotation or a secondary or tertiary sale, have proved challenging or economically unattractive for sponsors, a high-yield issuance has also provided an attractive alternative route to return value to investors by way of a refinancing to pay a distribution or repay shareholder debt (a 'dividend recapitalisation', discussed in more detail below) – further increasing the upper market's familiarity and comfort with European high-yield debt and its particular dynamics.

In the mid-market, while mezzanine debt continues as a potential source of debt finance, it has also seen its position challenged by a rise in alternative lenders, in the form of specialist debt funds who operate in the shadow-banking sector. These lenders will often invest non-amortising, longer term debt priced at a level between senior and mezzanine debt and structured as traditionally tranched senior debt, or as a unitranche term facility coupled with a super senior working capital facility. Mezzanine debt has continued to feature in bigger-ticket transactions with debt financing of £200 million and above, although its subdivision into senior and junior mezzanine is now rare due to the liquidity available for larger transactions and the smaller deal size where used in the mid-market.

For larger deals, cross-border financings also featured increasingly in 2012 and 2013 in the UK and other European debt markets, due to the depth of liquidity and comparatively more borrower-friendly pricing and terms available in the US markets. In these financings, lenders in the US debt market finance European transactions that are documented under US-style credit agreements governed by New York law. Any associated working capital facilities and the intercreditor arrangements will typically be documented on Loan Market Association (LMA)[2] terms under English (or local European) law.

2.2 Loan finance

The use of a multi-layered loan finance package offers sponsors a flexible and relatively cheap source of finance. The key benefits of the use of loan finance are:

- the ease and speed of implementation and the ability to retain confidentiality – compared to implementing a securitisation finance structure or issuing high-yield bonds or equity instruments, loan finance can be put in place relatively quickly, with a minimal number of advisers and with few public disclosure requirements; these features are essential to meeting the demanding timetables on which most private equity transactions are run;
- depending on the tax regimes applicable, most – if not all – of the interest costs that accrue on, and the deal fees associated with, the raising of the loan finance can be deducted against the taxable profits generated by the target group;
- flexibility – the structure, quantum, pricing and terms of a loan finance package can be negotiated to suit the transaction in hand, from jumbo facilities totalling billions of pounds to more moderate facilities offering millions, tens of millions or hundreds of millions of finance. The wide range of liquidity offered by loan finance caters for a range of risk profiles, allowing the use of multiple layers of debt instruments with different risk profiles. All but the more subordinated layers of debt allow the loans to be repaid early to allow exit opportunities to be taken.

2.3 Syndication

The amount of funding available for larger leveraged loan finance debt packages would not be achievable without the ability to syndicate the debt, since, for all but the smaller deals, one lender would not wish to fund the entire debt required because of capital adequacy and risk management concerns. A loan syndicate is a group of lenders who each fund a portion of the debt being made available. These lenders each become a party to the loan documents, assume a separate and independent participation in the loans comprising the financing package, and together make these loans available to the borrowers. The fundamental concept is that in forming a syndicate, the lenders do not enter into any form of partnership and do not assume any liability or responsibility for the actions or omissions of their fellow syndicate members. Each of their participations forms a separate loan from each of them to the relevant borrower (although in practice, the lenders advance their loans to a single bank – the agent bank – which then advances the funds to the borrowers as a single loan).

Generally, a loan finance package will be structured, arranged and underwritten

---

[2] The Loan Market Association (LMA) was created in 1996 to foster the development of a secondary market in Euromarket syndicated loans. It is responsible, in consultation with its members and the LMA steering committees on which they sit, for the production and promotion of a number of market standard documents. These include a suite of leveraged acquisition finance facilities documents drafted for senior/mezzanine deals (and produced in several alternative versions governed by other key European laws, as well as English law) and a related intercreditor agreement template. These are regarded as a leveraged loan market standard, albeit (particularly from a sponsor's perspective) only as a starting point for negotiations. The LMA's purpose is to improve the efficiency of the loan markets through the development of standard document templates that have been scrutinised by groups representing borrowers and lenders, although from the borrower side the role is chiefly performed only by the Association of Corporate Treasurers (ACT) in an investment grade context, which is of limited direct application in a leveraged finance context.

by one or several banks (commonly called the arrangers, mandated lead arrangers or MLAs). Different lenders will typically arrange the senior and the junior or mezzanine layer of debt. Senior debt will typically be arranged by banks, while mezzanine debt tends nowadays to be arranged by specialist mezzanine houses, alternative lenders and funds.

The commitment by the arranger will usually be made on a fully underwritten or a best efforts basis. Sponsors are generally keen to secure the debt funding required for a transaction on a fully underwritten basis, but if the arranger is unwilling or unable to underwrite the entire balance of the loan, it may be sufficient for the arranger to commit to use its best efforts to form a syndicate to provide the funding. The banks that fulfil the roles of arranger and underwriter receive a fee for their services – commonly referred to as an arrangement and underwriting fee. If offering a fully underwritten commitment, these banks are willing to commit themselves to lend the full amount of the debt on the basis that they are confident, based on prevailing market conditions and the experience of their syndication teams, that they will be able to syndicate the debt, thus reducing their exposure – potentially to zero, but more commonly to a targeted hold level.

The sponsor will appoint the chosen arranging and underwriting bank(s) at an early stage of a transaction, usually after a short competitive tender process (frequently termed a request for proposals), involving a number of competing banks who will offer term sheets (or comment on/complete a pro forma term sheet provided to the sponsor) setting out the key terms on which they are willing to arrange and underwrite the debt finance package.

More aggressive sponsors might run two or more competing arranging and underwriting banks for a longer period – sometimes until the day of signing the loan documents – before deciding which of them is offering the best terms. This strategy can result in two or more sets of bankers being run all the way to the point of having agreed full-form, final loan documents, with full credit committee approval (in larger bid situations, it can also result in the banks involved themselves running parallel processes, separated by information barriers, for more than one sponsor – known as running trees). The cost of this strategy can be more, since two or more sets of loan documents will require more time from the lawyers; and the bankers – however confident they might feel of success – will often require their out-of-pocket expenses to be reimbursed by the sponsor and for a fee to be paid to the loser(s).

In either strategy, sponsors seek to take advantage of the competitive tension between the competing banks in order to strengthen their negotiating power, and will aim to ensure that the terms offered (in terms of pricing, structure, covenants and the amount of debt) are as favourable to the sponsor as possible.

These appointments will be documented by mandate letters, which will set out the terms of appointment, the conditions on which the underwriting commitment is being offered, the exclusivity of the appointed banks, the underwriter's right to syndicate the debt, the fees payable for the arrangement and underwriting commitments, costs indemnities and confidentiality undertakings.

If a sale is being run as an auction, sellers will frequently require comfort as to the committed nature of the bidder's debt financing. Given the complexity of financing packages and the related expense of negotiating and agreeing the documentation, if the timetable for completing a transaction is particularly short and/or the bidder does not wish to incur unnecessary expense before knowing its bid has been accepted, the underwriting bank may be willing to lend the debt finance on the back of a so-called funded term sheet. In these circumstances, the debt finance is made available pursuant to a short-form loan agreement known as an interim loan agreement or interim facility agreement, and based on the terms set out in an agreed term sheet. This offers more certainty for vendors than a bid supported by a commitment letter and attached term sheet (which is a weaker alternative in a European context than in a US context), but is not intended ever to be drawn down. Instead, in the weeks or months after signing of the sale and purchase agreement and the interim loan agreement (but before first drawdown to achieve completion), the full-form loan, security and intercreditor documents will be negotiated (based on the agreed term sheet), drafted and signed, and will replace the interim arrangements. The use of interim loan agreements has become less common since the global financial crisis, although they may feature as part of a 'stapled financing' package where sellers pre-negotiate an interim facility for bidders to adopt, in order to make the transition from bid to completion smoother and more certain.

Syndication of most debt finance structures for private equity transactions will commence formally after signing of the main loan facilities (although initial market soundings by syndication teams will have taken place at a much earlier stage). This will involve the arranger(s) organising a primary syndication of the facilities (save for the amount which it or they intend to retain) to a number of other financial institutions. The number and make-up of the financial institutions approached during primary syndication will depend on the amount of debt to be syndicated and the composition of the debt – the more sophisticated the financing structure, particularly the subordinated layers of debt, the more specialised the financial institutions that will be targeted. Depending on how attractive to the market the credit is, primary syndication may be completed even before first drawdown, although a period of up to six months or so post-completion is often agreed with the sponsor, during which time the sponsor agrees to provide its assistance with the syndication efforts, such as making senior management available for investor calls.

An alternative approach that gained traction in the aftermath of the global financial crisis was for a group of lenders, termed a club, to arrange and hold debt on some deals, without a subsequent syndication. This approach remains widespread today in the mid-market, where institutions will often wish to hold debt while retaining the ability to sell down at a later date. Increased liquidity and the availability of additional debt funding sources (such as high-yield bonds) have seen club deals disappear from bigger transactions as greater willingness to underwrite deals has re-emerged. However, very large deals often still feature a relatively large number of arrangers – at least in part due to the desire by banks to be involved in arranging the financing of good credits.

2.4 Senior debt

The key features of senior debt are as follows:

- It is the first ranking layer of debt, unsubordinated and secured on a first ranking basis.
- It usually comprises several term loans and revolving credit facilities, offering cash and non-cash facilities (such as letters of credit and bank guarantee facilities), with a mix of amortising and bullet repayment profiles.
- The margin range is generally between 400 and 550 basis points, with amortising and revolving facilities skewed to the lower, and non-amortising facilities at the higher end of that range.
- The tenor range is usually between four and six or seven years.
- There is generally no call protection.[3]

The senior debt will form the core, and often the largest, part of the debt finance structure and will usually consist of:

- Acquisition finance – this is the finance required to purchase the target and is usually provided by way of secured term loans. The total amount of this type of debt is usually split into several tranches of debt, each with its own pricing, repayment profile and ranking in respect of certain types of prepayment – often denoted Facility A (usually the lowest priced tranche with an amortising repayment profile),[4] Facility B (usually with increased pricing and a bullet or semi-bullet repayment),[5] Facility C, and so on.
- Working capital and ancillary finance – this is the finance that will be required by the target group after the acquisition has completed for its day-to-day operational, working capital and general corporate needs. It is provided under a revolving credit facility that is made available during the life of the senior facilities, or by way of a separate overdraft facility, often on the bank's standard terms, alongside any other ancillary facilities that are required by the target group's business.
- Capital expenditure and acquisition finance – this may be provided to support the target group's capital expenditure requirements and sometimes also to finance bolt-on acquisitions, which will normally be projected in the financial model and/or business plan supporting the acquisition. If required, it is usually provided by way of secured term loans (although in the case of capital expenditure facilities, these are sometimes re-drawable term loans).

These sources of debt finance will be made available under separate facilities contained in a single senior facilities agreement, which will contain many of the standard provisions found in a conventional loan facility agreement. The LMA produces standard form senior facilities agreements for leveraged acquisition finance, and these are invariably used in the London and wider European market as the basis

---

[3] Call protection commonly refers to prepayment fees borrowers must pay if prepaying debt before the end of its scheduled term. Lenders negotiate call protection so that the return on their loan investment (including the upfront time and expense they incur in conducting their credit checks and investigations on the borrowers and their market segment) is protected to a degree in the event that the borrowers refinance earlier than expected.
[4] See "Repayment and prepayment" section below for an explanation of this term.
[5] See "Repayment and prepayment" section below for an explanation of this term.

for this agreement (although smaller transactions may be based on a single lending bank's standard, often shorter-form documents).

Given that the newcos are off-the-shelf shell companies with no assets of their own other than the target shares that they acquire, the terms of the senior facilities agreement are relatively restrictive (compared to those that could be expected to be offered to a corporate or investment-grade borrower). The sponsor will not offer any form of credit support from itself, from the funds that it advises or manages or from its other investments, so the lenders will only have credit support from, and recourse to, the value in the target group. As a result, lenders are particularly concerned to ensure that:
- the profits generated by the target group, and the cash held by it, are protected to ensure that they are available to service the fees, interest and principal payable on the debt finance;
- the target group does not do anything that might harm its financial position, or change its nature and therefore its credit profile (judged by reference to the status of the target group at the time of its acquisition, as set out in the financial model and the business plan);
- lenders receive an agreed package of regular financial information to allow them to monitor the performance of the target group against the financial model and business plan and to identify, as early as possible, any potential difficulties;
- lenders receive the benefit of a comprehensive guarantee and security package so that, should the target group run into financial difficulties, their position will be protected from the claims of other creditors, and they will be able to control any restructuring.

2.5   Second lien debt

The key features of second lien debt are as follows:
- It forms part of the senior, first ranking layer of debt, but is subject to a degree of subordination to the rest of the senior debt and is secured on a second ranking basis.
- It generally only comprises a single term loan, drawn in cash at closing, repaid in a bullet instalment at maturity.
- The margin range is priced above senior but below mezzanine debt.
- The tenor typically ends six months after the longest dated tranche of the priority senior debt.
- Call protection applies during the first one or two years (usually at a lower level than might apply to mezzanine debt).
- It is still relatively infrequently encountered in European markets.

Second lien debt was widely employed in mid- and upper-market transactions before the financial crisis, both as an alternative to mezzanine finance and in conjunction with it to form a third distinct layer of finance sandwiched between the senior and the mezzanine debt.[6] Second lien lending was originally dominated by hedge funds, but the investor base grew to include a variety of institutional investors such as insurance companies, pension funds, mutual funds and investment vehicles known as collateralised debt obligations (CDOs) and collateralised loan obligations (CLOs).[7] Traditional lending banks and mezzanine funds also participated in second lien debt, attracted by its enhanced margin and unique position in the debt-funding structure.

During the years running up to the pre-crisis height of the leveraged finance market in 2007, second lien debt became a common feature of debt finance packages and the documentation of it became fairly standard. Most commonly in the London market it was structured as a Facility D in the senior facilities agreement (particularly where there was a layer of mezzanine debt ranking after the second lien debt), thus forming part of the senior debt for many decision-making procedures, but being subject to a degree of contractual subordination to the rest of the senior debt. However, it can be documented separately, as is more common in the US debt markets. In any event, the second lien debt is subordinated to the priority senior debt, and benefits from the same guarantees and security that are granted to the senior lenders, but on a second ranking basis and with restricted rights of enforcement. It is usual for the second lien debt to be borrowed by the borrowers of the senior debt – it is not common for it to be structurally subordinated[8] – and it will generally have a maturity falling six months after the longest dated priority senior debt.

Following the global financial crisis, second lien decreased significantly as a feature of the London and European markets. Arguably this was attributable in large part to the withdrawal of traditional CLO and CDO institutional investors as they reached or neared the end of their investment periods,[9] while increased intercreditor protections negotiated by independent mezzanine funds in terms of voting, enforcement and valuation processes with regard to senior lenders, coupled with lower mezzanine pricing, made investment in mezzanine debt a more economically attractive proposition than subordinated senior debt. However, instances of new

---

6   For example, in 2005, Weather Investments HH Sarl acquired Italian telecommunications group Wind for around €3 billion, partly funded with €700 million of second lien debt.
7   CLOs and CDOs are funds that issue asset-backed securities, backed by a pool of bonds, loans and related assets.
8   In the European debt markets, it has been customary for certain debt that is to be subordinate to senior debt (such as high-yield bonds) to be borrowed by a holding company of the senior debt borrower, such that the senior debt is loaned at (or nearer to) the assets and cash generative business at the operating company level, whereas the subordinated debt is lent at a higher, holding company level, one step removed from (or structurally subordinated to) the operating companies. This structuring technique is called structural subordination. Contractual subordination may be used as an alternative, whereby the parties agree that the senior and subordinated debts are borrowed at the same level and the subordination is created by contract, such as under an intercreditor agreement.
9   The decline in the European CLO investor base underwent a reversal over the course of 2013 as pricing and other commercial factors began to make new issuance economically attractive and investors started to develop structures appropriate to address new European regulatory requirements introduced after the crisis (notably the 'skin-in-the-game' requirements of Article 122a of the Capital Requirements Directive or "CRD" (2006/48/EC) as amended by CRD II (2009/111/EC)) together with other features of the new European 'CLO 2.0'. Issuance subsequently slowed in mid to late 2013 due to a continuing lack of supply of underlying transactions combined with amendments to the skin-in-the-game requirements being proposed under CRD IV (which came into effect in January 2014, although certain of its elements and specific requirements remain subject to consultation). While a number of new fundraisings have been announced, it remains to be seen how strong the volume of issuance of new European CLO 2.0s will be. In contrast, new CLO issues in the United States are significantly advanced over the European position. See also the discussion in relation to "Syndication and transferability of loan participations" below.

CLOs and (although still comparatively rare in a purely European context) second lien financings have increased of late.

2.6 Mezzanine debt

The key features of mezzanine debt are as follows:

- It ranks after the senior (and, if present, second lien) debt, subordinated and secured on a second ranking basis.
- It generally only comprises a single term loan, drawn in cash at closing, repaid in a bullet instalment at maturity.
- The document terms (representations, covenant terms, events of default) mirror those in the senior facilities agreement, modified to reflect the subordinated ranking of mezzanine debt.
- The cash pay margin range is generally a number of percentage points higher than senior debt (and second lien debt), an increase that will be reduced if the mezzanine debt is also issued warrants to acquire shares in the target group's holding company (although this feature is less frequently seen in current markets).
- The margin comprises part cash pay and part capitalising/payment-in-kind interest.
- It can share in the potential equity upside through warrants.
- The tenor ends six months to a year after the longest dated tranche of senior (or, if present, second lien) debt.
- Call protection applies for up to three years.

Mezzanine debt was originally introduced into debt finance structures during the 1980s to fill the funding gap between the amount of senior debt that lenders were willing to lend and the amount of equity that private equity investors were prepared to provide (bearing in mind the investors' aims of minimising their investment capital and maximising the debt leverage so as to enhance potential returns).

At the high point of mezzanine financing before the crisis, market commentators estimated that nearly a quarter of UK private equity acquisitions and around 15% of European private equity acquisitions included mezzanine debt in their debt finance structure, and in 2006 over €12 billion of European mezzanine loans were made.[10] Since the crisis, mezzanine debt has not recovered to these levels, having been challenged by other debt finance options such as payment in kind, high-yield bonds and alternative lenders, as well as by increased investor equity cheques.

In common with senior debt, mezzanine debt is relatively easy to implement (as described above, being substantially based on the senior covenant and security package), its impact on cash flows is softened by the non-cash pay (capitalising or payment in kind) element of the interest charge, it accommodates early exits and recapitalisations (subject to any prepayment fees that may apply during the early years

---

10 The buy-out of Spanish IT travel business Amadeus included €900 million of mezzanine debt in its debt finance package. A €1 billion mezzanine offering followed shortly thereafter in 2006 with the mezzanine finance for the Casema acquisition – a far cry from its inception as a specialised form of funding-gap finance. Market data provided by S&P LCD.

– although these fees, when compared to those applicable to high-yield bond non-call protections, are not prohibitively expensive), and does not require a public credit rating.

Mezzanine debt is subordinated to the senior debt (including any second lien debt), but ranks ahead of the equity, including any equity investor loan notes and vendor loan notes. The subordination of the mezzanine debt is usually achieved by contractual subordination, under an intercreditor agreement, but the mezzanine may also be structurally subordinated by being borrowed by a holding company of the senior borrowers.

The mezzanine debt will generally consist of a single term loan (or, for some cross-border acquisitions, one loan in each currency required to fund the acquisition) and will usually share (to the extent legally possible in the relevant jurisdictions) the same guarantee and security package with the senior debt, but its interest in and rights to it will rank behind the senior debt. As a result of its second ranking status, mezzanine debt has a greater risk profile. Consequently, the mezzanine lenders receive a higher interest margin to compensate them for this risk.

In addition to receiving interest, mezzanine lenders historically received some kind of performance-related reward, often in the form of warrants to subscribe for shares in the target group's holding company at the time of, for example, a sale or listing (this is often called an equity kicker). These warrants could typically allow the mezzanine lenders to subscribe for up to 5% of the holding company's equity share capital. However, increased liquidity in the debt markets, increased competition between debt finance providers and the willingness of some CLOs/CDOs to lend mezzanine debt without receiving warrants (as their constitution was often not set up for the uncertainty of investing in warrants) enabled sponsors to retain the potential rewards of holding equity for themselves, and to negotiate mezzanine debt without accompanying warrants. This has generally remained the case since the financial crisis.

If of sufficient size, the mezzanine debt will be syndicated in a similar manner to the senior debt.

The mezzanine debt will be documented in a mezzanine loan agreement, which will be based on, and will contain substantially the same terms as the senior facilities agreement (particularly, the prepayment terms, representations, covenants and events of default). In practice, the first draft of the mezzanine loan agreement is produced at a relatively advanced stage of the negotiations, when the senior facilities agreement is in a near final form. Amendments will be made to the senior facilities agreement to tailor it to the structure of the mezzanine loan and its financial terms. These amendments are likely to include:
- adding additional conditions precedent to provide for the granting of the mezzanine lenders' warrants (if any) and to confirm that the senior debt has become unconditional, save for any condition relating to the funding of the mezzanine loan;
- deleting any margin ratchet;[11]

---

[11] A margin ratchet (or pricing grid) is a provision providing that, as the borrowers hit certain financial targets, the margin – the portion of the total interest cost to the borrower represented by an amount of basis points over funding costs, which is usually represented by LIBOR (the London interbank offered rate) or EURIBOR (the euro interbank offered rate) – decreases.

- changing the repayment profile to a single bullet repayment of the full amount of the mezzanine loan at the end of its term (which is usually six months to one year after the final repayment of the senior debt);
- providing that prepayments of the mezzanine debt will be subject to the prior repayment in full of the senior debt;
- adding the right to appoint a board director or observer to the board of one of the holding companies of the target group, to represent the interests of the mezzanine lenders; and for this person to receive notice of, and any papers for, these board meetings;
- notching down (ie, relaxing) the financial covenants (other than any cashflow covenant and capital expenditure covenant) to a level 10% to 15% below those applicable to the senior debt;
- amending the cross-default terms so that they are not automatically triggered by a default under the senior facilities agreement.

2.7 Unitranche debt

The key features of unitranche debt are as follows:

- It is non-amortising or limited amortisation senior term debt, generally comprising a single term loan only, drawn in full at closing and repaid in a bullet instalment at maturity.
- It may have a longer tenor than standard senior debt, of up to six or seven years.
- Its margin range is generally between 700 and 800 basis points. Margin ratchets are uncommon.
- A make-whole amount or prepayment premium may apply. These vary according to lender policy, but an example might be a prepayment premium of 2% and 1% respectively over principal prepaid during the first and second years of the facility's lifetime.
- It is provided by a single lender and not syndicated, but will be documented so as to be capable of transfer on terms comparable to other senior debt.
- The single lender structure brings with it an inherent size limitation, hence it is predominantly a feature of the mid-market.

Unitranche debt is typically provided by specialist debt funds or alternative lenders (lenders other than the main investment and commercial banks, who operate in the shadow-banking sector). Although unitranche debt has a number of distinguishing features, as outlined above, it is usually documented using as a base document the same standard leveraged LMA facilities agreement used by both senior and mezzanine acquisition financings. As a result unitranche debt is equally suitable for financing acquisitions, and shares many of the structural features of senior debt described below.

Although unitranche lenders may be able to fulfil the roles of facility and security agent, they are typically funds and are not usually geared up to provide revolving working capital and ancillary facilities. Unitranche debt is therefore often combined with a revolving facility provided by a bank lender (which may also take the agent role). For ease, efficiency and cost both these facilities are usually documented in a single facilities agreement.

The revolving facility is usually far smaller (typically between 5% and 10% of the size of the unitranche) and will usually be loaned on a super senior basis, meaning that it shares in the same guarantees and security equally with the unitranche debt, but ranking ahead of it in order of payment on any enforcement. Consequently, their respective rankings are documented in a separate intercreditor agreement similar to that governing the relationship between senior and mezzanine debt.

The single lender structure for all or the vast majority of a borrower's senior debt that unitranche facilities provide offers greater flexibility during the loan negotiation and execution process, as well as going forward over the lifetime of the loan.

3. The structure of the senior facilities agreement and the mezzanine loan agreement

3.1 Parties

The original parties to the senior facilities agreement and the mezzanine loan agreement will typically be the lead arranging bank or the club of banks – who will also fulfil the roles of arranger, facility agent, security trustee, issuing bank (if letters of credit are to be directly available under the senior facilities, rather than under an ancillary facility provided thereunder on a bilateral basis) and original lender(s) – and the newcos as guarantors and, where appropriate, borrowers. As these agreements will usually be entered into before the acquisition is completed, the members of the target group will not be original parties, but will (to the extent required) become parties (as guarantors and, for those companies that need direct access to the funds either to refinance existing debts or to finance working capital and capital expenditure, as borrowers) by way of an accession mechanism. Each of the syndicate of lenders will become a party to these agreements by way of an individual or a global transfer certificate during syndication of the facilities.

3.2 The facilities and the stated purposes

The loan agreements will set out a description of the facilities being made available and a detailed description of the purpose to which they are to be applied, in order to ensure that the funds lent are applied in the manner envisaged by the lenders. The stated purposes for a leveraged acquisition financing will include funding the cash consideration due to the seller, the payment of related transaction costs and, usually, to refinance existing bank debt in the target group.

3.3 Conditions precedent

Conditions precedent are intended to confirm the legal, financial and commercial condition of the borrowers and guarantors before any of the debt is lent, and they must be satisfied (or waived by the facility agent) before the facilities become available to be drawn down. The extent and type of conditions precedent will largely depend on the type of transaction being financed. As a result of the complexity of private equity financing structures, the conditions precedent are invariably extensive.

Debt finance

The conditions precedent will be divided into two main types:
- initial conditions precedent, which must be satisfied before the first drawdown of funds can be made, typically by delivery of appropriate documents and evidence for matters falling under the following categories:
- legal conditions precedent, including the constitutional documents of the borrowers and each company giving guarantees or security, all necessary corporate and shareholder authorities for each of these companies, in cross-border transactions the documents for any applicable financial assistance whitewash procedure[12] and legal opinions from each relevant jurisdiction (usually provided by the lenders' counsel);
- transactional conditions precedent, including the senior, any additional second lien and mezzanine debt documents, mandate, fee and certain other side-letters, intercreditor and priority documents, security documents, equity and quasi-equity documents and acquisition or, as the case may be, offer documents;
- financial conditions precedent, including the target group's recent financial statements, the financial model, budget and business plan and a completion funds flow statement;
- information conditions precedent, including certificates of title for real estate, documents of title, share certificates, 'know your customer'[13] information and due diligence reports, which may include an accountants' report, a legal report (often incorporating a review of tax and pensions issues), a market analysis, an insurance review, an environmental report and property valuations; and
- additional conditions precedent, which require the continued accuracy of a selected number of the representations and warranties and the absence of any potential or actual event of default. These must be satisfied at the time of, and immediately following, the drawings made at closing, at selected periods during the life of the facilities and before any subsequent drawing can be made after completion.

3.4 Interest

The total interest charge on each facility is invariably a fluctuating rate, which is the aggregate of:
- the margin applicable to that facility;
- the lenders' cost of funds, usually calculated by reference to LIBOR or, for loans denominated in euro, EURIBOR – this rate may be subject to a LIBOR/EURIBOR floor, to clarify that for the purposes of calculating the

---

12 Many jurisdictions prohibit a company from giving financial assistance (which may include any upstream or cross-stream guarantees and security granted by the relevant companies that are members of the target group) for the purchase of its own shares or those of any of its holding companies. In some of these jurisdictions, a private company may be able to give such financial assistance if it undertakes a statutory whitewash procedure (as used to be the case with English private limited companies when a comparable statutory prohibition, now removed, applied).

13 Lenders are subject to extensive regulatory requirements in relation to due diligence on borrowers as part of European-wide efforts to combat money laundering.

interest costs, the rate cannot go either below zero or, for some financings where the lenders' lending criteria demands this, below a set minimum rate;
- potentially, depending on the lenders involved, mandatory costs, which are the costs of complying with the requirements of the Bank of England and the Financial Conduct Authority and the Prudential Regulation Authority (the successors of the Financial Services Authority) (in respect of loans funded in the London market) and the European Central Bank (in respect of loans funded in the Eurozone).[14]

The margin is the number of basis points above the cost of funds determined by the second and third points above, and it represents a lender's notional profit on the loans, on the assumption that the lender has match-funded its participation in these loans in the relevant interbank market and that it is subject to no, or only average, mandatory costs. For any one lender these assumptions may or may not apply in practice, but the principle that debts of this nature bear interest at a fluctuating rate represented by cost of funds plus a fixed margin is the market standard approach to loan pricing.[15]

Interest will be payable in arrears at the end of sequential periods selected by the borrowers as interest periods (which are usually of one, three or six months' duration).

LIBOR and EURIBOR will be set by reference to a screen rate. The LIBOR screen rate is set by reference to the rate determined by the applicable rate administrator[16] and EURIBOR by the rate determined as such by the European Central Bank. Alternatively, and if these rates are not available for any reason (for example due to the suspension of the service or where a rate is needed for a non-standard interest period), two or three reference banks, which are generally members of the lending syndicate located in London (for LIBOR) or in the Eurozone (for EURIBOR), will be selected to provide an average rate. Many deals (particularly those where US lenders participate) have seen the inclusion of a LIBOR or EURIBOR floor, whereby the rate is deemed not to fall below an agreed minimum (eg, 0.75% or 1%). Borrowers have increasingly resisted the inclusion of these floor rates, and in the UK market a number of major lenders now prefer not to include them in facilities in which they participate.

It is fairly common for the margin applicable to one or more of the senior facilities to be subject to a margin ratchet. A margin ratchet provides for stepped

---

14 Previously a standard feature of the LMA loan documentation, mandatory costs provisions were deleted in 2013 in response to requests by lenders active as agent banks, who found themselves subject to an increasing administrative burden as a result of the complexity of calculations across syndicates of lenders. Mandatory costs provisions are now absent from many new deals, either because lenders have decided as a matter of policy that they will not charge them or because the lenders in question are not subject to applicable requirements.

15 Lenders do not fund every loan from deposits, but typically access the interbank market for loans for short-term periods that broadly correspond to the applicable interest periods chosen by the borrowers.

16 Historically this was BBA LIBOR, the British Bankers' Association interest settlement rate. Following extensive regulatory investigation into allegations of rate submission manipulation by some contributing banks, ICE (formerly NYSE Euronext) Rate Administration Limited took over administration of LIBOR from the British Bankers' Association in early 2014 and LIBOR is now known as ICE LIBOR.

reductions in the margin (usually three or four steps) if the target group meets agreed financial performance objectives. These targets are often set by reference to the leverage ratio[17] of the target group; the understanding being that as the leverage of the target group falls (as a result of a combination of the repayment of part of the debt and increased earnings, as would be projected by the original business plan and financial model) and the creditworthiness of the target group improves, the lenders should receive a reduced margin reflecting the reduced credit risk they are exposed to. If performance worsens (as well as, typically, while an event of default is continuing), the margin increases accordingly, up to its maximum (ie, day one) level.

3.5 Repayment and prepayment

The senior debt facilities will be repayable by way of regular, fixed instalments (often called an amortising repayment profile), on a semi-amortising basis (where the instalments are weighted toward the end of the debt's maturity), in a single lump sum at maturity (often called a bullet repayment) or, for revolving credit facilities, on a revolving basis, all falling over a period of between four and seven years (compared to typical periods of between six and nine years before the crisis, although tenors have started to open out again from the sharp contraction seen immediately after the collapse of Lehman Brothers).

Mezzanine (and unitranche and second lien) debt is invariably repayable in a single bullet instalment, falling after the repayment in full of the prior ranking debts.

Once repaid, term loans cannot usually be re-borrowed (an exception to this would be a re-drawable capital expenditure facility, although these are not common). Advances drawn under revolving credit facilities are usually repayable at the end of a short term (usually one, three or six months), but once repaid, they may be re-borrowed – and this cycle may continue until the final maturity date. Revolving credit facilities are therefore more flexible for the borrowers and allow them to meet their fluctuating working capital requirements.

Generally no repayments of the senior term debt will be scheduled for a period of between six and 12 months following completion, to allow the target group's cashflow some breathing space before it is required to service the repayment of these debts.

The loan documents will allow the borrowers to prepay the debts (in their order of priority) before their respective scheduled repayment dates. This is an essential feature of private equity financing structures, allowing all the debts to be repaid if an opportunity to exit or to refinance the existing debt package on more favourable terms arises, and allowing the borrowers to repay part of the debts to reduce the target group's leverage if cash becomes available to do so – perhaps as a result of out-performing the business plan or as a result of disposals being made.

A prepayment fee is generally payable to the relevant lending group (known as 'call protection') if mezzanine (or any unitranche or second lien) debt is prepaid during the first few years following completion. This fee may be negotiated to apply only to prepayments funded by the proceeds of a third-party bank refinancing, so

---

17   The ratio of debt (or net debt) to earnings before interest, taxes, depreciation and amortisation (EBITDA).

that it would not fall due on an exit. Prepayment fees are not usually levied on senior debt, although they may be present where an alternative lender is providing the financing.

In addition to scheduled repayments, certain events will trigger an obligation to prepay part or all of the debts. These are referred to as mandatory prepayments and may include the prepayment of:

- all the debts on the occurrence of a change of control, listing or flotation of any of the holding companies of the target group or the sale of the target group – these heads aim to cover the most common exit routes pursued by sponsors;
- part of the debts from the cash proceeds received from the disposal of assets (over and above an agreed threshold and net of costs and taxes incurred – cash proceeds that are used for re-investment in the target group's business are usually excluded from this obligation;
- part of the debts from the cash proceeds received from warranty claims, such as claims against the seller(s) for a breach of warranty or under an indemnity in the acquisition agreement or from insurance claims (in each case, often above an agreed threshold and net of costs and taxes incurred) – cash proceeds that are used for re-investment in the target group's business or are applied in meeting any loss or liability relating to the claim are usually excluded from this obligation;
- part of the debts from the excess cashflow generated by the target group's business (this prepayment obligation is called the 'cash sweep') – after an initial grace period, a proportion (often 50%, or a ratcheting percentage set by reference to the leverage ratio, which can reduce the proportion down to zero) of the cashflow generated by the target group's business over and above amounts applied to service the debts (and often also after deducting a negotiated amount that may be retained in the business) are required to be applied in prepayment of the debt.

3.6 Representations

A principal reason to include representations is that under English law there is no general duty to disclose to the other contracting party when entering into a contract – for example, a borrower is under no obligation to tell the lenders that it knows of a potential liability, claim or lawsuit that it expects to be incurred by or made against it.

Representations are therefore intended to concentrate the borrowers' minds on ensuring that certain factual matters are as the lenders believe them to be, and to ensure that borrowers disclose to the lenders everything that the lenders need to know before committing to lend. The representations will be made at the time the loan documents are entered into, and a selected number of them will be repeated (the 'repeating representations') on the date of each drawdown and at the start of each interest period. Certain representations may also be repeated more frequently, but this is a matter for commercial negotiation. The occurrence of a misrepresentation that is not remedied within any applicable grace period (often 10 to 20 business days' grace is given for remedial misrepresentations) will lead to an event of default being triggered.

Examples of standard representations are:
- corporate status of the borrowers and guarantors;
- due corporate authority and legality, validity and binding nature of the loan and related finance documents;
- the borrowers' tax position;
- that there is no default existing;
- that all information provided to the lenders is true and accurate;
- equal ranking of the debts;
- compliance with all laws and regulations (including environmental laws and, increasingly, anti-corruption laws and international sanctions);
- that good title is owned for all assets (including shareholdings and intellectual property);
- the absence of material litigation; and
- the centre of main interests[18] and FATCA[19] status of the borrowers and guarantors.

3.7 General covenants

Loan covenants are intended to protect the lenders' loan investment, and they are binding on the borrowers (and, by way of procurement obligations under which the borrowers will covenant to ensure that their subsidiaries also comply with the covenants, effectively on all the other members of the target group) throughout the life of the facilities. The wording of these covenants – usually split into positive covenants (setting out what the borrowers and their subsidiaries must do) and negative covenants (setting out what the borrowers and their subsidiaries must not do) – is where the views of the lenders will be most at odds with those of the borrowers. The sponsor and the borrowers will want to be free to run the business of the target group in the manner that they see as best serving their interests; and the lenders will want to maximise their control over the target group in order to protect their investment in it. Counsel for each of these sides will spend considerable time negotiating the wording of the covenants to balance these opposing demands while meeting the needs of the underlying business and the business plan.

---

[18] 'Centre of main interests' is a term and a concept used in the EU Regulation on Cross-Border Insolvency and the UNCITRAL Model Law on Cross-Border Insolvency, to determine which insolvency proceedings opened in an EU member state (excluding Denmark) will take precedence if competing proceedings are opened in more than one EU jurisdiction. Accordingly, the location of the centre of main interests of borrowers and guarantors, and ensuring that it does not change following entry into the loan (since this is the position on which credit risk analysis will have been based), is of key concern to lenders.

[19] The US Foreign Account Tax Compliance Act (FATCA) of 2010 imposes a system of information reporting to the US Inland Revenue Service on certain financial institutions, and withholding taxes on entities not complying with such requirements, in order to compel non-US entities (over which the United States typically has no jurisdiction) to report information regarding US source income of US account holders and owners. These obligations can also be fulfilled via reporting procedures subsequently set up within the scope of inter-governmental agreements (for example between the United Kingdom and the United States). The LMA and the London loan market generally have now developed fairly standard positions in respect of FATCA and lenders' and borrowers' expectations as to how its application, or potential risk of application, is most appropriately dealt with in loan documents.

The borrowers will undertake to provide the lenders with a regular package of information, typically comprising financial and operational information useful to the lenders in overseeing covenant compliance, with the overall objective of giving the lenders advance warning of possible debt service or repayment problems.

The occurrence of a breach of covenant that is not remedied within any applicable grace period (as with remedial misrepresentations, often 10 to 20 business days' grace is given for remedial breaches other than key failures such as non-payment) will lead to an event of default being triggered.

Examples of common covenants are:
- maintenance of the borrowers' and the guarantors' corporate status;
- compliance with laws (including environmental laws and, increasingly, anti-corruption laws and international sanctions);
- a restriction on the creation of security (the 'negative pledge');
- restrictions on disposals, acquisitions, mergers, joint ventures and the incurrence of further debt;
- a prohibition or restriction on dividends and other payments to the equity investors and the subordinated lenders;
- the maintenance of a minimum level of guarantor coverage;
- a restriction on changing the target group's business;
- maintenance of at least equal ranking of the debts.

3.8 **Financial covenants**

In addition to the general covenants, a suite of financial covenants will be set. These apply for defined periods, usually rolling periods of 12 months, tested quarterly throughout the life of the facilities. The financial covenants are tied to selected balance-sheet and income statement levels and ratios, and are designed to monitor the target group's financial performance against the financial model and business plan and the borrowers' ability to meet their payment obligations under the debt finance package.

On leveraged transactions, the level of the covenants will change over time, in line with the business plan underlying the transaction – for example, the leverage and interest cover ratios would be expected to improve over time (as earnings become enhanced and the debt is reduced by repayments and prepayments) and the restrictions on capital expenditure may relax.

The definition of each element of these covenants is thoroughly negotiated, often with the guidance of the reporting accountants advising the sponsor. The LMA has produced a template suite of definitions, and these are usually the starting point for negotiations. The lenders will be seeking to ensure that the financial covenant ratios give a true reflection of the borrowers' financial performance and creditworthiness and that they impose a strict discipline on the target group to meet its business plan. The sponsor and the borrowers will be seeking to ensure that the definitions give maximum flexibility to allow them to meet the test levels and to absorb one-off hits that they expect will or could arise and that could affect the covenant ratios.

Examples of common financial covenants are:

- the ratio of total debt to EBITDA (the leverage test);[20]
- the ratio of EBITDA to total debt finance charges (the interest cover test);[21]
- the ratio of cashflow to total funding costs (the cashflow cover test);[22] and
- a maximum annual level of capital expenditure.[23]

Generally, the better the creditworthiness of the target group, the more relaxed the financial covenants. Most private equity transactions involve an initially high leverage and as a result have relatively restrictive financial covenant controls. The leverage test, interest cover test and cashflow cover test are employed almost universally in the loan documents for leveraged finance debt packages.

Failure to meet a financial covenant will lead to an event of default being triggered. Although no grace period is given, as such a failure is not remediable, it has become common for an equity cure right to be included, which allows the sponsor to inject further equity into the target group, which is applied to notionally increase one or more of the variables constituting the relevant financial covenant that is not met – for example, by inflating cashflow (or, less commonly, EBITDA) or reducing total debt on a deemed basis by the amount of the cash injection (and, in the case of a reduction in total debt, also requiring up to 100% of such a cure amount to be applied in an actual debt prepayment). Any equity cure right is intended to be used as a quick fix for any blip in financial covenant compliance and, as such, its availability is usually limited to ensure that the lenders' rights to take action in respect of systematic underperformance is not curtailed (for example, it may be permitted a maximum of three or four times during the life of the facilities, and not in successive testing periods).

3.9 Events of default

These are an essential part of the lenders' protection, giving the lenders the right, upon the occurrence of the events or circumstances specified as being an event of default, to cancel the commitments and to demand (or have the right immediately to demand) immediate repayment of outstanding debts (this is called accelerating the debts).

The right to place the debts on demand or to accelerate is a powerful remedy for lenders, otherwise relying on the uncertainties inherent in exercising their rights at law, such as the right to obtain an injunction or specific performance, terminating

---

20 This tests the aggregate amount of debt to the target group's earnings. Leverage covenants are key indicators of the viability of the target group's debt structure and its ability to service and repay the debt finance. Total debt is often calculated on a net basis (ie, net of cash held by the borrower/obligors).
21 Interest cover tests show whether earnings are sufficient to service the debt, and are often an early warning of cashflow problems.
22 Cash cover ratios (sometimes called fixed charge ratios) measure operating cashflow against financial costs. Cashflow calculations usually take the accounting measure of profit (EBITDA) and convert it to a cash measure of profit. The lender is thus able to calculate the number of times that a company's cashflow covers total funding costs (ie, servicing and repaying the target group's debts), though in most leveraged deals this is usually set at 1:1.
23 Capital expenditure covenants restrict the amount that can be spent on long-term assets such as equipment or machinery. These are often limited in highly leveraged financing structures to ensure there is enough cash to service debt, though these levels will be set at industry standards and based on the company's business plan.

the loan documents on the basis of a repudiatory breach of contract, suing for damages arising from a non-repudiatory breach of contract or suing for damages or rescinding the loan documents on the basis of misrepresentation.

The events that could trigger an event of default may relate to some action or omission by the borrowers or any other member of the target group, or they may relate to external circumstances (such as a deterioration in trading conditions) that materially and adversely affect the creditworthiness of the target group.

If repayment is not made following acceleration of the loans, the lenders will have an action against the borrowers for non-payment of a debt.

Examples of standard events of default are:
- non-payment of amounts due under the loan documents;
- breach of the terms of the loan documents (often subject to a remedy period for remediable breaches);
- misrepresentation (often subject to a remedy period for remediable misrepresentations);
- cross-default and cross-acceleration;
- the occurrence of insolvency events affecting any member of, or any material member of, the target group;
- auditors' qualification of audited financial statements;
- departure of key members of the management team without satisfactory replacement;
- the occurrence of a material adverse change.

4. Other considerations in relation to loan financing

4.1 The security package

The debt in private equity transactions is invariably supported by a guarantee and security package granted by the newcos and (subject to legal restrictions applicable in the relevant jurisdictions, such as restrictions and prohibitions on granting financial assistance) the target group over all, or substantially all, of their respective assets and shareholdings. This security from the target group is required as the newcos are shell companies without any assets (other than, in the case of the newco which bids for and purchases the target, the shares it acquires in the target) against which the lenders could have recourse in the event of insolvency.

Typically, the newcos and other members of the target group that are English companies grant a guarantee and a debenture in support of their own borrowings and those of the other borrowers. In addition, any members of the target group that receive funds (for example, under intercompany loans, rather than as direct borrowers) or are material to the target group's business will do likewise. The debenture is a standalone document encompassing fixed and floating charges and the guarantee is (usually) contained in the loan documents. In cross-border transactions, the nature of the security package granted by companies incorporated in an overseas jurisdiction will be dictated by the type of assets located in that jurisdiction, the type and extent of security interests available under the laws of that jurisdiction and the costs and taxes which will be incurred in connection therewith.

This structure gives the lenders an unsecured claim (under the guarantee) and a secured claim (under the debenture or other security agreement or instrument) against each of these companies. The security and guarantee package should help ensure that any material assets on which the target group's forecast performance is based are retained and that the lenders' charges take priority over any interests of other creditors (such as trade creditors) in an insolvency, except for the prescribed part of any insolvent borrower's floating charge assets required to be made available to unsecured creditors (under Section 176A of the Insolvency Act 1986, as introduced by Section 252 of the Enterprise Act 2002).

It will also give the lenders an element of control over any restructuring, as they will be able to appoint an administrator if they hold a floating charge over all, or substantially all, of the assets of a company (a 'qualifying floating charge' under Paragraphs 14 to 21 of Schedule B1 to the Insolvency Act 1986, as introduced by paragraphs 14 to 21 of Schedule 16 to the Enterprise Act 2002). Although the insolvent company can also appoint an administrator, it must notify the secured creditors holding the qualifying floating charge before doing so, who may in turn nominate an administrator of their choice.

Where the debt is to be syndicated to new lenders, a security trustee will be appointed to hold the security on trust on behalf of all the lenders. Where there are secured senior and junior debts, the security trustee (usually being a senior lender that arranged the senior debt package) will hold the security on trust for all those lenders, and this arrangement will be governed by an intercreditor agreement entered into between the borrowers, the guarantors and security providers, the security trustee, the senior and junior lenders and certain other creditors of the newcos and the target group (such as hedging providers and the sponsor and members of the management team where their investment takes the form of shareholder debt or loan notes). If the security trustee enforces the security, the proceeds of enforcement (net of the security trustee's costs) will be held by the security trustee on trust and applied in accordance with the provisions of the intercreditor agreement.

As a consequence of the way public acquisitions are structured and for a variety of reasons in private acquisitions (such as the need to obtain competition clearances), there can be a gap between the time that the lenders commit to lend the debt finance and the date the acquisition completes and the debt finance is borrowed and paid to the seller(s). This means that the guarantee and security package is often put in place in a number of phases, as follows:

- The newcos will enter into the relevant guarantee and security documents at the time the lenders commit to lend the debt finance (ie, at the time of signing the loan documents).
- The target and other relevant members of the target's group will enter into the relevant guarantee and security documents at or immediately after completion of the acquisition.

The second of these phases may, depending on the laws applicable to the guarantee and security package being put in place, be further split, as follows:

- in cross-border transactions where financial assistance prohibitions apply, the target and relevant members of the target group will enter into the relevant guarantee and security documents in respect of that part of the debt finance that is not affected by any applicable legal restrictions relating to financial assistance. This debt could comprise debts that have not been used to acquire shares in the target, such as amounts borrowed to refinance the target group's existing debts or working capital facilities.
- Once any necessary procedures available in any affected jurisdiction have been completed to allow guarantees and security to be granted in respect of affected acquisition debt (ie, financial assistance-tainted debt), the relevant members of the target group will enter into further guarantee and security documents, or will amend the terms of the documents entered into in the phase above, in respect of the balance of the debt finance.

In many overseas jurisdictions there will be restrictions on the ability of target group companies to grant upstream security, or security over certain classes of assets. It is important that lenders and borrowers carry out a thorough analysis of any such limitations and potential ways to mitigate these limitations as part of their initial due diligence.

4.2 Certain funds

If a sponsor wishes to acquire a public company listed on the London Stock Exchange, it will need to comply with the City Code on Takeovers and Mergers and the Takeovers Directive (Interim Implementation) Regulations 2006. In a public acquisition funded with cash (in whole or in part), Rule 24.8 of the Code requires an appropriate third party (typically the offeror's financial adviser) to confirm that the bidder will have resources available to satisfy full acceptance of the offer. This 'certain funds' requirement means that the cash must be in place by the time the offer is made and the bidder's financial adviser must confirm that the bidder has sufficient resources in place to fund the bid.

This phrase 'certain funds', when applied to loan documentation, describes the concept of the lending banks committing to make the debt facilities available subject only to a very limited set of conditions. This is achieved by satisfying many of the usual raft of funding conditions at the time of signing the loan documents (or, at the latest, before the announcement of the offer) or deferring their satisfaction until after funding, in order to leave only conditions precedent to funding that are technical or entirely within the newcos' control to satisfy, and by disapplying all but the more fundamental drawstop defaults.

The use of the public acquisition certain funds technique has been wholeheartedly adopted by the London and (frequently wider European) private acquisition market, particularly on larger transactions, notwithstanding that its use is not a statutory or regulatory requirement. Private acquisitions often need a period of time between signing the acquisition agreement and actually completing the acquisition – for example, where the parties may need to obtain competition authority clearances or satisfy other conditions to closing – and during that time the newcos will complete all the conditions required by the lenders to make the facilities available. Sellers are therefore keen to ensure that, where exchange and completion take place in stages, the company that signs the sale and purchase agreement (which will inevitably be a newly formed newco with no assets) will have the required debt financing available to it to pay the purchase price. Although funding is never absolutely certain, limiting the funding conditions to those used in a public acquisition certain funds scenario provides the seller with an enhanced degree of comfort. The protection afforded by a certain funds commitment by the lenders also benefits the sponsor, as it reduces the risk that the debt finance package might be terminated for some reason before it is drawn down.

In summary, under certain funds style drawdown conditions, only those events of default that relate to the following apply (these are the 'drawstop' events):

- a breach of certain undertakings by or in respect of the newcos;
- certain misrepresentations by or in respect of the newcos; and
- any insolvency event affecting the newcos.

By limiting the remit of these conditions to the newcos, the target and its subsidiaries are purposely excluded; any such events affecting them may or may not result in a condition of the offer (or, in the case of private acquisitions, of the sale and purchase agreement) being breached, and the lenders will seek some protection by controlling whether or not the offer (or obligation to purchase) remains open (ie, by the condition being waived by the purchaser).

Changes affecting the lenders or the wider debt finance or capital markets (for example material adverse change in the market clauses) are also excluded from being drawstop events.

The relevant undertakings and representations are either those of fundamental importance to the lenders (such as illegality and corporate status) or are in the control of the newcos (such as restrictions on mergers, security interests, loans, guarantees, indebtedness, share capital, changing business, disposals, joint ventures and maintenance of insurance). The insolvency events capture solvency tests and insolvency-related steps and proceedings.

The risk of such a condition being triggered should be minimised by the newcos' careful management of their activities (which is ultimately a question of sponsor control) during the period from signing to funding, ensuring that none of these drawstop events occurs.

4.3 Hedging

The rate of interest on debt finance is usually a floating rate, exposing the borrowers to a potentially increasing cost of servicing their debt if underlying interest rates rise. The lenders will require the borrowers to mitigate this exposure by entering into interest rate hedging arrangements in respect of some or all of their debt obligations.

A hedging strategy will be agreed between the borrowers and the lenders, which may employ interest rate caps, collars or swaps (or a combination of any of them). The usual benchmark is to hedge two-thirds of the term debt finance package, for at least the first two or three years of the relevant facilities. Although sponsors are careful to avoid being obliged to undertake this hedging with the arranging bank(s), as a commercial matter it is common for the borrower to do so. The borrowers' liabilities to the hedging counterparty (or counterparties) will be secured on a first ranking basis, alongside the senior debt.

Currency (or foreign exchange) hedging is not usually required – instead, the debt finance package will be denominated in currencies that generally match the predicted currencies of the target group's cash flows, creating a 'natural hedge'.

4.4 Syndication and transferability of loan participations

Part of the reason that commercial and investment banks are willing and able to underwrite and take on to their balance sheet large debt financings is the liquidity of the debt capital markets, which (in the absence of any adverse factors such as the shock and contraction caused by the global financial crisis) enables them to sell their loans in primary syndication and, if required thereafter, in the secondary market. As mentioned earlier in this chapter, the market's capacity in this regard has fallen significantly since the onset of the global financial crisis – but this 'originate, arrange and distribute' model remains valid and active.

Lenders are keen to ensure that they have freedom to manage their balance sheets and credit exposures, as well as to comply with regulatory capital risk management requirements. In addition, both lenders and sponsors are acutely aware of the potential in current markets for distressed debt funds to buy the debt of groups that may be struggling; and therefore also of the importance of freedom to transfer (for lenders) on the one hand and controls on who might purchase a borrower's debt (for sponsors) on the other.

Consequently, although sponsors generally prefer their relationship banks to retain a meaningful participation in the debt package and borrowers may try to insist that they have the right to approve any potential transfer and transferee, lenders have increasingly sought to ensure that the transfer provisions of loan documents permit the loan to be freely transferable without any attached conditionality, or subject to only minimal borrower protections.

Typically, loan documentation will permit transfer of the loans by the lenders subject to a borrower consultation right (rather than a requirement to obtain the borrower's consent to the transfer). In conjunction with this, the lenders may agree that they will retain a minimum amount of their loan commitment, or that they will only transfer an agreed minimum amount. A minimum credit rating of the transferee may also be set. Lenders may also agree a list of permitted transferees (a 'white list', which is often extremely long) or (less frequently, for understandable reputational and relationship reasons) of prohibited transferees (a blacklist). However, the level of protection these afford in practice is less than might be expected as they will usually cease to apply while an event of default is continuing.

Investment vehicles known as CLOs (collateralised loan obligations) and CDOs (collateralised debt obligations), which buy groups of loans and sell exposures to layers of the pooled loans with distinct risk profiles, have historically accessed the loan market via the secondary market (by purchasing loans after they have been made) and have targeted only non-amortising or longer dated, higher priced, term loan tranches of debt. Before the crisis, some CLOs would also participate in the primary syndication of deals, taking all tranches of debt, including 'A' tranches of amortising term debt and revolving credit tranches. Following the crisis, new CLO issuance fell massively and CLO participation in leveraged finance contracted sharply, coupled with increased regulation in Europe and the United States. CLO issuance increased in 2013, as innovative structures were developed to address the changed regulatory requirements, and investor confidence in CLOs and the debt in which they invest as an asset class improved as pricing and other commercial factors made CLOs more economically attractive. However, it inevitably remains difficult to be certain that CLOs will resume their former levels of importance as a source of leveraged debt funding.

4.5 Market flex

'Market flex' terms allow the underwriters of a transaction to renegotiate the structure, terms, pricing and tenor of a deal if they decide that this is necessary in order to complete a successful syndication. This right is granted in mandate or commitment papers, before the loan documents are entered into and the related acquisition has completed, and is particularly common in high-risk financings or event-driven financings, during periods of uncertain or volatile market risk, or where there is a long commitment period between signing and drawdown of the debt.

Market flex was first employed in the UK debt markets of the 1980s, during the market instability resulting from the UK property crisis and Gulf War, and emerged again during the early and later 1990s in response to various other local and global economic conditions, and is now an established feature of the debt markets.

A properly negotiated flex will balance the needs of the underwriting bank and the borrowers' desire for certainty as to the terms of the deal which they have signed up to. As a result, the terms of the right to flex may:

- specify the parameters of any flex, such as agreeing which terms of the loan documents can be changed and which cannot – the flex is commonly limited to a specified maximum uplift in the margin (or specified margin(s) or weighted average margin), but may allow changes to the tenor or structure of the facilities; the number of times, and period during which, the flex can be exercised are commonly limited;
- agree a definition of 'successful syndication', often by reference to the underwriter's target hold level and the timeframe to achieve it;
- allow the borrower to walk away from the deal if it does not agree with the proposed flex (with or without reimbursement or waiver of underwriting, arrangement and commitment fees);
- agree that the underwriter will act reasonably in exercising the flex and will provide the borrowers with reasonable details of the changes that have occurred in the relevant commercial bank market, syndicated loan market, financial market or capital market that justify the need to flex, and that the changes proposed as a result are necessary or advisable in order for syndication to be completed successfully.

In times of strong institutional and other debt investor demand, mandate letters frequently include an obligation on the underwriter to use its best efforts to achieve a reverse (or downward) flex of the pricing of the debt, in the event that syndication of the debt is oversubscribed. In return, the sponsor may agree to share some of the benefit of any cost saving arising from a reverse flex with the underwriter.

5. Extensions and refinancing

5.1 Amend and extend
In the years following the global financial crisis, while bank debt liquidity continued to be severely constrained and the growth in sub-investment grade high-yield debt was in its early stages, many private equity portfolio companies were refinanced on an 'amend-and-extend' basis. This involved incumbent lenders (or a majority of them) agreeing to extend the maturity of existing loan facilities in return for fees and frequently an adjustment to ongoing pricing and/or financial covenant levels. 'Forward-start' facilities were a refined version of amend-and-extend facilities. Amend-and-extend remains the only refinancing technique for some less attractive credits that are unable to attract new debt (whether via loan facilities or issuance of high-yield bonds).

5.2 Dividend recapitalisations
The restructuring of debt financing packages via dividend recapitalisations (or 'recaps') was a significant part of annual debt volumes in the years leading up to the global financial crisis, but fell out of favour for many years, resurging again in 2012 as lender and debt investor sentiment towards them again improved and reaching 15% of new leveraged debt issuance over year-to-date by August 2013 (the highest proportion since 2007).

Dividend recaps are a useful tool to extract value from private equity portfolio companies, where the net enterprise value of the target group has increased since the original acquisition as a result of increased asset values, improved business performance and/or reduced debt levels (which may have been achieved as a result of repayments or prepayments of debt via improved cashflow and/or disposals).

Several additional market features have also driven the resurgent volume of dividend recaps, among them suppressed deal-flow and exits via stock market flotation, investors searching for yield, increased alternative lender activity and buoyant US debt markets.

A further advantage of dividend recaps for sponsors has been the opportunity to improve the debt terms put in place in the aftermath of the financial crisis, including higher leverage and improved pricing levels.

At its most straightforward, a dividend recap may consist of an increase in the amount of an existing debt facility or the addition of a new tranche, which may be coupled with other amendments. Alternatively, a full refinancing may be carried out, whether as a loan refinancing or a high-yield bond refinancing (discussed further below). In either case, the new debt will include an additional dividend recap element that will ultimately be paid to the sponsor as a dividend on its equity stake

Debt finance

in the target group or, more frequently, by way of a redemption of its shareholder debt or loan notes.

6. European high-yield debt

The key features of European high-yield debt are as follows:
- It consists of debt capital markets instruments, issued by sub-investment grade European issuers to European and US institutional investors (via Regulation S or Rule 144A offerings), typically governed under New York law.
- It is usually subject to a fixed rate of interest (currently higher than senior bank debt levels).
- It is non-amortising debt with a bullet maturity and longer tenor than bank debt.
- It carries a prohibition on redemption for an agreed 'non-call' period of between three and five years, coupled with a reducing redemption premium.
- It includes a requirement to offer to redeem the bonds at a premium (typically 1% or 2%) on a change of control of the issuer, sometimes coupled with the need also for a ratings downgrade trigger, unless the bonds feature a portability mechanic (a bondholder put).
- It provides the ability to offer to repurchase a proportion of the bonds (typically 35% to 40%, frequently also subject to a redemption premium) from proceeds of equity issuance or offering (known as an 'equity claw').
- The minimum issuance size has decreased, but is still around €100 million to €150 million, with an average issuance size of around €300 million and above.
- It is usually listed (eg, in Luxembourg or Ireland) for tax reasons.
- Where it is used to finance an acquisition, bond issuance will usually (but not always) be bridged by dedicated bank facilities governed by English (or other local) law and containing market-standard bond transition mechanics and exploding margins.
- It is typically structurally subordinated to the bank debt in the capital structure – in other words, it is issued by a holding company higher in the group structure than the bank debt borrower(s) and therefore further away from the operating group than the bank debt borrower.
- It may or may not be secured, but security (except at the level of the high-yield debt issuer) and guarantees will often also be subordinated to the bank debt in the structure.
- Due to its historical US provenance, it is still predominantly arranged and underwritten by the major US investment banks, although major European banks are typically also involved.

High-yield bonds (historically known as 'junk bonds', due to the sub-investment grade rating status of their issuers) have increasingly developed from being used as a source of refinancing for existing acquisition bank debt, to forming part of an initial leveraged acquisition finance structure. Where this is the case, the high-yield debt may be issued to investors shortly before closing and held in escrow until completion, when it is released in order to fund the acquisition.

More commonly, in order to take advantage of the speed, ease, expediency and efficiency associated with the inception of debt finance (as discussed above), the acquisition of the target is funded initially by a dedicated high-yield bridge bank facility. The high-yield bonds are then issued as soon as possible following completion (usually subject to a longstop date) and applied to repay the bridge facilities.

These bridge facilities are usually arranged by the same banks that arrange and underwrite the subsequent high-yield issue. Typically in a European acquisition financing context they will follow European norms and be documented based on the standard LMA leveraged facilities agreement containing 'certain funds' provisions and subject to English (or other applicable local European) law. They will therefore contain some of the key representations, undertakings and events of default seen in a typical leveraged acquisition facility agreement (as discussed above), but not necessarily the full suite. Instead, the positive and negative undertakings that will govern the high-yield bonds, when issued, will also be incorporated into the bridge facilities and these will be expressed to be construed in accordance with New York law (assuming that is the law that will ultimately govern the bonds).

The terms of mandate, commitment and arrangement of high-yield bridge facilities and of the high-yield bonds intended to take them out will be documented separately to those documenting the comparable arrangements in relation to the acquisition bank debt in the structure, on standard high-yield market terms, and will typically be subject to New York law. In addition to mandate documentation, high-yield bond issuance will also require the preparation of an extensive offering memorandum accompanied by an international marketing process, each requiring significant input by the senior management of the issuer. Other key documents include the bond indenture or trust deed containing the terms and conditions of the high-yield bonds, and the purchase agreement under which the investment banks underwriting the issue will agree with the issuer to subscribe for the initial issuance of bonds, also typically subject to New York law.

Inherent in high-yield bond issuance are extensive initial and ongoing capital markets, regulatory and listing authority diligence and disclosure requirements, together with relative difficulty in obtaining investor consents and waivers (due to a widely dispersed investor base and the freedom of transferability of high-yield bonds). These are execution and operational challenges not associated with debt finance packages, where it is much more straightforward to obtain consents and waivers.

Furthermore, even where there is no term debt other than the high-yield bonds, issuers will typically require working capital facilities to be provided by bank lenders. It is usual for these to be provided by the borrower's relationship banks on a super senior basis, such that the high-yield debt (insofar as it is secured) ranks equally with the bank debt, but is subordinated in order of payment. In such cases, the relative intercreditor positions of bank and bond debt will be heavily negotiated and documented in a separate intercreditor agreement, which will also usually seek to cater for a variety of potential future loan and bond refinancings of the high-yield debt. All of this adds significant complexity, time and cost to the inception of bank high-yield bond financings. The high-yield markets are also notoriously susceptible to investor sentiment, particularly around macro-economic factors, another reason for the tension in an acquisition financing context between the need for certainty of funding and the desire to issue bonds to repay bridging debt as soon as possible.

The significant benefits for sponsors in relation to high-yield financings lie in the far greater flexibility of a typical out-of-the-box high-yield covenant package, which is both more limited in application and wider in terms of permissibility than a typical European leveraged debt finance package. This is because a high-yield covenant package is intended to balance creditor protections against flexibility to enable the issuer group to grow, hopefully encouraging and allowing the issuer group's capital value to increase and therefore also making its bonds more attractive in the secondary market.

In particular, a high-yield covenant package will not include the 'maintenance' financial covenants found in loan facilities (the quarterly and annual testing of financial ratios, often tightening as the term of the facilities elapses, which must be complied with on an ongoing basis). Nor will it contain a comparably extensive suite of restrictive covenants (for example limiting the incurrence of additional financial indebtedness). Instead, the covenant package will contain fewer restrictions, which often need only be complied with if and to the extent the proposed action would otherwise contravene them. An example of such 'incurrence' covenants would be a limitation on incurring additional debt to the extent it would cause an agreed (and often fairly high) leverage ratio to be breached, and usually subject also to an extensive list of market-standard exceptions.

Examples of typical high-yield covenants include the following, all of which will follow accepted high-yield market norms and will also be subject to market-standard exceptions, which may in some cases (eg, indebtedness, restricted payments, restrictions on dividends etc and liens) be very extensive:

- limitation on incurring indebtedness;
- limitation on restricted payments (dividends, distributions and other payments flowing out of the issuer group);
- limitation on restrictions on dividends and other payment restrictions affecting restricted subsidiaries (subsidiaries other than those designated as unrestricted, which are exempted from the high-yield provisions applicable to the restricted group but are therefore treated like third parties and ring-fenced as far as the restricted group is concerned);
- limitation on liens (ie, on granting security, which could otherwise effectively subordinate the high-yield debt);
- limitation on transactions with affiliates;
- limitation on consolidation, merger and sale of assets and on change in business activities;
- limitation on issue or sale of capital stock of restricted subsidiaries;
- limitation on issuance of guarantees of indebtedness by restricted subsidiaries (typically requiring them also to be granted to the bondholders);
- limitation on sale and leaseback transactions; and
- an anti-layering covenant (prohibiting the incurrence of additional subordinated debt that is not also subordinated to the high-yield bonds).

High-yield bond terms will also require the provision of a less onerous set of financial and other information reporting obligations, and will contain a more limited set of events of default than a typical European leveraged facilities agreement.

Examples of typical high-yield debt events of default include the following:

- non-payment of principal (whether or not prohibited by the payment blockage mechanism);
- non-payment of interest (after a grace period);
- breach of a covenant;
- cross-acceleration or cross-payment default (ie, acceleration or non-payment, rather than simple cross-default, of other material financial indebtedness);
- judgments for material amounts entered and not satisfied or stayed (after a grace period) – comparable to the creditors' process event of default under a loan facility;
- insolvency proceedings and related events; and
- events of key business relevance to a particular issue, such as loss of licences or regulated status.

7. Intercreditor agreements

Key features of intercreditor agreements include the following points:

- They are a key structural element of European financings, used to rank different layers and types of secured debt as against each other and between themselves (for example, senior and mezzanine; senior and second lien; super senior revolving debt, senior term debt and senior secured high yield bonds; super senior working capital and senior unitranche term debt – plus secured hedging).
- They are also used to subordinate sponsor (ie, private equity investor) debt (whether or not secured) and intra-group debt.
- Subordination and ranking is purely contractual.
- They are vital in multi-jurisdictional financings in order to regulate enforcement and valuation procedures where differing local insolvency regimes would otherwise apply (notwithstanding the application of the EU Regulation on Cross-Border Insolvency and the United Nations Commission on International Trade Law Model Law on Cross-Border Insolvency).
- They are typically based on an LMA standard intercreditor agreement (although this is typically extensively stripped down if only senior secured and subordinated unsecured debt feature in the capital structure, when it becomes more akin to a simple subordination agreement).

The intercreditor agreement is an essential part of all but the most simple secured financings. Its primary purpose is to govern the relative ranking and priority of secured debt between senior and junior creditors, and to subordinate unsecured investor and intra-group debt.

The LMA form of intercreditor agreement for senior and mezzanine leveraged acquisition financings was first introduced to the market in 2009, in response to judicial scrutiny of a number of litigated pre-crisis proprietary intercreditor agreements that revealed certain weaknesses in their structure. This form was developed further in 2012 in response to the increasing sophistication of senior and mezzanine positions and expectations.

In 2013 an additional form of LMA intercreditor agreement was released for super senior bank debt and secured high-yield bonds (an area that had hitherto been catered for predominantly by various law firms' standard documents).

However, it is standard within the London market and for European cross-border financings to use the LMA senior/mezzanine form of intercreditor agreement as at least the starting point in leveraged financings, and increasingly common to see a variant of the LMA bank/bond form of intercreditor agreement used in more straightforward bank and bond structures.

Notwithstanding that an LMA form will typically be used as a starting point, the intercreditor agreement will always be negotiated and will be more or less complex depending on the requirements of any particular capital structure; for example, including super senior revolving and senior term bank debt and other combinations of secured bank, bond, alternative lender, second lien, payment-in-kind and investor debt.

The final position will frequently recognise the relative bargaining power of the parties, within the context of recognised market norms applying to specific structures; albeit norms that are continually evolving in response to market developments.

Among other things, the intercreditor agreement will typically include the following key features, each subject to a greater or lesser degree of negotiation:
- ranking and relative priority of security and payments on enforcement;
- subordination upon the insolvency of debtors of claims of junior creditors to those of more senior creditors;
- turnover of receipts between creditors to maintain priorities;
- permitted payments and conditions in which they are blocked;
- security enforcement through the security trustee only;
- security enforcement instructions – who may give them (ie, the composition of an instructing group) and how they may be given (ie, through relevant agents; composition of the applicable majority);
- security enforcement standstill periods applicable to actions by junior creditors (ie, where action is permitted following the elapsing of an agreed period without action by the senior creditor);
- restriction on the grant of security and guarantees not granted to all secured creditors;
- valuation of secured assets and release of security and liabilities on enforcement;
- creation of security trust; sharing and equalisation between secured creditors;
- rights of more junior creditors to acquire prior ranking debt; and
- deemed consent and override provisions, to ensure uniformity of application of senior consents and waivers (to junior debt, so that junior debt cannot block the agreement of debtor and senior debt) and of intercreditor provisions over terms differing between the various debt documents (so that the provisions of the intercreditor agreement will prevail).

Acquisition documentation

Richard Lever
Lorraine Robinson
King & Wood Mallesons LLP (formerly SJ Berwin LLP)

This chapter reviews the acquisition documentation involved in a management buyout in the United Kingdom, and looks in particular at how the involvement of a private equity provider will impact on the main terms. It focuses on purely private deals; public-to-private transactions are very different, and are the subject of the chapter "Public-to-privates".

1. **Basis of valuation**

    It is important to understand the basis of valuation that has been adopted for a target business, as it will have a direct impact on the terms of the acquisition agreement. In particular, it will affect financial adjustments that may be required to the consideration, the scope of the warranties and the recourse on a breach of warranty, and the terms of any tax indemnity.

    There are many ways to value an acquisition target, but a common approach taken by private equity buyers is to use a multiple of profits or, more commonly, a multiple of the earnings of the target before interest, tax, depreciation and amortisation (EBITDA). This sets the 'enterprise value' of the business, which is the value that it has irrespective of how the business has been financed, or the level of its net assets. The price will then be fixed on the assumption that the business has no debt, no excess cash and a normal level of working capital – the so-called 'cash-free, debt-free, normal to actual working capital' model.

    As the target business is likely to have some debt and excess cash, the price will need to be adjusted to take account of the amount of cash and debt in the business either at completion or at some identified time before completion (the principle being that the buyer should pay for any excess cash in the business but receives a price reduction for any debt). Different price adjustment mechanisms are discussed below, but in either case the definitions of 'debt' and 'cash' will require detailed analysis and negotiation between the parties. For example, does debt include break costs or prepayment penalties, finance leases, unfunded pension liabilities or provided-for or deferred tax; and does cash exclude trapped cash that is not available for distribution? The basis of valuation will also include an assumption about the normal level of working capital that the business requires (ie, the level needed to support the sustainable profits of the business). Adjustments will also need to be made to the price to reflect whether or not the actual level of working capital reflects the agreed norm.

2. Acquisition structure

A key issue when a private equity provider makes an acquisition is tax efficiency. Therefore, consideration needs to be given to the choice of an appropriate acquisition vehicle and structure. This may depend on the profile of the investors in the private equity provider itself. Additionally, the provision of an advantageous tax and business environment for directors and certain employees of the company to be acquired will also be considered.

Buyouts are usually structured as share acquisitions and in consequence all of the target's assets, liabilities and obligations are automatically acquired. Effectively, the buyer acquires a company that owns a business and is running it as a going concern. Alternatively, however, a buyer may choose to acquire the assets that make up the business and not buy the company itself. The significant difference between this route and a share sale is that where the transfer of an undertaking is chosen, the assets that are being acquired and the particular liabilities that are being assumed by the buyer are defined by the acquisition documentation. This may be unfavourable to the seller and its shareholders, which must retain any liabilities that have not been transferred after sale. In addition, the taxation consequences of either type of acquisition must be considered carefully as they will influence a transaction significantly. This chapter largely focuses on buyouts by way of a share sale as these are significantly more common.

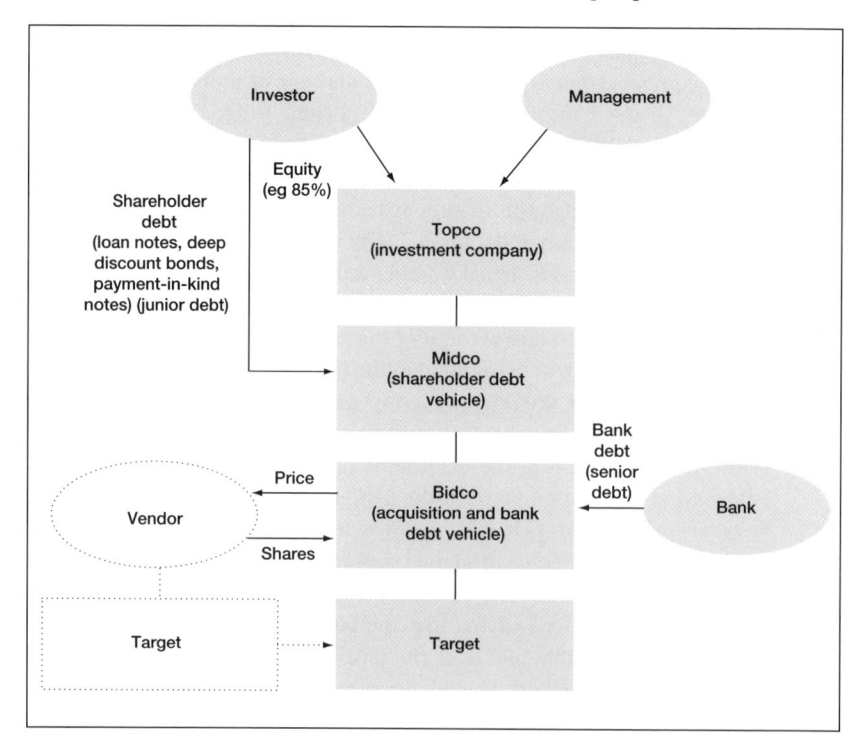

It is usual for a group of newly incorporated companies ('newcos') to be established for the purpose of the acquisition. Often the group of newcos takes the form of a chain of three (or more) companies, which we will refer to as 'Topco', 'Midco' and 'Bidco', each being a 100% subsidiary of the previous entity. The benefit of Bidco is that it provides a clean company with no previous trading history into which funds can be introduced to finance the acquisition. The private equity provider and the management team will invest in the equity of Topco, with the funds invested being fed down the chain to Bidco to finance the acquisition. The function of Midco is to be a separate vehicle into which debt finance (whether from the private equity provider or externally) may be introduced.

The main advantage of using this structure is to facilitate structural subordination, so that payment on the debt financing can be made lower down the chain and, therefore, in priority to returns on the equity investment in Topco. Midco may be replaced by several midcos facilitating further structural subordination between different types of debt finance (eg, senior, mezzanine and shareholder debt).

In addition to the benefit of structural subordination, the structure has advantages in tax and banking regulation compliance, although the United Kingdom's worldwide debt cap rules also need to be considered from a tax perspective.

Detailed consideration should be given to the ability of the buyer and the seller to recover value added tax (VAT) on legal and professional fees incurred in relation to the sale and purchase of shares. The legal position is unclear, but there are steps that can be taken to improve the arguments in favour of VAT recovery.

3. Buyout process

Before going through an expensive due diligence exercise and preparing contract documentation, a private equity provider may require that heads of terms be agreed. The heads of terms will generally be a non-binding statement of an 'in-principle' agreement, but may include binding confidentiality and exclusivity provisions. They may also include breakfee provisions and provisions for the non-solicitation of employees, customers and suppliers. Alternatively, separate exclusivity and confidentiality agreements may be entered into at the same time.

It has become common for businesses to be sold by way of auction, sometimes with no bidder being granted exclusivity until signing of the acquisition agreement, or for a very limited period only. The impact of an auction on the sale process and the terms of the acquisition agreement is discussed below.

The heads of terms will usually take the form of a letter or memorandum of terms signed by the seller and Bidco (as buyer) or, if Bidco has not yet been incorporated, the private equity provider. This will be separate from any heads of terms between the private equity provider and the management team relating to the equity aspects of the deal. The heads of terms will include details of the key terms of the deal – the price, the basis of valuation and any other important issues that have been agreed between the parties – as well as the process towards exchange of contracts and completion of the acquisition.

3.1 Confidentiality agreement

The potential buyer will want to have as much commercial and financial information about the business as possible to enable it to make a detailed evaluation of the target. The seller will insist that any potential buyer enters into a confidentiality undertaking as a prerequisite to the release of any sensitive information (whether in the form of an information memorandum, release of disclosure bundles or access to a data room or, increasingly, a 'virtual' data room, which is provided via a website). The seller will be particularly concerned to prevent a prospective buyer from disclosing or misusing information such as customer lists, pricing policies or costs of sale.

Among the most important provisions in the confidentiality undertaking from the seller's point of view are:

- the limits on the buyer's rights to disclose or use information (including the fact of the potential transaction) and the exceptions to them; and
- the seller's right to demand the return or destruction of confidential information on request or if the buyer does not proceed with the deal.

The prospective buyer's duty to return or destroy confidential information (including confidential information held by its advisers or bankers, or materials generated by its advisers or bankers from the confidential information) is a key provision, since the terms of the undertaking are likely to become an issue only if the deal does not go ahead with that particular buyer. A private equity provider will resist being liable for the actions of its advisers or its bankers, including procuring the return of confidential information; but if it is forced to accept some liability for its advisers, it will seek back-to-back undertakings from them. The seller may, in any event, require the private equity provider's bankers to enter into a direct confidentiality agreement with the seller.

Only the parties to the confidentiality undertaking will be bound by it. If the letter is sent to potential buyers by an investment bank on the bank's letterhead, the bank will usually act as the seller's agent so that the seller (and possibly also the target) will be able to enforce it.

Confidentiality obligations in transactions in the United Kingdom and Europe are usually drafted to expire around one to two years after completion of an acquisition or termination of negotiations between the parties, although there is no legal obstacle to imposing a confidentiality obligation that is unlimited in time. A prospective buyer may expressly require that the confidentiality undertaking expire automatically after completion of the acquisition by the buyer, as much of the due diligence information will lose its confidential status.

Some sellers may seek to include an indemnity in the confidentiality agreement, in an attempt to make it easier to enforce and recover against a prospective buyer for a breach. Private equity providers will typically resist this, arguing that specific performance (eg, a court order to prevent use or disclosure) or damages on the usual contractual basis should provide adequate protection. In reality, confidentiality obligations can be very difficult to enforce, given the need to show proof of breach. From the sellers' point of view, an information leak is irreversible, but the damage suffered can be difficult to quantify.

Separate rules, incorporating confidentiality undertakings, will be prepared governing access to a data room (whether physical or virtual). A prospective buyer will have to sign up to abide by these rules before being granted access.

3.2 Exclusivity/lockout agreement

Exclusivity agreements, also known as 'lockout' or 'noshop' arrangements, are commonplace in many forms of commercial negotiation, including buyouts. An exclusivity agreement prevents the seller from actively seeking or negotiating with any other potential buyers for a specified period. This allows the private equity provider to conduct its due diligence and negotiate the acquisition agreement (with the resulting advisers' costs), with the comfort that for a limited period the seller cannot negotiate with any other potential buyer.

From a legal perspective, a lockout agreement (ie, an agreement by one party with a second party not to negotiate with anyone other than the second party) is enforceable in the United Kingdom, but it should be stated to apply for a specified period that is reasonable in the circumstances, and it should either be supported by good consideration (eg, by reference to the buyer's costs in conducting due diligence) or the agreement should be executed as a deed.

In contrast, a positive obligation to negotiate, like an agreement to agree, is unenforceable because it lacks certainty. The concept of a duty to carry on negotiations in good faith is inherently repugnant to the adversarial position of the parties involved in negotiations, as confirmed by the House of Lords decision in *Walford v Miles* [1992] 2 WLR 174. This decision confirmed that each party to the negotiations is entitled to pursue its own interests as long as it avoids making misrepresentations. To advance that interest, each party must be entitled, if it thinks it appropriate, to threaten to withdraw from further negotiations, or actually to withdraw, in the hope that the opposite party may seek to reopen the negotiations by offering improved terms.

However, in contrast to the position under English law described above, some other jurisdictions recognise an obligation to negotiate in good faith, so this should always be considered if any of the parties involved in the negotiations is located outside the United Kingdom. There can, in some circumstances, be an implied agreement not to walk away from negotiations without good reason.

If an exclusivity agreement is breached, a buyer might attempt to seek an injunction against the seller to stop the breach, but injunctions are available only at the court's discretion and must be reasonable in the circumstances. The standard remedy would be damages equal to the wasted costs of the buyer. It is advisable for the agreement to include a list of the items for which damages can be claimed in the form of a liquidated damages clause, but this should not go as far as quantifying the likely costs, as if these costs are not incurred the clause could be construed as a penalty. Alternatively, the parties might agree a daily rate at which costs will be incurred and this might form the basis of a liquidated damages claim.

3.3 Break fees

Break fee agreements can be used to protect a private equity provider against abort costs in the event that a transaction fails to reach signing or completion, although such agreements were historically more common in public-to-private deals when they were permitted by the UK Takeover Code. For the current position on break fees in public-to-private transactions, see the chapter on such transactions. It may be appropriate to seek a break fee on a private deal if the acquisition is subject to some significant conditions precedent that must be satisfied by the seller; for example, shareholder approval if the seller or its parent is a quoted company. A break fee agreement can give additional comfort to a buyer before it incurs significant costs. It may also be appropriate in larger deals, when in the final round of an auction bidders can be required to do a substantial amount of work and incur substantial costs.

In order to be enforceable, as with exclusivity agreements, it is important that break fee terms are not drafted so as to be punitive. Instead, care should be taken when drafting break fee provisions to ensure that only reasonable costs and fees incurred in relation to the acquisition can be recovered should the transaction abort.

3.4 Acquisition agreement

The acquisition agreement is the principal contractual agreement setting out the terms of the transaction. Usually, separate documentation is required to transfer legal ownership of the shares (eg, a stock transfer form) or the assets in a business transfer (eg, property transfer documents). Typically, but certainly not invariably, the acquisition agreement is drafted by the buyer's lawyers, except on a sale by auction where the process is seller-driven (see below).

The key commercial terms may have been agreed previously in heads of terms. The acquisition agreement will include the following principal terms:

- sale of the shares or business;
- price and any financial adjustments that may apply to the price;
- any conditions precedent to which the purchase is subject;
- detailed completion mechanics;
- detailed warranties regarding the nature of the target business;
- restrictive covenants that bind the parties post-completion; and
- if relevant, specific pension and insurance arrangements.

Additionally, a number of ancillary documents traditionally accompany an acquisition agreement, including:

- the tax deed, if one will be provided; and
- the disclosure letter.

There may also be other key documents, depending on the nature of the deal; for example, a transitional/interim service agreement, which provides for certain arrangements between the target and the seller's group to continue for an interim period, where the target and the seller's group have been to some extent operated together.

4. Usual provisions of an acquisition agreement

4.1 Agreement to sell and purchase

This provision is one of the most important operative provisions in the acquisition agreement, but is usually one of the shortest and simplest. In a share sale, the buyer's priority is to ensure that proper title to the shares is transferred without any encumbrances and that the shares are transferred with all rights attaching to them. The buyer will generally seek an absolute covenant or warranty as to title, and will want to ensure that any limitations of liability in relation to the warranties and other provisions of the acquisition agreement generally are not applicable to the covenant or warranty as to title to the shares. By selling with 'full title' guarantee, there are certain title covenants implied by law (under the Law of Property (Miscellaneous Provisions) Act 1994), although the buyer will usually want to see these backed up with specific title warranties. A private equity provider will want to ensure that there are no risks to title, as these could impact on its ability to make a clean exit from the target. When buying shares in a company, full title guarantee gives several important protections for the buyer:

- The disposing party has the right to dispose of the property.
- The disposing party will do all that it reasonably can to give the title it purports to give, at its own cost.
- The disposal is free of all charges, encumbrances and adverse rights, except any charges, encumbrances or adverse rights about which the seller does not know and could not reasonably be expected to know (ie, free from all known encumbrances).

The buyer should also consider whether it needs to acquire title to any other assets which are not owned by the target directly (eg, any intellectual property rights), and will therefore not pass with the shares. This can be achieved either by making the relevant company a party to the agreement or by imposing a procurement obligation on the seller.

The contract should also address the treatment of dividends in the lead-up to completion. The basic principle is that the seller will be entitled to any dividend declared before the date of completion (even if unpaid), and the buyer will be entitled to dividends declared after completion unless otherwise agreed (*Black v Homersham* (1878) 4 ExD 24). In practice, if the seller wishes to effect a dividend strip it will, for tax reasons, wish to declare, and in most cases pay, the dividend before the contract is signed.

4.2 Conditions precedent

If the parties are in a position to sign and complete the agreement simultaneously, this will simplify the terms of the agreement considerably and should therefore be done whenever possible. Where exchange and completion are not simultaneous, the agreement will need to address matters that may arise in the period between exchange and completion, and to allocate risk between the seller and the buyer. Clearly, the longer the period between exchange and completion, the more likely it is that something will happen to affect the basis upon which the terms of the acquisition agreement were struck.

(a) **Common conditions precedent**

Where exchange and completion cannot be simultaneous, there will be one or more conditions to be met before completion can take place. The most common conditions precedent are as follows:

- Regulatory approval from competition or other authorities – unlike in many other jurisdictions, where there is a statutory obligation on both a seller and a buyer to refer matters to competition authorities, under English law any filing to the UK competition authorities is voluntary (other than in certain circumstances). However, if the buyout meets the test for a qualifying merger under the Enterprise Act 2002, the buyer can be required to divest, post-completion, the target or any part of it. Consequently, a private equity provider may seek to avoid the risk of being forced by the regulator to make divestments post-completion by requiring a condition precedent that the transaction is given regulatory clearance. Where there is a concern that the transaction contemplated may constitute a 'concentration with a European Union dimension', it is imperative to include a condition precedent that can be removed only if the parties are clear that the EU Merger Regulation does not apply. If the target group has any turnover outside the United Kingdom, it is important to consult early in a transaction with competition law specialists, as it is possible that, when aggregated with the private equity provider's other portfolio companies, a threshold may be met that will require filing with, and clearance by, non-UK competition authorities.

    Where the target group operates in a regulated industry such as insurance or banking, or where there is an entity in the target group that is regulated by the Financial Conduct Authority or the Prudential Regulation Authority, the relevant regulator's consent may be required.

- Tax clearances for the seller – if the sellers (usually management sellers) are taking some consideration in the form of securities in Bidco or another company in the acquisition structure, such as loan notes or shares, then normally no immediate chargeable gain will arise and no tax will arise in relation to the deferred consideration until the consideration shares or loan notes are disposed of (ie, the gain is rolled over). The sellers may want clearance to be obtained from Her Majesty's Revenue and Customs (HMRC) (under Section 138 of the Taxation of Chargeable Gains Act 1992) to the effect that HMRC will not apply the anti-avoidance provisions of Section 137 of the Taxation of Chargeable Gains Act 1992. These provisions prevent a seller who holds 5% or more of any class of shares or debentures of the target company from rolling over the gain on the disposal of those shares into new securities on the basis that the exchange was not for bona fide commercial purposes, or was part of a tax avoidance scheme or arrangement. However, if the principal seller is a private equity house, it will often object to tax clearance being a condition precedent, and will require management sellers

either to obtain clearance prior to exchange of contracts or to proceed without clearance.
- Stock exchange requirements – where the target is part of a group of companies whose parent is listed on a stock exchange, the relevant rules may stipulate that the consent of the parent company's shareholders is needed and require that certain specified information be provided to those shareholders before consent can be given. Where shareholder consent is required, a circular to shareholders of the listed company is usually sent out immediately after entering into the share acquisition agreement and the relevant shareholders' meeting is held two to three weeks later. Accordingly, the acquisition agreement will need to be conditional on shareholder approval being obtained. Under the Financial Conduct Authority's Listing Rules, shareholder consent is required for a 'class 1 transaction', that is to say one where the size of the business being sold by the listed company is substantial in percentage terms in relation to the size of the listed company's overall business. Listed companies also require shareholder approval for certain 'related party transactions'; for example, where the buyer is an existing or former director or substantial shareholder of the listed company.
- Third party consents with respect to change of control or assignment of a contract – in certain circumstances, particularly where there is a change of control provision in any of the target's existing contracts, on a share sale transaction, or prohibition on assignment in an asset sale transaction, the consent of a major customer or supplier will be required before the transaction can be completed. Practically, the private equity provider may prefer to obtain that consent prior to signing the agreements. However, consideration needs to be given in situations where a listed company is involved, as there are likely to be inside information restrictions on providing information on the deal before it is made public. Similarly, disclosure to an important customer or supplier of the existence of a potential sale may be a very sensitive issue that should be dealt with at a time when all other negotiations are all but finalised, or after signing of the acquisition agreement.
- Defined benefit schemes and the Pensions Regulator where an acquisition target has a defined benefit scheme (ie, a pension scheme providing benefits according to a formula, as opposed to a money purchase scheme) – the pensions aspects should be considered early in the transaction process. Actuarial advice should be taken in relation to the funding of the scheme since, if it is not funded sufficiently, plans will need to be made with the trustees of the scheme in order to address this. The Pensions Regulator has powers to impose financial sanctions on employers with pension schemes and parties that are associated or connected with such employers in order to ensure these schemes are properly funded.

By a contribution notice, the regulator may require all or part of the full deficit (calculated on the onerous buyout basis) to be paid to the trustees if it considers that an act (or a failure to act) is materially detrimental to the likelihood of a person receiving their accrued scheme benefits. The regulator must determine whether or not it can use its powers by reference to a list of factors. There is a statutory defence if the potential recipient of the contribution notice can demonstrate that it gave consideration to any potential detriment and concluded that there was no impact, or that it took steps to minimise or eliminate it. Contribution notices may also be issued if the regulator considers that an act (or a failure to act) has taken place with the intention of evading responsibility for statutory debts arising under Section 75 of the Pensions Act 1995; and in these circumstances, the statutory defence previously mentioned does not apply.

Of potentially greater risk in transactions is the Pensions Regulator's power to impose a financial support direction on corporate entities associated with the employer of the pension scheme. This may occur when a pension scheme is underfunded and there are insufficient free (unsecured) assets of the employer(s) to meet a proportion of the deficit. No act or failure to act is therefore required in order for a financial support direction to be imposed, but an action can create a situation in which the risk of the imposition of a financial support direction is increased. For example, if an employer has unsecured assets and then in a buyout those assets are secured against debt obtained to implement the buyout, the financial security of the scheme is reduced. The risk of a financial support direction being imposed in these circumstances will not be one that a private equity provider will be prepared to accept, particularly given the levels of leverage used in buyouts.

In these circumstances, applying for clearance from the Pensions Regulator should be considered early in the transactional process. If satisfied with the application, the regulator will be bound, in light of the circumstances set out in the application, not to issue a contribution notice or financial support direction (usually both), provided that the circumstances are not materially different from those set out in the application. For a clearance application to succeed, it will almost always require the support of the trustees, who may see in the transaction an opportunity to improve their pension scheme's security; they will at least be concerned to ensure that the scheme is not put at financial risk. Negotiating with the trustees (which may require a confidentiality agreement) and applying for clearance require extra work and time, and a separate focus in the transaction process (a clearance application takes some weeks at a minimum; possibly longer). It is therefore well worth addressing early on the question whether clearance will be required and commencing the process as soon as possible if it is. See the chapter 'Due diligence' for further explanation and analysis of the pensions aspects of buyouts.

There may be other situations where the acquisition agreement is not subject to competition or regulatory conditions, but where a gap is required between exchange and completion; for example, to enable necessary structuring or tax planning to take place or to enable a private equity buyer to draw down funds.

(b) **Risks with conditions precedent**

It is advisable for there to be a longstop date beyond which the agreement will terminate if the conditions are not satisfied (or waived) and, as previously mentioned, the period between exchange and completion should be kept as short as possible. Conditional agreements may be problematic in buyouts because a private equity provider is unlikely to be prepared to enter into a binding commitment to provide funds for the acquisition unless all conditions to draw down under its banking facilities have been satisfied. The risk to the seller is that the terms of the buyer's bank finance may include a material adverse change condition, whereby the bank is not obliged to fund if there is a material adverse change in either the financial markets or the target group.

(c) **Controls between exchange and completion**

Where there is a period between exchange and completion, the buyer will require some degree of control over how the target's business is run during that time, in order to protect its interest. Because due diligence and warranties are often tied to the date of the acquisition agreement, the business could in theory be run down in the period between exchange and completion. This could leave the buyer obliged to complete the acquisition and without a remedy, unless the seller agrees to repeat the warranties at the date of completion. On a secondary buyout, where management are rolling over a proportion of their interests into Bidco, the private equity provider may take some comfort from management's involvement in the business during the period prior to completion and merely seek a covenant from the seller that it will operate the business in the ordinary course. More commonly, however, a private equity provider will require detailed covenants regulating key aspects of operating the business, such as consent rights over:

- entry into or termination of material contracts;
- additional debt that is to be incurred;
- any alterations to the target's share capital; and
- undertaking any material litigation.

The scope of these covenants may depend on what financial adjustments will be made to the price.

(d) **Satisfying conditions precedent**

Where conditions precedent are contained in the agreement, there must be complete certainty as to when they have been satisfied (ie, objective standards against which satisfaction of the condition can be tested) or are no longer capable of being satisfied. The agreement should also state which of the parties is responsible for satisfying each condition and, where appropriate, provide a right to waive a condition precedent. The respective parties should be obliged to use all reasonable endeavours to procure satisfaction of the relevant conditions precedent by a specific longstop date. Depending on the nature of the conditions precedent, more detailed provisions may be required on the steps that each party needs to take in order to achieve satisfaction of the conditions. Additionally, it should be acknowledged that if all the conditions precedent have not been satisfied by that date, the agreement falls away (other than in respect of any other existing breaches).

4.3 Termination rights

Where there is a gap between exchange of contracts and completion, the buyer will seek termination rights in certain circumstances. However, particularly on secondary buyouts where a financial seller is involved, the buyer will encounter significant resistance to the inclusion of any form of termination right.

Buyers sometimes seek to include a material adverse change clause that would allow them to terminate the deal if there is a major change impacting on the target after they sign. Although they remain much less common in UK buyouts than in US buyouts, material adverse change clauses have become less unusual in the United Kingdom (and elsewhere in Europe) since the financial crisis. Material adverse change clauses are often required by a bank as part of the terms on which it will provide finance. This sometimes leads to the express inclusion of a material adverse change clause in the acquisition agreement, mirroring the bank's material adverse change clause. Alternatively a similar result can be achieved if the acquisition agreement contains a finance condition. Perhaps unsurprisingly, material adverse change clauses are more common in deals where there is a US acquirer, or there will be a lengthy delay between signing and closing, especially when long clearance procedures may be required by competition authorities. Sellers are very resistant to material adverse change clauses that can be triggered on adverse changes in general market conditions and, if they agree to include a material adverse change clause at all, will seek to restrict it so that it is closely related to changes in the target's business, and it is drafted to be as narrow as possible.

Whether or not the buyer is successful in negotiating a material adverse change clause, it may seek the ability to terminate the acquisition agreement in other limited circumstances – for example, on a breach of warranties or pre-completion undertakings which gives rise to a loss above a certain threshold. Any ability of the buyer to terminate will attract much negotiation, and, as with material adverse change clauses, on a secondary buyout a financial seller will be highly resistant to the inclusion of any such right.

If a termination right is agreed, both parties will want to ensure that the circumstances in which it can be invoked are clear enough to prevent unnecessary litigation. The seller may prefer there to be a fast-track expert process to determine whether a termination right has arisen. The buyer may argue that it should have the right to terminate and for the seller's recourse to be limited to issuing proceedings against the buyer where the buyer has terminated in breach of the terms of the acquisition agreement. If the seller agrees to this, it may seek to include a liquidated damages clause that applies if the buyer terminates in breach of the acquisition agreement, rather than having to try to recover its loss on a normal contractual basis.

4.4 Completion

The nature of a buyout means that if any problems are encountered at completion, the seller could be faced with claiming against a newly incorporated bidco buyer that has no cash. The seller may seek to cover this risk in different ways. It may seek a direct undertaking (what is often called an equity commitment letter) from the private equity provider that it will provide the equity at completion, assuming that all conditions precedent in the acquisition agreement have been satisfied. Some private equity providers will not agree to a contractual commitment to fund the equity, but may offer a non-binding comfort letter to the seller. The seller's primary comfort may be the reputational risk that the private equity provider would suffer if it did not meet its obligations. The seller may also require sight of the conditions precedent in the banking documentation to assess the risk of the bank finance not being available and may back this up with a restriction on the buyer amending these conditions precedent.

In most buyouts, the terms of the buyer's financing will depend on the existing security over the target's business and assets having been removed. Conversely, the seller will be unable to release this security until the incumbent bank has been repaid. While this situation is customarily resolved by the use of solicitors' undertakings, the logistical issues should be addressed well in advance to ensure completion proceeds smoothly.

4.5 Financial assistance

Previously it was illegal for a company to provide a person proposing to acquire shares in that company (or its parent company) with financial assistance. 'Financial assistance' was broadly defined, but included the situation where a target company and its subsidiaries provided security for the buyer's debt finance. Although there was some limited scope for private companies to provide financial assistance if they complied with a statutory procedure, this was cumbersome and costly, involving auditors reporting on the company and the directors making statutory solvency declarations.

The prohibition on financial assistance was abolished in relation to private companies in the Companies Act 2006 and is no longer a concern in relation to private companies; however, the provision of financial assistance by public companies or their subsidiaries is still prohibited. Therefore, in a public-to-private transaction, where a listed company is to be acquired by a private equity buyer, the public target entity will still need to be re-registered as a private company before it can give financial assistance. As discussed above, this financial assistance is usually in the form of security granted by the target company over its assets in relation to the debt used to finance the take-private.

Even though a transaction involving a private company may no longer be subject to the prohibition against financial assistance, the transaction should still be analysed to ensure that it does not infringe capital maintenance rules, which ensure that moneys subscribed for shares can only be paid back to shareholders in certain circumstances. For example, these rules would prevent a private company (with insufficient distributable reserves) from guaranteeing a loan made to a shareholder, if the company was aware at the time it gave the guarantee that the borrower would be unlikely to be able to repay the loan (as the company would be required to make a provision in its accounts in respect of its exposure under the guarantee). This would amount to an unlawful return of capital, unless the amount of the provision was covered by the company's distributable reserves (profits available for distribution to shareholders).

Directors must therefore still consider and minute any decision to grant a guarantee or security to the company's future parent entity as part of a leveraged acquisition, to ensure that accounting for the transaction will not reduce the company's net assets (or if it is likely to do so, to ensure that the reduction is covered by distributable profits). The directors must also comply with their duties to the company when considering whether or not to approve the guarantee or security, not least their duty to act in the way they consider "in good faith, would be most likely to promote the success of the company for the benefit of its members as a whole" (Section 172 of the Companies Act 2006).

4.6 Consideration

The most common forms of consideration on buyouts are cash and shares and/or a form of debt instrument (eg, loan stock) issued by Bidco or, depending on the structure, an intermediate holdco. The form of any securities issued will be influenced by tax considerations. In particular, individual sellers may want the loan notes to be drafted so that they do not constitute qualifying corporate bonds. This protects the seller from being taxed on amounts they do not receive if for some reason the loan notes are not repaid in full.

4.7 Deferred consideration

The majority of buyouts are highly leveraged and the ability to defer part of the purchase price can be advantageous for the private equity provider. Sellers, on the other hand, will usually seek payment of the full amount of the consideration at completion (even if this is subject to post-completion adjustment). Even if the seller accepts that the full amount will not be paid immediately at completion, it may require the balance to be paid into an escrow account pending agreement of the completion accounts and any other adjustments.

There are a number of reasons why part of the consideration may be deferred.

(a) *Seller incentivisation*

Where a seller is, or includes, an individual considered to be key to the business, the private equity provider may link part of the consideration to the achievement of certain financial targets following completion. Practically, however, it is not always tax-efficient to structure additional consideration in this manner (for which see below) and incentivisation of management is more often achieved by individuals receiving equity in Topco, thereby aligning their interests with the private equity provider.

(b) *Earnouts*

Earnouts are structured in such a way that if the target achieves certain financial targets over a stated period after completion, the seller becomes entitled to receive additional consideration based on those targets. Earnouts are not generally considered to be appropriate for private equity transactions because they do not reflect the commercial intentions of the acquiring group: it is not usually desirable for a seller to participate in the potential upside of the business going forward unless the seller is also contributing to that success. Additionally, if there is an earn-out, sellers may well want some controls over the target during the earn-out period. These controls will not be attractive to private equity-backed buyers.

Earnouts involving individual sellers may also not be efficient from a tax perspective, as HMRC may in some circumstances seek to categorise the amounts received on the earnout as income rather than capital, to the extent that the individual continues as an employee or director of the group or continues to provide services to it. Tax on any income characterised as employment income may have to be accounted for under the Pay-As-You-Earn system and employee's and employer's national insurance contributions may also arise.

Even if income treatment does not apply, where the consideration for the acquisition includes an earnout right, there are complications with the capital gains tax treatment for sellers. Often, deferred consideration is satisfied by the issue of shares or loan notes or other debentures by the buyer, rather than cash, so as to enable a seller to defer any tax liability on the earn-out consideration until the amount of the earn-out has been determined and the consideration shares or loan notes are sold or redeemed. However, there are also concerns that a payment received under the earnout right may not benefit from entrepreneurs' relief (which, where available, can operate to reduce the effective rate of tax on certain sale proceeds from 28% to 10%, at current rates), so a seller may want to consider electing to be taxed on the earn-out at the time of the original sale – the downside here being that the seller may end up overpaying tax if the earn-out target is not actually achieved.

4.8 Completion balance sheets/accounts

Completion accounts are an important price adjustment mechanism. They provide a statement of the target's financial position on or around the day of completion. This then allows the consideration to be adjusted upwards or downwards based on the completion accounts.

Completion accounts may consist of a balance sheet or profit and loss account (or both) showing the net asset and profit positions, levels of cash and debt, and working capital as at the date of completion.

The completion accounts clause will specify the timeframes within which the accounts are to be prepared and provided to each of the seller's and the buyer's accountants for review. In the event of disagreement between the accountants, the matter is usually referred to an independent accountant who is required to resolve the issue. Since the price payable for the target is often based on an expected net asset value or profit figure, level of cash and debt or working capital, the acquisition agreement details the appropriate figure expected at completion and the mechanism for adjustment if that figure is not met. When finalised, the adjustment amount will be paid within a short period, failing which default interest becomes payable.

The accounting policies used in valuing the assets and liabilities of the target are of crucial importance and are often heavily negotiated. They should be checked with the accountants throughout negotiations and before they are agreed. The usual criteria applied are consistency with the target's annual accounts and the application of generally accepted accounting practice. However, these will be subject to specific provisions relevant to the transaction and agreed between the parties.

4.9 **Locked box mechanism**

A 'locked box' mechanism is an increasingly common way to set the price paid for a company, which avoids the need for completion accounts to be prepared. Here, the price paid by the buyer is agreed before signing on a cash-free, debt-free, tax-free, normal to actual working capital basis by reference to a balance sheet as at an effective date before completion (the 'locked box date'). Although legal title to the business does not pass until completion, the idea of this structure is to ensure that, economically, the business passes to the buyer at the locked box date.

The seller therefore typically demands some form of additional payment on top of the agreed price in respect of the period from the locked box date until completion to compensate for the delay in getting paid. In return, the buyer will want certain protections to make sure that the seller is not extracting value from the business between the locked box date and closing (commonly referred to as 'leakage'). These take the form of warranties and pre-completion covenants in the acquisition agreement. Unlike the more usual business warranties contained in the acquisition agreement, the buyer will usually be entitled to a pound-for-pound recovery of amounts extracted by a seller from the business in breach of these warranties/covenants. In addition, these warranties/covenants will be subject to few, if any limitations on liability, other than a relatively short period of time (eg, within six months of completion) in which the buyer can make a claim for leakage.

The agreed price is not subject to subsequent adjustments relating to working capital, cash or debt of the target as at closing, and completion accounts are not required. That means that the buyer must be very confident about the financial position of the business on the locked box date, either through warranties from the seller or its own due diligence or (commonly) both. It is also critical to define very carefully the extent of any permitted leakage (ie, legitimate payments out of the business) from the business between the locked box date and closing. Permitted leakage usually includes items such as ordinary-course payments of salary and directors' fees, amounts already provided for in the locked box accounts, and other items specifically agreed with the buyer and taken into account in the pricing.

4.10 **Warranties and indemnities**

Warranties and indemnities are typically the most heavily negotiated aspects of a share or asset acquisition agreement and should be considered in parallel with the disclosure letter, under which the warranties are qualified by the seller's disclosures of general and specific matters. English law provides very little protection for a buyer of the shares of a company (or the assets and liabilities of a business) and, therefore, extensive contractual statements in the form of warranties provide the buyer with an important form of protection if any of those statements proves to be untrue.

(a) **Warranties**

Warranties are statements made by the seller about the specific state of affairs of the target or business. Their purpose is:
- to allocate risk between the seller and the buyer as to who takes responsibility for the financial state of the target company; and
- to elicit disclosure of information that otherwise might not be made available on the target and its subsidiaries.

A buyer will only be able to bring a successful claim for damages if it can show that the warranty was breached (ie, the statement is proved to be incorrect) and that the result of the breach is to diminish the value of the company or business acquired. Therefore, the burden is on the buyer to show both a breach of warranty and a quantifiable loss.

In a share purchase, warranties are particularly important because the buyer acquires the company as a going concern, with all of its assets, rights and liabilities, both past and present.

Although in an asset purchase the buyer does not inherit all the liabilities of the business (unless it agrees to accept them), warranties remain very important. First, there are a number of exceptions to the general proposition that liabilities stay with the seller on an asset sale. The most important of these is that the buyer will take on employment liabilities if the Transfer of Undertakings (Protection of Employment) Regulations 2006 apply, as they normally will when a business is acquired as a going concern. The buyer will therefore require warranties as to the employees' terms and conditions of employment, employment disputes and benefits (including pension entitlements). Secondly, through the novation or assignment of contracts, the buyer will be responsible for contractual liabilities and therefore the buyer will require some warranties as to the state of those contracts. Additionally, the buyer will require the seller to warrant title to the assets, the absence of liabilities and the adequacy and state of the assets that it is buying.

As with any other buyer, a private equity provider will usually seek contractual protection from the seller in the form of warranties, although (especially when private equity providers sell to each other in secondary buyouts) it has become increasingly common for deals to be done with very little warranty protection being provided by a private equity seller. This is because private equity providers do not give detailed warranties as a matter of policy (because they want to return the proceeds of sale in full to their investors without clawback under warranty claims). As a result, it is generally understood between the parties on secondary buyouts that limited warranty protection will be provided by a private equity seller, such protection as there is usually coming from the management shareholders, where only limited financial protection is usually available. This 'warranty gap' is considered further below.

In addition to warranties from the seller, private equity providers will often also seek additional comfort in the form of warranties in the investment agreement from the management team that are rolling over their investment into Bidco.

Warranties are often accompanied by the retention (sometimes called an escrow) of some of the purchase price by the private equity provider to cover risks under warranty claims or specific liabilities. In the absence of a retention, Bidco will take the credit risk of enforcing against the seller and, perhaps, multiple individual sellers.

If the buyer can show that there has been a breach of warranty, the measure of damages is that the buyer must be put in the same position as if the contract had been performed properly. Damages for breach of warranty are therefore the amount by which the actual value of the shares bought is less than it would have been had the warranty been true. Warranties thus provide a form of retrospective price adjustment. However, the buyer is required under duties of common law to take steps to mitigate its loss, and for this and other reasons it may not be able to recover its entire loss.

Where the warranties constitute misrepresentations that have induced the buyer to enter into the acquisition agreement, the buyer may be able to sue for misrepresentation, giving rise to damages in tort. The measure of damages in tort is the sum that will put the buyer in the position it would have been in had the tort not been committed (ie, the representation not been made). In this situation damages will be the amount by which the actual value of the company bought is less than the price paid for it. Where the buyer has made a bad bargain, this may lead to a higher level of damages than that available on a contractual basis (which will generally be preferable where the buyer has paid less for the target than its true market value). The other main disadvantage of a claim for misrepresentation from the seller's point of view is that the buyer may, with the court's permission, be able to rescind the contract, although this is not generally practical after completion and is likely to be strongly resisted by the seller. Where there is a gap between exchange and completion, the buyer may wish to have this option, but in these circumstances it is more usual to include an express right of termination in the contract.

A seller is likely to require that remedies for misrepresentations be excluded and that the buyer's only remedy be damages for breach of contract. The seller's justification for this will be that the basis of the transaction between the parties should be set out in the contract (and any related documents such as the disclosure letter), and the buyer should not have the ability to elect which sort of damages constitutes a better remedy.

An important covenant often sought by a buyer is that the seller agrees to waive all claims against the continuing management team – be they directors or employees – in respect of any information supplied, other than in circumstances of fraud. In the event of a claim by the buyer for breach of warranty, the buyer will want to prevent the seller being able to sue individuals who are continuing to run the business, as this is likely to cause major disruption to the smooth running of the organisation and jeopardise the private equity provider's investment.

(b) *Indemnities*

Warranties should be distinguished from indemnities. In contrast to a warranty, an indemnity is a promise to reimburse the buyer in respect of a specific type of liability, should it arise. The purpose of an indemnity is to give a guaranteed remedy (on a pound-for-pound basis) for the buyer in circumstances where a breach of warranty may not lead to a successful claim in damages, or to provide a specific remedy which may not otherwise be available. There is also no requirement for the buyer to take any steps to mitigate its loss on an indemnity claim. Damages may not always be available even in the event of a clear breach of warranty – the most obvious example being where a defect in an asset acquired, which has been the subject of the warranty, does not affect the value of the company (because, for example, the company has been valued on a multiple of profits). In this situation, an indemnity, which gives an automatic right to a payment in prescribed circumstances, should be sought by the buyer. Equally, where the sellers' disclosure against a warranty of a potential liability (eg, environmental cleanup costs) would prevent a warranty claim, a specific indemnity provides a means of redress for the buyer. The process of due diligence and disclosures made by the seller against the warranties can signal to the buyer specific areas where warranties would not be sufficient.

In a traditional share acquisition, it is usual for the seller to provide a tax indemnity in respect of the tax liabilities of the target relating to the period prior to sale (or other date used to fix the consideration), to the extent that:
- they are not provided for in the most recent set of audited accounts; and
- they do not arise in the normal course of business since the date of those accounts; or
- they are not provided for in any completion accounts that adjust the consideration.

However, tax indemnities have become much less common on larger buyouts and on secondary buyouts, for the reasons discussed below. Where one is agreed, the details of the tax indemnity will depend on the commercial terms of the transaction.

Other risks that may be covered by indemnities include:
- environmental risks;
- repayment of loans by the target;
- product liability claims in respect of products sold before completion; and
- doubtful book debts.

Buyers sometimes seek to include a contractual provision that gives them the option, if there is a breach of warranty, of recovering damages either on the usual basis or on an indemnity basis. It is unusual for sellers in transactions in the United Kingdom to agree to provide warranties on an indemnity basis, but this is fairly customary in US transactions.

(c) *Levels of warranty and indemnity protection*
Financial sellers, such as private equity providers, will generally refuse as a matter of policy to give warranties and indemnities, except for a warranty that they own the shares they are selling and that the shares are being sold free from third-party rights. They may argue that the management team should have a better knowledge of potential liabilities and other matters affecting the business, as they have been involved in day-to-day operations. However, the rationale is largely financial – the financial seller wants to distribute the proceeds from the sale immediately after

completion to its investors without having to meet a warranty or indemnity claim. Leaving part of the proceeds of the sale with the seller or in escrow will also impact on the internal rate of return of the funds invested, although a short escrow is sometimes acceptable. The upshot is that financial sellers will generally only give warranties as to title and capacity, leaving the management to give the business warranties. If the financial seller owns the majority of the target, the amount that the buyer can recover from the management for breach of warranty or on an indemnity claim will be limited, as management will not accept liabilities in excess of their share of the consideration (and often, below this level).

(d)   *Warranty and indemnity insurance*

Various mechanisms are used to fill this 'warranty gap' on a secondary buyout. These might include obtaining full warranties from the financial seller but with a low cap on liability (perhaps covered by an escrow), or requiring the financial seller to place funds in escrow but not to give the warranties. More commonly, the gap is filled by warranty and indemnity insurance.

The warranty and indemnity insurance market has grown significantly in the last decade and a key set of insurers offer this specialised insurance. The amount insured is limited to a specified amount, and will be subject to an excess dependent on the insured party's appetite for risk. The aggregate limit for claims under the policy may be set at the amount of the consideration, but will usually be less, depending on the types of risk involved. Buyer policies (see below) typically cover up to around 30% of the enterprise value. A single premium is payable when the insurance policy is taken out, and premiums will vary depending on the level of risk to the insurer. In the London market, premiums were normally somewhere between 0.9% and 1.6% of the level of cover required in 2013. The insurer will take a number of factors into account when setting a premium, such as:

- the type of business being sold;
- the complexity of the transaction;
- the excess payable;
- the financial stability of the parties to the transaction; and
- the scope of cover agreed.

Much of the negotiation with the insurers will be dealt with in the lead-up to exchange of contracts, as the insurers will want to review the documents in as final a form as possible. An insurance policy will generally set out the main operative clause followed by a list of exclusions: specific matters for which the insurers are unwilling to accept the risk, such as any forward-looking warranties, fraud and inadequacy of insurance cover. The policy is negotiable and the insurer may remove exclusions if it is given sufficient comfort, or a higher premium is paid.

Warranty insurance can be taken out by either the buyer or the seller, and this may be the subject of negotiation, although buyside policies have become more common. Sellside policies are less popular with sellers, as the seller remains liable to the buyer on a warranty claim if for any reason the policy does not pay out. A recent trend on auction sales has been for sellers to prearrange a warranty and indemnity policy that the successful bidder can then take up. Whether the policy is for the seller's or the buyer's benefit, the insurers will usually want to see that the warrantors take on some financial risk to ensure they negotiate the warranties and the disclosure letter diligently. This generally is dealt with by ensuring that the insurance is subject to an excess. In the London market in 2013, excesses were around 1% of the deal enterprise value.

(e) **Warranty and indemnity limitations**
It is standard practice for a seller to seek to limit its liability under the warranties and indemnities, not only by seeking to reduce the scope of the warranties or by including materiality thresholds within the warranties, but also by placing certain limits on the buyer's ability to bring a claim. There are a variety of common limitations, the most important of which are discussed below.

Awareness of the seller: It is common for a seller to qualify certain warranties on an awareness basis, so that it is not liable for things it did not know about, or could not have known about, at the time of the acquisition. What is meant by the term 'so far as the seller is aware' will need to be negotiated carefully and each warranty should be reviewed in this context. The buyer will want the seller's awareness to include the knowledge and awareness it would have had if it had made due and careful enquiry. If there is no express statement to that effect, a court will imply into the statement of awareness a provision that the seller has made only such an investigation as could reasonably be expected (*William Sindall Plc v Cambridgeshire CC* [1994] 1 WLR 1016 (C)).

A compromise is for the seller to be deemed to have the knowledge and awareness it would possess had it made due and careful or reasonable enquiries of a group of identified persons, such as specific directors and employees with knowledge of the matters referred to in the warranties. This does not normally limit liability under tax or other indemnities. It is common for auction draft acquisition agreements (which will be drafted by the sellers' lawyers) to restrict awareness to the actual knowledge of those giving the warranties and a list of additional individuals of whom they are expected to make enquiry. (See the end of this chapter for more on auction sales.)

Disclosure: A matter that is properly disclosed by the warrantors in a disclosure letter against the warranties prevents the buyer making a claim in relation to the matter that has been disclosed. In an auction sale or secondary buyout, the buyer will often be expected to accept greater deemed disclosure against the warranties; for example, the content of any data room and any vendor due diligence reports. This transfers the risk of the matters in the disclosed documents back to the buyer, which may not be in a position to make a judgement about all such matters in the context of the warranties. To protect itself against this risk, the buyer will seek to set a standard of disclosure so that only matters specifically and fairly disclosed qualify or limit the warranties, but this will be subject to negotiation.

If there is a gap between signing and completion, on a buyout the seller will often resist having to repeat the warranties at completion. When repetition of warranties is agreed, the seller will often seek the right to disclose against the repeated warranties any new matters that have arisen between exchange and completion. If it agrees this, the buyer may then seek a right to terminate the contract, if the matter disclosed is significant. Again, disclosure does not normally limit liability under tax or other indemnities.

Awareness of the buyer: The buyer's starting position will be that any knowledge it derives from sources outside the disclosure letter should not prevent it from bringing a claim against the seller for breach of warranty. The buyer will argue that its employees and advisers will come across a wide variety of information through the formal due diligence process, or through less formal conversations or correspondence with management, the significance of which may not always be clear at the time. As a result, the buyer will often seek to include a clause in the agreement providing that the warranties are only qualified by matters disclosed in the disclosure letter and that the knowledge of the buyer (whether actual, constructive or imputed) will not prevent it bringing a claim for breach of warranty.

However, in *Eurocopy Plc v Teesdale* [1992] BCLC 1067 the court cast some doubt on whether this type of clause would enable a buyer to bring a claim for breach of warranty where it had actual knowledge of a matter that was not disclosed in the disclosure letter. Although the decision was a ruling on a preliminary matter, and it has more recently been questioned in *Infiniteland Ltd v Artisan Contracting Ltd* [2005] All ER (D) 236, the issue remains problematic for buyers. Even if the buyer would not be prevented from making a claim, *Infiniteland* suggests that where a buyer brings a warranty claim having had actual knowledge of the breach at the time of acquisition, this will be a significant factor for the court in deciding what level of damages (if any) should be awarded.

What amounts to the actual knowledge of the buyer was also considered in *Infiniteland*. The majority of the Court of Appeal thought that actual knowledge did not include the knowledge of an agent (eg, the buyer's lawyers and accountants); this amounted to imputed knowledge only. A buyer will usually seek to prevent its imputed knowledge, or its constructive knowledge (knowledge it ought to have had if it had made proper enquiry), from limiting the warranties. However, sellers are often successful in obtaining the buyer's agreement that matters in the buyer's actual knowledge should qualify the warranties. Where a buyer agrees this, it will seek to negotiate that the buyer's actual knowledge should only be deemed to include that of a small group of named individuals who have worked closely on the transaction and have an understanding of the matter concerned (and its implications). For obvious reasons, this group should specifically exclude the target managers who are joining the board of Bidco.

Infiniteland also made it clear that the level of disclosure required in each case depends on the precise wording of the sale documentation and is not determined by the courts by reference to an objective standard. The language used in the acquisition agreement and the disclosure letter itself as to what constitutes sufficient disclosure is therefore critical. The case also demonstrates that if the buyer expressly provides for disclosure to be made directly to an expert such as its accountant, the knowledge and expertise of that expert will be taken into account in determining whether an adequate disclosure has been made (in *Infiniteland*, the disclosure letter provided that it was deemed to include "all matters from the documents and written information supplied" to the buyer's accountants).

As a general point, a buyer and its advisers must be sure that they have not been informed of anything during the due diligence exercise that might give rise to a claim. If a buyer does become aware of an undisclosed issue that is of concern, the only safe course is for the buyer to seek a specific indemnity from the seller in respect of the matter.

Financial limits on warranty claims: It is usual to find that a seller will not be liable under the warranties until the aggregate value of claims that may be made exceeds a certain amount, commonly known as the 'threshold amount'. Market trends suggest that a common threshold level is around 1% of the acquisition price. Additionally, a seller will seek that individual claims below a certain amount do not count towards establishing the threshold (this amount is often around 10% of the threshold, but from the buyer's point of view it is important to consider the type of business and whether this level is appropriate if, for example, multiple small claims are more likely than large claims). Once the threshold has been met it will be a topic for negotiation whether liability is 'over and under' or 'only over'. This refers to whether, once the threshold is met, the seller is liable for all the warranty claims or whether the seller is liable for claims only to the extent that the value is in excess of the threshold amount.

In the past it was common for the buyer to want the seller to be liable under the warranties up to the total consideration paid or perhaps the total enterprise value (ie, equity and debt). However, in particular on a secondary buyout or a competitive auction sale, the sellers will seek to cap their liability at a significantly lower amount – this may be significantly below 50% of the purchase price. Where a lower cap is agreed, the buyer should take care to exclude from the cap the title and capacity warranties (and potentially other warranties, such as those relating to indebtedness or insolvency).

Time limits on warranty claims: It is customary for the acquisition agreement to specify a time limit for bringing a claim under the warranties; often this is in the region of between 15 and 30 months, based on the accounting periods of the target. It is common to see enhanced limitation periods for warranty claims connected with specific issues; for example, environmental concerns. The period allowed for claims under the tax warranties or tax indemnity is usually four to seven years, to allow time for challenges by HMRC to the tax affairs of the target group.

On a secondary buyout or competitive auction, the sellers typically seek to limit exposure to one clear audit period following the acquisition.

4.11 Multiple sellers

Where there are multiple sellers of shares, the acquisition agreement needs to stipulate how their obligations are given and how their liability is to be shared. A buyer will often require that each seller be joint and severally liable under the warranties so that each seller is treated as having assumed the obligations both collectively and individually. This means that the buyer may pursue any one or more of the sellers for the whole loss or damage arising from a breach of warranty. In these circumstances it is sensible for the sellers to agree separately between themselves as to how they will share liability in the event that a claim is brought, by way of a contribution agreement. However, in buyouts involving financial sellers, it is common for obligations and liabilities to be expressed to be on a several basis, with each seller's liability being capped at a maximum amount (which may be tied to the consideration it receives). Although this does not provide true several liability, the sellers may be able to improve their position further if their individual liability is also restricted to a specific proportion of any claim that is made (again, linked to the proportion of the consideration each receives). In addition, some liabilities will be on a true several basis only (so that each party is responsible only for its own failings), for example, title and capacity warranties in relation to the shares sold.

4.12 Restrictive covenants

Restrictive covenants typically involve a requirement that the seller of a company or business undertakes not to compete with the target by, for example, setting up a similar business in relation to the products or services provided by the existing business, in a geographical area associated with the existing business, for a certain length of time. Other common covenants include obligations not to deal with or solicit the company's customers or its employees or a category of them. They are designed to protect the confidential information and goodwill of the business acquired and, under ordinary common law principles in relation to restraint of trade, will be enforceable only if they go no further than is reasonably necessary for this purpose. A private equity seller will typically not enter into such restrictive covenants, as it will not want to limit its opportunities to invest.

(a) Permitted restrictive covenants

Depending on the precise nature and length of the covenants, the size of the business acquired, its markets and the parties involved, the covenants may need to be reviewed to ensure that they comply with Articles 101 and 102 of the Treaty on the Functioning of the European Union.

Article 101 provides for the prohibition of restrictive agreements and Article 102 concerns the abuse of a dominant position. The Competition Act 1998 provides that the prohibitions that the treaty contains do not apply to:
- transactions that are mergers under the Enterprise Act 2002;
- concentrations with an EU dimension under the EU Merger Regulation; or
- restrictions that are directly related and necessary to the implementation of the merger or concentration (ancillary restraints).

If an agreement contains restrictions that may not be considered to be ancillary, or if the agreement is particularly anticompetitive (eg, if it contains price-fixing or market-sharing elements), appropriate advice should be sought.

(b) Enforceability of restrictive covenants

Restrictive covenants must be carefully drafted to avoid being excessive in scope or duration and thus unenforceable. This will always involve a consideration of the specific circumstances of the transaction and the relevant business sector. In this regard, all covenants in restraint of trade are, in principle, void as contrary to public policy (*Nordenfelt v Maxim Guns and Ammunition Co* [1894] AC 535), and will be enforceable only if they go no further than is reasonably necessary to protect the legitimate business interests of the buyer (namely, the value of the company by reference to its confidential information, client base and the stability of its workforce).

Under EU competition rules, if a sale includes both goodwill and know-how, a non-compete clause is acceptable for a period of up to three years, but the period for goodwill is limited to two years. A longer period may be acceptable in exceptional circumstances, for example, if customer loyalty to the seller will continue for more than two years, or for more than three years where the scope or nature of the know-how acquired justifies a longer protection period. In practice, the agreed period is likely to be between one and three years.

While the non-compete clause is considered to be the most important restriction (and is generally viewed more strictly by the courts), it will also be important for the buyer to prevent the seller from actively soliciting key employees or key customers or suppliers. It is generally understood that the maximum length of time for a non-solicitation restrictive covenant is between two and three years (provided that this can be justified in all the circumstances). In light of the difficulty for the buyer of showing that solicitation has occurred, it is increasingly common for non-dealing covenants to be requested. Even if a customer approaches the seller directly following the sale (ie, there is no solicitation), the seller would be prevented from working with the customer for a specified period. As with other restrictive covenants, the length of time of the non-dealing and non-solicitation clauses will be the subject of negotiation between the parties.

When drafting restrictive covenants, each should be set out in a separate subclause so that a court can sever a provision that is found to be unenforceable using the so-called 'blue-pencil test', which allows the reasonable provisions to remain in force. In particular, a court cannot rewrite a restrictive covenant, or substitute a lesser restraint that would be enforceable. Following the case of *Francotyp-Postalia Ltd v Whitehead and others* [2011] EWHC 367 (Ch), careful drafting of restrictive covenants is particularly important so that each is capable of standing independently (and does not rely, for example, on inappropriate shared definitions). In *Francotyp-Postalia*, the High Court ruled that the offending wording in one restrictive covenant that was unenforceable could not be severed because it would result in the alteration of other restrictive covenants that were enforceable.

The courts will generally look favourably on a reasonable restrictive covenant if a buyer is buying the goodwill as well as other assets from the covenanting seller. The goodwill would be worthless if the seller could compete with the buyer without hindrance.

In most transactions, the buyer will be prepared to leave it to the courts to decide the remedy if there is a breach of restrictive covenant (eg, damages and/or an injunction). More unusually, the buyer may wish to specify the consequences of breach in the agreement. Where this is the case, it is important to note that if the contract stipulates an amount that is to be payable by the party in breach, this must not amount to a penalty. In *El Makdessi v Cavendish Square Holdings BV and another* [2013] EWCA Civ 1539, the Court of Appeal held that certain clauses – which provided that, if the seller breached certain restrictive covenants, the buyer did not have to pay deferred consideration to the seller and could buy the seller's remaining shares at a discounted price – amounted to an unenforceable penalty. The court found that, looking at the agreement as a whole, these clauses were not a genuine pre-estimate of the buyer's loss, they were extravagant and unreasonable and (importantly) they lacked commercial justification. Their main function was to deter a breach of the restrictive covenants, and the amount the seller would lose under these clauses was out of all proportion to the loss attributable to the breach. As a result, the court held that the relevant clauses amounted to penalties and the buyer could not enforce them.

The key lesson from this case is that any similar provision, if it does not amount to a genuine pre-estimate of the buyer's loss in the event of a breach, must be otherwise commercially justified if it is to avoid being an unenforceable penalty. This applies to any other provision in an acquisition agreement as much as it does to restrictive covenants.

4.13 Rights of assignment

A seller will generally resist the buyer having the ability to assign its rights under the acquisition agreement, although it may be prepared to allow the buyer to assign within its group and/or to the buyer's lenders. The lenders will often require the buyer to assign its rights under the acquisition agreement as part of the security package. A seller will often agree to this, provided that the liability it assumes is not greater than it would have been without the assignment.

5. Other key documents

5.1 Tax deed

The generally accepted position is that tax on the pre-completion activities of the target business is borne by the seller and the tax on its postcompletion activities is borne by the buyer. In the past it was market practice for the buyer to be given a tax indemnity, in addition to the tax warranties, to indemnify the buyer against any tax liabilities within the target and its subsidiaries relating to the period leading up to completion. However, in recent years tax indemnities have become much less common, in particular on secondary and larger buyouts. Exiting private equity funds generally refuse to give a tax indemnity.

Where one or more sellers agree to give a tax indemnity it will usually be contained in a separate deed, but it can be included as a schedule to the acquisition agreement. Where this is the case, the acquisition agreement should be executed as a deed in order to permit claims under the tax indemnity to be made after the six-year statutory limitation period.

The main advantage of the tax indemnity is that it provides a pound-for-pound reimbursement to the buyer in respect of any unforeseen pre-completion tax liabilities of the target company. In addition, in contrast to the position under the tax warranties, disclosure of a matter to the buyer will not prevent the seller being liable to the buyer in respect of that matter under the tax indemnity, and the buyer has no duty to mitigate any loss arising under the tax indemnity.

Before the decision in *Zim Properties Ltd v Procter* [1984] 58 TC 371, the buyer would normally be protected by an indemnity given by the seller to the target in respect of any unforeseen pre-completion tax payable by the target. However, *Zim Properties* made it clear that payments directly to the target would comprise taxable receipts in the hands of the target, meaning that the target would need the payment to be increased under a grossing-up provision in order to be fully compensated. Under an HMRC extra-statutory concession (ESC D33), payments from the seller to the buyer are deemed to be a reduction in the purchase price, to the extent possible; this means that there is no requirement to gross up a payment to the buyer unless the total indemnity and warranty payments would exceed the consideration (which can arise where a target company is sold subject to a significant amount of debt). This treatment is also tax-advantageous for the seller because it reduces its capital gain on the sale of the shares, although this is now often less of a consideration given the substantial shareholdings exemption often available on the sale of shares in trading companies. For these reasons, where a tax indemnity is to be provided, it is now usual for there to be a covenant by the seller to pay the buyer an amount equal to the unforeseen pre-completion tax suffered by the target (or to pay it to the target at the option of the buyer), and for such payments to operate as an adjustment to the purchase price.

5.2   **Disclosure letter**
The scope and terms of the disclosure letter are negotiated carefully between the parties. The seller will try to include in the disclosure letter all matters that are seen as being inconsistent with the warranty statements, whereas the buyer will want to ensure that disclosures are specific and clear enough for it to understand the consequences of the matter disclosed, so that it can decide how best to proceed (whether this means renegotiating the price, seeking a specific indemnity or pulling out of the transaction).

The disclosure letter usually takes the form of a letter from the seller to the buyer. It is normally divided into two parts – general disclosures and specific disclosures – and will have appended to it copies of the documentation being disclosed (known as the 'disclosure bundle') or a copy of the relevant virtual data room appended on a disk. The general disclosures will include such matters as public registries, company books, replies to due diligence enquires and any data room. The buyer will want to protect itself by resisting the level of general disclosures and, as discussed above, by negotiating the standard of disclosure required.

There have been a number of cases on the standard of disclosure required in order for disclosure to be effective. One case has suggested that it is not enough that the buyer be given notice generally, or that it be given the means or knowledge to enable it to work out facts and draw conclusions itself (*Levinson v Farin* [1978] 2 All ER 1149). Another has indicated that there must be fair disclosure of sufficient facts and circumstances to identify the nature and scope of the matters disclosed so that the buyer can form a view (*Edward Prentice v Scottish Power* [1997] 2 BCLC 264). However, the Court of Appeal's decision in *Infiniteland* is particularly noteworthy. It provides that there is no set standard of disclosure; rather, the fair standard of disclosure in any case will depend on what has been agreed between the parties, which might agree for example, that general disclosure will be enough, or alternatively that detailed specific disclosure will be required.

This is of particular interest in recent years, where there has been a marked reduction in the time taken to reach exchange of contracts, and a corresponding lessening in the amount of time that can be spent on disclosure and due diligence exercises. It is increasingly common for the parties to accept that a lower standard of disclosure will be achieved, but that the price may be adjusted accordingly. This is particularly common in distressed sales following the appointment of insolvency practitioners.

6. Impact of auction sales on acquisition terms

Auction sales, conducted by the seller, have become increasingly common for corporate disposals and private equity providers frequently participate in these auction sales. This has resulted in the seller having a significant influence on the way in which an acquisition agreement is drafted, with the seller's solicitors preparing the first draft, which will be more seller-friendly (with more limited warranties and more extensive limitations of liability). The due diligence process will be streamlined with the use of a data room (or more commonly, an electronic or virtual data room), vendor due diligence reports on which the successful bidder may rely and a tight timetable that restricts the scope of the due diligence.

Generally, an auction process will start with the seller or its advisers providing a short teaser document to potential buyers to gauge interest. Potential buyers that express an interest will be required to enter into confidentiality and non-reliance letters before being provided with an information memorandum discussing the target in some detail, the vendor-produced due diligence report and access to any data room. Following review of the information provided, a prospective buyer will submit an indicative offer, normally by expressing a range within which an offer might be made, based on the due diligence and the assumptions underpinning its offer. The seller, together with its advisers, will review the indicative offers and produce a shortlist of potential buyers. These shortlisted potential buyers will receive a set of draft documents prepared by the seller and its advisers, and possibly any further information considered too sensitive to disseminate earlier in the process. The potential buyers will submit a formal bid, together with a markup of the terms of the acquisition agreement and the disclosure letter. The seller will then review the bids and will open negotiations with one or possibly more potential buyers.

If the seller is a financial seller, such as a private equity provider, it will consider carefully the extent of the markup provided by a potential buyer, particularly to avoid the bid carrying too much execution risk (for example, where the buyer sought to include conditions, such as a financing condition, or a material adverse change clause).

The seller will resist any bidder being given exclusivity, and it is not uncommon for two or more bidders to negotiate right up to signing of the acquisition agreement, with the seller proceeding with the most competitive bid (highest price or lowest execution risk). A seller may even offer to pay a bidder's costs in some circumstances, in order to maintain the auction process, as a private equity provider may be reluctant to continue in the final stages of an auction sale without exclusivity.

Due diligence

Tom Evans
Benedict Nwaeke
David Walker
Latham & Watkins

In today's difficult deal environment due diligence continues to be of crucial importance for private equity houses when investing in a target, refinancing or restructuring an existing investment. When investing in a target, the private equity house will want to build up a clear picture of what it is actually buying, in particular to identify any issues that may impact on either the value of the target or the ability of the private equity house to effect a future exit. This includes seeking to understand the liabilities and obligations of the target, some of which could ultimately flow through to the private equity house itself. In the case of a refinancing or restructuring, the private equity house will want to understand their impact on its existing investment. Add to this greater risk-focus than ever from the debt investors who provide acquisition or refinancing debt for such transactions, and the need for a careful and integrated approach by private equity houses and their professional advisers in the due diligence process becomes all the more apparent.

1. What is due diligence?

The due diligence process described in this chapter is conducted by professional advisers on behalf of private equity houses. In the context of private equity transactions, due diligence most commonly involves professional advisers reviewing an agreed range of information in relation to the potential investment target. The advisers report their findings to the private equity house in order that it may decide whether and on what terms to invest in the target. The findings are typically shared with any other debt and/or equity investors in the transaction process.

Due diligence may also be carried out on behalf of a potential target or seller to facilitate a sale or investment (otherwise known as 'vendor due diligence'). Vendor due diligence allows a potential buyer to make an assessment of the target before (in some cases) carrying out its own due diligence exercise. From a seller's perspective, vendor due diligence gives the seller more control over the transaction timetable and it allows competing bidders for a target to bid from a level playing field, which is intended to create competitive tension and therefore maximise the value realised for the seller and the speed of execution of the transaction.

Following any investment, due diligence may also be conducted on behalf of investors or classes of investor (eg, debt investors), particularly if the target does not perform in accordance with expectations, and potentially if the funding invested in the target needs to be restructured or refinanced.

In this chapter we focus on the due diligence process generally undertaken by a private equity house considering investing in a target (which for these purposes includes any form of investment or acquisition). Where relevant, we discuss the role of vendor due diligence and we also outline the vendor due diligence process itself. For the purposes of this chapter we refer to private equity houses in general, without distinguishing between their constituent parts (typically limited partners, general partners and managers).

2. **Why conduct due diligence?**

While the answer to this question may appear self-evident, it provides a useful focus for the due diligence process. The purpose of due diligence may be best encapsulated in the 'so what?' question: having identified an issue during the due diligence process, a professional adviser must ask itself, "So what?". What is the potential impact of the issue on the target business and how, if at all, should the terms of the transaction change to address that issue (and in extreme cases, should the transaction proceed at all)? We set out below a number of responses to this question relevant for any investor and then concentrate on those that tend to be the most important for private equity houses.

3. **Types of due diligence**

For a typical private equity investment, due diligence will be carried out by a number of professional advisers. The core advisers will be independent specialists in legal, accounting, commercial and taxation matters. Depending on the target business, its industry and the associated risks, additional advisers may be retained to report on pension, insurance, environmental, property, ethical compliance/anti-bribery, executive remuneration and/or technical matters. Commonly, and particularly in the case of transactions involving the acquisition of a target whose equity securities are traded on a recognised investment exchange, a financial adviser will also be retained. The due diligence process will usually be coordinated by either the financial adviser, where one has been appointed, the legal advisers or a combination of the two. As set out below, a thoughtful and integrated coordination of the due diligence process is crucial to its success.

4. **The role of due diligence in private equity transactions**

Due diligence carried out on behalf of a private equity house is important for the same reasons as it is important for other buyers of assets. These include the following:
- Confirmation of what is being acquired – verification is needed to ensure that the target has legal and beneficial title to the assets necessary to carry on the business following completion of the transaction and to plan the integration of the target business. From a legal perspective, an investor will want to be confident that in return for the funds it invests, it will receive good title to the target and the assets necessary to carry on the underlying business. The investor will want to be sure that the target business can be carried on following acquisition in the same or a predefined manner, and that the revenue, costs and profit targets may therefore be reliably predicted from past performance of the target business.

- Identification and allocation of risk – there are risks in the acquisition of any business. The due diligence process aims to identify those relevant to the business carried on by the target, assess the likelihood of such risks materialising and consider the severity of the potential impact on both the business and the acquirer itself. This then helps in determining both the allocation of risk between the parties to the transaction and what contractual protection is required by the buyer, whether by way of warranty, indemnity or otherwise. In simple terms: should the buyer or seller take the risk? It will also help to determine whether and how risk may be insured.
- Price negotiation – where risks are identified or liabilities unearthed, these may be reflected in the purchase price, such as by a price reduction or an alteration to the method of payment (eg, part of the purchase price may be deferred until it becomes clear whether a particular contingent liability is real).
- Disclosure of further information – for a transaction involving a target that is not listed on a recognised investment exchange, due diligence allows a buyer to frame warranties in order to elicit further information in the form of a disclosure letter prior to entering into the acquisition agreement. Where the target is listed on a recognised investment exchange, it will be impractical to procure warranty protection due to the likely high number of shareholders and their limited involvement with the management of the target, although very occasionally a significant shareholder may be persuaded to do so. Special care will need to be taken with any information received from the seller and target to ensure that the implications of the information are clearly understood in the context of any warranty protection. Case law supports the contention that in the absence of specific provisions relating to the standard of disclosure required, where a matter is fairly disclosed (whether to the buyer itself or its advisers) it will constitute adequate disclosure against warranties and therefore limit the ability of a buyer to recover any losses through a warranty claim.[1] The English courts have applied an objective test and held that the disclosure requirement would be satisfied if it could "fairly be expected" that the adviser in question would become aware, from an examination of the relevant documents provided in the ordinary course of carrying out a due diligence exercise, of the existence of an exceptional item and the implications of that item. This clearly impacts on the drafting of any acquisition documentation and highlights the fact that the actual knowledge of an adviser, in so far as it is knowledge obtained in the ordinary course of carrying out a due diligence exercise for which the buyer's professional adviser is acting, will be deemed to be knowledge of the buyer.
- Discharge of legal duties – to limit its liability and minimise its tax profile, a private equity house is likely to invest in a transaction by way of a newly incorporated company (Newco) or a series of such companies. In the United Kingdom, the directors of Newco will be under a duty to act in good faith to

---

[1] *Infiniteland Limited v Artisan Contracting Limited* [2005] EWCA Civ 758. Please refer to the chapter, "Private equity angles of acquisition documentation", for further details.

promote the success of the company for the benefit of its members as a whole and to carry out their functions with reasonable skill and care; similar rules apply in most other jurisdictions. Carrying out due diligence will provide useful evidence that the directors have discharged this duty when deciding whether to enter into the transaction. Similarly, a private equity house is likely to be under an obligation to one or more of its investors, whether by way of a fiduciary or contractual obligation, to undertake due diligence in accordance with agreed parameters before making any investment.

Private equity houses will have different specific perspectives on the due diligence process, although generally the areas set out below are likely to be considered significant.

4.1 The 100-day plan

A private equity house will have definite views on its plan for a target following completion of any transaction. Advice given to private equity houses commonly indicates that significant change will have the greatest effect if made within a short period following completion, usually discussed in the context of the first 100 days. The view is that managers and employees are predisposed to change during this period and the lack of any entrenched positions as between managers and the new investors means that change is easier to implement. The opportunity of the first 100 days is therefore significant for the success of the target where this relies on the adoption of new methodologies.

Issues identified during the due diligence process and capable of remedy are often included in the 100-day plan and will be highlighted in professional advisers' reports. To the extent there have been any shortcomings in the due diligence process or any potential warranty claims, these will start to become apparent during the 100-day period once the private equity house has been given complete access to the accounts and documents of the target and it can then conduct a post-completion audit of the target. Professional advisers will seek to follow up promptly with the private equity house post-completion of a transaction to ensure that the private equity house has a clear action plan to remedy the issues identified and agree who is to action each step of the plan.

4.2 The model

A significant focus of a private equity house during the due diligence process is to incorporate information arising from due diligence into the financial model, which is typically generated to assess the value of the target, project the returns from the investment on an exit, and assess the value and terms of debt which may be used to fund the transaction. As a result, for each issue identified during due diligence that involves a future material commitment, actual liability or contingent liability, the private equity house will be keen to understand:

- where the liability is contingent on an event or circumstance occurring, the likelihood of that event or circumstance occurring;
- the amount of the actual liability, contingent liability or commitment and each payment in respect thereof;

- when the target will be obliged to make any payment in respect of the liability or the commitment; and
- whether there is any commercially reasonable way that the target or the private equity house could reduce its exposure to the actual liability, contingent liability or commitment.

4.3 **Exit**

Unlike many other buyers, a private equity house will invest in a target in a manner that permits a suitable exit from that investment. This is because private equity funds are established for a finite period, during which funds will be drawn down from the fund investors, invested, realised and then returned. As a result, the average investment horizon for a private equity house in the United Kingdom is estimated to be between three and five years.

Depending on the exit strategy for the investment, during the due diligence process certain issues may be of greater significance to the private equity house than others, as the following examples illustrate:

- Where an exit is likely to take place by way of a number of disposals of different parts of the target, it will be important to understand how and by which entity within the group shared services (eg, insurance, information technology, human resources and payroll) are provided, and which group entities are the significant employing entities. It will be important to a potential future buyer that the appropriate management, employees and other assets be transferred with the business; and rights to these assets should be identified. It will also be important to identify any impediments to such disposals. For example, will extensive employee consultation be required, is there a lease that cannot be assigned or is there a material contract that will be terminable by the counterparty as a result of the disposal?
- Where the exit is likely to be by way of an initial public offering of shares in the target or a parent of the target, the private equity house may be particularly interested in the existing corporate governance arrangements, ethical/anti-bribery compliance, and accounting practices of the target so that suitable arrangements can be put in place to establish a track record ahead of listing on the relevant investment exchange.
- Where the investment may be realised in several tranches, it will be important that investors in the private equity fund are not taxed on any capital gains until funds are actually received by them. To avoid so-called 'dry gains', it may be necessary to carry out a pre-acquisition reorganisation to increase the base cost of the assets and/or to create structural protection from any capital gains being attributed to them until funds are actually received. The results of due diligence will influence how any such reorganisation or structuring will be effected.

4.4 **Banks, co-investors and managers**

In addition to Newco and the investing private equity house, potential equity co-investors and debt providers will be keen to review the due diligence reports provided by professional advisers. Disclosure of draft reports to such further investors usually occurs following review by the private equity house, so that the due diligence reports disclosed may incorporate any proposals to mitigate the risks identified.

Typically, senior managers who are asked to invest in the target alongside the private equity house will be requested to review the final due diligence reports and to warrant for the benefit of other equity investors that such reports are accurate in all material respects and draw reasonable conclusions, and that there are no material omissions therefrom.

4.5 Reliance

A further key element of the due diligence process is reliance on any due diligence report produced in relation to the transaction. While any such report will be designed to assist with structuring the transaction, assessing the value of the target and improving the business following completion, the private equity house will want comfort that the due diligence process has been carried out by its advisers with due skill and care, and that in entering into the transaction it can rely on such reports.

The classes of person that may rely on the due diligence reports issued by professional advisers will vary depending on the relevant market. In the United Kingdom, the dominant practice is that in making their respective investments, the following parties will be entitled to rely on such reports:

- Newco;
- the investing private equity house or consortium of private equity houses;
- the debt providers and their primary syndicates (where relevant); and
- equity co-investors that invest at completion of the transaction and any person to which equity is syndicated within a reasonable period after completion.

Commonly, Newco and the investing private equity house(s) will be distinguished from the other classes of reliance party as 'addressees' of the due diligence report. This is because the professional adviser will be keen to record that the report has been prepared in accordance with the instructions of the addressees (but not the other reliance parties), and that the addressees are liable for its fees. Typically, the remaining classes of reliance party will be entitled to rely on the report subject to agreeing that the aggregate liability of the adviser in relation to any event or circumstance will not be more than that which would have been payable to the addressees.

In contrast to the practice in the United Kingdom, in the United States typically only the investing private equity house(s) will be entitled to rely on the due diligence report prepared by its legal and accounting advisers. The legal due diligence report is often shared with debt providers and other equity investors, but those recipients are required to execute non-reliance letters stating that the legal adviser does not owe a duty to such recipient as a result of access to the due diligence report and has no liability to the recipient with respect to the due diligence report.

In the United Kingdom, the liability of advisers for loss arising from a due diligence report will ordinarily be capped. For accounting advisers, pursuant to a memorandum of understanding between the Big Six accounting firms (now the Big Four) and the British Venture Capital Association[2] which, while not legally binding, sets out a framework of reference, the caps for private equity transactions are invariably as follows:

- where the aggregate new equity and debt invested or agreed to be invested pursuant to the transaction ('transaction value') is £10 million or less ('smaller transactions'), an amount equal to the transaction value;
- where the transaction value is between £10 million and £55 million ('mid-market transactions'), £10 million plus one-third of the amount by which the transaction value exceeds £10 million, subject to a maximum of £25 million; and
- where the transaction value is more than £55 million ('larger transactions'), £25 million, subject to variation in exceptional circumstances.

In the case of legal and taxation advisers, liability is also likely to be capped. Other professional advisers will usually cap their liability at a significantly lesser amount than that of accounting, tax and legal advisers. In the United States, by contrast, the liability of professional advisers to the private equity house(s) for loss arising from a due diligence report is uncapped.

An area of fundamental importance when reviewing vendor due diligence for an investing private equity house is reliance: a private equity house will want to know whether it may rely on any vendor due diligence report in sufficient time to conduct its own detailed due diligence exercise if reliance is not permitted. The scope of any vendor due diligence will also be critical (see below).

Despite the apparent equality of reliance parties in relying on the due diligence report, those parties will commonly enter into a proceeds-sharing letter or agreement. The letter usually provides that any proceeds received from a professional adviser arising from any claim in connection with its report will be distributed between the reliance parties in accordance with their agreed ranking as creditors.

In the case of due diligence reports disclosed to parties (eg, potential debt providers to a private equity house) who ultimately may not come to rely on the report and therefore do not require reliance in the first instance, release (otherwise known as 'hold harmless') letters are often a mechanism utilised. In this instance due diligence reports are released to the relevant party on a non-reliance basis (which also avoids delays to the sharing of such reports, which may otherwise be caused by negotiations relating to the terms of reliance letters where these may not ultimately become necessary).

5. Due diligence process

Given the significant time and resources expended in carrying out due diligence and in light of how broad the due diligence process can be, particular focus should be placed on making the process as efficient as possible. Efficiency is usually maximised when the parameters (eg, materiality thresholds) of the due diligence exercise are

---

2   Dated February 16 1998 and effective from February 18 1998.

agreed between the private equity house and each of its advisers prior to work commencing, and clear communication lines are set out among the parties. With that in mind, set out in this section is a summary of the typical due diligence process and scope, which may be sculpted according to the demands or issues of a particular transaction.

5.1 What happens when?

Where there are competing bidders or potential competing bidders, the due diligence process undertaken on behalf of a private equity house buyer and Newco typically is divided into three phases:

- Initial phase – during this phase professional advisers are retained by the private equity house and the scope of their work is settled. The scoping of the diligence exercise is important from a time and cost perspective, and the most valuable advisers to a private equity house will be those that can quickly identify the key areas of focus. Typically the professional advisers will review the initial material available regarding the target, which in the case of an unlisted target is likely to include an information memorandum and, where available, any due diligence reports produced for previous transactions involving the target or a vendor due diligence report. The initial period will often end with the submission of an indicative offer by the private equity house on behalf of Newco. In the case of a target whose equity securities are listed, the initial review will usually be limited to publicly available material – in particular, the last issued annual report, regulatory announcements and documents underlying any publicly traded debt securities. In such a case the initial period may conclude with an approach to the target's board of directors.

During the initial period professional advisers will generally provide feedback to the private equity house by way of regular teleconferences and a 'red flag' report. This due diligence report will outline any issues identified that are sufficiently material to influence the price that a private equity house is prepared to offer, or indeed whether it is willing or able to pursue the transaction at all. To the extent that sufficient information on the target is available, advisers may also produce a fuller draft due diligence report at this stage.

- Second phase – the bulk of the due diligence takes place during this phase. Access is usually granted by the seller or target to additional information that is not public. The information is invariably disclosed subject to a confidentiality agreement and is usually included in a data room, either in physical or, more likely these days, in electronic form. The seller or target will usually allow the private equity house and its advisers to ask questions of the relevant managers and advisers of the target to clarify any issues raised by the documents. The questions may be submitted in written question-and-answer format or during scheduled meetings with the managers and/or the seller's advisers. Given that the recipient of the questions raised by the private equity house and its advisers tends to be the management team of the target, it is of course important that they are not made to feel under siege from the private equity house or its advisers (particularly on an auction where management are having to deal with the requests of several bidders). It is crucial therefore to avoid asking irrelevant or immaterial questions (which can be avoided by ensuring that there is a clear scope, and questions raised mirror the materiality thresholds agreed for the due diligence process).

During this phase advisers will report on a regular basis on any material issues identified, and will usually produce a draft and final draft of their written due diligence report. It is important that professional advisers provide regular updates to the private equity house in 'real time' between draft due diligence reports in respect of any key issues arising from the due diligence process, so as to alert the private equity house to any potential deal-breaking (or price-altering) issues. In the case of an unlisted target, the second phase typically concludes with the submission of a (binding) offer by the private equity house on behalf of Newco. In the case of a listed target, a bidder will typically be required to reconfirm to the target board the price at which it is prepared to make an offer for the relevant securities.

- Final phase – in the case of an unlisted target, a private equity house will move into the final phase if it is a preferred bidder in an auction process, or if the seller indicates that it is prepared to proceed with the transaction on the basis of the binding offer submitted at the end of phase two. During this phase, the private equity house and its professional advisers may be given the opportunity to discuss with the relevant managers and advisers of the target any material outstanding due diligence matters that may affect the price to be paid for the target, the transaction documents or the structure of the transaction.

At the end of this phase the advisers will issue their final due diligence report, and the transaction documentation will be entered into by Newco and the seller; or in the case of a listed target, the offer to existing security holders will be announced.

5.2 Engaging professional advisers

Agreeing the terms on which a private equity house engages its professional advisers may take considerable time. Negotiation of some of the terms of engagement will inevitably occur close to signing or announcement, and may therefore distract from the principal elements of the transaction at this key time. To avoid unnecessary cost and to minimise the burden at signing or announcement, in most instances private equity houses and their advisers will be prepared to proceed on the basis of previously agreed terms, as amended for the peculiarities of the transaction in question. Typically a private equity house will engage professional advisers on the basis that on completion, their engagement will novate to Newco. Newco will then gain reliance on the due diligence report produced and will be responsible for any liabilities under the engagement, such as payment of adviser fees and any indemnities given.

Any scope of due diligence will be heavily influenced by the particular transaction. Rather than set out a standard form scope here, we have set out in the following section those matters that are of particular concern to private equity houses and which will therefore usually be the subject of the due diligence exercise.

Key findings from one professional adviser will affect the findings of another. Due diligence coordinators should therefore actively seek to cross-pollinate the work streams of the different advisers to maximise the value of the work conducted by each adviser and avoid any duplication of work. This emphasises why professional advisers should be adopting an integrated approach rather than working on a silo basis. Key synergies that are often realised when this integrated approach occurs include:

- focusing the legal review of commercial arrangements on those documents that evidence relationships that are responsible for providing material revenue or supplies for the target;
- providing enhanced data and analysis for consideration as part of the commercial and financial due diligence;
- assessing the likely pension contributions for the target by coordinating the actuarial analysis and the legal analysis of the constitutional documents establishing the relevant scheme(s);
- increasing understanding of actual and potential instances of trapped cash for consideration in the financial due diligence; and
- making more reliable the assessments of the exposure of the target to current and future civil litigation and regulatory/criminal enforcement based on insurance claim histories and litigation searches.

By the same measure, the private equity house and its professional advisers will be keen to avoid any so-called 'white space' developing between the work streams of its respective advisers, which could result in certain due diligence matters being inadequately considered. The phenomenon of white space is most often minimised by the disclosure among the professional advisers of respective due diligence scopes, red flag and draft due diligence reports, and regular invitations for advisers to share information with each other.

Where vendor due diligence has been undertaken, this is likely to impact on the scope of due diligence undertaken by buy-side professional advisers. Buy-side advisers will usually assess the quality of the vendor due diligence provided by considering the methodology used to select the material that is subject to the vendor due diligence, the relative involvement of managers of the target in contributing to the vendor due diligence and its scope, and the applicable materiality thresholds. The buyer and its professional advisers will also be conscious of the fact that the vendor due diligence report provided will only represent a snapshot of the target at the time it was prepared and may therefore be potentially stale. The scope of the buy-side adviser will also be determined by whether and on what terms Newco and the private equity house may rely on the due diligence report produced as part of the vendor due diligence. Depending on these factors, there are a number of options for the scope of the due diligence required of the buy-side adviser, for example:

- the private equity house may be satisfied with the vendor due diligence and therefore not require a professional adviser to undertake any due diligence (although this would be unusual, particularly given the historical and therefore potentially stale nature of the vendor due diligence);

- the professional adviser provides a summary of the scope and any key limitations of the vendor due diligence, using the expertise gathered from previous transactions and experience of current market practice;
- in combination with the review referred to above, a professional adviser provides a red flag report that identifies the key issues set out in the vendor due diligence;
- the professional adviser carries out top-up due diligence to address any deficiencies in the vendor due diligence; or
- the professional adviser carries out an independent, comprehensive due diligence process.

5.3 Sources of information

(a) *Confidentiality and non-disclosure agreements*

In addition to any available vendor due diligence report, information regarding a target will be acquired from a number of sources. Any non-public information made available by the target or seller will invariably be subject to a confidentiality or non-disclosure agreement (which may include the ability to share material without waiver of privilege). In agreeing the terms of the confidentiality agreement, the focus of each private equity house will differ slightly; however, it is important that:

- the agreement be with the appropriate entities within the private equity house's structure;
- the seller be party to the agreement; if only the target is a party and there is a breach of confidentiality, the private equity house does not want to find itself only having a claim against the target it is acquiring (although it is helpful to have the target as a party in addition to the seller, particularly in an auction so that the successful buyer can then step into the shoes of the target and enforce the terms of the confidentiality or non-disclosure agreement against unsuccessful bidders);
- disclosure be permitted within the private equity house and to appropriate external parties (usually the private equity house's professional advisers and its potential providers of finance, co-investors, consortium members and syndicate members, as relevant, and each of their professional advisers); and
- appropriate carve-outs be included for disclosure as required by law or regulation, or where information has entered the public domain otherwise than by way of a breach of the confidentiality or non-disclosure agreement.

Each private equity house will have a view on whether it will agree to take responsibility for breach of confidentiality obligations by its professional advisers and financiers and their own professional advisers. Where it does so, it will often require back-to-back undertakings in its favour from any such persons. Where the confidentiality agreement between the private equity house and the seller expressly provides that a back-to-back agreement be entered into by the private house with its advisers before it passes confidential information to such advisers, such an arrangement should be procured. In a recent case, the failure of a party to procure such a back-to-back agreement on terms equivalent to those contained in the original confidentiality agreement (as expressly provided for in the original confidentiality agreement) was held by the English courts to be a breach of contract.[3]

Non-solicitation of customers or employment restrictions (subject to standard carve-outs for employing in response to general advertisement, etc) are increasingly common in confidentiality agreements, as are requirements that use of the disclosed information be restricted to use in connection with the proposed transaction. Together with any standstill for trading of securities in the target (which is particularly important in the case of a listed target where the private equity house will need to be mindful of the fact that any information provided by the vendor or target may well constitute inside information), these obligations should not normally apply to professional advisers or financiers. A private equity house will invariably resist giving any indemnity or liquidated damages undertaking, on the basis that damages for breach of contract (or injunctive relief) should be an adequate remedy for the disclosing party.

(b) *Data rooms*

Once relevant information is collated, it will usually be made available to the private equity house and its advisers in the form of a data room. The data room may be electronic, and thus accessible from users' desktops, or physical, requiring users to attend the data room and sign in and out in person.

In recent years, electronic (otherwise known as 'virtual') data rooms have become increasingly prevalent to the point that today, on the majority of transactions, it is typical that the data room will be in an electronic rather than physical format. The increasing popularity of electronic data rooms stems from the fact that such a format makes the process of providing due diligence materials for review to a private equity house and its professional advisers far easier and less expensive. For example, electronic data rooms can be accessed simultaneously by a number of users at any and all times. This is particularly useful in an auction where there may be a number of potential bidders together with their advisers, and/or where the transaction is cross-border with advisers spread across several jurisdictions. In the past, utilising the physical data room format (particularly on an auction) would have entailed several physical data rooms having to be opened and manned with personnel for the period of access granted, as well as bidders and their professional advisers incurring a significant amount of time travelling to and from a physical data room. Private equity houses should of course bear in mind that with an electronic data room, the vendor is able to monitor and measure the amount of time a bidder and its advisers are actually spending in the data room, which enables the vendor to assess the true extent of a bidder's interest in the target asset.

In any data room the key elements that will need to be addressed by the advisers of the private equity house are as follows:
- Terms of access – on top of any applicable non-disclosure or confidentiality

---

[3] *Dorchester Project Management Ltd v BNP Paribas Real Estate Advisory Property Management UK Ltd* [2013] EWCA Civ 176.

agreement, additional data room rules will inevitably apply. These may be in hard-copy form; or users may be required to click "I Accept" or "I Agree" before accessing an electronic data room. At this point, the desire to access the data room may need to be weighed against accepting terms that cut across the previously negotiated non-disclosure or confidentiality agreement. Terms reviewed by the authors have included, for example, personal confidentiality undertakings that restrict the disclosure of information "to any other person"; such a restriction would prevent disclosure to the user's client, its potential finance providers or any other professional advisers on the transaction (which is unhelpful in the context of a due diligence exercise and subsequent negotiations of the acquisition documents). To try and negate this at the outset of a transaction (particularly in the context of an electronic data room where this issue is more common), a private equity house may wish to negotiate into the non-disclosure or confidentiality agreement a form of 'anti-click through' language. This would provide that the non-disclosure or confidentiality agreement takes precedence over any additional purported confidentiality or non-disclosure requirements that may be imposed by any electronic data room to which a private equity house or its professional advisers are granted access notwithstanding clicking on an "I Accept" or "I Agree" icon or any other indication of acceptance of such additional confidentiality conditions. This would ensure that the confidentiality obligations of the private equity investor are exclusively governed by the non-disclosure or confidentiality agreement and may not be extended except by a mutual agreement executed between the parties.

- Terms of access – another common issue is that the terms of access may include a statement that the entire contents of the data room may be disclosed against any warranties contained in the acquisition documentation. It would be unfortunate for a private equity house or its professional advisers to concede such a point inadvertently so, where practicable, it is advisable for the private equity house to seek a copy of the terms of access at the outset of the transaction so these can be reviewed in conjunction with the non-disclosure or confidentiality agreement. The private equity house can then resist commercial points like disclosure of the data room against the warranties so as to ensure its negotiating position is not weakened further down the line of the transaction process.
- Responsibility for reviewing documents – to minimise duplication of work between its professional advisers, the financial adviser or legal adviser of the private equity house will maintain a master data room index setting out who is responsible for reviewing each document. The index will be updated as the contents of the data room are updated throughout the due diligence exercise. This helps to ensure that all information has been reviewed, thereby reducing the risk that any white space develops between the advisers of the private equity house.
- Redacting of information – documents made available in data rooms will often be redacted to retain the privilege and/or confidentiality of

commercially sensitive information. This is more likely to be the case where a potential bidder is in the same industry as the target (and so may apply to private equity houses with portfolio companies that are competitors of the target). It will be particularly so in the case of listed targets in the United Kingdom, as in such cases Rule 20.2 of the City Code on Takeovers and Mergers requires that information provided to one offeror or potential offeror be provided (on request) equally and promptly to other offerors or bona fide potential offerors (even where such other offerors are less welcome). While information will be unredacted as a transaction process moves forward and a preferred bidder is identified, it is good practice for the buyer to query timing in the process for full disclosure of any redacted materials to the extent this is not mentioned by the seller at the outset.

Arrangements will be established with the seller or target to provide further information requested in a set form as a result of the review of the information provided in the data room. It will usually be the responsibility of the financial adviser or legal adviser of the private equity house to collate requests from other professional advisers and forward these to the relevant contact at the seller or target. There is often a set timetable for advisers to provide questions to the seller/target to ensure the seller/target is not flooded with questions, particularly if it is an auction process where there may be several bidders.

(c) *Information requests*
Historically, when a due diligence process was initiated the buyer would prepare a checklist of documentation necessary to complete the due diligence exercise. While it is now more usual for a predetermined range of information to be provided by the seller/target, advisers are likely to maintain extensive checklists in order to assess and cross-check the scope of information disclosed to assess if there are any material gaps (and to elicit information from a seller or target when commencing any vendor due diligence).

To the extent the transaction is proprietary in nature and diligence questionnaires are required to be sent by the advisers of the private equity house to the seller/target, it is important that professional advisers do not simply send their standard form diligence questionnaires without first checking to ensure that all the questions are material and match the thresholds agreed upon for the due diligence reports. It is also helpful, where practicable, for the advisers of the private equity house to share their proposed diligence questionnaires with each other prior to these being shared with the seller/target, in order to limit any duplication of information requests.

(d) *Interviews with managers of the target*
Interviews with managers of the target are of significant value, particularly at the start and conclusion of a due diligence process. At the beginning of the process, asking open questions such as "What are the material risks to the business from your perspective?" and "What do you consider to be the most material assets of the

business?" usually provides useful material to inform and to focus further the scope of the due diligence exercise.

At the conclusion of the due diligence process, background to the written material provided will assist in establishing the significance of particular issues – for example, the risk that a change of control right may be exercised on completion, or the likely response of pension trustees to the transaction.

Given the more subjective nature of information provided during interviews, in advisers' due diligence reports it will usually be attributed to the interviewee, or at least indicated as having been provided by way of interview rather than in written form. Furthermore, in management buyouts, managers will commonly be asked to warrant the accuracy of the various diligence reports.

(e) *Public information*

To the extent to which it is accessible, publicly available information may provide an additional perspective on the target or may verify information provided elsewhere. Key sources of public information available in most jurisdictions include the following:

- commercial register – this will usually evidence a target's constitutional documents, share or other ownership interests, officers, registered office, security over its assets and current status (including whether a company is in good standing);
- intellectual property register – this will identify intellectual property over which a target has the benefit of registration, in addition to any rights at common law (registrable intellectual property usually constitutes patents, trademarks and designs);
- litigation searches – commercial providers in a number of jurisdictions maintain a database of court proceedings, which may provide an indication of the number and value of claims against (or brought by) a target, and whether any winding-up petition has been issued against the target in any insolvency/bankruptcy courts;
- credit agency searches – where the creditworthiness of a target is questionable, such a search will usually reveal relatively current information;
- land registry – this will provide details of title and encumbrances in relation to freehold property and usually leases over a specified duration.

5.4 Presenting the results of due diligence

Reporting by professional advisers can broadly be divided into two categories: 'by-exception' reporting and descriptive reporting. By-exception reporting is a short-form due diligence report that will include only those issues that, in the opinion of the adviser, are material in the context of the overall transaction (including whether the issue would be material to the private equity house in its decision whether or not to proceed with the transaction and/or would have a material impact on price). Materiality should be discussed at the outset of the transaction between the private equity house and each professional adviser (for example, if there are hundreds of commercial contracts but the target contracts on a purchase order basis with no guaranteed revenue streams and the contracts are terminable on notice, a private equity house is very unlikely to want its advisers spending much time, if any, reviewing these contracts). The parties will be guided by:

- thresholds in the case of any item of expenditure, revenue or value by an amount per year or in aggregate in respect of that matter/contract;
- guidance from the private equity house and industry experience that may identify particular matters involving risk to the private equity house's reputation;
- guidance from managers within the target who may identify particular assets, contracts or matters as being particularly material; and
- matters that will have a material impact on timing or deliverability of the transaction, such as required third-party, shareholder or regulatory consents.

Descriptive reporting involves summarising the terms of existing arrangements in order to provide the private equity house with a comprehensive summary of certain aspects of the target. Most due diligence reports will be a combination of the by-exception and descriptive approaches. So, for example, in a legal due diligence report it is common to report on a by-exception basis, but with a descriptive summary of the material terms of the commercial arrangements with material customers and suppliers. Not every document will need to be reviewed in detail and/or reported on.

5.5 Preparing vendor due diligence

Whereas previously control of the transaction process and preparation of the transactional documents commonly lay with buyers, during the 1990s sellers began to take control of the transaction process and responsibility for drafting the transaction documents. As a result, sellers could communicate to a number of potential buyers information about the target and the terms on which they were prepared to dispose of the target. Auctions became prevalent as a means of creating competitive tension to increase the price that would be paid for the target. As part of this process, sellers found that they could encourage numerous potential buyers to make bids that were more informed, and less likely to be reduced later, where the majority of the due diligence exercise had already been carried out. Potential buyers could spend less time and money on due diligence – costs that would be written off unless the potential buyer became the actual buyer – before making a bid. As a result of cost pressure on buyers and the desire of sellers to control sale processes, vendor due diligence became more common.

Vendor due diligence undertaken on behalf of a seller or the target differs from due diligence undertaken on behalf of a potential buyer principally because there will usually be only a limited answer to the "So what?" question. After identifying an issue for a potential buyer, a vendor due diligence adviser is unlikely to advise on the implications of the issue in question; this will be a matter for buy-side advisers to address (although, where possible, the vendor's advisers may seek to solve identified issues as part of any pre-sale planning before the release of the vendor due diligence report in order to make the target look as attractive as possible for sale). Instead of being reflected in the vendor due diligence report, the answer to the "So what?" question is likely to be reflected in advice to the target/seller and may be reflected in the seller's approach to the proposed transaction documents.

Further differences between vendor due diligence and buy-side due diligence include:

- reporting style – because vendor due diligence is intended to make a potential buyer familiar with the relevant target, any report produced is likely to be more factual compared to buy-side due diligence and will include more descriptive content (rather than simply being written on a by-exception basis);
- access to managers of the target – it is likely that there will be greater access to managers when preparing vendor due diligence than in a buy-side process because vendor due diligence advisers are effectively on their side at this stage of a transaction, and because the intention will be that a well-managed vendor due diligence process should minimise the potential burden of responding to queries from multiple potential buyers;
- data room – vendor due diligence advisers are likely to assist with establishing a data room holding the information on which their vendor due diligence reports are based.

(a) **Process**

The vendor due diligence process is typically broken up into two phases. During the first phase, vendor due diligence advisers will discuss with managers of the target an appropriate scope for the vendor due diligence, appropriate materiality thresholds for vendor due diligence and subjective assessments of the key aspects and risks to the target business. Based on discussions with managers and the vendor due diligence adviser's experience of what will be considered material from a potential buyer's perspective, vendor due diligence advisers will circulate a draft scope for vendor due diligence and circulate to the target a request for documents reflecting the scope.

During the second phase of vendor due diligence, the information provided by the target will typically be compiled in a data room for ease of access by vendor due diligence advisers (and at a later date, potential buyers and their professional advisers). Where the initial information is deficient or discloses a potential issue, further information will be requested by the vendor due diligence advisers. Vendor due diligence advisers will prepare and revise a draft vendor due diligence report for review by the target and seller. That draft report will be provided to potential buyers, usually during phase two of the buy-side due diligence process – at that stage on a non-reliance basis by way of a release/hold harmless letter.

(b) **Data rooms**

When establishing a data room, the vendor due diligence adviser responsible will be keen to ensure that only information that would be considered material by a potential buyer is included in the data room. Where an abundance of information (which may not be material) is included in the data room, such information will delay the due diligence process conducted by potential buyers and may lead to further information requests and unnecessary effort.

Often, certain documents (eg, those relating to employees) contain personal data, as defined in data protection regulations. According to data protection rules in some jurisdictions, personal data may be communicated to third parties (eg, the potential buyer of the target) only with the relevant person's prior consent. Since obtaining this prior consent will in most cases be inappropriate in practice due to sensitive business issues or the confidentiality of the transaction, data covered by data protection regulations is often made impersonal (eg, by presenting the information in an abstract manner or by deleting names or other information that may identify individuals). This approach is likely to be acceptable for all but the most senior or key employees, whose consent should be obtained, albeit such information is typically provided only at the later stages of the due diligence process.

6. Key areas

Due diligence carried out by professional advisers on behalf of a private equity house will tend to focus on the same areas of importance as due diligence carried out on behalf of other investors, buyers and sellers. However, a number of areas are of particular significance to private equity houses, because of a material impact on:

- the cashflow of the target (and therefore the target's ability to service payments required in respect of debt finance);
- the ability of the private equity house to exit from its investment and to be confident that no further liabilities will be incurred following exit; and
- the potential for the private equity house itself or other portfolio companies of the private equity house to be affected.

6.1 Pensions

Perhaps the most important question for a private equity house in the employee benefits piece of the due diligence process will be whether the target operates a UK defined benefit pension scheme. As well as factoring in the size of any deficit when considering the price it is prepared to pay for the business, there are a number of key compliance and regulatory issues the private equity house will need to look out for. In practice, the legal advisers will work together with an actuarial firm, which will likely also have a team that specialise in reviewing the 'employer covenant' of the employers that participate in the pension scheme, to provide the necessary specialist advice.

(a) Pension scheme documentation

The first point to check for a private equity house and its professional advisers is whether the shares of the principal employer participating in the pension scheme are being purchased. If they are, the pension scheme will, unless otherwise agreed, also transfer as part of the transaction. If only a participating employer is being purchased, the pension scheme itself will remain behind with the seller but there may still be pensions issues to consider (eg, any debt on the departing employer that may arise under Section 75A of the Pensions Act 1995).

A detailed review of the pension scheme documentation will be required to ensure the pension scheme has been administered in compliance with applicable legislation. One particular area of risk to check is whether benefits have been correctly equalised between men and women. Prior to May 17 1990, it was accepted practice for men to retire at 65 and women at 60 until the Barber[4] judgment held that this was unlawful sex discrimination. If the benefit structure has not been correctly altered, both men and women would, in summary, be entitled to retire on a full pension at 60, which can significantly increase the pension scheme's liabilities.

Also critical will be an analysis of the wind-up powers in the trust deed, or any other 'poison pills'. If the trustees have a unilateral power to wind up the pension scheme, this will trigger the full buy-out deficit (known as the 'Section 75 debt', so-called because it arises under Section 75 of the Pensions Act 1995) as due and payable from the employers. The trustees may seek to use such a power as leverage in any discussions with the private equity house regarding the transaction.

(b)   *Effect of the transaction*
In the ordinary course, the employer's main obligation to the pension scheme is to pay the contributions required by the schedule of contributions agreed with the trustees as part of the triennial actuarial valuation process. The actuary will calculate the pension scheme's scheme-specific deficit which will then need to be made good over a set period (typically five to 10 years from the effective date of the valuation).

If the trustees become concerned that a private equity transaction will lead to a weakening of the employer covenant to the pension scheme, they may call for a new actuarial valuation to be carried out using more conservative assumptions. This would lead to a higher deficit figure and higher employer contributions (reducing the funds available to the employer to service the debt that will likely be introduced as part of the transaction). In addition, the trustees have the power to set the scheme's investment strategy (although they must consult with the employer in doing so) and may move to a more conservative strategy such as investing in bonds rather than equities. This can have the effect of locking in the existing deficit.

Private equity transactions are typically highly leveraged, meaning the amount of secured debt in the target group will increase. This is commonly viewed as weakening the employer covenant because, among other things, the pension scheme deficit is unsecured and will only recover in an insolvency after secured creditors have been made whole. Therefore in practice there will need to be detailed discussions by the private equity house with the trustees prior to completion of the transaction (and in some cases prior to signing) to ascertain their likely approach to the transaction and agree any mitigation to be provided to the pension scheme. Mitigation will typically take the form of a substantial one-off contribution at completion and/or increased contributions. Increased security such as guarantees or giving all or part of the pension deficit equal ranking with secured debt can also be offered (although the latter approach would need to be agreed with the debt investors).

---

4   *Barber v Guardian Royal Exchange Assurance Group* [1990] IRLR 240 ECJ.

Due diligence

(c) *The Pensions Regulator*

The Pensions Regulator has the power, in certain circumstances, to issue financial support directions or contribution notices to either the pension scheme employers or 'connected' or 'associated' parties. The definitions of 'connected' and 'associated' are from the Insolvency Act 1986 and are very wide. In the case of both a financial support direction or a contribution notice, as well as encompassing all companies in the portfolio group, their directors, shadow directors and employees, the definitions will also likely extend to the private equity house itself, any individuals that control the funds, and other portfolio groups.

A financial support direction can be issued at any time where the employer is either insufficiently resourced (meaning, broadly, that its net assets are less than 50% of its share of the buy-out deficit, and another connected party has sufficient assets to make up the difference) or if the employer is a services company (meaning a group company that derives most or all of its income from providing the services of its employees to other group members). A contribution notice can only be issued where there is a specific act or omission that either reduces the amount of the Section 75 debt or prevents its recovery, or is otherwise materially detrimental to the pension scheme. In either case, the Pensions Regulator can only act if it is reasonable to do so.

In order to obtain certainty that the Pensions Regulator will not use its powers in relation to the proposed private equity transaction, it is possible for the private equity house to apply for a clearance statement from the Pensions Regulator to that effect. Clearance is only appropriate where the private equity transaction is materially detrimental to the pension scheme, which, as noted above, may be the case for a highly leveraged private equity transaction. The Pensions Regulator will not grant clearance unless it believes sufficient mitigation for the detriment is being provided, and the trustees' views on the application will also be sought.

Clearance is only relevant to the facts described in the application, so will not protect the private equity house in respect of future events such as the granting of additional security, payments of dividends, restructuring or any eventual exit. Clearance is therefore most commonly sought by sellers on an exit to ensure a clean break. Without clearance, sellers potentially remain at risk of the Pension Regulator's powers for two years after completion in respect of financial support directions, and six years in respect of contribution notices. Whether or not an application for clearance is made, it is likely the transaction will need to be notified to the Pensions Regulator. Notification is a far simpler process than clearance and involves the seller completing an online form.

(d) *Auto-enrolment*

Private equity houses should be aware that, with effect from October 1 2012, every employer in the UK must auto-enrol its eligible workers in a qualifying pension scheme and make contributions to that scheme for each worker. The precise date by which an employer must comply with this obligation will depend on its 'staging date' which is calculated based on the number of employees the employer had at April 1 2012. The Pensions Regulator has the power to issue significant fines, of up to £10,000 per day, for non-compliance, so it will be a key part of the due diligence process for the private equity house and its professional advisers to determine whether the target has met its obligations under this regime.

6.2 **Environmental/health and safety liability**
Depending on the activities of the target and the previous history of its properties, there may be the potential for the target to have significant liability (whether civil, criminal or statutory clean-up liabilities) for environmental damage (eg, soil, groundwater or water pollution). As a result, environmental due diligence is high on the agenda of any private equity house, particularly given the ever-increasing public scrutiny and awareness of environmental issues. It will also be important to understand if any environmental consents or licences are required to operate the target and if any conditions attach to such consents or licences, in order to determine environmental compliance issues.

An environmental review of the target's properties is usually carried out initially by conducting a desktop-based assessment of information (eg, a review of information including surveys, historical maps and process information) to identify properties where pollution is likely to be an issue. Where the target's activities are potentially polluting, a specialist environmental consultant commonly conducts a site walk-over to assess any evidence of pollution. Where there are particular concerns, a more invasive assessment may be undertaken (and may be required by any debt investors) – provided that it is permitted by the target (which may be reluctant to do so, because if pollution is found the target may be under an immediate obligation to remedy it).

Liability to remedy pollution problems generally rests with the polluter or the party that knowingly permits it to be present (the 'knowing permitter'). However, in some cases where the polluter or knowing permitter cannot be found, the owner or occupier of the site will be liable. Liability may be complicated due to the terms of occupation by the target or its tenant/sub-tenants, which can sometimes have the practical effect of altering the general statutory position.

Depending on the nature of the target's activities, due diligence may also be necessary to establish whether the target's activities or its properties are compliant with health and safety laws. For example, from April 6 2012 the Control of Asbestos Regulations 2012 imposes certain duties on non-domestic property owners and tenants in relation to the removal and/or management of asbestos. As part of the due diligence process a private equity house would want to see evidence of any asbestos reports and compliance with their recommendations. Failure to comply with the requirements of the 2012 Regulations constitutes a criminal offence and the enforcing authority can therefore bring criminal proceedings against the target, which if successful could result in imprisonment for the target directors responsible and/or an unlimited fine. In addition to criminal proceedings brought by the enforcing authority, those affected such as employees can themselves take civil action for breach of the 2012 Regulations.

6.3 **Ethical/anti-bribery compliance**
Ethical – or anti-bribery and corruption – due diligence seeks to identify the risk that

individuals associated with the target may engage in criminal activity, in particular bribery. This is particularly important for private equity houses for a number of reasons. Either they, the target or its personnel could face investigation and prosecution in relation to the wrongdoing, with attendant legal and professional costs. As a result this may lead to conviction, fines and, in the case of the concerned individuals, imprisonment, which could in turn lead to debarment from public and other procurement processes. This could also lead to enforcement authorities seeking civil recovery in respect of gains derived from the wrongdoing, including dividends, or to third parties bringing claims for losses arising from the wrongdoing.

More indirectly, investigations in themselves can lead to severe reputational damage for the target and for the private equity house itself. If left unchecked, bribery and corruption can also significantly increase the day-to-day costs of doing business.

It is also particularly important for the private equity house and its professional advisers to understand ethical compliance risks prior to completing an acquisition since, depending on the contractual governing law, it may be unlawful to enforce indemnities obtained as contractual protection for the private equity house in respect of fines flowing from any bribery/anti-corruption legislation. There is also no limitation period in some jurisdictions, including the United Kingdom, for prosecuting criminal offences.

Furthermore, where bribery continues following completion of a transaction, the private equity house could potentially be liable under Section 7 of the Bribery Act for failing to prevent the actual bribery so it will want to ensure that adequate procedures (as discussed below) are put in place promptly following completion to the extent there are none already in existence.

(a) *The legal framework*

Ethical due diligence has taken on renewed significance in recent years, owing to a variety of factors, not least the continued enforcement of the US Foreign Corrupt Practices Act 1977 and the coming into force in July 2011 of the UK Bribery Act 2010. Both these statutes create criminal offences with potentially global effect. The Bribery Act also has wider scope than the Foreign Corrupt Practices Act, in that it criminalises commercial bribery (as well as bribery of public officials), and also criminalises the receipt of bribes.

Of particular concern to private equity houses is the offence of failure to prevent bribery under the Bribery Act, by which a target could be criminally liable for bribery carried out on its behalf anywhere in the world by persons 'associated' with it (ie, without the need to prove dishonest corporate intent), which could include employees, subsidiaries, and third-party agents. This has led to potential criminal liability of the target arising from bribery within its own business, either committed by its own employees, subsidiaries or third-party agents, and potentially liability for private equity houses themselves.

In addition, new laws will soon empower UK prosecutors to enter into deferred prosecution agreements, offering corporates an alternative to the risk of conviction, but at the cost of admitting wrongdoing, paying a fine and related recompense. This may have the knock-on effect of increasing investigatory activity in this area.

The only defence to the offence of failure to prevent bribery is for the target to demonstrate that (despite the bribery) it had 'adequate procedures' designed to prevent the bribery from occurring. Such adequate procedures should follow international best practice, including:

- top-level commitment at or near board level, including adequate compliance resource;
- risk assessments, to determine what bribery risks the business faces;
- proportionate policies and procedures, including anti-bribery policies and procedures such as financial controls, internal reporting, and record-keeping;
- due diligence on those who perform services for the business;
- communication and training, to ensure that personnel follow the policies and procedures; and
- monitoring and review, to ensure improvements where the bribery risks change.

(b) *Identifying the risks*

Ethical compliance risks (together with the adequate procedures defence) have increased the need for private equity houses to conduct detailed ethical due diligence on targets. This is commonly incorporated into the standard due diligence process, supported by an outline analysis of the potential bribery risks that the target might face. The private equity house typically provide a summary of the work done in this area to its investment committee before approval is then given by the investment committee for the private equity house to proceed with the proposed transaction. For a private equity house, ethical due diligence is more than a tick-the-box exercise.

It is vital for private equity houses and their professional advisers to identify if the target has low organisational controls and a low-compliance culture. The absence, or poor quality, of written policies and procedures may indicate ethical compliance risks but, conversely, good quality written compliance materials may not necessarily reflect reality. Such policies and procedures must not only be fit for purpose, but must also work in practice.

Accordingly, a data room review alone is not sufficient, and it is often essential to conduct interviews with top-level compliance personnel and country managers in order to identify the true risk areas, any historical problems (not limited to publicly reported matters) and the general compliance culture of the target, its agents and employees (among others).

(c) *Common risk areas*

Every target has different ethical compliance risks, and different ways for its policies and procedures to mitigate those risks. However, common risk areas for a private equity house and its professional advisers to be aware of include:

- operations in high-risk geographical regions, often assessed by reference to the annual Transparency International Corruption Perception Index;
- high-risk sectors, for example the extractive/natural resource industries, infrastructure sectors, or certain unregulated sectors;

- use of agents or joint ventures (commonly overseas), in particular for liaising with potential customers or with government officials, where there is little oversight of the relationship, or where the agent/partner controls the external relationship;
- high-risk transactions, for example where customers are states or state-owned enterprises, where government licences or permits are required in order to conduct business, or where dealings with government officials are common such as shipping across borders, as these can commonly involve facilitation payments (ie, payments to secure routine governmental functions) which can also constitute bribery;
- extensive use of corporate hospitality – legitimate expenditure on hospitality is generally not a priority for prosecutors, but it can be used to disguise bribery, in particular in relation to public officials (including employees of state-owned enterprises).

6.4 International sanctions

International sanctions due diligence is aimed at identifying the risk that the target is engaged, or may have engaged, in transactions or dealings in breach of international sanctions, or anticipates carrying out business which may be in breach of international sanctions. If any such conduct is identified, there is the risk that the target could face investigation and prosecution, which could result in imprisonment of relevant individuals and/or potentially substantial fines. Aside from potential criminal liability, sanctions violations may result in significant reputational consequences, which in turn may damage the target's business, and affect the private equity house itself.

In light of the far-reaching consequences of sanctions violations, it is very important for the private equity house and its professional advisers to understand the legal risks associated with doing business with countries and persons subject to sanctions. Given the nature of global finance and business, it is likely that the private equity house will need to consider risks under different sanctions regimes.

The most extensive sanctions are imposed unilaterally by the United States and the European Union. These sanctions are often aimed at restricting business with specified countries or persons, and are likely to be highly relevant if the target is engaged in business with a country subject to sanctions.

(a) EU sanctions

The substantive prohibitions of the EU sanctions are contained in EU Council decisions and regulations. For practical purposes, the key legal instruments are Council regulations, which have direct effect in each EU member state and are binding on individuals and corporate entities in the same way as the domestic law of those member states.

Although EU sanctions apply throughout the European Union, the competent authorities of individual member states administer and enforce the sanctions contained in Council regulations. Penalties for breach of EU sanctions are contained in the domestic legislation of each member state. As such, it is important for the private equity house to be aware that the consequences of breaching EU sanctions vary across the European Union, as different member states adopt different approaches to non-compliance with sanctions.

As part of the due diligence, it is important to consider the wide-ranging scope of the jurisdiction of EU sanctions. Council regulations are generally stated to apply:

- within the territory of the European Union, including its airspace;
- on board any aircraft or any vessel under the jurisdiction of an EU member state;
- to any person inside or outside the territory of the European Union who is a national of an EU member state;
- to any legal person, entity or body that is incorporated or constituted under the law of an EU member state; and
- to any legal person, entity or body in respect of any business done in whole or in part within the European Union.

EU sanctions are constantly being modified. Currently, the EU sanctions regime against Iran is the most wide-ranging, but other sanctions regimes, in particular the one aimed at Syria, pose significant risks to companies wishing to conduct business with such countries.

The main provisions of the EU sanctions against Iran include:

- export and import restrictions, including an embargo on Iranian crude oil, petroleum products, petrochemical products, and natural gas;
- a prohibition on the supply of key equipment for certain industrial sectors, including the Iranian oil and gas sector;
- restrictions on financing of certain enterprises (including Iranian entities engaged in the petroleum or petrochemical industries);
- an extensive asset freeze in respect of persons and entities associated with Iran's nuclear programme and with serious human rights violations;
- a prohibition on EU credit and financial institutions transferring funds to or from Iranian banks; and
- restrictions on transfers of funds and financial services, including requirements that transfers of funds to or from Iranian entities over certain thresholds be notified to or approved by a competent governmental authority.

If, in the course of due diligence, it appears that the target has business in countries subject to more extensive sanctions, this business will need to be considered carefully to ensure that it has complied with EU sanctions.

A private equity house requires clarity on these issues before it can be confident that it will not be buying a company that has engaged in conduct in breach of EU sanctions. It also needs to satisfy itself that the target has adequate policies and procedures in place to ensure that its employees are aware of sanctions issues and the company's compliance obligations. The asset freeze is an integral element of most EU sanctions regimes, and companies need to ensure that monitoring and screening procedures catch any transactions with designated persons or entities subject to an asset freeze.

Once the due diligence review and question and answer phase with the target's management has been completed, the private equity house and its professional advisers need to consider the risk that the target has engaged in conduct in violation of applicable sanctions, and include appropriate representations and covenants in the contractual documentation.

(b) **US sanctions**

Due diligence on compliance with US sanctions seeks to identify risks that a target company has engaged or is engaging in transactions or dealings that would violate the various US government primary sanctions regimes targeting various countries, entities, and individuals worldwide. The due diligence process will subject any US-based company to questions about its compliance with those sanctions regimes. Because of the potential broad scope and extraterritorial reach of certain US sanctions programmes, it is important for a private equity house to be aware that non-US companies often face questions about their compliance with those sanctions regimes even if they are not formally required to comply with them. Banks involved in private equity transactions routinely undertake their own investigation of a target's sanctions compliance, to avoid taking on liability for supporting prohibited activities or playing a part in a lending transaction where funds will be used to further dealings or transactions with markets or persons subject to US sanctions.

The US Treasury Department's Office of Foreign Assets Controls (OFAC) is the lead agency responsible for administering and enforcing primary US sanctions. While the various OFAC embargo programmes are addressed to "United States persons", this is broadly defined and, for example, covers not only US entities organised under the laws of the United States and their foreign branches (but generally excluding parents and subsidiaries) and any party physically located in the United States, but also US citizens and permanent residents wherever resident or employed. The US sanctions programmes against Cuba and Iran are broader and generally reach any person, including a foreign entity a US person owns or controls. As a result, virtually any transactional involvement (ie, support, facilitation or approval) by a US person in conduct that would be prohibited if undertaken directly by a US person would itself violate the OFAC-administered sanctions programme.

Because the details of the various US sanctions regimes vary greatly, due diligence investigations in this area often begin with questionnaires that seek to identify high-risk areas and topics for more targeted interviews with the company's senior management and trade compliance personnel. Data room reviews alone are normally insufficient to identify and to assess accurately sanctions-related risks. Due diligence investigations typically review the last five years of activities (the default statute of limitations period), and financing documents often include representations regarding sanctions compliance over a similar time period as well as covenants for forward-looking conduct.

The scope of the diligence review usually depends on the profile of the target involved, the industry or industries involved, the nature of the target's products and services, and the location of its customer base. For example companies with operations in, customers in, or other connections to countries subject to comprehensive primary US sanctions (currently Cuba, Iran, North Korea, Sudan, and Syria) will face a detailed review of every aspect of those operations, whereas investigations in respect of other countries that are regarded as high-risk will scrutinise carefully operations in these countries to verify that no business has taken place with individuals or entities subject to sanctions.

Any due diligence exercise should also take account of the fact that OFAC also maintains and regularly updates a list of 'specially designated nationals' and 'blocked persons', with whom US persons may not transact business without US government authorisation. These persons may be located in countries partially or completely subject to sanctions or in countries not targeted by US sanctions. A target should be asked to explain how it ensures compliance in this area, such as using 'interdiction' software that screens parties to a contemplated transaction against the list of specially designated nationals and against other US and non-US government blacklists. If a target undertakes activities in these countries or with specially designated nationals under the terms of US licensing or other authorisation, the diligence investigation will review compliance with those licences or authorisations.

Investigations into sanctions compliance will also seek to assess a target's level of understanding as to its obligations, typically through reviews of compliance procedures and processes as found in written documents and actual practices. As with the anti-bribery reviews described above, the key issue is to ensure that sanctions compliance procedures and processes are effective in practice.

6.5 **Carve-out of a target from an existing corporate group**

In the case of a target that is integrated into the seller's overall corporate group, the due diligence process will identify the services provided to the target by other members of the seller's group that are not being acquired and arrangements with third parties from which the target benefits by virtue of its status as a member of the seller's group. In the case of a private equity house this is particularly significant, because unless the acquisition is a bolt-on acquisition for an existing portfolio company, the acquisition undertaken by Newco will then be expected to stand alone, without ongoing support from the private equity house. A corporate buyer may be able to provide support to an acquired target through its existing infrastructure; in contrast, a private equity house's portfolio company will need to provide the services internally, procure them from a third party or – usually for an interim period only – procure them from the seller.

Typical services that are provided on a group-wide basis are back-office functions such as logistics, information technology services (eg, support, maintenance, data processing, personnel, payroll, accounting and disaster recovery) and human resources.

Arrangements with third parties that are commonly negotiated on a group-wide basis, the right to which may terminate following completion, include:
- insurance cover – typically, the target will benefit from group-wide insurance cover or cover provided by a captive insurer within its existing corporate group; the terms of existing cover applicable up to completion and appropriate cover from completion will be established by insurance advisers;

- information technology, to the extent that these processes are outsourced by the selling corporate group, including licences to use third-party software and arrangements granting access to source code and data required to develop information technology necessary for the target's business;
- licences for intellectual property used by the target; and
- supply agreements that include discounts based on consumption by the selling corporate group.

In the case of services provided to the target by other members of the seller's corporate group, to allow the transaction to proceed quickly the seller may be willing for the seller group to provide the services to the target on an interim basis under a transitional services agreement. From a private equity investor's perspective, a key issue where services are provided by the seller's group for such a period will be guarding against any permanent transfer of employees under the Transfer of Undertakings (Protection of Employment) Regulations 2006 (TUPE) in the United Kingdom and equivalent provisions in other jurisdictions (see below).

In the case of arrangements with third parties, the private equity house will want to establish during due diligence:

- whether and for how long the target is intended to have the benefit of the relevant arrangement following completion;
- whether any third-party consent is required for the arrangement to continue, the process for procuring such consent and the likelihood that such consent will be granted; and
- the cost of those arrangements, including payments to be made to the seller during any transitional period and payments to be made to third-party providers on an ongoing basis.

6.6 Corporate matters

From a corporate perspective, the following matters will be particularly relevant:

- Joint ventures – issues in this regard include the cashflow impact of joint venture arrangements; whether profits will be able to be extracted going forward; and whether the target group will be obliged to contribute further funding to the joint venture in the future.
- Warrants, options and minority shareholdings – fundamentally, a private equity house will want to be comfortable that the entirety of the share capital will be delivered on completion. From a legal perspective, particular attention will be paid to the enforceability and timing requirement under any provision in a target company's articles of association permitting a seller to drag other shareholders into a sale. Where a minority shareholder remains in the target, this will have implications for corporate governance, may result in leakage of value and, depending on the size of the shareholding, in some jurisdictions may prevent taxation grouping which allows interest payable on debt by one company to be offset against profits of another within the relevant taxation group.
- Acquisitions and divestments – where the target has engaged in recent

acquisitions and divestments, the private equity house will want to understand the cashflow impact of these going forward – regardless of whether any liabilities are likely to arise under any divestment agreement or any deferred consideration is payable under any acquisition agreement – and any restraints on the expansion and operation of the target's business going forward.
- Change of control – generally a private equity house will want to be comfortable that its proposed acquisition will not give rise to a right for a third party to be able to terminate a material commercial contract with the business (eg, a customer contract, supply contract, a joint venture agreement or lease) it is acquiring on a change of control of the target, or that a change of control of the target will entitle any managers or other individual(s) to significant bonuses or other benefits payable by the target.

6.7 Debt finance

The expectation for a private equity house on an acquisition is to repay the existing facilities of the target and to arrange for Newco to enter into new facilities. As such, the terms of the existing debt are largely irrelevant, save in the case of arrangements for pre-payment (although a change of control clause in a bank loan document, following the recommended Loan Market Association form, triggers an immediate requirement to prepay all amounts outstanding) and any early termination fees payable. However, as a result of market conditions for debt finance over recent years, there have been an increased number of capital structures utilised by private equity houses that employ high-yield bonds where the terms typically only require a change of control offer (often at 101% of the face value of the bonds) to be made on a change of control (with no obligation on the bondholders to accept such offer), and in certain recent deals, 'portability' has been introduced to allow a change of control to occur without this offer needing to be made if certain conditions are satisfied. As a result, private equity houses are not necessarily able to assume that the existing debt arrangements of the target can be taken out and easily replaced with their proposed new capital, and therefore there may need to be an increased focus on the target's debt arrangements compared to previous practice.

6.8 Employment

The most complex employment-related issues are likely to apply where the transaction is structured as an asset sale, due to the application of the EU Acquired Rights Directive[5] (implemented in the UK as TUPE). This will require an assessment of which employees are assigned to the business being sold, and an information and consultation exercise will need to be carried out before completion (and even before signing in some jurisdictions). There will also be a negotiation as to which party is responsible for employment-related liabilities. Although TUPE itself requires the purchaser to inherit all such liabilities, in practice it is typically agreed in the acquisition agreement that the seller retains responsibility for pre-completion

---

5 Directive 2001/23/EC.

liabilities. TUPE may also apply where services are to be provided between the parties through a transitional services agreement for a period after completion.

A private equity house will also wish to understand the key terms and conditions of employment of the target's senior management team. Typically these senior managers will be invited to invest alongside the private equity house and become co-owners of the target. The private equity investor may propose amendments to those employment terms in order to align the interests of senior managers with the private equity house more fully (eg, by replacing elements of remuneration with 'sweet equity' or adjusting bonuses and incentive targets to mirror the interests and investment timescale of the private equity house). With effect from September 2013, senior managers may be invited to enter into new employee shareholder contracts under which they relinquish certain statutory employment protections in return for shares worth at least £2,000 in the target.[6] There are certain tax incentives attached to these arrangements which can be beneficial to the employer and the employee. It may also be necessary to revise the senior manager employment contracts in line with recent legislative developments or to provide adequate protections for the target (eg, suitable notice periods, effective post-termination restrictive covenants should the senior manager leave the target, robust confidentiality provisions and specific allocation of rights in connection with any intellectual property created by the senior manager). The private equity house will also need to be familiar with the terms of employment relating to any underperforming managers in order to assess the cost of terminating their employment.

Full due diligence of standard employment contracts, handbooks, bonus plans and other related documents will also be required to assess related costs and any compliance issues for the private equity house following closing of the transaction. Senior employees may, for example, be entitled to significant bonuses or other benefits on a change of control of the target. In addition, employee claims, for example discrimination claims, can be very high-value and should be thoroughly investigated.

6.9 Regulatory consents

Where the target or part of the target includes a regulated business – such as an airport, a financial services provider, a utilities provider or a communications provider – it is likely that consents will be required from the relevant regulatory authority either before completion or following completion, but subject to the risk that the regulator directs that the transaction or part thereof be varied or unwound. During the due diligence process, professional advisers will identify:

- whether any such consents are required;
- the consequences of not receiving those consents before completion of the transaction;
- the likelihood that consent will be given; and
- the time required for the regulatory authority to grant such consent, or a structural solution to avoid the need to obtain any such consent.

---

[6] Please refer to the chapter, "Tax Structuring and Management", for further details.

The time taken for such consents to be given can be considerable; for example, in the United Kingdom the acquisition or increase of control in a firm authorised under the Financial Services and Markets Act 2000 is subject to a statutory process with the Financial Conduct Authority or the Prudential Regulation Authority (as applicable) that may take up to three months. Failure to obtain such consent constitutes a criminal offence, and depending on the consents required, the private equity buyer is likely to include as a condition in the acquisition documentation that the necessary regulatory consent is received.

6.10   **Assets or shares?**
The focus of a due diligence process for an asset transfer will differ from that for a share transfer. Where the buyer is to acquire the shares in the target, the assets, liabilities and obligations of the target will also be acquired. The due diligence for a share transfer will therefore be more detailed in order to uncover current and historical liabilities (in particular, tax) and the current and historical activities of the target and its subsidiaries.

In the case of an asset transfer, the focus will instead be on identifying the assets required to undertake the target business and understanding the mechanism for their transfer. An asset transfer is likely to be significantly more complicated, given that each asset will need to be individually transferred, appropriate consents received from counterparties and any registration obligations complied with. The benefit to the private equity buyer should be that it acquires only the assets and liabilities identified under the acquisition document and those which transfer by operation of law (eg, employees and associated liabilities under TUPE). However, sellers will often try to draft such agreements so that all liabilities bought with a business transfer to a private equity buyer as if the transfer were in effect a share transfer, in which case the due diligence process will need to be more like that undertaken for a share transfer.

7.   **Conclusion**
Due diligence goes to the heart of a private equity house's ability to manage and allocate risk. The scope and scale of due diligence will of course vary significantly from transaction to transaction but should be viewed as more than a simple box-ticking exercise. It is important that the due diligence conducted is tailored to the target, with regular communication between the private equity house and its professional advisers.

The due diligence performed by the private equity house and its advisers is an audit of the target and will ultimately determine whether the private equity house proceeds with the transaction and, if so, the terms and shape of such a transaction (including determining the structure, logistics, protections and price associated with the transaction, and the likely form of a subsequent exit from the target). The need for a diligent and integrated approach by private equity houses and their professional advisers to the entire process should be a priority in any transaction, and if performed properly can ensure significant added value to the overall deal.

Performance of private equity

Barry Griffiths
Landmark Partners LLC
Rüdiger Stucke
Warburg Pincus LLC

1. Introduction

Compared to other asset classes, such as public equities or bonds, the measurement of returns from private equity has developed in a fundamentally different way, and remains less sophisticated in quantitative terms. The main reason is the private nature of private equity funds, which are typically not traded on an organised exchange. Instead of observing actual trading prices, limited partners in private equity funds receive estimates of net asset value from the general partners who manage these funds.

By construction net asset values represent, at best, estimates of the actual fair value of a fund; however, in reality they are often lagged and smoothed as well. This is especially the case if a general partner uses precedent transaction or past-quarter earnings measures, as well as maybe having different expectations about the development of certain industries or the economy as a whole. Moreover, different appraisers may use completely different approaches to value the same asset.[1]

As a consequence the calculation of periodic returns series in private equity is highly unreliable, and so therefore is the calculation of all of the time-weighted returns statistics that form the armamentarium of public-market equity analysis. It is clear that differentiating two unreliable quarterly net asset values must result in a very unreliable quarterly return, and that these in turn must result in extremely unreliable regression statistics. So while concepts that are useful in the analysis of public equity, such as alpha and beta, may still be valuable in private equity, it has proven very much more difficult actually to produce estimates of these quantities that are accurate enough to be useful.

In addition to the problem of unobservable fair market values comes the fact that the general partner, rather than the limited partner, is responsible for the timing of the actual cash flows in a private equity fund. This raises additional questions about the appropriateness of time-weighted return statistics in general.

As a result, return measures in private equity have developed around the observed cash flows between a private equity fund and its investors. In private equity, cash flows are facts but valuations are opinions. Private equity investors understandably prefer to focus on measurable facts, and to minimise reliance on unreliable opinions.

---

1 Although under generally accepted accounting principles (GAAP) general partners are required to produce net asset values that estimate the fair market value, and since 2007 have had guidance on how to meet this requirement in the form of Financial Accounting Standard (FAS) 157, there can be a wide range of estimates for the fair market value of an asset.

The contractual structure of private equity funds adds further complexity. Funds typically have an investment period of between five and six years, during which the fund manager calls the committed capital, as well as an overall lifecycle of between 10 and 12 years – or even beyond, until all investments have been realised. As a result the true returns of private equity funds are very uncertain when the fund is young, and they generally become more meaningful as the fund ages. But they are only known with certainty when the fund has been fully liquidated. Even the best estimates of interim return for private equity investments must be approached with caution.

2. Absolute measures of private equity fund returns

The two standard return measures in private equity are the ratio of total value to paid-in capital, and the internal rate of return. Both of these return measures are based solely on the cash flows of a private equity fund, plus the residual net asset value at the time of analysis. As discussed above, both of these measures are money-weighted, since the responsibility for cash flow timing rests with the general partner.

The ratio of total value to paid-in capital (TVPI), also known as money multiple or multiple of invested capital, is the ratio of the sum of a fund's capital distributions (D), plus a residual net asset value (NAV), over the sum of a fund's capital calls (C). By construction, the TVPI describes the overall value created by a private equity fund: a TVPI of 1.0 means that a fund has distributed or contains exactly as much wealth as was originally invested. The major limitation of TVPI is that it contains no information about the rate at which this value has been generated.

The internal rate of return (IRR), also known as money-weighted rate of return, is the discount rate at which the present value of a fund's capital distributions (D), plus a residual net asset value (NAV), equals the present value of a fund's capital calls (C). In other words, the IRR represents the compound rate on the stream of capital calls from the fund with respect to the timing and the size of the capital distributions back to investors. As a rate of return, the IRR is an annualised measure of a private equity fund's performance.

The IRR is not an uncomplicated measure of returns. As a single number that describes the rate of return over the whole life of the fund, it is oversimplified – it does not account for the ups and downs of the equity markets over decade time scales. The IRR is sensitive to comparably early and large distributions back to fund investors, and rather insensitive to distributions towards the end of a fund's life. In addition, the IRR carries no information about the overall value that has been created in absolute terms.

Finally, there are some practical issues associated with calculating IRR. In some cases there is no result for IRR; in other cases there can be more than one result. A correct solution for IRR must select the most economically meaningful solution, if one exists. For example, economically meaningful solutions must produce a positive IRR for TVPI greater than 1.0, and negative IRR for TVPI less than 1.0. Some commercially-available software is known to be unreliable in this regard, so users need to check their results carefully.

Because of their complementary strengths and weaknesses, IRR and TVPI are typically used alongside each other. Exhibit 1 briefly summarises the advantages and weaknesses of both return measures.

Exhibit 1: Advantages and weaknesses of traditional return measures

	Advantages	Weaknesses
Internal rate of return (IRR)	• Annualised measure of return	• Sensitive to early distributions • Not always unique solution
Ratio of total value to paid-In (TVPI)	• Overall measure of return • Single, valid solution • Always defined	• No information on the rate of value creation

Statistics for TVPI and IRR for individual private equity funds, and for groups of funds, are available from a number of commercial providers. These include Burgiss, Preqin, Pitchbook, Bloomberg, and Thomson Reuters. Once again, however, the private nature of private equity means that all such services have inherent limitations. Private equity managers are not required to report their results to anyone but their limited partners, and those limited partners may be under contractual prohibitions from sharing those results. This means that no commercial provider can cover the entire universe of private equity funds, although some cover a large fraction. Results included in a commercial service may only reflect the experience of a single limited partner, and not the experience of the whole fund. Furthermore, some services appear to have issues concerning data inclusion and dropouts that may limit their usefulness.[2]

Finally, commercial services that provide TVPI and IRR statistics can only provide the roughest of comparison sets. For example, it may be possible to find the quartile boundaries of European buyout funds formed in 2007, but it's not possible to use these services to compare based on industry exposure or relative use of financial leverage. An investor who consistently invests with groups whose predecessor funds were in the top-quartile for their year, fund type, and geography may simply be chasing groups who used high leverage in industries that were hot over the prior three years. This is not necessarily a winning strategy.

3. **Relative measures of private equity fund returns**

A key drawback to using absolute return measures in private equity is that private equity is not an absolute return class. Transactions in private equity are based in large part on the values of comparable public companies. It is also clear that when the

---

[2] Rüdiger Stucke, "Updating History", working paper (2011).

public market goes up, private equity values go up; and when the public market goes down, the private market goes down as well.

This is an important issue because not all private equity funds are the same. For example, consider the possible behaviour of two 2007 buyout funds. Fund A might have invested most of its capital before the 2008 public market crash, while Fund B might have invested most of its capital after the crash. It is easy to imagine a situation where Fund A has outperformed the public market and Fund B has underperformed, yet Fund B has a higher TVPI and IRR than Fund A. Analogous situations arise not just across time, but also across portfolios with different exposures in terms of size, geography and industry. In such a situation, reliance on simple absolute return measures like TVPI and IRR is not likely to lead to intelligent investment decisions.

In recent years, various approaches have been developed to account for the effect of changes in the public market throughout the life of a fund. These methods, commonly referred to as public market equivalents (PME), aim to adjust the size of a fund's capital distributions and its net asset value by the returns that public markets would have generated instead. Conceptually, the notion is that when the effect of the public market is removed, whatever is left must be due to the specific return contributions of the particular fund or fund manager. Due to the wild profusion of public-market indexes, reference benchmarks can be constructed to represent any desired combination of size, geography, industry concentration, leverage and so on. The reference benchmark represents the return that the investor could have obtained with much lower cost and much better liquidity in the public market. Whatever is left over is the value added by the private fund.

Two measures that are useful in this regard are the public market equivalents measure of Kaplan and Schoar[3] (2005), commonly referred to as KS-PME, and the Direct Alpha measure devised by Griffiths[4] and developed by Gredil, Griffiths, and Stucke.[5] These two measures are analogous to TVPI and IRR. KS-PME is a ratio that measures the wealth generated in a private fund compared to what would have been generated in a public market benchmark. Direct Alpha is a rate of return that measures the outperformance of a private equity fund compared with the public market benchmark.

Both KS-PME and Direct Alpha are calculated in a similar way to the regular TVPI and IRR of a private equity fund. The key difference is that, instead of using the actual cash flows of a fund, both methods use a capitalised version of its cash flows. That is, capital distributions and capital calls are either discounted or compounded by a reference benchmark to the same single point in time, for example, their future value at time n:

---

3 Steven Kaplan and Antoinette Schoar, "Private Equity Performance: Returns, Persistence, and Capital Flows", *Journal of Finance* Volume 60, Issue 4, pp1791–1823 (2005).
4 Barry Griffiths, "Estimating Alpha in Private Equity", in Oliver Gottschalg (ed.), *Private Equity Mathematics* (PEI Media, 2009).
5 Oleg Gredil, Barry Griffiths, and Rüdiger Stucke, "Benchmarking Private Equity – The Direct Alpha Method", working paper (2014).

$$KS-PME: \quad \frac{\sum_{t=0}^{n} FV(D_t) + NAV_n}{\sum_{t=0}^{n} FV(C_t)}$$

$$Direct\ Alpha\ (DA): \quad \sum_{t=0}^{n} \frac{FV(D_t) - FV(C_t)}{(1+DA)^t} + \frac{NAV_n}{(1+DA)^n} = 0$$

with

$$FV(C_t) = c_t \cdot \frac{m_n}{m_t} \quad and \quad FV(D_t) = d_t \cdot \frac{m_n}{m_t}$$

based on the time series of values of the reference benchmark; for example, the total returns of a public equity index

In academic work, KS-PME is commonly quoted using the Standard & Poor's 500 Total Return Index (S&P 500) as the reference benchmark. However, KS-PME and Direct Alpha can be used for any benchmark. If the user wants to measure the performance of a private equity portfolio against a leveraged benchmark of small-cap European retailers, that can be done quite readily. Economic interpretation of KS-PME and Direct Alpha measures depends heavily on understanding the relevance of the selected benchmark.

Direct Alpha can be computed using the same software used for computing IRR. As a result, many of the same practical considerations for computing IRR arise when computing Direct Alpha. There may be many solutions for Direct Alpha, or there may be none. An economically meaningful solution for Direct Alpha must be positive when KS-PME is greater than 1.0, and negative when KS-PME is less than 1.0. The user of commercial software should take care that correct results are reported.

Exhibit 2 compares the four introduced return measures along their two distinguishing dimensions.

Exhibit 2: Traditional return measures and market-adjusted return measures

	Absolute return	Market-adjusted return
Rate of return	IRR	Direct Alpha
Total return	TVPI	KS-PME

There are several other flavours of public market equivalents that are often cited. Historically, the idea of adjusting private equity returns for the behaviour of the public market came from Long and Nickels[6] in their index comparison method, now

---

[6] Austin M Long and Craig J Nickels, "A Private Investment Benchmark", working paper (1995).

recognised as the first of various public market equivalents methods. Later methods included PME+ by Rouvinez[7] and Capital Dynamics, and mPME by Cambridge Associates.[8] All of these methods were designed to measure the outperformance of a private equity portfolio compared with a specified public equity benchmark. All of them are closely related mathematically, and all of them suffer from various drawbacks due to their reliance on heuristic approximations. KS-PME and Direct Alpha are unique in that they actually solve the index-outperformance problem without introducing unnecessary and inaccurate approximations. Further details on how the different public market equivalents approaches compare to each other can be found in Gredil, Griffiths, and Stucke.[9]

Relatively few sources currently provide computed statistics for public market equivalents measures. As of this writing, Burgiss reports both the Long-Nickels index comparison method and the KS-PME for selectable fund aggregates, using the S&P 500 as the reference benchmark. The implementation of the Direct Alpha and further public equity indices is current work in progress. However, investors doing due diligence on a fund can usually obtain detailed cash flow data at the level of underlying deals, making it possible to compute both Direct Alpha and KS-PME against whatever benchmark is desired. As a result, the relative unavailability of commercial aggregates for public market equivalents data is not a major stumbling block for investors.

4. A numerical example for the return measures in private equity

Exhibit 3 presents an illustrative, simple private equity fund with actual capital calls (C), capital distributions (D), and a final net asset value over a 10-year period. Based on the annual net cash flows of the fund, its IRR is 17.5%. The TVPI of the fund is (425+75)/250 = 2.00.

Using the total returns of a public equity index, such as the S&P 500, the future values of the private equity fund's capital calls and capital distributions, FV(C) and FV(D), are calculated as of December 31 2010. In this example the (arithmetic) Direct Alpha is 12.6%, representing the annualised rate of return (beyond the public equity returns) that is solely attributable to private equity. Similarly, the KS-PME is 1.67, indicating that the final wealth is 1.67 times what would have been achieved by investing in the public equity index.

5. The returns of private equity funds

In the following we present descriptive statistics on the returns of US venture capital, buyout, and private real estate funds, as well as western European buyout funds. The data has been provided by Burgiss, a leading provider of portfolio management software, services, and analytics to limited partners investing in private capital. Burgiss solutions streamline the investment process, provide transparency into

---

7	Christophe Rouvinez, "Private Equity Benchmarking with PME+", *Venture Capital Journal*, August 2003, pp34–38.
8	Cambridge Associates, *Private Equity and Venture Capital Benchmarks – An Introduction for Readers of Quarterly Commentaries* (2013).
9	*Op cit.*
10	David Hartzell and Lynn Fisher, "Real Estate Private Equity Performance: A New Look", working paper (2013).

Exhibit 3: Illustration of a private equity fund's cash flows and return measures

	Actual Values					Future Values			
	C	D	NAV	Net CF	Index	FV (C)	FV (D)	NAV	FV (Net CF)
Dec-31, 2001	100	0	...	-100	100	131	0	...	-131
Dec-31, 2002	0	0	...	0	78	0	0	...	0
Dec-31, 2003	100	25	...	-75	100	130	33	...	-98
Dec-31, 2004	0	0	...	0	111	0	0	...	0
Dec-31, 2005	50	150	...	100	117	56	168	...	112
Dec-31, 2006	0	0	...	0	135	0	0	...	0
Dec-31, 2007	0	150	...	150	142	0	138	...	138
Dec-31, 2008	0	0	...	0	90	0	0	...	0
Dec-31, 2009	0	100	...	100	113	0	115	...	115
Dec-31, 2010	0	0	75	75	131	0	0	75	75
Total	250	425				317	453		
		IRR:	17.5%		Direct Alpha (arithmetic):				12.6%
		TVPI:	2.00		KS-PME:				1.67

portfolio holdings, and enable data-driven decisions. The fund cash flow data underlying these statistics is widely recognised as the most accurate and representative data in the industry.

We present pooled and median IRR and TVPI numbers for funds with vintage years from 1992 to 2008, as of December 31, 2013. We also present Direct Alpha and KS-PME numbers. As noted in Section 3, the economic interpretation of Direct Alpha and KS-PME results depends heavily on selecting a reference index that represents the systematic risk of the portfolio in question. While there has been a great deal of discussion about the appropriate benchmark for private equity with respect to industry, size, and risk exposure, we present market-adjusted returns relative to the S&P 500, which has been the lowest common denominator in both academia and industry practice.

5.1 Returns from US venture capital funds

Venture capital refers to equity investments into companies that are at an earlier stage of their corporate lifecycle. The current and historical returns of US venture capital funds show one of the most striking patterns in the industry, as presented in Exhibit 4. Median IRRs achieved by funds raised until 1997 range between 20% and 60% in all but one vintage year. IRRs at the top quartile have a peak above 120% for funds from 1997. This material difference reflects the fact that larger funds tended to generate higher returns than smaller funds, which is in line with the common wisdom that better managers use to attract more capital, and there has been persistent success across subsequent funds by the same manager.

Venture capital funds from 1998 that invested most or all of their capital before the bursting of the so-called 'new economy' bubble show correspondingly poor returns, the median of which was even negative for three consecutive years. While some of the more recent vintage years show slightly positive median IRRs again, the top quartile has not exceeded 10% until recently. However, those funds increasingly carry unrealised investments. Nonetheless, it is surprising that funds that invested and realised most of their capital in the flourishing economy between 2003 and 2008 have not achieved higher IRRs.

The Direct Alphas of US venture capital funds present their returns without any positive or negative impact by movements in the general public market. Up until 1998, the majority of venture capital IRRs represented excess returns over and above the S&P 500. Since 1999, the top quartile has hardly generated such excess returns, implying that 75% of all venture capital funds returned less capital than the S&P 500.

By definition, IRRs and TVPIs are highly correlated measures of returns. Consequently, TVPI multiples have a very similar pattern across vintage years to IRRs. Until 1996, median TVPIs were above 2.0 in all but one vintage year. The top quartile was substantially higher, and even above 5.0 from 1993 to 1996, having returned more than five times the invested capital back to limited partners. From 1998 to 2000, median TVPIs were slightly below 1.0, and have been slightly above 1.0 since 2001. As for the top quartile, TVPI multiples have been around 1.5 since 2001.

As explained above, the KS-PME is a multiple that indicates to what extent the returns of a private equity fund have exceeded, or not, those of the public market over its entire life. For the median US venture capital funds this was the case in all but one vintage year until 1997, with a peak at 2.63 in 1996, indicating that the median fund from this vintage year generated returns that were 163% higher than those of the S&P 500. Top-quartile public market equivalents have been above 1.0 for funds from every vintage year.

5.2 Returns from US buyout funds

Exhibit 5 shows the quartiles achieved by US buyout funds. Buyouts typically represent investments in mature companies involving material fractions of debt in addition to a fund's equity piece. In contrast to venture capital, median buyout IRRs have been positive for funds from all vintage years. Similarly, TVPIs for funds raised between 1992 and 2008 have been above 1.0 in every vintage year. At first sight, the returns of buyout funds across vintage years appear to be inversely correlated to public equity and general economic cycles. However, the opposite is the case. Funds from the first half of the 1990s and 2000s show higher returns, since they invested most of their capital at rather moderate conditions in equity markets and realised most of their investments during the late 1990s as well as in the years leading up to the recent financial crisis when equity markets were booming.

In addition to the observed wave pattern of absolute buyout returns, we note a long-term downward trend in returns. While this trend is in line with a generally decreasing risk-free rate over the same period, this observation is interesting given that buyouts are primarily funded with debt. The most likely explanation is the significant inflow of capital into this asset class, causing an increased competition among buyout investors for suitable companies. But also a general uplift in the enterprise value-multiple environment may have contributed to this trend.

Median Direct Alphas are positive in almost all vintage years and, similarly, median KS-PMEs are above 1.0 relative to the total returns of the S&P 500. In contrast to absolute IRRs and TVPIs, relative returns show a much less pronounced wave pattern and some of the highest returns relative to the S&P 500 were delivered in the early 2000s. However, it needs to be stressed that our Direct Alphas and KS-PMEs, relative to the S&P 500, implicitly assume private equity to have the same exposure to market risk as the benchmark. For both venture capital and buyout funds this is unlikely to be the case. Consequently, the presented excess returns should not be interpreted as alpha in the sense of traditional asset pricing models, such as the capital asset pricing model. In that model the alpha intercept is defined as that part of an asset's return that cannot be explained by the return from the market portfolio (or a certain exposure thereto) in combination with the return from the risk-free asset. We will return to the risk of private equity investments in the next section.

5.3 Returns from US private real estate funds

While the emergence of US venture capital funds reaches back to the 1970s, and US buyout funds started becoming mainstream in the 1980s, private US real estate funds have only arisen since the 1990s. As shown in Exhibit 6, IRRs and TVPIs of this type of fund were comparably stable between 1994 and 2000. Returns of funds since 2004 fell off sharply due to decreasing values in the US real estate market by mid-2007. Funds starting to invest in 2007 and 2008 have shown some recovery, though most of their investments are still unrealised.

Direct Alphas and KS-PMEs show an interesting pattern relative to the total returns of the S&P 500. The median private real estate fund up until 1995 did not deliver returns in excess of public equities. Funds around the vintage year 2000 show some of the best returns relative to the S&P 500. Since 2004, median returns have again been lower in each vintage year. Hartzell and Fisher[10] provide a more detailed comparison of the returns of private real estate funds, among others, against indices of publicly-listed real estate investment trusts.

5.4 Returns from western European buyout funds

In contrast to the US market, the market for leveraged buyouts in western Europe developed in the 1990s, with a delay of approximately a decade. Exhibit 7 shows fund returns for the vintage years 1994 to 2008. As a result, IRRs and TVPIs are at elevated levels relative to US buyout funds until the mid-2000s. This is particularly the case for funds from the late-1990s whose drop in performance has been much less pronounced. Along similar lines, the dispersion in returns (ie, the interquartile range) has been larger for buyout funds from western Europe.

On the other hand, the pre-crisis vintage years 2006 and 2007 show a worse performance for western European funds. The main reason is likely the slower recovery of the European economies compared to the US economy. But also credit contracts of deals prior to the financial crisis have been more rigid for leveraged buyouts in Europe.

Performance of private equity

Direct Alphas and KS-PMEs are at correspondingly higher levels for most vintage years. Note that both relative return measures have also been calculated against the total returns of the S&P 500.

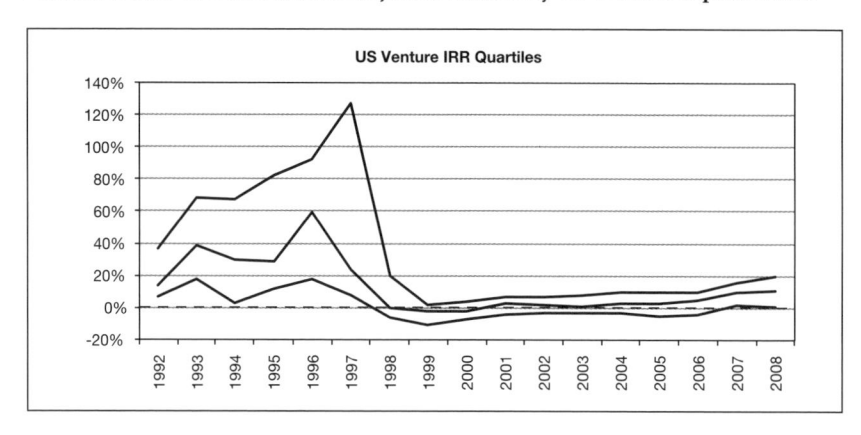

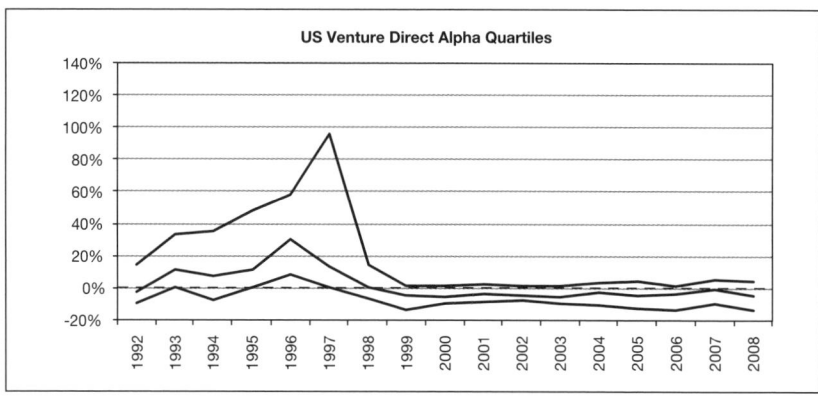

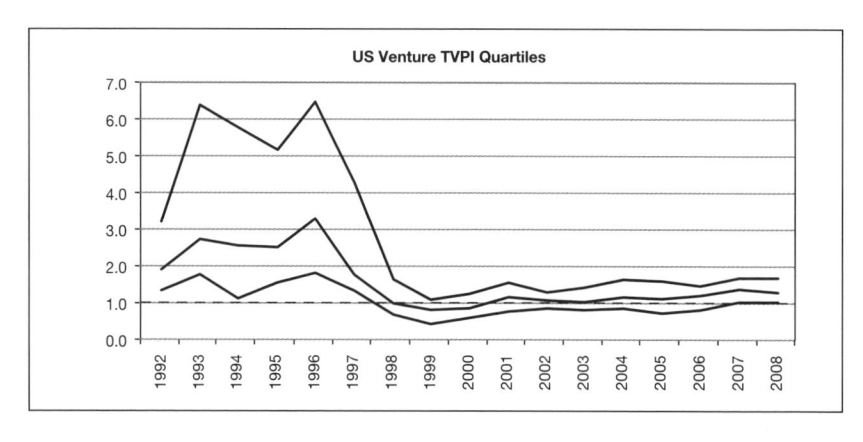

Exhibit 4: Absolute and market-adjusted returns by US venture capital funds

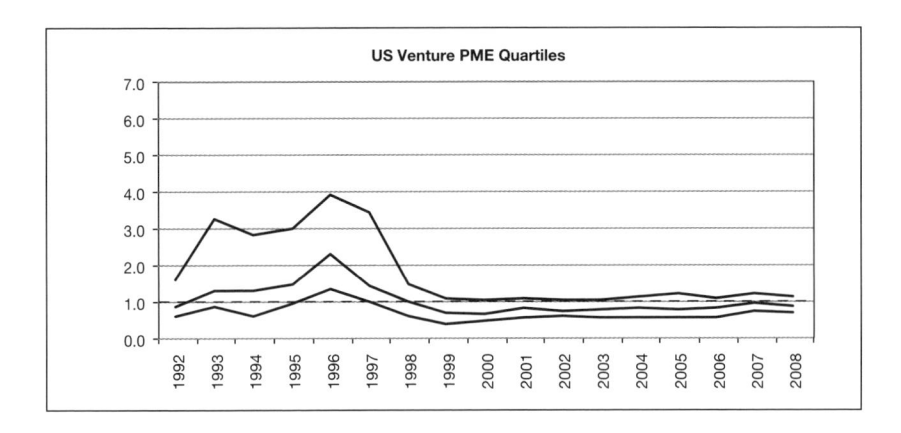

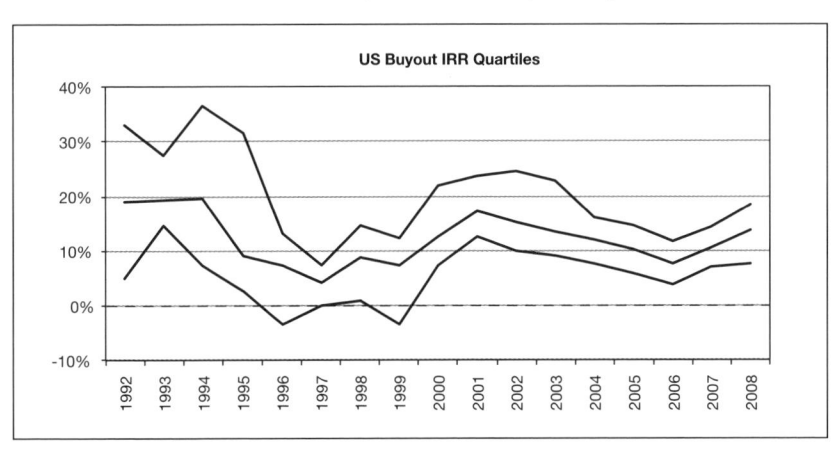

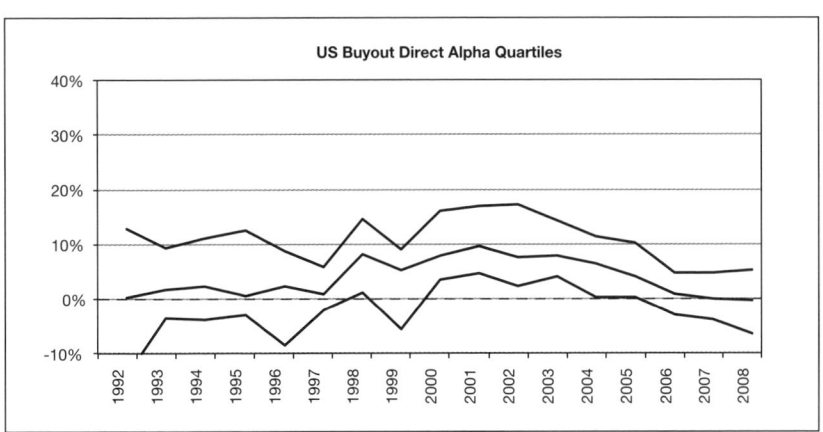

Exhibit 5: Absolute and market-adjusted returns by US buyout funds

Performance of private equity

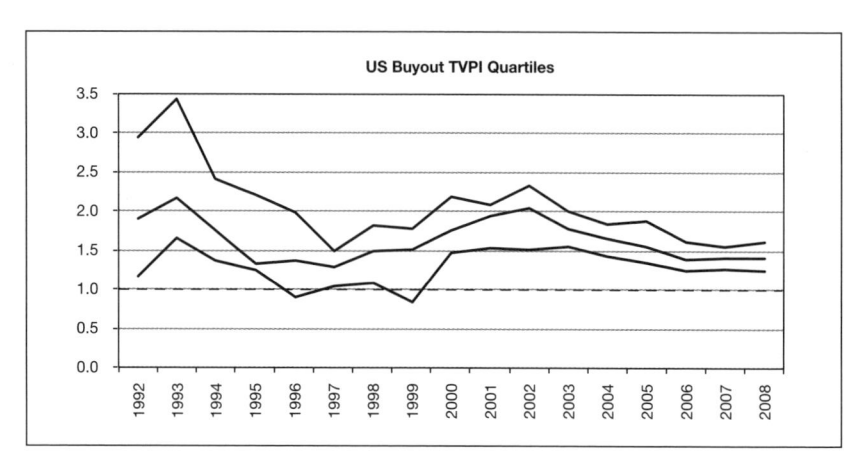

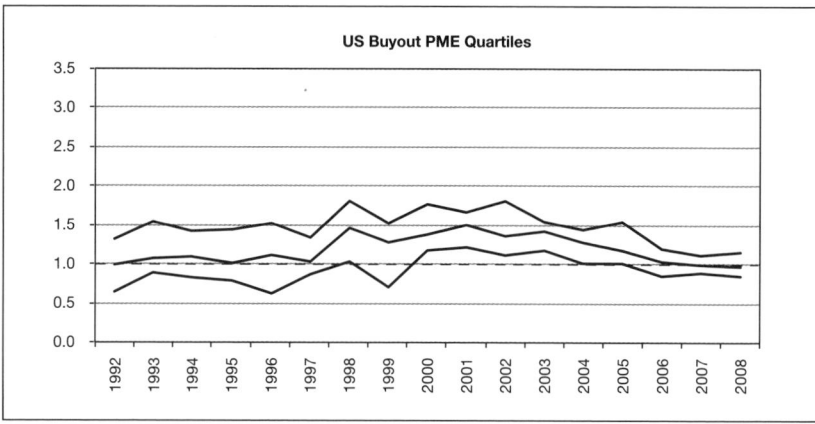

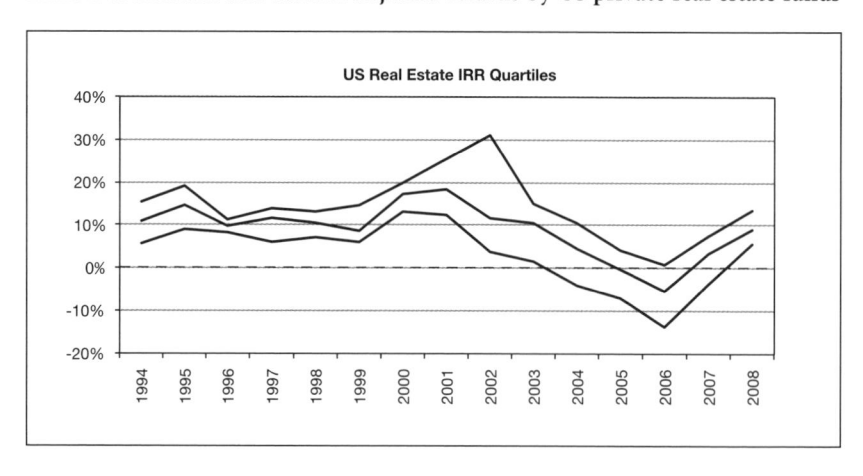

Exhibit 6: Absolute and market-adjusted returns by US private real estate funds

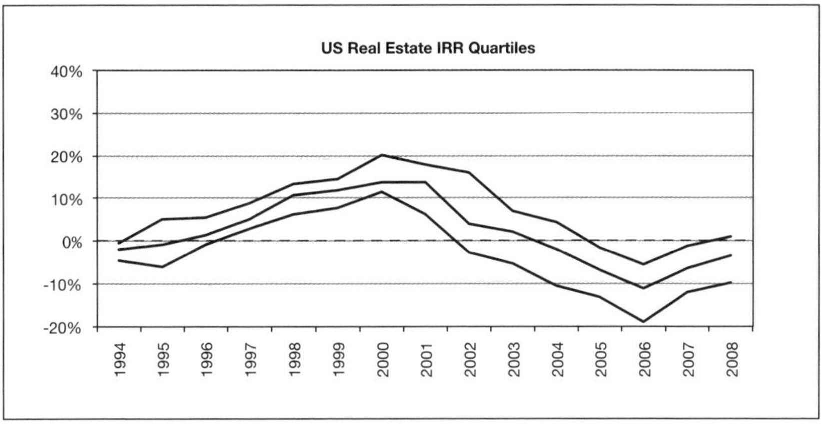
US Real Estate IRR Quartiles
40%
30%
20%
10%
0%
-10%
-20%
1994
1995
1996
1997
1998
1999
2000
2001
2002
2003
2004
2005
2006
2007
2008

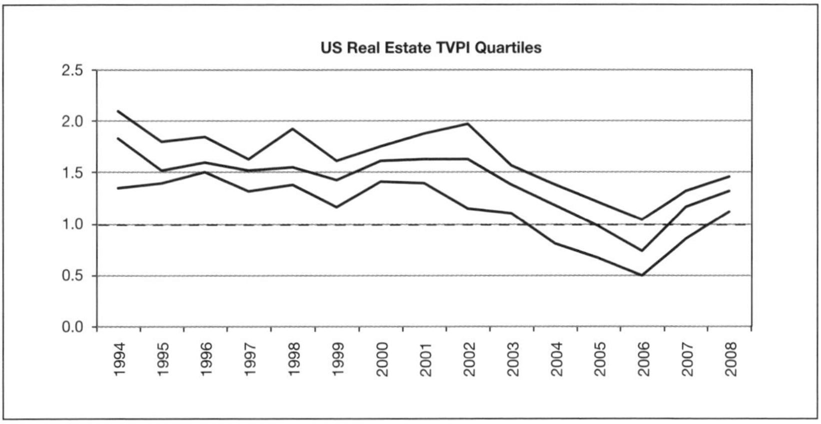
US Real Estate TVPI Quartiles
2.5
2.0
1.5
1.0
0.5
0.0
1994
1995
1996
1997
1998
1999
2000
2001
2002
2003
2004
2005
2006
2007
2008

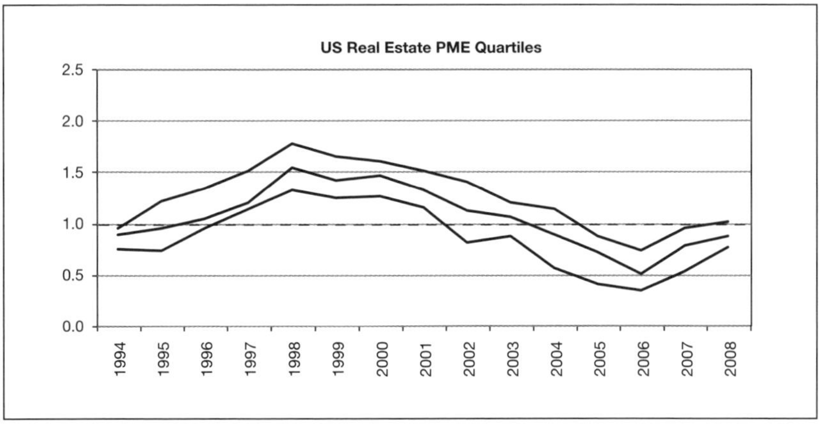
US Real Estate PME Quartiles
2.5
2.0
1.5
1.0
0.5
0.0
1994
1995
1996
1997
1998
1999
2000
2001
2002
2003
2004
2005
2006
2007
2008

Exhibit 7: Absolute and market-adjusted returns by western European buyout funds

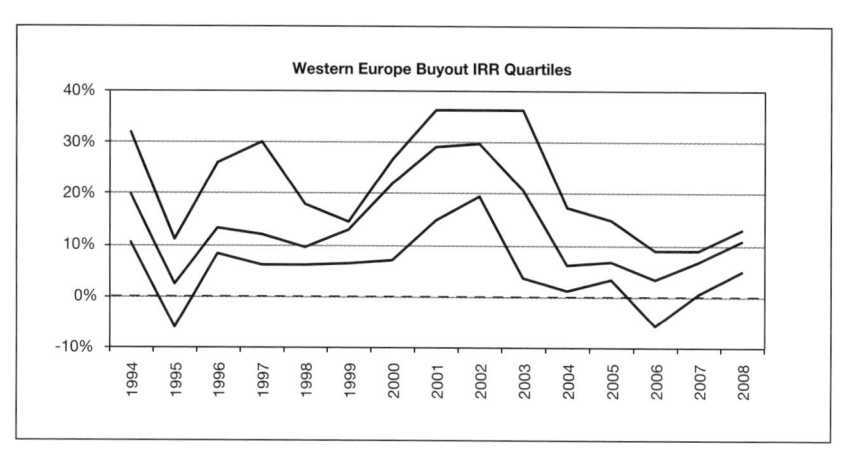

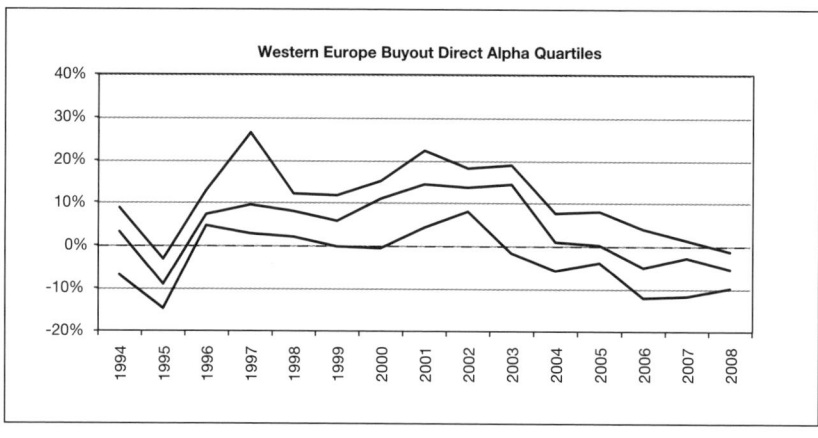

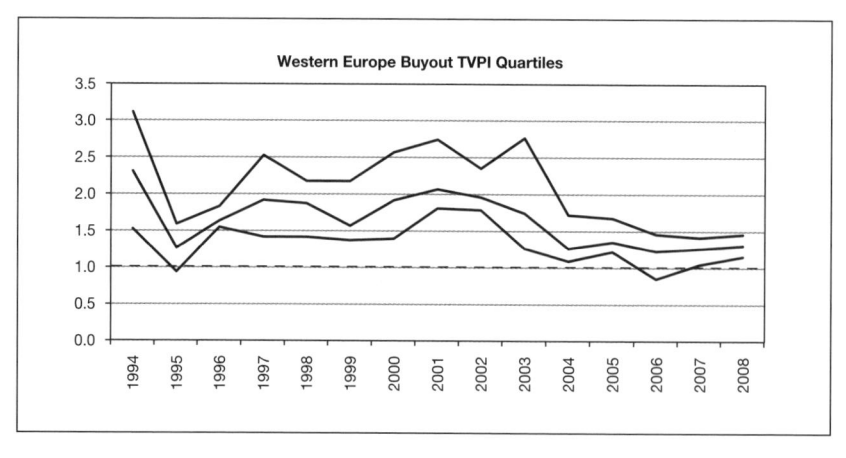

Western Europe Buyout PME Quartiles

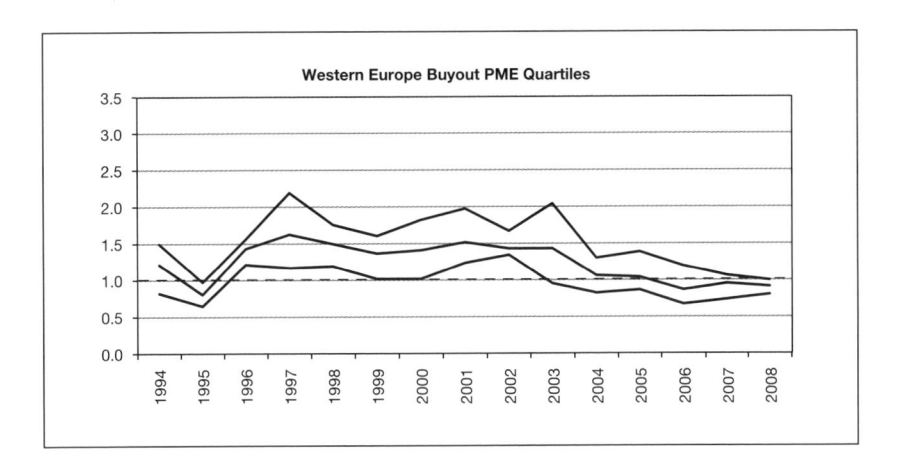

6. The risk of private equity

In the previous section we have compared the returns from US venture capital, buyout, and private real estate funds, as well as western European buyout funds, against the S&P 500. This is useful to the extent that many investors believe that their objective is to beat the S&P 500. However, it is really only a valid measure of risk-adjusted return if the S&P 500 represents the systematic risk inherent in private equity. It seems clear that the risk in private equity can be usefully related to some broad public index, but it can reasonably be argued that the beta of private equity should be materially higher than 1.0.

For example, leveraged buyout and private real estate investments typically involve significant amounts of debt, which makes the equity contribution of such funds particularly sensitive to changes in the equity market and the overall economy. Venture capital funds invest in young and risky companies, which are also highly sensitive to the overall market conditions. So the fact that a private equity fund has delivered returns above the S&P 500 is not indicative that it has also delivered better returns on a risk-adjusted basis.

Buchner and Stucke[11] provide an overview of beta estimations in the academic literature, as well as own estimations based on deal and fund level data.

In addition to the market risk, the illiquid nature of private equity adds a liquidity risk to an institutional investor's portfolio. In contrast to publicly-listed securities such as stocks and bonds, selling the interest in a private equity fund during its lifetime is less straightforward and typically associated with a certain discount on the position. Although secondary markets for limited partner interests in private equity funds have become increasingly liquid in recent years, reducing the exposure to private equity and turning a part of the portfolio into liquidity can require a certain amount of time.

Finally, investing in private equity is associated with a certain funding risk. Private equity funds typically call their capital over a five to six year investment period with only a short notice. To the extent to which such capital calls do not

---

11 Axel Buchner and Rüdiger Stucke, "The Systematic Risk of Private Equity", working paper (2014).

match with distributions from mature funds in an investor's portfolio, certain amounts of capital need to be held in liquid assets ready to be sold, or a credit facility needs to be in place.

We would like to thank James Bachman and Julia Bartlett from Burgiss for providing statistics of private equity fund returns.

This chapter reflects the personal experience and views of Barry Griffiths and Ruediger Stucke. It does not reflect the official position of Landmark Partners or Warburg Pincus LLC.

Regulation

Amy Mahon
Clifford Chance LLP

In the past year we have seen a number of regulatory changes which are of interest to the private equity community. The most fundamental of these was the coming into force of the EU Alternative Investment Fund Managers Directive 2011/61/EU (the AIFMD) on July 22 2013, which was implemented (in part) by the UK Alternative Investment Fund Managers Regulations. The second phase of the UK's carbon reduction programme, called the CRC Energy Efficiency Scheme, has also come into force and there have been some developments in merger control regulation and the approach taken on transactions. This chapter looks at these developments in turn and considers their implications for private equity transactions.

1. The Alternative Investment Fund Managers Directive (AIFMD)

1.1 Background

Very broadly, the AIFMD creates a panEuropean regulatory regime for managers (AIFMs) of alternative investment funds other than retail funds (AIFs), including private equity, hedge and real estate funds, that are managed or marketed in the EU. Much of the impact of the AIFMD is on the management and marketing of funds, but this chapter focuses on the impact the AIFMD has on merger and acquisition transactions involving AIFs or AIFMs.

The AIFMD imposes new notification, disclosure and anti-asset-stripping obligations on AIFMs in relation to acquisitions by AIFs of certain levels of voting rights in EU companies. These obligations are implemented in the United Kingdom by the Alternative Investment Fund Managers Regulations, which apply to UK AIFMs who hold a permission from the Financial Conduct Authority (FCA) to manage an AIF under the AIFMD (unless the AIFM has assets under management of less than €100 million or, for certain closedended, unleveraged AIFs, €500 million) and to AIFMs with a registered office outside the EU in relation to AIFs marketed by them in the UK on or after July 22 2013 using a private placement route prescribed under the Regulations. It therefore has implications for financial sponsors across the globe, unless they have no connection with the EU via the manager, fund entities or marketing activities.

There is a *de minimis* exemption for small and medium sized enterprises with fewer than 250 employees in the European Union and either an annual net turnover not exceeding €50 million or a balance sheet not exceeding €43 million.

Regulation

1.2 FCA notification obligations

The FCA voting rights notification provisions give rise to notification obligations in relation to non-listed companies (being companies whose shares are not admitted to trading on an EU regulated market) and apply throughout the life of the relevant portfolio investment. When an AIF of a relevant AIFM acquires, disposes of or holds shares in a nonlisted company, its AIFM must notify the FCA when the proportion of voting rights held reaches, exceeds or falls below the thresholds of 10, 20, 30, 50 and 75 per cent.

This obligation is most likely to be triggered where the percentage of voting rights held by the AIF reaches or crosses a relevant threshold as a result of the acquisition or disposal of a corresponding number of shares. However, the trigger is voting rights, which may not correlate to the number of shares acquired or disposed of. It could also be triggered as a result of events changing the breakdown of the nonlisted company's total voting rights in issue, such as a new issue of shares or buyback or redemption of existing shares. It is important, therefore, to bear this requirement in mind across a range of corporate actions of portfolio companies, as well as on merger and acquisition transactions.

Each AIF that becomes subject to a relevant notification obligation must notify the FCA by completing and filing a separate form. Where two or more AIFs of the same AIFM jointly have voting control, the FCA has confirmed that it is possible to complete the same form.

1.3 Disclosure obligations on acquisition of control

When an AIF of a relevant AIFM acquires control of a nonlisted company or an issuer (being a company whose shares are admitted to trading on an EU regulated market such as the London Stock Exchange), the FCA disclosure and anti-asset-stripping rules apply. 'Control' means holding more than 50% of the voting rights of a nonlisted company or between 30% and 33% of the voting rights of an issuer (depending where in the European Union the issuer's registered office is and how that jurisdiction has implemented the EU Takeovers Directive). For a company listed on the London Stock Exchange, the level is 30%. Voting rights held in a nonlisted company are calculated on the basis of all shares in the relevant company to which voting rights are attached, even if the exercise thereof is suspended. This is generally understood to include voting rights actually held by the AIF (even if the AIF has agreed not to exercise them), but to exclude contingent voting rights, for example, where it is contemplated that the AIF will or may acquire additional voting rights on the occurrence of specific future events such as pursuant to a ratchet or hurdle share structure or preference share terms. The acquisition group structure is looked through for the purposes of calculating the AIF's voting rights in the relevant nonlisted company. In relation to an issuer, the percentage of voting rights held is determined by, and calculated in accordance with, the provisions adopted in the Member State in which the issuer has its registered office to implement the provisions of the EU Takeovers Directive.

Under the disclosure provisions, the AIFM must notify the company, its shareholders and the FCA of the acquisition of control and provide them with details of the voting rights in the company, the identity of the shareholders and any person entitled to exercise voting rights on their behalf, any conditions subject to which control was acquired and the date on which control was acquired. The notifications must be given as soon as possible and at the latest within 10 working days of the date on which control is acquired. In the vast majority of private equity transactions the target company and its shareholders will be well aware of the transaction and therefore this notification obligation has little practical significance other than the notification to the FCA.

In addition, certain information must be provided to the company, its shareholders and the FCA upon request, including the identity of the AIFM, the policy for preventing and managing conflicts of interest, details of the safeguards to ensure that any relevant agreements are on an arm's length basis and the policy for communications, in particular as regards employees.

Where the target is a nonlisted company, the AIFM must, within 20 working days of the date on which control is acquired, also disclose its intentions with regard to the future business of the nonlisted company and the likely repercussions on employment, including any material change in the conditions of employment to the nonlisted company and its shareholders. It must also provide the FCA and the AIF's investors with information relating to the financing of the acquisition. It will be interesting to see the level of disclosure that results from this obligation.

For nonlisted companies, the AIFM must ensure that on an ongoing basis the company's annual report contains a fair review of the development of the nonlisted company's business, reference to any important events that have occurred during the year, information regarding the nonlisted company's likely future development and information concerning acquisitions and disposals of the nonlisted company's own shares.

The AIFM must ask the board of directors of the nonlisted company or issuer to give this information to the employees' representatives or the employees themselves without undue delay, and the AIFM must use its best efforts to ensure that the board complies with this request. However, where the communication of information to the employees' representatives (or employees) would "seriously harm the functioning of, or would be seriously prejudicial to" the company, the board of directors is not obliged to comply with the AIFM's request. Furthermore, the employee notification obligations are subject to certain confidentiality provisions,[1] which require Member States to prevent employee representatives from revealing to employees or third parties information that, in the legitimate interests of the relevant undertaking, has been expressly provided in confidence.

1.4 Prohibition on asset-stripping

The anti-asset-stripping provisions are triggered when an AIF of a relevant AIFM individually or jointly acquires control of a nonlisted company or an issuer. Relevant AIFMs with portfolio companies with minority or consortium investors whose

---

[1] These are the confidentiality provisions set out in the Information and Consultation of Employees Directive (2002/14/EC).

constitution provides for differentiated or fluctuating voting rights will obviously need to consider these provisions carefully. For the two years following the acquisition of control, the AIFM must not facilitate, instruct, or vote for any distribution, capital reduction, share redemption or acquisition of own shares by the nonlisted company or issuer subject to some limited carve-outs. As a consequence, private companies under the ownership of relevant AIFs are effectively subject (for a two-year period) to the same restrictions on distributions to which public companies are subject under the Companies Act 2006, losing the benefit of various relaxations on distributions and equivalent corporate actions otherwise enjoyed by private companies in the United Kingdom. These provisions restrict the ability of an AIF to do a dividend recapitalisation of a portfolio company where such recapitalisation involves a distribution on shares or a return of share capital, for a period of two years. As with other capital maintenance rules however, these prohibitions do not limit AIFs receiving returns from, or being repaid, shareholder loans. In practice therefore, while the anti-asset-stripping rules severely limit the flexibility that would otherwise be available to AIFs under English law, where a refinancing is contemplated within the first two years of control, equity funded by way of a shareholder loan may be refinanced in the same way as has historically been the case.

Distributions that reduce net assets below the level of subscribed capital plus undistributable reserves (as determined by reference to the company's annual accounts on the closing date of the last financial year) are therefore prohibited. Distributions that exceed distributable profits plus any profits brought forward and sums drawn from reserves available at the end of the last financial year are also prohibited. Furthermore, distributions will not be permitted by reference to interim accounts if the most recent audited accounts do not show sufficient surplus net assets or distributable profits. While it is open for a company to change its year-end to facilitate a distribution that would be justified by more recent accounts, this may have some other unwanted consequences.

Acquisitions of own shares or share redemptions that reduce net assets below the level of subscribed capital plus undistributable reserves, as determined by reference to the company's annual accounts, are also prohibited. This broadly correlates to the existing restrictions for UK public companies incorporated under the Companies Act 2006 on acquisitions of own shares and share redemptions out of capital. Again the impact of this is that the flexibility afforded to private companies to perform share buy-backs out of capital under the Companies Act 2006[2] is negated for two years following the acquisition.

All capital reductions are prohibited other than where the purpose is (i) to offset losses incurred, or (ii) to credit an amount (being not more than 10% of the reduced subscribed capital) to a non-distributable reserve of the company. From the wording of the Regulations, it appears that a capital reduction will be subject to the prohibition even where there is no actual distribution to shareholders. For example, a capital reduction for the purpose of creating a reserve in excess of the permitted 10% to improve the relevant company's balance sheet, rather than to distribute cash

---

2   Section 709 of the Companies Act 2006.

to the AIF, is prohibited. The impact of this is that private companies lose the relatively recently introduced but frequently used 'solvency statement' route of reducing capital under English law[3] for two years following the acquisition.

At the time of writing there is some uncertainty around which companies these restrictions apply to. Neither the AIFMD nor the Regulations address how these provisions should apply where a target group rather than a single entity is being acquired, which will be the case in the vast majority of private equity transactions. Under the AIFMD and the Regulations the anti-asset-stripping restrictions are expressed to attach to the EU nonlisted company or issuer in respect of which the acquisition of voting control by the AIF has triggered the application of the regime. Where a target group is being acquired, the industry view appears to be that the restriction attaches to the 'top' qualifying nonlisted company (with a registered office in the European Union and not qualifying for the *de minimis* exemption) that has been the subject of the change of control and, importantly, not also to its subsidiary undertakings. This is thought to be consistent with the political objective behind Article 30 of the AIFMD, which is to prevent AIFs from acquiring an existing business and extracting value in a way that affects its viability, rather than potentially preventing ordinary course intra-group activities below that level, including declaring dividends from one group company to another, provided there is no distribution up to the AIF itself.

The anti-asset-stripping restrictions apply for two years following the acquisition of voting control. However, the AIFM's obligations are not expressly linked to the period within which its AIF retains a controlling (or indeed any) interest in the company, and the AIFM is obliged to use its best efforts to prevent the company effecting any restricted transactions during the two-year period. It seems logical that the anti-asset-stripping restrictions should fall away if the AIF ceases to have a controlling interest in the company, but the Regulations do not expressly state this to be the case. Despite this 'best efforts' obligation, it is difficult to see industry practice moving to a position where private equity sellers would need to extract mirror undertakings from third-party purchasers for the remainder of the two-year period. On secondaries, a new private equity buyer within the scope of these rules will be subject to a new two-year restriction itself in any event.

The FCA has indicated that it will be providing guidance on these and other provisions in the Regulations, which will hopefully confirm the general consensus.

The notification and disclosure obligations will need to be built into the transaction process on merger and acquisition transactions to ensure these disclosures are not impacted by any sale documentation. It will also be advisable for AIFs to include in the investment agreement for the portfolio company provisions facilitating the relevant disclosures that are required by the AIFM. It may be appropriate to include contractual obligations prohibiting the breach of the anti-asset-stripping rules particularly on consortium transactions and in arrangements with management.

---

3   Section 642 of the Companies Act 2006.

2. The CRC Energy Efficiency Scheme

The CRC Energy Efficiency Scheme is central to the UK's strategy for improving energy efficiency and reducing carbon dioxide emissions, as set out in the Climate Change Act 2008. The CRC Scheme is intended to incentivise greater energy efficiency in large non-energy-intensive organisations operating in the United Kingdom in both the public and private sectors. The CRC Scheme has caused some disquiet among private equity funds (now as well as when it was first introduced) as it requires undertakings to participate in the scheme on a group basis, as one 'CRC participant'. Broadly speaking, companies controlled by a general partner (or fund manager) will be grouped together for the purposes of the CRC Scheme and liability for compliance with the scheme is placed jointly and severally on all entities within the relevant CRC participant. While private equity firms are not opposed to the CRC Scheme as such, the concern is the requirement to group portfolio companies together rather than treat them as separate standalone entities (which is the reality of how they are operated). This grouping caused some consternation for private equity funds when the CRC Scheme was first introduced (and subsequently) as it undermined a number of important principles underpinning private equity fund structures, namely that each portfolio company in a fund is separate to every other portfolio company in such fund, that parallel partnerships or other vehicles comprising a fund are treated independently and, even more critically, that independent funds managed by the same general partner or general partners in the same corporate group might be aggregated, depending on the structure. Having joint and several liability across distinct businesses is problematic and inappropriate for many reasons. This grouping arises because of the definition of 'group' that is used by the CRC Scheme, which is derived from the definitions of parent and subsidiary undertakings in Section 1162 of the Companies Act. There was significant lobbying on behalf of the private equity community to try to explain that this particular group definition was not appropriate in the context of private equity funds, but the Department of Energy and Climate Change declined to amend it.

The CRC Scheme has been reformed for its second phase (confusingly renamed to be called the 'initial phase') and now operates effectively as a tax on energy consumption (rather than a 'cap and trade' scheme as it was originally envisaged). Under the reformed scheme for the initial phase, any business that exceeded the trigger amount of electricity consumption in the qualification year (April 1 2012 to March 31 2013) is caught by the CRC Scheme and will have to register and comply with it. The trigger amount is annual UK electricity consumption exceeding 6,000 megawatt hours (MWh) in total across the group during the qualification year, which is equivalent to an annual bill of approximately £500,000. This applies to all UK companies, irrespective of where the parent company of the CRC participant is based, which means that any non-UK portfolio companies with UK subsidiaries will be caught. Phase 1 runs from April 1 2010 to March 31 2014. Phase 2 (the 'initial phase') runs from April 1 2014 to March 31 2019.

2.1 Implications of the CRC Scheme for a general partner

As a first step, a general partner needs to analyse which entities within its group (as defined under the CRC Scheme) should form part of a potential CRC participant. Each portfolio company must be analysed up the chain of control to assess where the ultimate parent undertaking is, and is then grouped with every other undertaking controlled by such parent undertaking. That entire group is a potential CRC participant, which must then:

- analyse the electricity consumption of the combined group and determine whether its organisation therefore qualifies for the CRC Scheme based on its electricity consumption;
- consider what changes to its structure – such as acquisitions, disposals, or restructurings at fund or portfolio level – have occurred since March 31 2013, as these may be relevant for identifying the structure and members of the relevant CRC participants, and to information required for registration;
- choose a 'primary member/compliance account holder' for each CRC participant to act as the principal liaison with the regulator; this must be a member of the CRC participant with its principal place of business in the UK;
- register online for the CRC Scheme: the registration period started on November 4 2013 and ended on January 31 2014 for the initial phase; and
- from April 2014 (and in each April thereafter), estimate its annual energy consumption, determine its CRC-regulated consumption and acquire allowances to cover that consumption; a new twice-yearly fixed-price sale of allowances is being introduced from the initial phase.

The first sale applications took place during April 2014 with payment in June 2014. Compliance sale applications (at a slightly higher price) will be made in June/July 2015 (after the end of the 2014/2015 compliance year) with payment in September 2015. This twice-yearly sale structure is intended to encourage accurate forecasting of energy consumption at the beginning of the year and reductions in energy consumption, with the second annual sale allowing CRC participants to acquire the balance of allowances where necessary for compliance purposes. Trading of surplus allowances and banking for future years will be permitted subject to certain rules and restrictions.

A general partner can decide to elect that certain undertakings within a CRC participant (for example whole portfolio groups) should take part in the CRC Scheme on a standalone basis. In order for this to be effective from the beginning of the initial phase, the relevant CRC participant must have registered as a whole by January 31 2014 and consent to the 'disaggregation', and the disaggregating entities must have registered separately by April 30 2014. A positive development for the initial phase is that there is much greater flexibility to disaggregate groups of undertakings from the CRC participant than there was in relation to Phase 1, which is helpful in assisting funds achieve the aim of treating funds separately and the portfolio companies within a fund separately. In particular, CRC participants are now given an opportunity for disaggregation on an annual basis.

It will be important to put in place a compliance function for each CRC participant and reporting lines through the organisation to ensure ongoing compliance and supply of relevant information, and to consider whether environmental advisers are required to assist with this.

2.2 Impact on transactions

Although the CRC Scheme may not be the most business-critical focus of a due diligence exercise, CRC participant status and the level of emissions should be covered as a diligence item on transactions, including bolt-ons or disposals. Consideration should be given to whether warranty and indemnity protection is appropriate, although it is rare to request or obtain any suitable warranties and indemnities in relation to compliance and scheme costs. Transactions involving 'participant equivalents' (those individual undertakings that would have passed the qualification threshold on their own) need to be notified to the regulator.

It is important to ensure that the investment documentation for portfolio companies provides the sponsor funds with sufficient information and record-keeping requirements to enable the primary member to perform its obligations, and addresses funding and allocation of allowances to enable future compliance. Loan facilities and other financing documentation also need to permit the funding and allocation of allowances.

3. Merger control

On every merger and acquisition transaction, the antitrust position must be considered, and many transactions involving private equity funds will trigger filings given the turnover of the funds involved. In the United Kingdom, a new competition regulator, the Competition and Markets Authority (the CMA), took over from the Competition Commission and assumed certain consumer functions of the Office of Fair Trading in April 2014. The CMA has jurisdiction to carry out all reviews under UK merger control laws (and all market investigations), with enhanced powers to freeze integration by imposing hold-separate obligations on the merging parties and, in some cases, preventing completion during the Phase I review – something that cannot be prevented under the current regime – as well as Phase II. A binding review deadline of 40 working days and information-gathering powers will be introduced for Phase I. While this should result in faster Phase I reviews, as at EU level, pre-notification is likely to become standard practice such that the overall time period in front of the regulator is unlikely to change materially. Of note is the sharp increase in filing fees – up to as much as £160,000 for deals involving targets with turnover of over £120 million. The regime will remain voluntary, and consequently these changes are likely to be of most relevance to private equity funds in the context of portfolio companies doing bolt-on acquisitions where there is overlap and a strategy to achieve synergies. In such cases, private equity funds may be more inclined to pre-notify and complete only after clearance has been obtained given the likely significant burdens on the parties associated with the CMA's enhanced hold-separate powers.

In addition to the new UK regulator, there has also been a proliferation of merger control regulation generally. Over 100 jurisdictions worldwide now have merger control laws, and many have foreign investment restrictions that must be considered. On that basis, it seems we should expect antitrust regulation to play an increasing role in private equity transactions.

Protectionism is also increasing. This can take the form of standalone foreign investment rules, which exist in various jurisdictions including Canada, the United States (the Committee on Foreign Investment in the United States), Brazil (for rural property), Russia (for 'strategic entities'), Finland, China and Australia. Some jurisdictions such as China and South Africa also include factors other than competition in their merger control reviews (such as, in South Africa, impacts on employment, small businesses and national champions). As a consequence, numerous filings and regimes may be required on transactions, which will impact on timing and transaction certainty.

On many private equity transactions there is no substantive risk and yet, particularly in an auction sale context, falling outside the scope of certain regimes usually provides a bidder with a competitive advantage. As a consequence, on consortium deals it is not unusual for private equity funds to adopt a shifting alliance structure such that, at least for the purposes of the EU Merger Regulation, there is no controlling shareholder and as such no notification is required. It is worth noting, however, that the European Commission is currently consulting on possible amendments to the EU Merger Regulation to capture non-controlling minority stakes. The proposals range from a German-style system of mandatory filing for all minority interests meeting certain criteria – which would be immensely disruptive for private equity consortium bids – to a UK-style voluntary filing regime, with reviews limited to those transactions that are most likely to harm competition, such as minority stakes in direct competitors. This is an area worth monitoring. In deciding whether to pursue particularly competitive auction processes, many private equity funds will assess the regulatory position of the competing bidders to determine whether their own filing requirements and consequent conditionality on deals means they are at a significant disadvantage to the rest of the field.

3.1   **Impact on transaction documents**
Most sellers will require comprehensive disclosure of a private equity buyer's regulatory position, and it is a market norm in the United Kingdom (if not also Europe) for the only conditions to a sale and purchase agreement to be mandatory and suspensory regulatory conditions. In certain regulated sectors, such as utilities or financial services, consent from the industry regulator will be required, and many private equity funds will require antitrust clearance in various jurisdictions also.

Where a private equity fund has overlaps in its portfolio that might present a risk of a merger clearance being denied or delayed, it is increasingly common for the seller to demand 'hell or high water' provisions, which shift risk to the private equity buyer which is required to use its best efforts to obtain clearances, including offering divestments and remedies in connection with its entire portfolio in addition to the specific target. Many funds shy away from agreeing to this as a precedent, but on competitive sale processes some private equity fund bidders will agree to these provisions where they are confident that there is no overlap or risk of the regulator requiring remedies to clear a transaction.

An alternative method of providing comfort to a seller is for a buyer to provide a reverse break fee payable if the buyer fails to satisfy a condition. However reverse break fees remain very unusual on deals in the UK market, particularly with financial sponsor buyers. The EMI/Universal deal involved a take-or-pay provision, which shifted financial risk to the buyer. Under a take-or-pay provision, the buyer pays the seller full price for the target, even if clearances are not obtained by the longstop date. Such clauses are unlikely to be seen on private equity transactions and they need to be structured so as to avoid gun-jumping concerns. Nonetheless, with an increased focus on merger control globally, we should expect to see private equity buyers being forced to assume greater risk on merger control issues on more transactions. This being the case, early planning of merger strategy, ensuring a consistent narrative across various jurisdictions and a consistent approach to filings will be important for private equity funds.

Tax structuring and management

Kathleen Russ
Travers Smith

The UK tax issues that arise in relation to private equity deals are broadly the same as those that would arise in relation to any other merger or acquisition. The significant differences that arise on private equity deals flow from the tax considerations of the private equity fund investors and the managers. These can be summarised as follows and are discussed in more detail below:
- The private equity fund's tax structure and investors' tax requirements will affect the deal structure;
- The acquisition structure must optimise leverage and minimise tax leakage during the investment period;
- The UK managers' tax aims are to minimise the tax charges on acquiring their equity and only capital gains tax on the sale; and
- The structuring must be exit focused.

A typical tax structure for private equity deals given these considerations is outlined in the diagram below and each issue noted is described in more detail.

1. **The current climate**
   UK government's need to increase its tax revenues, coupled with press criticism of any company perceived as not paying its 'fair share' of tax, has made tax avoidance a hot topic in recent years. Companies that have been publicly shamed for minimising the amount of tax they pay have suffered reputational damage; as a result, private equity firms are increasingly cautious about this issue. In addition, the UK government is tightening up its tax legislation to reduce the opportunities available to companies and individuals to mitigate their tax liabilities. Examples of this changing legislative landscape are discussed in this chapter, including the introduction of a general anti-abuse rule (see Section 3.1) and the barring of individuals from claiming compensating adjustments in certain circumstances (see Section 3.5).

2. **Tax structure of private equity fund and investors' tax requirements**
   Most private equity funds are structured in the form of one or more limited partnerships. The investors in the private equity fund are the limited partners. The limited partnership as such is generally not subject to tax at the partnership level, as it is fiscally transparent. This means that the fund cannot benefit from tax treaties, because tax treaty protection can be invoked only by the investing entities or persons that are subject to tax in their country of residence.

Tax structuring and management

Broadly speaking, limited partners receive two types of returns: income-type returns (dividends and interest) and capital returns.

If the private equity fund receives interest or dividends from Newco, Newco may be obliged under local rules to withhold tax on the interest or dividend payments. In some situations, the withholding tax liability is partially reduced because some of the investors can claim double taxation treaty protection under the tax treaty concluded between their home country and the country in which Newco is situated, as the fund is tax transparent. For other investors, the withholding tax will be a real cost, and private equity funds therefore seek to avoid such withholdings. This is discussed in more detail below.

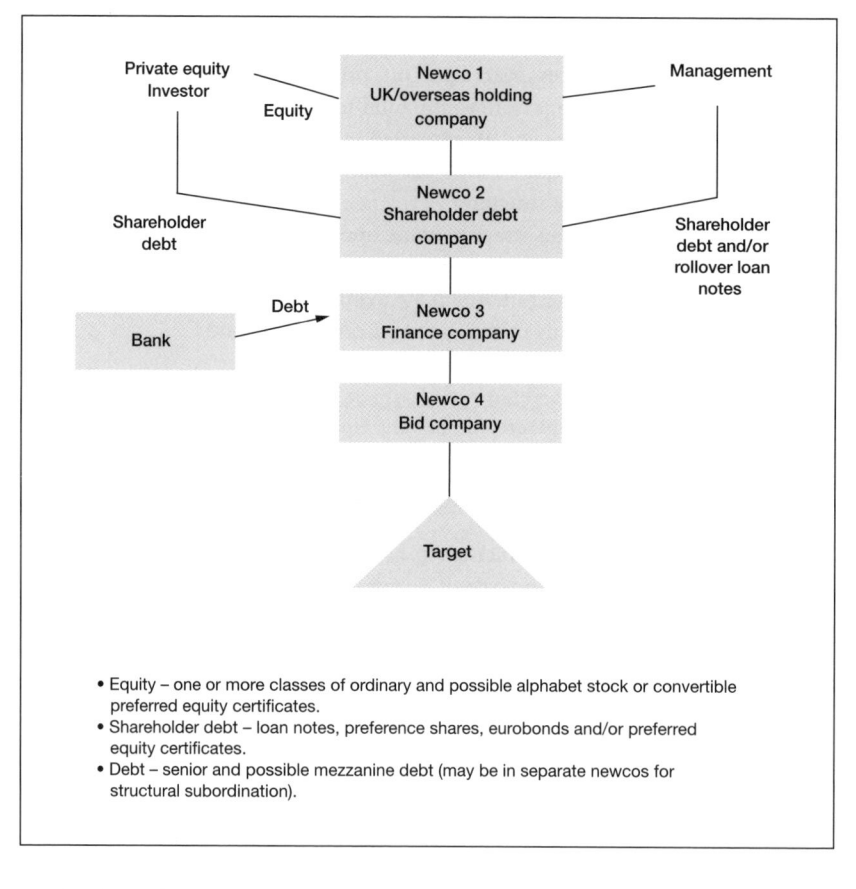

```
                Private equity              Newco 1                  Management
                  Investor              UK/overseas holding
                              Equity        company


              Shareholder              Newco 2                    Shareholder
                 debt               Shareholder debt              debt and/or
                                       company                    rollover loan
                                                                     notes

                              Debt        Newco 3
                 Bank                  Finance company


                                          Newco 4
                                         Bid company


                                           Target
```

- Equity – one or more classes of ordinary and possible alphabet stock or convertible preferred equity certificates.
- Shareholder debt – loan notes, preference shares, eurobonds and/or preferred equity certificates.
- Debt – senior and possible mezzanine debt (may be in separate newcos for structural subordination).

Similarly, the private equity fund will wish to ensure that there is no local capital gains taxation on exit, when the fund sells the shares of Newco 1. A number of Organisation for Economic Cooperation and Development countries (but not the United Kingdom) still apply such a capital gains tax charge, but structuring should ensure that treaty protection against such capital gains taxation can be obtained by interposing a holding company between the fund and Newco 1. Whatever jurisdiction is chosen for the location of the offshore holding company, it is important to provide the offshore holding company with sufficient 'substance' in order to qualify as a genuine treaty resident of the chosen country.

Assuming that non-resident capital gains tax charges can be avoided, limited partners will be subject to capital gains on investments under the rules governing their state of residence. As a general principle, capital treatment is preferable to income treatment. Capital treatment is normally available on complete exits or divestments. However, planning is also often implemented to deal with partial exits with a view to seeking capital (rather than income) treatment on that partial exit.

Examples include the use of 'alphabet stock' or convertible preferred equity certificates that are drafted so that, under local law, they can be redeemed by class, converted or bought back to return value in a way which is a return of capital.

Other issues requiring consideration are those that affect US investors in private equity funds. These include the potential for US investors to suffer tax on an accruals basis (a 'dry tax' charge) if the investment gave rise to original issue discount. Other issues that US investors in private equity funds need to consider include the need to avoid unrelated business income tax arising (usually by ensuring that debt finance is issued by a corporate entity rather than the fund) and the controlled foreign corporation and passive foreign investment company anti-deferral regimes.

In all jurisdictions, it is important to check the tax position of the private equity fund's executives to ensure that the appropriate elections are being made to protect any co-invest or carried interest taken under the laws of the relevant jurisdiction. For example, elections under Section 431 of the UK Income Tax (Earnings and Pensions) Act 2003 or Section 83(b) of the US Internal Revenue Code should be considered at both fund and management level.

3. Structure of acquisition to optimise leverage and minimise tax

3.1 General anti-abuse rule (GAAR)

The GAAR legislation, contained in Part 5 of the Finance Act 2013, is intended to target 'abusive tax arrangements' that avoid the payment of income tax, corporation tax, national insurance contributions and capital gains tax (among others) and were entered into on or after July 17 2013. The legislation is widely drafted, and will therefore need to be considered by tax advisers when implementing any arrangement that tries to reduce the tax liabilities of the institutional investors, management and the investee company.

In order to fall within the provisions of the GAAR, there must be an abusive tax arrangement that gives rise to a tax advantage:

- Tax arrangement – arrangements are 'tax arrangements' if it can be reasonably concluded that obtaining a 'tax advantage' was the main purpose, or one of the main purposes, of the arrangements.
- Tax advantage – the legislation states that a 'tax advantage' includes any relief or increased relief from tax, any repayment or increased repayment of tax, any avoidance or reduction of a charge/assessment to tax, any avoidance of possible assessment to tax, any deferral of a payment of tax or any avoidance of an obligation to deduct or account for tax.

- Abusive arrangements – tax arrangements are 'abusive' if they are arrangements the entering into or carrying out of which cannot reasonably be regarded as a reasonable course of action in relation to the relevant tax provisions (the 'double reasonableness test'). This should take into account the principles (express or implied) and policy objectives of the provisions, any contrived or abnormal steps taken to receive a tax advantage and any exploitation of shortcomings in the provisions. However, the GAAR guidance does recognise that:

    > under the UK's detailed tax rules taxpayers frequently have a choice as to the way in which transactions can be carried out, and that differing tax results arise depending on the choice that is made. The GAAR does not challenge such choices unless they are considered abusive.

An independent advisory panel has been established and is tasked with reviewing and updating the GAAR guidance as well as receiving referrals from officers of Her Majesty's Revenue and Customs (HMRC) (who have been specifically appointed for the purposes of the GAAR) on which they provide non-binding opinions as to whether or not arrangements constitute a reasonable course of action.

The GAAR guidance sets out HMRC's and the advisory panel's interpretation of the GAAR provisions, as well as setting out examples of arrangements that those parties currently consider to be abusive/non-abusive under the GAAR. While the legislation obliges courts and tribunals to take the guidance into account when considering whether the GAAR applies to any particular arrangements, they are not bound by its content.

If any abusive tax arrangements are subject to counteraction under the GAAR, any tax advantage created by such arrangements would be subject to such adjustments as are just and reasonable.

3.2 Acquisition vehicle

A new company is invariably incorporated to acquire the target group or its assets rather than the shares or assets being acquired direct. The reason for this is that it provides a clean vehicle into which debt can be lent, and in which management and the private equity house can subscribe for equity in the appropriate proportions.

The question of the jurisdiction in which Newco should be incorporated depends largely on the jurisdictions in which the target business is operated and where effective management and control can practically be maintained. The structuring will also take account of jurisdictions with high tax bills and the ability to use leverage to reduce certain tax liabilities. As noted above, the holding jurisdiction should also allow investors to take out proceeds in a tax-efficient form prior to exit and to receive gross proceeds from the sale of their shares in Newco.

3.3 Shares or assets

There are significant differences from a tax perspective between acquiring shares and assets of a target. These are outlined below, but Newco will invariably acquire the shares in a target. The main consequences are as follows:

- A UK corporate seller may be able to sell shares in a subsidiary without crystallising a charge to corporation tax if the conditions of the substantial shareholding exemption are met. This relief cannot generally be claimed on the sale of assets, and an asset sale may therefore generate a significant corporation tax charge where the base cost in the assets is low. However, since July 2011, if a degrouping charge arises in a corporate seller as a result of a previous intra-group asset transfer to a subsidiary that is now being sold, that degrouping charge may be extinguished if the conditions of the substantial shareholding exemption are met.
- An individual seller cannot benefit from the substantial shareholding exemption and will instead look to benefit from capital gains tax treatment. If assets are sold, a double layer of tax will arise – that is, the company will suffer tax on the sale of the assets and the individual will suffer tax on the extraction of the proceeds of sale (which would usually take the form of a dividend taxed at an effective rate of 30.6% (at the rates applicable for 2014/15) for higher-rate taxpayers).
- A purchaser inherits the tax history of the target when shares are acquired, but not when assets are acquired. However, the practicalities of transferring the assets of a large business usually favour a share sale. On a share sale, a purchaser often requires the seller to protect the purchaser from inherited tax risks by entering into a tax indemnity and tax warranties. By contrast, a purchaser may benefit by inheriting tax losses in the target (although whether these will be available going forward requires detailed analysis).
- A purchaser may benefit from capital allowances or corporation tax relief on the acquisition of certain capital or intangible assets such as intellectual property and goodwill, but the seller may suffer balancing charges or realise a disposal under the same regime. This relief is not available for investors on an acquisition of shares.
- A purchaser will have to pay 0.5% stamp duty on the consideration paid on the acquisition of shares, whereas most assets can be acquired free from stamp duty (save for land and certain debts).

3.4 Debt or equity funding

The extent to which a deal should be debt-funded rather than equity-funded will be driven by both commercial and tax considerations. The commercial advantage of using debt funding as opposed to equity funding in UK private equity transactions is the greater flexibility offered by company law in repaying debt. From a tax perspective, the historical advantage is that the interest costs of the debt funding can be tax deductible, thereby reducing the target group's taxable profits. In addition, the costs incurred in relation to raising finance are deductible, whereas those in relation to equity will be capital in most situations. However it is now more difficult to obtain a deduction for debt financing costs.

3.5 Availability of UK corporate tax deductions for debt interest

The tax treatment of interest (and related costs) under UK law is complex, but starts from the position that Newco should be able to obtain corporation tax relief for interest on an accruals basis in line with the accrual treated as a debit for accounting purposes.

However, the availability of this relief is subject to a number of restrictions.

First, the UK loan relationship rules disallow interest relief for a borrowing taken out for a tax avoidance purpose (Section 441 of the Corporation Tax Act 2009). The scope of this provision is outside the scope of this chapter, but should be considered in relation to re-financings in a private equity context.

Secondly, interest payments can be re-characterised as a distribution under UK rules (and those of certain other jurisdictions). If these rules apply, the borrowing company will be unable to claim relief for these purposes.

Interest can be re-characterised as a distribution under UK tax law where, broadly:
- the rate of interest is excessive, in which case distribution treatment applies to the extent that it exceeds a reasonable commercial return for the use of the principal secured;
- the rate of interest is dependent on the results of the group, except where the rate increases if the results deteriorate or decreases if the results improve, or where certain exceptions apply such as the interest being paid to another UK corporation taxpayer;
- the debt instrument carries rights to further shares in the borrower or loan stock with conversion rights into shares or loan stock in the borrower (unless the loan stock is listed on a recognised stock exchange or the terms of the loan stock are comparable to those of listed debt, or unless the lender is a UK corporation taxpayer); or
- the debt is stapled to equity (which means that the terms of the debt instrument require the holder to transfer shares it holds in the borrower if it transfers the debt instrument or if it would be advantageous for the holder to do so), unless the lender is a UK corporation taxpayer.

Thirdly, the UK transfer pricing rules deny the corporation tax deduction for interest payable between connected persons to the extent that it exceeds the interest that would have been payable if the transaction were between the parties at arm's length. The rules require an examination of the rate of return, level of debt and terms, on a transaction-by-transaction basis, as compared with those with a notional third-party lender not investing in equity (including considering whether a third party would have lent at all).

For the purposes of the UK transfer pricing rules the private equity fund investors, mezzanine lenders and management are treated as connected with the investee company so that the transfer pricing rules apply. Given the UK tax authorities' position, transaction modelling tends to assume deductions on a worst case basis until agreement can be reached with the tax authorities on the facts of that transaction.

Before October 25 2013, where interest deductions were denied in whole or part to the investee group under the transfer pricing rules, UK-resident holders of loan notes in respect of which that interest was due could sometimes reduce their taxable interest receipts by corresponding amounts. However, legislation introduced in the Finance Act 2014 implements new proposals that apply for any interest that accrues from October 25 2013 onwards – for this interest, individuals within the charge to income tax will not be able to claim corresponding adjustments where the other party to the transaction is a company, although receipt of the excess interest (above arm's length) will be charged as dividend income rather than interest income. The new provisions will not apply to interest that has accrued before October 25 2013 but which has not yet been paid (so that corresponding adjustments claims can still be made).

Fourthly, the leveraged nature of private equity transactions means that the banking documentation will invariably limit the investee group's ability to pay interest to connected lenders ahead of the bank lenders. This means that some or all of the interest rolls up until exit or an earlier refinancing. The question of whether a UK corporation tax interest deduction is available for the interest as it accrues, or only when it is paid, is governed by the late interest loan relationship rules in Part 5, Chapter 8 of the Corporation Tax Act 2009.

The UK loan relationship rules allow a corporation tax deduction for interest in line with the accounts accrual if the interest has been paid (in cash or in kind as described below) within 12 months of the end of the accounting period, or if the lender brings into account the full amount of the interest for corporation tax purposes, or is not connected to the borrower. These rules mean that without further planning (eg, by the issue of funding bonds providing for the payment of interest by the issue of further bonds), typical private equity deal structures funded by debt from a limited partnership, management shareholders or foreign lenders will often not benefit from the cashflow advantage of a deduction before the interest is paid.

The worldwide debt cap, contained within Schedule 15 of the Finance Act 2009, can also restrict further the tax deductions that UK corporate borrowers may claim in respect of interest costs. However the measures imposed by the worldwide debt cap do not have a material effect on most private equity backed groups.

Fifthly, the payment of interest in a UK company is subject to the obligation to withhold income tax at the rate of 20% unless one of the following exceptions applies:
- The interest is 'short interest' (where the term of the loan is not expected to exceed one year). This is unlikely to be the case in private equity transactions;
- The recipient is a UK-resident company or a UK permanent establishment subject to corporation tax on the receipt; or
- The recipient qualifies for double taxation treaty relief or satisfies the requirements of the EU Interest and Royalties Directive.

As most private equity transactions are funded by limited partnerships, the 20% tax withheld can be a real cost to investors, whereas the lending banks can often be paid gross within one of the exceptions above. Historically, many transactions were funded using deep discount bonds, as the repayment on redemption is a discount rather than interest and therefore is not subject to withholding tax. These have been used less frequently since the amendment to the late interest rules to deny a tax deduction for accruing interest or discount payable to a connected person.

As discussed above, some private equity funds have been able to use offshore funding vehicles in double taxation treaty jurisdictions, such as Luxembourg, to fund transactions. In such cases interest can be paid gross, subject to the application of the decision in *Indofood International Finance Limited v Chase Manhattan Bank* NA [2006] STC 1195. In order to benefit from treaty relief, the recipient must be the beneficial owner of the interest. HMRC's view of *Indofood* is that it establishes a principle in UK law that when interpreting double taxation treaties, beneficial ownership should be given an "international fiscal meaning", which requires that the recipient enjoys "the full privilege to directly benefit from the income". This means that if the non-UK (eg, Luxembourg) resident vehicle receives interest from a UK-resident company and has "clear obligations" or is "predestined" to forward that interest to a party that is not entitled to the benefit of a double taxation treaty with the United Kingdom (even if the vehicle makes a turn on the loan), there may be arguments that the interest will not benefit from the relevant (eg, Luxembourg–UK) treaty and must be paid net of UK withholding tax.

Another alternative is the use of quoted loan notes to fund the transaction. Provided that the notes are listed on a recognised exchange, such as the Channel Islands, payments of interest can be made gross in accordance with the quoted eurobonds exemption. This alternative is commonly used. Listing on the Channel Island's Securities Exchange was, until recently, straightforward and inexpensive. Changes to the listing regime in the Channel Islands mean that other exchanges may now be the preferred choice.

4. Managers' tax considerations

The satisfaction of managers' tax considerations is key to recruiting and incentivising the team from acquisition through to a successful exit. There are a number of ways in which the managers' UK tax position can be improved by ensuring that the deal structure takes account of managers' tax considerations. In those cases where the managers are resident in more than one jurisdiction, it will be important to coordinate the international tax advice in the best interests of all. For example, elections may be required to improve the tax position on a future sale of US managers' shares.

There are broadly two ways in which managers may fund their investment in Newco:

- Managers who are shareholders in the target vehicle may 'roll over' their holding of shares in the target vehicle by exchanging those shares for shares (and loan notes, if relevant) in Newco, in order to defer the payment of tax on the shares until the shares or loan notes are sold or redeemed.
- Managers may invest directly in shares and loan notes, using either their own funds, borrowed funds or the cash proceeds from the sale of shares in the target vehicle.

The UK managers' tax considerations on such investments generally relate to some or all of the following issues.

4.1 Funding investment in Newco

Managers who are shareholders in the target vehicle will be concerned to optimise the tax treatment on their proceeds. In those cases where the managers are required to reinvest all or part of their proceeds in exchange for shares and possible loan notes in Newco, the tax payable on their proceeds will affect the size of their reinvestment.

UK-resident manager shareholders in the target may be able to roll over their shares in the target for shares and/or loan notes in the acquiring company on a tax-free basis if the conditions in Section 135 of the Taxation Chargeable Gains Act 1992 can be satisfied. In order to ensure that this rollover is effective where there is more than one Newco in the acquiring structure, the UK managers must initially exchange their shares for loan notes issued by the acquisition Newco in the structure, and then exchange a proportion of those loan notes for shares up the corporate chain to the holding Newco (in the case of a double or triple Newco structure).

Advance clearance can be sought under Section 138 of the Taxation Chargeable Gains Act that the tax-free rollover treatment will not be denied on the grounds that the transaction is for the avoidance of tax or not for genuine commercial purposes. This will be relevant only to those managers who hold 5% or more of any class of the target's shares or securities. If this clearance is obtained, it will confirm that HMRC will not seek to set aside a rollover on the grounds that it was effected otherwise than for genuine commercial purposes, but clearance gives no comfort that the technical requirements of the relief have been satisfied.

The time taken to obtain clearance needs to be built into the transaction timetable. HMRC is entitled to take up to 30 days to review a clearance application and, if it seeks further information, is entitled to an additional 30 days upon receiving that further information. While HMRC will try to speed up its consideration of clearances where possible, this can never be guaranteed.

If the managers hold share options that are not HMRC-approved options or enterprise management incentive options or held interests under a long-term incentive plan, the managers' advisers should take account of the income tax and national insurance contributions (if any) deductible from their proceeds.

UK-resident managers that need to borrow to fund their investment in Newco 1 may be able to claim income tax relief for the interest on their borrowings. Interest relief is available if, among other things, the following conditions are satisfied:

- The relevant manager spends the greater part of his time in the actual management or conduct of the business, or controls more than 5% of the ordinary share capital of Newco 1.
- The manager's borrowings are in the form of a loan taken out specifically for the purpose of investing in Newco 1 (ie, not overdrafts, credit card or general borrowings).
- Newco 1 is 'close' for tax purposes at the time the shares are acquired. In broad outline, Newco 1 will be close if five or fewer shareholders, or directors who are shareholders, together hold more than 50% of the share capital of Newco. In order to ensure that Newco is close at the time the managers make their investment, it is generally necessary for them to invest before the institutional investors have subscribed for their shares.

- Newco 1 must also exist wholly or mainly for one or more of the purposes set out in Section 34 of the Corporation Tax Act 2010 (broadly, trading or the holding companies of one or more trading companies), which means that it must not be a close investment-holding company. On a strict interpretation of the law, this requirement may not be satisfied if Newco 1 is the top company of a triple/quadruple newco stack, because in order to be the holding company of a trading company (which would mean that a close company is not a close investment-holding company), Newco 1 must control a company that carries on a trade, which, in the case of Newco 2 or Newco 3 in the diagram shown above, would not be the case.

Where shares are subscribed to enable a shell newco that has not yet traded, but will acquire a trading business or trading subsidiary, the purpose of that company may still be the carrying on of such trading (*Lord v Tustain* [1993] STC 755), but in these circumstances it is important that Newco's memorandum of association or articles state that the object of the company is to be a holding company investing in a trading group.

Further, it is important that a corporation tax accounting period has commenced at the time the managers invest. This can be achieved by funding Newco with a small initial investment to buy a source of income (eg, a gilt) which will trigger the commencement of an accounting period.

4.2 Tax treatment of investment in Newco

A typical private equity transaction will involve the management team investing in ordinary shares in Newco. In addition, management may invest in:
- loan notes and/or preference shares issued by the acquiring vehicle, often on identical terms to those issued to the private equity house – these may be issued in proportion to additional ordinary equity as part of the 'institutional strip'; and
- guaranteed loan notes in lieu of cash consideration for any existing shareholding in the target vehicle – this will generally be to allow managers to realise gains in a later tax year.

Legislation in Part 7 of the Income Tax (Earnings and Pensions) Act 2003 deems that the acquisition of shares, loan notes or other securities by any UK-resident manager in a Newco group is made available by reason of employment. This means that the acquisition, holding and disposal of the shares may give rise to income tax and associated national insurance contribution liabilities. The aim for managers will be to avoid these charges so that the investment is subject only to capital gains tax, so that the tax charge on exit is now at 28%.

Entrepreneurs' relief was introduced with effect from April 6 2008 following the withdrawal of taper relief. This reduces the effective rate of capital gains tax to 10% on the disposal of qualifying business assets, provided that certain conditions are met. The qualifying capital gains for individuals are subject to a lifetime limit of £10 million for disposals on or after April 6 2011. If a manager benefits from entrepreneurs' relief, the importance of achieving capital gains treatment is therefore all the greater.

The potential income tax charges arise in the following way.

The acquisition of shares or securities by reason of employment at less than their market value is a taxable benefit. However, shares in a private equity-backed newco will usually constitute 'restricted securities' by virtue of the restrictions on their transfer, good leaver/bad leaver provisions and possible voting, dividend or other restrictions which reduce their value. The consequence of a security being restricted is that managers can elect, under Section 431(1) of the Income Tax (Earnings and Pensions) Act, to be charged income tax up front on the difference (if any) between the price that they pay and the security's initial unrestricted market value (ie, value ignoring the depressing effect on value of the restrictions), on the basis that any growth in value following the acquisition should then be subject only to capital gains tax.

If no election is made, the income tax charge is deferred until the removal of the restrictions or disposal of the shares, if earlier, and is on the proportion of the value of the shares when the disposal or removal of restrictions occurs that the undervalue paid for the shares originally represented as a proportion of the full value. So if the manager paid half of the initial unrestricted market value, half of the market value is subject to income tax on the disposal or removal of the restrictions. In practice, this can mean that if shares are acquired at an undervalue, an income tax charge can arise even if, when the shares are sold, their value has decreased. If the shares are readily convertible assets at the time a charge arises, employee and employer national insurance contributions (13.8% employer rate in 2014/15) will be due in addition to income tax. As this would represent a real cost for Newco on exit, private equity transaction documents invariably require all UK-resident managers to make elections under Section 431 of the Income Tax (Earnings and Pensions) Act within the 14-day time limit after the acquisition of the securities, even in cases where it is clear that the initial unrestricted market value has been paid or that the memorandum of understanding between the British Venture Capital Association and HMRC (see below) applies, making it strictly unnecessary.

Where the managers make Section 431 elections and have paid less than the initial unrestricted market value – or where it is unclear what the initial unrestricted market value is – a valuation will be required in order to determine the tax payable. An independent valuation is generally considered appropriate for these purposes, but as HMRC may later challenge it, the managers and the private equity house often agree in the documentation on who should bear the tax risk of a higher valuation and tax charge.

In order to avoid the costs of such valuations across all private equity transactions, the British Venture Capital Association agreed a memorandum of understanding with HMRC (published July 2003), which sets out the circumstances in which HMRC will accept that the price paid by managers in private equity transactions is not less than the initial unrestricted market value. Where the managers are within the memorandum of understanding, they are taken to have paid the initial unrestricted market value for their securities in Newco; accordingly, no income tax should be payable on acquisition of the securities and any subsequent growth in value should be subject to capital gains tax. Where the transaction is not within the memorandum of understanding and the price paid by the managers is less than the initial unrestricted market value, but a Section 431 election has been made, the managers will be liable to income tax up front (if any) but should still benefit from capital gains tax on the future growth in value.

(a) *Conditions to be satisfied to fall within the memorandum of understanding*
The memorandum of understanding describes and is designed to apply to typical venture capital or private equity-backed transactions in which managers acquire securities. Not all private equity deals fall within the memorandum's scope or spirit and, as the memorandum is concessionary, it will not apply where it is considered that a significant purpose of the arrangement is to avoid tax.

There are several conditions that must be satisfied for HMRC to accept that the price paid by managers for ordinary shares which do not carry ratchet rights is equal to initial unrestricted market value (or their market value where they are not restricted).

First, managers' shares must be ordinary capital. 'Ordinary capital' means ordinary shares, leveraged by all other capital of the company, including senior debt, junior debt such as mezzanine and preferred capital invested by the private equity house such as preferred shares or subordinated debt. This condition needs to be read within the spirit of the memorandum of understanding, as HMRC intends this to refer to shares which offer the potential for growth in value and not to shares which, while labelled 'ordinary', form part of the leverage and do not increase in value and carry a return.

Secondly, where leverage is provided by holders of ordinary capital, in the form of preferred capital, this must be on commercial terms. It will be taken to be on commercial terms if the coupon or the expected rate of return on it is not less than the most expensive financing provided to the company by investors (including lenders) that do not hold ordinary capital (provided such investors are unconnected with the managers). This condition requires that the rate of return on any amount invested in debt or preference shares by the private equity house and managers be at least as high as the rate of return on the debt provided by any lender that is not also acquiring shares. The comparison must be made with bank debt and other third-party debt (senior bank debt and mezzanine debt, most commonly). Where there is no funding from debt providers that do not also take equity, HMRC has not indicated what evidence it would need in order to be satisfied that the private equity house lending is on commercial terms. This is a particular concern in 'integrated finance' transactions, where the senior debt is provided by a bank that is connected with the equity investor (although HMRC may provide guidance on a case-by-case basis).

Where the return on the private equity house's funding is expressed as a blended rate on, say, preference shares and loan notes, this must be broken down into its constituent parts and compared against third-party debt on that basis.

The memorandum of understanding sets out guidance on how to compare the rates of return as follows:
- The comparison of the rates should be measured as at the time when the

managers acquire their shares. Any later changes as a result of subsequent changes in market interest rates need not be taken into account.
- Where the third-party debt terms include an equity kicker (eg, a warrant entitling the lender to acquire shares), it is accepted that such equity kickers that have an uncertain outcome will be ignored.
- The comparison of the rates should be adjusted according to whether the debt is, in principle, tax-deductible. Most commonly, the bank debt should be tax-deductible, whereas the coupon on preference share funding will not be tax-deductible.

The consequences of complying with this condition on the expected return on the ordinary shares to be acquired by managers will need to be considered when they are negotiating their equity share with the private equity house.

Thirdly, the price paid by the managers for their shares must not be less than the price that the private equity house pays for its ordinary capital shares, being shares of the same class as the managers' shares or shares of another class, but having substantially the same economic rights as the managers' shares. This condition is self-explanatory, and the only complication in practice is to ensure that the managers' share price is compared against the highest price paid by the private equity house.

Fourthly, the managers must acquire their managers' shares at the same time as the private equity house acquires its ordinary capital.

Fifthly, the managers' shares must have no features that give them or allow them to acquire rights not available to other holders of ordinary capital. Examples of preferential rights include anti-dilution rights and enhanced proceeds of sale if the managers' pot of shares has not been allocated by that date.

Finally, the managers must be fully remunerated by salary and bonuses (where appropriate) through a separate employment contract. The principal concern here is to check that the managers' salary or bonus rights have not been reduced in favour of enhanced sweet equity rights.

(b) *Ratchets*

Memorandum of understanding ratchets: Ratchet arrangements, while not a feature of most transactions, are used periodically in private equity deals. The structure of the ratchet may vary, but its commercial purpose is invariably to provide management with an increased share of the proceeds on an exit if specified business performance targets are met.

The memorandum of understanding lists three examples of ways in which ratchets may be structured:
- Managers subscribe for 15% (B ordinary shares); private equity house subscribes for 85% (A ordinary shares). A term in the share rights requires that a set number of the managers' shares automatically convert into worthless deferred shares in the event that the company does not meet certain performance targets, leaving management with 12% of the equity and the private equity house with 88% of the equity.

- As above, but rather than a proportion of the managers' shares converting to deferred shares, the terms of the private equity house's shares allow it to subscribe for additional shares in the event that the company does not meet certain performance targets. This additional subscription has the effect of diluting the managers' shareholding so that management is left with 12% of the equity and the private equity house is left with 88%.
- Managers subscribe for 12% (B ordinary shares); private equity house subscribes for 88% (A ordinary shares). A term in the share rights requires that a set number of the private equity house's shares convert into worthless deferred shares in the event that the company does not meet certain performance targets, therefore increasing the percentage of the company's share capital managers' shares represent to 15%.

In order to fall within the memorandum of understanding, ratchet arrangements must satisfy several conditions.

First, the ratchet arrangements must be arrangements under which the participation of different holders of ordinary capital in the profits and assets of the company might vary according to the performance of the company or the private equity house's investment. This means that the participation cannot vary by reference to personal performance.

Secondly, the ratchet arrangements must exist at the time that the private equity house acquires its ordinary capital. In light of this condition, it is very important that post-transaction changes to ratchet arrangements are avoided if the memorandum is to be relied upon.

Thirdly, the managers must pay a price for their shares in the ordinary capital that, at the time of acquisition, reflects their maximum economic entitlement. This condition works as follows: in the first and second examples outlined above, the managers start with 15% of the shares and their percentage shareholding can be decreased only by the operation of the ratchet. Here, provided that management pays the same price per share as the private equity house for its shares on day one, the memorandum can apply (subject to other conditions being met); that is, the managers must pay for 15% of the shares at the same price as the private equity house, without any reduction to take account of the fact that the ratchet may operate to reduce their shareholding.

In the third example, the managers start with 12% of the shares, but if the ratchet operates, their shareholding may potentially increase to 15%. In order to fall within the memorandum, the managers must pay 'top of the ratchet' – that is, they must pay a price that reflects the current value of the maximum percentage of shares that they would obtain if the ratchet operates. Say, for example, 1% of management's equity is worth £1; management would need to pay £15 on day one but would get only 12% of the equity at that stage.

Problems can arise in relation to arrangements that give management the right to receive a percentage of the proceeds on exit above a specified hurdle (eg, where management has the right to 5% of the exit proceeds in excess of £100 million). In such case it will be impossible to say, when management subscribes for its shares, what proportion of the total proceeds the management shareholders will receive, and it is therefore very difficult for management to know what it needs to pay in order to have paid top of the ratchet. The only way in which management can obtain complete comfort that it has paid top of the ratchet is to pay a premium for its shares equal to the current value of 5% of the whole of the company, even though it will never receive the whole of this on an exit.

Non-memorandum of understanding ratchets: For ratchet arrangements that do not fall within the memorandum of understanding, the tax treatment that HMRC will seek to apply is currently unclear. This is because HMRC had published guidance suggesting that it could tax the 'benefit' received on the operation of such a ratchet, the tax being determined by reference to the proportion of the share capital for which the managers paid when they first acquired their shares. Many advisers considered that HMRC's approach in relation to ratchets was technically wrong, on the basis that a ratchet right is inherent in the shares from the outset and is not a benefit provided in relation to the shares. HMRC took two cases on this point but, following receipt of counsel's advice that its position was not sustainable, withdrew this guidance in August 2006. The replacement guidance maintains that income tax charges under Chapters 3B, 3D and 4 of Part 7 of the Income Tax (Earnings and Pensions) Act may apply to ratchets outside the memorandum, but does not explain the basis on which they may be applied and notes that such cases will need to be considered on their own facts.

(c) *Post-transaction valuation checks*

HMRC will generally not agree the market value of shares in advance of a transaction. However, where managers or employees have acquired shares in circumstances in which their employer would have to account for tax under Pay as You Earn (PAYE) if the shares were acquired at an undervalue, it is possible to apply for a post-transaction valuation check. This provides confirmation of whether, in the view of HMRC's shares and assets valuation department, a value is a 'best estimate' for the purposes of operating PAYE. As these valuation reviews are necessarily brief given the date by which the PAYE must be accounted for, they are not agreed on a formal basis and do not bind the shares and asset valuation department for self-assessment purposes.

4.3 **Possible post-acquisition tax charges**

Various income tax charges may arise in relation to managers' shares if certain events occur following the acquisition of the shares. These can apply even if the transaction falls within the memorandum of understanding or an election under Section 431 of the Income Tax (Earnings and Pensions) Act has been made.

(a) *Convertible securities (Part 7, Chapter 3 of the Income Tax (Earnings and Pensions) Act)*

These provisions impose a charge on convertible securities. The charge will arise when the securities convert or are disposed of, or the holder accepts a payment in exchange for the release of the entitlement to convert or in connection with the right to convert. Any gain arising on the occurrence of the chargeable event (such 'gain' being, broadly speaking, the difference between the market value of the securities prior to the chargeable event) will be subject to income tax and (if the shares are readily convertible assets at that time) national insurance contributions. By way of example, if an employee holds loan notes that, under their terms, convert into equity at exit then there will be an income tax charge at the date of conversion on the value of the equity at exit less the face value of the loan notes.

(b) *Securities with artificially depressed market value (Part 7, Chapter 3A of the Income Tax (Earnings and Pensions) Act)*
This charge applies where the market value of securities is reduced by at least 10% by something done otherwise than for genuine commercial purposes in the seven years before the acquisition. The definition of 'otherwise than for genuine commercial purposes' includes transactions carried out for tax avoidance purposes and transactions carried out by companies that are members of the same group otherwise than at arm's length.

The aim of the charge is to catch transactions in which artificial steps have been taken to reduce the market value of shares when managers acquire them, with a view to minimising the tax charge on managers when they acquire their shares.

The charge arises on the acquisition of the shares and is broadly based on the difference between their actual market value when they are acquired and the market value that they would have had if the artificial depression in the market value had not occurred.

(c) *Securities with artificially enhanced market value (Part 7, Chapter 3B of the Income Tax (Earnings and Pensions) Act)*
This charge applies where the market value of securities is enhanced by at least 10% by something done otherwise than for genuine commercial purposes (see above).

The aim of the charge is to catch transactions in which management acquires shares and something is done after acquisition to increase the market value of the shares, thereby putting additional value into the hands of the managers. This is particularly relevant in circumstances where a private-equity-backed company is controlled by a corporate entity. In those circumstances, care will need to be taken to ensure that transactions carried out by group companies are on arm's-length terms. The charge to income tax (and national insurance contributions, where the securities are readily convertible assets) arises broadly on the difference between the enhanced market value and the market value that the securities would have had if the artificial enhancement in value had not taken place.

(d) *Securities acquired for less than market value (Part 7, Chapter 3C of the Income Tax (Earnings and Pensions) Act)*
This charge applies where securities are acquired at less than their market value. A common example is where shares are issued as partly paid shares to employees.

Where the charge applies, the undervalue element will be treated as if it is a notional loan made to the employee. Income tax will be charged on the interest element of the notional loan (the interest element is at the official rate specified by HMRC).

The notional loan is treated as having been written off when the shares are disposed of (or the obligation to pay up partly paid shares is waived), and income tax (and national insurance contributions, if appropriate) is at that stage charged on the undervalue element.

(e) *Securities disposed of for more than market value (Part 7, Chapter 3D of the Income Tax (Earnings and Pensions) Act)*

This charge applies where a manager sells his shares and receives a price for them that is more than their market value. In those circumstances, an income tax (and, if appropriate, national insurance) charge will arise on the difference between the price paid for the shares and their actual market value on the date of disposal.

This section is designed to prevent a manager from being able to receive employment income in the form of extra capital gains consideration on the disposal of shares.

(f) *Post-acquisition benefits from securities (Part 7, Chapter 4 of the Income Tax (Earnings and Pensions) Act)*

This is the most broadly drafted anti-avoidance section and charges to income tax "benefits received in connection with employment-related securities". As discussed above, one controversial area in which HMRC has indicated that it will seek to impose a charge is on proceeds received in connection with ratchet arrangements where management has not paid top of the ratchet and cannot fall within the safe harbour in the memorandum of understanding. Less controversial examples are the application of Chapter 4 to special dividends or bonus issues received by employee shareholders to the exclusion of others.

(g) *Possible tax charges when shares are acquired from leavers*

The articles of most private-equity-backed companies will provide that the shares held by a manager must be offered for sale on cessation of his employment. The price at which the shares can be acquired may depend on whether the manager is leaving as a 'good leaver' or 'bad leaver', with the former receiving a greater amount per share than the latter. The tax treatment of the disposal of the shares by a manager in these circumstances will depend entirely on whether the amount paid represents an amount equal to or in excess of the market value of the shares at that time. If and to the extent that a leaver is paid more than the current market value of the shares held by him at that date, an income tax charge will arise on the difference between the price paid and their actual market value on disposal. It is important in this respect to consider the extent to which any rights are personal contractual rights, as opposed to rights attaching to the shares (*Grays Timber Products Limited v The Commissioners for HMRC* (2009)).

4.4 Disguised Remuneration

Care must also be taken in relation to the disguised remuneration legislation set out in Part 7A of the Income Tax (Earnings and Pensions) Act 2003. The introduction of this regime has been designed to counteract the deferral or reduction of employment taxes by employers and employees using third parties such as employee benefit trusts or pension schemes. Although the legislation was originally intended to target a number of identified tax reduction arrangements, it is extremely widely drafted and as a result can apply in a variety of circumstances. Management will therefore be inclined to exercise caution during the life of the investment when encountering situations that could be regarded as providing any reward or remuneration for their employment duties. In particular this may include:

- transactions with employee benefit trusts or other third parties to acquire shares (including the issue of partly paid shares to employees);
- bonus arrangements with employee benefit trusts or other third parties where the payment of a cash bonus is deferred; or
- loan arrangements with employee benefit trusts or other third parties.

4.5 Second-tier managers

Other issues that can arise in structuring a transaction can relate to incentivising the so-called 'second tier' layer of management – that is, those key managers below the primary tier.

The second tier (and other employees) will often be numerous, and giving them shares directly generates an administrative burden both during the investment and on a future exit or restructuring. If it is thought desirable to give them shares to bring their gains within the capital gains tax regime (and potentially allow them to benefit from employee shareholder status, discussed further at paragraph 5.2(b)(ii)), the administrative burden can be eased by the legal title to such shares being held by an employee-benefit trust as nominee for the second tier/other employees.

Issuing shares to the second tier often occurs after completion, and will give rise to potential income tax charges if the company has appreciated in value and the memorandum of understanding cannot be relied upon for that reason. Such charges would have to be funded by individuals' personal financial resources or their employer.

If an upfront charge is likely to be material, consideration should be given to granting options exercisable on an exit. Although the full value of the option will be subject to income tax and national insurance contributions on exercise, the tax charge arises only at a time when option-holders will be receiving cash proceeds with which to fund the tax charge. The company can also require the option-holder to pay the employer's national insurance contributions charge.

Options are also easier to administer as they can be structured to lapse if an option-holder leaves, whereas the compulsory transfer provisions in the company's articles of association would have to be relied upon to obtain shares from a leaving shareholder.

5. Exit focus from date of acquisition

When presented with a proposal for an exit, a tax adviser must consider the likely tax liability that will be incurred by each vendor on the sale of its shares in the target and whether this can be minimised. The tax issues affecting institutional shareholders and management shareholders will be different.

5.1 Institutional shareholders

(a) Capital return

It is difficult to set out any hard and fast rules about the tax effects of disposal by institutional shareholders, as the identity and tax status of such shareholders will vary significantly, as outlined above. As a general rule, such vendors ordinarily wish to ensure that the proceeds are in capital and not income form, and to secure a cash exit. This may be achieved by selling the whole group, or by selling part and using the structures outlined in Section 2 above to return capital to shareholders.

(b) Dividends and interest

In addition to the proceeds of their share sale, institutional investors are likely, on exit, to receive accrued preference dividends and/or rolled-up interest.

Where interest is due, the paying company will need to consider its withholding obligations. No interest should be paid out by the company gross until it has satisfied itself that it is entitled to do so (see above).

Unlike interest, there is no withholding obligation on the payment of UK dividends on preference shares.

5.2 Management shareholders

(a) Capital or income for managers?

Before considering the managers' tax position, it is important to confirm that management's shares are within the capital gains tax regime only and not in the income tax regime (whether to be taxed as employment income or dividend income).

If the shares are subject to income tax as employment income, management will ordinarily suffer income tax (at 45% in 2014/15 if they are higher rate taxpayers) at the point of sale, plus national insurance contributions on at least part of the increase in value. The target will also suffer employers' national insurance contributions (at 13.8% in 2014/15) on the same amount. Except in the case of options (see above), this national insurance contribution charge cannot be lawfully collected from the employee. This can accordingly be a significant cost for the target on exit.

Alternatively, managements' share proceeds could be taxed as dividend income (at an effective rate of 30.6% in 2014/15) in certain circumstances, such as where the proceeds arising on a share sale are re-characterised as dividend income (see paragraph 5.2 (c) "Clearances" below).

(b) Capital gains tax regime

If the UK managers' shares are subject only to capital gains tax on sale, the tax payable will depend on the base cost of the shares and the availability of any exemption or relief.

Entrepreneurs' Relief: As noted above, entrepreneurs' relief reduces the effective rate of capital gains to 10% on the first £10 million of lifetime gains. This relief has three principal conditions.

First, the company whose shares are sold must be a trading company (or the holding company of a trading group). To be treated as a holding company of a trading group:
- the company must have one or more 51% subsidiaries; and
- one or more members of the group must carry on trading activities.

It is also important that the company does not carry on non-trading activities (eg, investment activities) to a substantial extent. Although there are no statutory rules as to what is meant by 'substantial extent', HMRC has issued guidance stating that the threshold for non-trading activities can be taken to be approximately 20% of total activities. The 20% test can be applied in various ways by reference to the assets of the group, revenues received or management time incurred in relation to the non-trading activities.

Secondly, the shareholder must be an officer or employee of the company, or (if the company is a member of a trading group) any member of the trading group. For the purposes of this condition, an individual may be either a full-time or part-time employee and there is no requirement to devote a minimum amount of working time to the business.

Thirdly, the shareholder must hold at least 5% of the ordinary share capital of the company whose shares are sold, and at least 5% of the voting rights in that company, for one year before the date on which the shares are sold. This condition has three separate elements:
- The individual must hold at least 5% of the ordinary share capital of the relevant company. For these purposes the individual will own 5% of the ordinary share capital if they own 5% of the nominal value of all the company's issued share capital (however described) other than shares that give the holders a right to a dividend at a fixed rate but have no other right to share in the company's profits (eg, fixed-rate preference shares).
- The individual must hold at least 5% of the voting rights in the relevant company by virtue of their shareholding.
- The individual must have met both of these conditions for one year before the date of disposal.

For these purposes, the individual's shareholding will not be aggregated with that of a spouse. It also appears that a direct 5% holding is required in order for the test to be satisfied, and therefore that holdings through trusts other than bare trusts will not count towards the individual's 5% holding. Where an individual is the beneficial owner of shares under a bare trust or nominee arrangement, again, it is not entirely clear how the rules apply, but depending upon the nature of the trust arrangements and the extent to which the individual is entitled to call for the legal title to the shares and to determine how the voting rights are exercised, it may be possible to argue that such shares should count towards the beneficial owner's total holding.

The Finance Act 2013 extended entrepreneurs' relief to disposals of shares acquired under enterprise management incentives (EMI) options and relaxed the conditions that had to be met to qualify for the relief. To claim entrepreneurs' relief on the disposal of EMI options, option-holders need only be officers or employees of a trading company (or a company that is a member of a trading group) and have satisfied this condition for a period of one year before the date of disposal; in other words, the 5% shareholding and voting rights requirements do not apply.

The relevance of entrepreneurs' relief on a company flotation also needs to be considered. In many flotations, management will be obliged to accept a 'lock-in' such that they can only sell a percentage of their shares on the flotation. If they qualified for entrepreneurs' relief before the flotation, they should qualify for a 10% rate on the shares sold on the flotation. However, the manager is likely to fall beneath a 5% holding after the flotation, which means that without further planning, future gains will fall within the 28% regime.

Employee shareholder status (ESS): Although managers may be able to take advantage of the 10% entrepreneurs' relief rate, the introduction of a new employee shareholder status scheme by the UK government could mean that management benefit from a capital gains tax exemption on the disposal of shares that had a value of up to £50,000 on the day of issue. HMRC's shares and assets valuation department has established a specific valuation service to obtain a prior valuation ruling, although it is expected that this valuation will be significantly light touch and take at least four weeks to confirm.

The principles of the scheme are as follows:

- The individual must be an employee.
- That individual enters into an 'employee shareholder agreement' with their employing company whereby they must waive certain employment rights (including those relating to unfair dismissal, redundancy payments and certain rights to request flexible working time and time off for training) in consideration for shares in the employing company or its parent.
- No other consideration may be given by the employee for the shares (which in turn creates technical issues about how an employee obtains fully paid-up shares).
- The shares must be issued or allotted to the individual (not transferred), must be fully paid up, and must have a value on the day of issue of no less than £2,000.
- There is no restriction on the type of shares that may be issued under the employee shareholder status scheme (ie, growth shares and preference shares would both qualify).
- The recipient of the shares must not have a material interest in the company (or the parent) at the time of the acquisition. In the context of a close company, a 'material interest' means holding at least 25% of the voting rights in the company or having a right to receive 25% of the assets of a company on a winding-up. For companies that are not close, the material interest test is limited to the 25% voting test. The scope of the material interest test also

extends to whether there are arrangements in place for the recipient of shares to acquire a material interest in the company. Since management's future investment in the company will be governed by an investment agreement, lawyers acting for management will have to take great care in relation to how this document is drafted in order to ensure that the investment agreement does not constitute an arrangement to acquire a material interest on the date the shares are issued. Of course, given that the material interest test also considers any shareholdings of a person connected with the recipient of the shares, there is also a risk that employee shareholder status could be unavailable on the basis that the material interest test is triggered where management are, under the terms of the investment agreement, deemed to be connected with each other or with the private equity investors.

- The employee must receive independent legal advice on the content of the employee shareholder agreement, particularly in relation to the employment rights given up under that agreement. There must be a seven-day cooling off period between the employee receiving the legal advice and giving up the employment rights, which could create a further delay to the completion of any private-equity-backed transaction.
- The disposal of the shares by the individual will be exempt from any charge to capital gains tax.

Although the scheme was arguably primarily aimed at business start-ups, the potential utilisation of the scheme by managers of private-equity-backed portfolio companies or on a traditional buyout transaction has not gone unnoticed.

Aside from the technical difficulties, the availability of ESS will also depend on the impact of GAAR and the need for a private equity house to consider the reputational aspects of offering tax exemptions in return for what some might consider to be the waiver of management's fundamental employee rights.

Qualifying corporate bonds and non-qualifying corporate bonds: Regardless of the availability of employee shareholder status, where managers are required to re-invest by the private equity house (as is often the case), they may choose to do so by investing net cash proceeds in the new shares.

Alternatively, managers may decide that they do not want to pay tax now, but would prefer to defer paying tax until they sell the shares/loan notes in which they are required to re-invest.

In these circumstances, UK managers will need to decide between:
- crystallising a tax charge on the sale of their shares, but deferring the payment of the tax until the loan notes are redeemed (the 'qualifying corporate bond route'); and
- deferring the tax charge arising until the loan notes are redeemed (the 'non-qualifying corporate bond route').

The two options appear similar, but have radically different tax effects.

Under the qualifying corporate bond route, the amount of tax payable on the sale of the shares is determined at the point of sale of the managers' shares. The capital gains tax does not become payable until the loan note is redeemed. Managers therefore take a credit risk on the purchaser on the qualifying corporate bond route: even if the purchaser is later insolvent and the loan notes are never redeemed for cash, the tax will still be payable. A suitable guarantee is therefore advisable if the qualifying corporate bond route is adopted. However, if a manager qualifies for entrepreneurs' relief at the point of sale, so long as a claim for entrepreneurs' relief is made on or before the first anniversary of January 31 following the tax year in which the disposal was made, the gain will be taxed at 10%. If no claim is made within the specified time, the held-over gain will be taxed at the capital gains tax rate at the time (28% in 2014/15).

Under the non-qualifying corporate bond route, the amount of tax and rate of tax payable are not determined until the loan notes are redeemed. That means that if the purchaser is later insolvent and the loan notes are never redeemed for cash, there will be no tax to pay. A suitable guarantee may nonetheless also be advisable here for obvious commercial reasons. If, however, managers wish to claim entrepreneurs' relief on the exchange of their shares for loan notes (because they may not qualify for entrepreneurs' relief in the new structure or have concerns regarding a change of law), an election can be made under Section 169Q of the Taxation of Chargeable Gains Act 1992 to treat the exchange as a disposal for capital gains tax purposes, thereby triggering a capital gains tax charge at 10%. This election must be made on or before the first anniversary of January 31 following the tax year in which the exchange was made.

(c) *Clearances*

In order to achieve a deferral of tax when using the non-qualifying corporate bond route, well-advised managers will need to ensure that they can achieve a rollover under Section 135 of the Taxation of Chargeable Gains Act. In most circumstances the technical conditions can be achieved without undue difficulty. The next step is to receive confirmation from HMRC that, broadly, the transaction is being carried out for genuine commercial purposes. Managers will wish to obtain the benefit of a clearance on this point prior to completing the transaction. This is discussed in more detail in Section 3.1 above.

HMRC also has the power under Section 684 of the Income Tax Act 2007 to re-characterise consideration received by managers as a dividend taxed at an effective rate of 30.6% (at 2014/15 rates). This risk is particularly prevalent where the target group has distributable reserves, because HMRC argues that the sellers are trying to sell the reserves for a capital payment, whereas the target could have distributed the reserves before the sale by way of a dividend.

This point is particularly taken on secondary buyouts. In these circumstances, managers' percentage shareholding in the purchaser is often the same, or higher, than their shareholding in the target. HMRC may view the managers' position as unchanged economically in terms of share ownership, with any value received in relation to shares being potentially taxable as a dividend, rather than as a capital disposal.

Prior notification can be sought from HMRC (under Section 701 of the Income Tax Act 2007) that Section 684 will not apply to UK managers in respect of the transaction. If the notification is given and the taxpayer has made full disclosure, HMRC cannot subsequently seek to apply Section 684; if the notification is refused, HMRC may pursue the taxpayer for an adjustment under Section 684.

6. Refinancings and restructurings

Since the credit crunch, many private equity-backed groups have found it necessary to restructure their financing arrangements as trading performance has worsened. These restructurings take a variety of forms dictated by the commercial circumstances of each case, but the most common theme is the reduction of the overall level of indebtedness of the group.

Common forms of restructuring range from the capitalisation of existing debt, through the purchase by the group or its institutional backers of external debt or the injection of further equity to the group by its shareholders, to the simple resetting of financial covenants. More recently, private equity-backed portfolio companies have been carrying out dividend recapitalisations (partly as a result of stronger debt markets) in order to pay sums to the company's owners. These types of restructurings lead to tax issues arising for both the group and its shareholders and are discussed below in outline.

6.1 Investee group

There are two main ways in which an investee group might suffer a tax disadvantage as a result of a restructuring of its financing. The first of these is a charge under the corporate loan relationships regime (now found in Part 5 of the Corporation Tax Act 2009) on an actual or deemed release of all of part of its debt. The second is the possibility that the arrangements in the round might cause the transfer pricing regime to restrict interest deductions going forward more than was previously the case.

The Finance Act 2010 introduced new provisions in this area that have made significant changes to the former position. The circumstances in which debt can be bought into a group at a discount without a tax charge arising have been significantly narrowed, but there is greater flexibility in the availability of the relief from the charge on waiver where the debt is waived in consideration of the issue of shares.

The transfer pricing rules have already been discussed. The point to note in the context of a refinancing is whether the terms of any debt have been changed sufficiently so as to amount to a new provision for the purpose of those rules, such that it is necessary to reassess interest deductibility going forward.

In addition, a capitalisation of accrued interest is treated for tax purposes as a payment of that interest, so the company issuing shares will need to be satisfied that it has no obligation to withhold tax as a result.

Finally, in the unlikely event that the restructuring leads to any value passing to employee shareholders, the investee group may suffer a liability to PAYE and national insurance as a result.

6.2 Institutional shareholders

As in the case of an exit or other receipt of returns from an investment, it is difficult to set out a useful general summary of the issues for institutional shareholders due to the wide variety of different types and tax residences of such shareholders. To the extent it is possible to generalise, institutional shareholders' primary concern is normally the prevention of tax charges in the investee group, and if a restructuring is such as to prevent any problem for the group or the management it is unlikely to prejudice the institutional shareholders.

Where the institution's arrangements include a co-invest element for UK individuals, the income tax and accrued income scheme issues discussed below in relation to management shareholders may be in point. Any liability to PAYE and national insurance in relation to the co-invest will often fall on the institution rather than the investee group.

6.3 Management shareholders

The primary concern of management shareholders will be to prevent any charge from arising under the employment-related securities regime. This will be a question of valuation: if any employment-related securities (whether shares or debt) increase in value as a result of the restructuring, a charge under Part 7, Chapter 4 of the Income Tax (Earnings and Pensions) Act 2003 may arise. In practice, it is extremely unusual for this to be an issue as in restructurings it is normally clear that management's interests are of only nominal value both before and after the transaction. The widely held view is that no charge under Part 7, Chapter 4 can arise as a result of a transaction that, while leaving a security still worthless, increases the possibility that it might become worth something in the future, for example by reducing the net liabilities of the investee group. However, there are two other issues that can arise.

First, where individuals hold securities with accrued but unpaid interest, care will be needed to prevent their suffering a charge under the accrued income scheme set out in Part 12 of the Income Tax Act 2007 as a result of any restructuring. In the specific case where debt held by an employee or officer of the investee group (or an institutional shareholder) is capitalised, a new election under Section 431 of the Income Tax (Earnings and Pensions) Act 2003 will normally be appropriate in relation to the employee's new shares.

Secondly, individuals may in some circumstances be concerned to ensure that they are not treated as having disposed of any of their existing securities for capital gains tax purposes. A disposal will generally be a good thing in relation to shares (since where the investee group needs refinancing, it will probably crystallise a loss). However, where the individual holds loan notes that were consideration for a previous sale at a gain to the investee group and that were structured as 'qualifying corporate bonds' within the meaning of Section 117 of the Taxation of Chargeable Gains Act 1992, a disposal of those notes – even for consideration of minimal value – will trigger an unfunded liability to pay tax on the earlier gain.

Public-to-privates

Graham Gibb
Charles Martin
Macfarlanes LLP

1. Introduction

Public-to-privates are essentially transactions that take listed public companies into private hands. There are two principal routes for structuring a public-to-private: a traditional takeover offer and a court-approved scheme of arrangement. This chapter considers the key differences between these two routes, the regulatory regime in which they operate and the central issues and concerns that arise in their implementation.

Before the credit crunch, there was significant private equity involvement in the UK public company arena. This was partly due to the increased resources available to private equity and hedge funds as a result of their fundraising and the relative scarcity of opportunities for investment in the private arena. While overall deal volumes have remained relatively subdued in the years following the credit crunch, with some early indications of economic recovery and given the wealth of some of the funds and the attractiveness of many of the potential targets, public-to-privates are likely to remain popular in the longer term.

The most common types of public-to-private are:
- the traditional management buyout; and
- a consortium bid whereby a number of private equity funds join together to bid for a company – this is particularly prevalent with larger targets that may be too significant, expensive or complex for a single house to take on by itself.

This chapter begins by looking at the recently altered regulatory landscape in which these transactions take place.

2. Regulatory overview

Public-to-private transactions are much more heavily regulated than private transactions. The keystone in the UK regulatory system is the City Code on Takeovers and Mergers, but parties will also need to consider the Companies Act 2006, the Financial Services and Markets Act 2000, the Model Code on Directors' Dealings, the Listing Rules of the Financial Services Authority and the Criminal Justice Act 1993.

Virtually all takeovers of public companies in the United Kingdom, including public-to-privates, are subject to the City Code, which is issued and administered by the Panel on Takeovers and Mergers. The panel was established in 1968 and, until a few years ago, existed as a non-statutory body. However, the implementation of the

EU Takeovers Directive (2004/25/EC) into UK law on May 20 2006 gave the Takeover Panel statutory powers and gave the City Code, to the extent it is now derived from the directive, a statutory basis.

The City Code was subject to some quite significant changes in the latter part of 2011, the results of which are still being absorbed by the market. Those changes that are particularly relevant to public-to-privates are noted below.

2.1 The Panel on Takeovers and Mergers

The Takeover Panel consists of a chairman, other members appointed by the governor of the Bank of England and additional members representing institutions and professional and self-regulatory associations involved in the securities industry (eg, the Association of British Insurers, the National Association of Pension Funds and the British Bankers' Association). The Takeover Panel works on a day-to-day basis through its executive (its professional staff) headed by the director general.

2.2 The City Code on Takeovers and Mergers

The City Code on Takeovers and Mergers consists of six general principles, which match the general principles set out in Article 3 of the directive. These general principles are supplemented by 38 specific rules which in turn are accompanied by explanatory notes and supplemented by practice statements issued by the Takeover Panel.

The principal purposes of the City Code are:
- to ensure fair and equal treatment of all shareholders in the target;
- to provide an orderly framework for the conduct of takeover offers; and
- to enable shareholders to make an informed decision on the merits of an offer.

The introduction to the City Code makes it clear that its rules are not framed in technical language and are to be interpreted so as to achieve the underlying purpose: its spirit must be observed as well as its letter. The Takeover Panel encourages companies and their advisers to consult with it before and during an offer in relation to how the City Code should be applied in particular circumstances, rather than adopting a technical and legalistic approach to its interpretation.

Importantly, consideration of the commercial and financial merits of an offer is beyond the remit of the Takeover Panel and the City Code. The Takeover Panel is concerned only to ensure the process operates in a fair manner.

(a) Scope of application

In determining whether the City Code applies, it is the nature of the target or potential target (whether it is public, listed or unlisted or private) that is relevant, not the nature of the bidding entity, or 'offeror', to use the terminology of the City Code. English companies are designated as public or private by their certificates of incorporation, and not all public companies are listed.

With effect from September 30 2013, any company that has its registered office in the United Kingdom, the Channel Islands or the Isle of Man, and that has any securities listed on a multilateral trading facility in the United Kingdom (or on any market in the Channel Islands or the Isle of Man), will be subject to the City Code. One consequence of this is that an offer for a target company may be subject to more than one regulator, and in such cases it is necessary to liaise with the Takeover Panel at an early stage to establish which regulator will take the lead.

Additionally, the City Code applies to offers for any public company considered by the Takeover Panel to have its place of central management and control in the United Kingdom, the Channel Islands or the Isle of Man where that company's securities are traded solely on a market that is not a regulated market (in the United Kingdom or the European Economic Area), is not a multilateral trading facility in the United Kingdom or a stock exchange in the Channel Islands or Isle of Man.

Consequently, a number of companies that would not formerly have been subject to the City Code under the previous regime, for example, companies listed on the London Stock Exchange's Alternative Investment Market that were centrally managed and controlled from outside the United Kingdom, the Channel Islands or the Isle of Man, will now fall within the jurisdiction of the City Code.

Companies with a registered office in the United Kingdom, Channel Islands or the Isle of Man, but which are not centrally managed and controlled in the United Kingdom and have securities that are only traded on overseas markets, continue to fall outside the jurisdiction of the City Code.

In the absence of a waiver from the Takeover Panel, the City Code will also apply to private companies if, in addition to having their place of central management and control in the United Kingdom, Channel Islands or Isle of Man:
- their share capital has been admitted to trading on a regulated market or multilateral trading facility in the United Kingdom or any stock exchange in the Channel Islands or Isle of Man at any time in the last 10 years;
- dealings and/or prices have been published regularly for at least six months during the previous 10 years (whether via a newspaper, electronic price quotation system or otherwise); or
- a prospectus relating to the offer, admission to trading, or issue of securities in that company has been publicly filed with the registrar of companies or any other competent regulator at any point during the previous 10 years.

The City Code is concerned with all takeover and merger transactions involving relevant companies. These include, in addition to public-to-privates:
- other takeover bids;
- partial offers;
- offers by a parent company for shares in a partly owned subsidiary; and
- certain other transactions where control of a company is to be obtained or consolidated – for example, transactions creating dual-listed company structures or schemes of arrangement.

(b) *General principles*
The general principles demonstrate the fundamental concerns addressed by the City Code:

- All holders of the securities of an offeree company of the same class must be afforded equivalent treatment; moreover, if a person acquires control of a company, the other holders of securities must be protected.
- The holders of the securities of an offeree company must have sufficient time and information to enable them to reach a properly informed decision on the bid; where it advises the holders of securities, the board of the offeree company must give its views on the effects of implementation of the bid on employment, conditions of employment and the locations of the company's places of business.
- The board of an offeree company must act in the interests of the company as a whole and must not deny the holders of securities the opportunity to decide on the merits of the bid.
- False markets must not be created in the securities of the company, of the offeror company or of any other company concerned by the bid in such a way that the rise or fall of the prices of the securities becomes artificial and the normal functioning of the markets is distorted.
- An offeror must announce a bid only after ensuring that it can fulfil in full any cash consideration, if such is offered, and after taking all reasonable measures to secure the implementation of any other type of consideration.
- An offeree company must not be hindered in the conduct of its affairs for longer than is reasonable by a bid for its securities.

This chapter goes on to examine how some of these general principles manifest themselves in offers involving private equity bidders.

3. Structuring a public offer

The two principal methods of structuring the acquisition of a public company in the United Kingdom are by way of:
- conventional offer; and
- a court-approved scheme of arrangement under Section 895 of the Companies Act.

Provided that the target is a company to which the City Code applies, the City Code applies to both structures.

At its most fundamental level, the difference between the two structures can be summarised as follows: an offer is a corporate action of the bidder, inviting shareholders in the target to accept an offer for their shares and to receive consideration, while a scheme is a court-sanctioned action of the target company, which asks its own shareholders to vote in favour of proposals to effect a change of control as a result of which they will receive consideration.

Overall, the choice of structure will depend on individual circumstances, but the general observations outlined in the following table highlight certain of the key differences between the two structures.

Offer	Scheme of arrangement
Minimum acceptance level (ie, the lowest point at which the offer can become unconditional as to acceptances)	
The City Code provides that an offer must have a minimum acceptance condition that results, if accepted, in the bidder owning more than 50% of the voting rights of the target. However, in practice this is usually set at a higher level (see "Acquiring 100% of the target" below).	There is no minimum acceptance level. However, a scheme requires approval of 75% of the shareholders in value plus a majority in number of shareholders present and voting in person or by proxy at the relevant meetings. Non-voting shareholders and shares held by the bidder and its associates will not be counted in the calculation of the required level.
Acquiring 100% of the target	
Utilisation of the compulsory acquisition procedures is possible only if acceptances of 90% or more are obtained. Private equity bidders will almost invariably wish to gain full control of the target company, and their finance providers will often be wary of lending unless they are sure that it will be possible to obtain 100% of the shares. Accordingly, the finance documentation may restrict the ability of the bidder to declare the offer unconditional at an acceptance level lower than 90%, and will almost certainly restrict the bidder's ability to do so at an acceptance level below 75% (being the level at which a corporate action could be taken to delist the target company).	If the scheme is approved, then all shareholders will be bound. Therefore, structured properly, there is no risk of a continuing minority.
Financial assistance	
The bidder cannot use cash in the target to finance the offer before, or at time of, the offer. Cash resources of the target can only be extracted after the offer has completed and the company has been re-registered as a private company.	Actions that would otherwise be prevented by the United Kingdom's rules prohibiting financial assistance may be approved by the court as part of the scheme.

continued on next page

Offer	Scheme of arrangement
Hostile/recommended	
As the offer is a corporate action of the bidder, it can be hostile or recommended.	As a scheme is a corporate action of the target, the cooperation and support of the target's directors is required. While it is theoretically possible to mount a hostile scheme (and indeed an expression of intent to launch such a transaction has previously been announced), no such transactions have been formally attempted, or concluded, in the United Kingdom to date. Even if the scheme is initially recommended, it should be noted that it is possible that the target's directors may withdraw their recommendation for fiduciary reasons.
In practice, the UK market continues to see relatively low levels of hostile bidding activity, with the vast majority of completed deals being ones that were recommended.	
Stamp duty	
Stamp duty is payable at 0.5% of the consideration on the transfer of the shares in the target.	No stamp duty is payable if a cancellation scheme is used (as is usually the case). In practice, this can amount to a significant saving in the bidder's transactional costs.
Time period	
The timetable for an offer is more fluid and is therefore potentially shorter or longer than that for a scheme. The minimum time period from posting to declaring an offer unconditional is 21 days and the maximum period is 81 days. (Further details are set out in the section entitled "Timetable" below). NB: If an offer is made into the United States under Tier I (see "US shareholders" below), the offer must remain open for 20 business days, resulting in a slightly longer timeline.	The timetable for a scheme is less fluid and is usually seven to eight weeks from posting. While the timeframe for executing a scheme is generally longer than that required for implementing an offer, 100% control of a target (as opposed to *de facto* control at some lower level through an offer) is usually achieved more quickly by way of a scheme.
Court sanction	
No court approval is required.	Court approval is required. There is a risk that this provides a forum for disgruntled minority shareholders to object.

continued on next page

Offer	Scheme of arrangement
Flexibility in the event of a contested bid	
It is relatively simple to change the terms of the offer during the offer process.	It is more difficult to change the terms of an offer during a scheme process. It may be necessary to restart the timetable. In this respect a scheme may be more suitable if there is little or no risk of a competing bid. If a competing bid does arise, it is possible to switch to an offer. Consequently, bidders often reserve the right to switch between a scheme and an offer and vice versa.
US shareholders	
If less than 10% of the target shares are held by US persons, cash offers can be made into the US under a 'Tier I exemption'. This avoids the US Securities and Exchange Commission (SEC) registration requirements. If between 10% and 40% of the shares are held by US persons, then under Tier II most SEC requirements apply.	A scheme utilises the Regulation 3(a)(10) exemption to circumvent SEC registration requirements as it is a process that involves the sanction of the courts.
Who controls the process	
The offer document is issued, and the process is controlled, by the bidder.	The process is controlled by the target. The target and its directors are responsible for the scheme. In the past, it was commonplace for a bidder and target to enter into a merger agreement to impose mutual obligations to implement the scheme. Such agreements were prohibited in September 2011, with the Takeover Panel instead enforcing the timetable announced by the target company.
Satisfaction of conditions	
All conditions must be satisfied within 21 days of the offer being declared unconditional as to acceptances. At the very latest, this is 81 days after the posting of the offer document.	All conditions must be satisfied or waived by the time of the court hearing to sanction the scheme.

continued on next page

Offer	Scheme of arrangement
Market purchases	
Before the offer is announced: • acceptance condition: purchases will count towards the acceptance condition; • compulsory acquisition: purchases will not count towards the 90% limit. After the offer is announced: • acceptance condition: purchases will count towards the acceptance condition; • compulsory acquisition: purchases made after posting of the offer document (but not simply after announcement) will count towards the 90% limit. In some cases, this has led to a practice of announcing the transaction and posting the offer document on the same day, in conjunction with the purchase of a significant block of shares in the target, with the intention that the acquired shares could be counted towards the 90% threshold and also to deliver significant forward momentum from day one of the offer. NB: Insider dealings issues may prohibit market purchases.	Shares purchased before the shareholders' meeting to approve the scheme will not carry the right to vote at the shareholders' meetings to approve the scheme.
Lost and untraceable shareholders	
When calculating the 90% acceptance level, no account can be taken of lost or untraceable shareholders unless permission is sought from the court.	Lost and untraceable shareholders are not likely to be relevant when calculating the 75% acceptance level, as this level relates only to those shareholders that have voted.
Trading in target shares	
Accepting shareholders must submit their share certificates or transfer their shares into escrow on accepting the offer.	The target's shareholders can continue trading up to the final court hearing date.

Traditionally, the majority of takeovers were achieved by means of a conventional offer. There is no obvious reason for this except, perhaps, that the process of a scheme can appear more cumbersome and expensive. However, recent years have seen a rise in the number of takeovers that have been effected by way of a scheme.

The significant number of private equity houses effecting public-to-privates in the past undoubtedly contributed to the growth in the popularity of schemes.

First, these houses have traditionally shied away from hostile bids. This is mainly because they require both:
- a detailed due diligence process, which requires a friendly dialogue with the target; and
- the support of lending banks, which are often unwilling to commit to a leveraged buy-out without the comfort provided by sophisticated due diligence.

Additionally, some limited partnership agreements will prohibit the private equity fund from launching a bid that is not recommended by the target board.

The recommendation required for a scheme is therefore seen as more of a prerequisite than a burden for these bidders and, when combined with certainty of 100% control guaranteed by a scheme, the scheme route may be vastly more attractive than a traditional offer, especially to a private equity bidder, and can also offer an opportunity to save money on stamp duty which would otherwise have been payable under an offer.

Despite lower representation of private equity bidders in the UK public markets over the last few years, recent experience would suggest that schemes continue to remain the structure of choice for higher value recommended bids. Takeovers by way of an offer have, however, continued to remain more prevalent for lower value bids.

It remains to be seen whether the recent changes to the City Code shift the balance of negotiating power in favour of target boards, but increasingly, institutional shareholders are disinclined to rely blindly on recommendations from target boards to accept an original offer. For example, they may take and hold positions in companies that are, or are rumoured soon to be, subject to an offer in an attempt to be able to force the price upwards from the original recommended price and ultimately, if unsuccessful in increasing the bid price, they may retain their shares as 'silent investors' in the target, trusting the private equity house to increase the value of their holding over time. This scepticism often remains, irrespective of the support of the target's financial adviser or the existence of an independent committee of the target board.

A good example of activism arising from such scepticism was the shareholder revolt during Glencore's takeover of Xstrata, where very public intervention by certain of Xstrata's leading shareholders resulted in significant amendments being made by Glencore to the terms of the transaction and an increase in the offer price.

4. **Secrecy and possible offer announcements**

When involved in a public-to-private it is imperative to be aware of the Takeover Panel's rule on secrecy and the obligations to make announcements.

Rule 2.1 of the City Code requires that absolute secrecy be maintained before the announcement of an offer, and that all persons privy to confidential information concerning an offer conduct themselves in such a way as to minimise the chances of a leak of the information. Strict controls to ensure the security of confidential information should be in place and an 'insider list' keeping track of all persons with confidential information should be maintained.

The Takeover Panel must be consulted in cases where, before an announcement has been made, discussions are extended beyond six external parties or the potential target is the subject of rumour, speculation or an untoward movement in its share price. The Takeover Panel has set out detailed guidance on this area in Practice Statement 20.

Parties that count towards the six include potential providers of finance (equity or debt), shareholders in the target or bidder, potential management candidates, significant customers of, or suppliers to, the target and potential purchasers of assets. The Takeover Panel will not count professional advisers towards this number, and has said that it may be prepared also to exclude parties that have been approached but have declined to act (eg, financial providers). The Takeover Panel may allow an increase in the number of parties approached if it is satisfied that secrecy will be maintained, but it must always be consulted in advance.

Should there be a possible leak of information regarding a possible offer or a movement in the share price of the target company, the Takeover Panel may require an announcement to be made. Rule 2.2 of the City Code contains details of when an announcement may be required. Before the target is approached the obligation to determine whether any announcement is required lies with the bidder. Once an approach has been made, this obligation switches to the target unless the approach is unequivocally rejected.

The Takeover Panel introduced a fundamental change to the operation of the City Code in September 2011 through the strengthening of the so-called 'put up or shut up' regime to give it automatic application. These changes were introduced in order to prevent target companies from being subjected to protracted sieges by way of virtual bids, whereby an offeror would announce a possible intention to make an offer, thereby putting the target company into play, but would then delay making a formal offer for as long as it could in the hope of ultimately persuading the target company's directors to recommend a bid at a lower price.

Under the revised regime, when a target company announces to the market that it has received an approach relating to a possible offer, that announcement is required to name all potential bidders with whom the target company is either in talks, or from whom it has received an approach relating to a possible bid.

Upon publication of such an announcement, those bidders who have been named have a period of 28 days within which to announce a firm intention to make an offer. This 28-day period falls away if a firm intention to make an offer in respect of the relevant target company is announced during the period.

If the bidder is unable to reach a point where it can make such an announcement and is unable to convince the target board to support an application to the Takeover Panel for an extension (more on this below), it must announce that it has no intention to make an offer, in which case it is then locked out of the market, with respect to that particular target company at least, for a period of six months.

This lock-out period can be reversed, with the consent of the Takeover Panel, where there has been a material change in circumstance, or where, with the panel's consent, the locked-out bidder wishes to approach the target board with a view to discussing the parameters of a recommended offer.

A period of 28 days within which to move from preliminary discussions to the announcement of a firm intention to make an offer seems like a very short period of time indeed, especially for private equity bidders, who will typically wish to conduct a more involved and detailed due diligence exercise than a trade buyer might need to, and will also need to manage a parallel workstream arranging financing. However, the Takeover Panel has discretion to extend the 28-day period upon request and has indicated that where such a request has the support of the board of the target company, it will ordinarily grant an extension.

In fact, since the introduction of this new regime, the Takeover Panel has granted all requests for extension made jointly by the bidder and the target company.

While there has been insufficient deal flow under the new regime to gauge its impact on market practice fully, the put up or shut up period should arguably be viewed as imposing a shortened period during which bidders must engage proactively with the board of the target company in order to convince them that they are a credible offeror who will ultimately be capable of tabling an offer that would be recommendable.

Taken together with the prohibition on transaction-related arrangements discussed in more detail below, the introduction of this new regime should serve to improve the bargaining position of target boards on future public-to-privates.

5. Conflicts of interest

5.1 Independent advice – the 'Rule 3 adviser'

Whenever an offer is made that is subject to the City Code, the board of the target company is required, under Rule 3 of the City Code, to obtain competent independent advice on the offer, and the substance of such advice must be made known to its shareholders. This has been the unwavering view of the Takeover Panel for many years. In its 1995 annual report the Takeover Panel stated that it "has always regarded it as of paramount importance that the adviser should be sufficiently independent so that its advice should be objective beyond question". Further, the Takeover Panel has noted in Note 1 to Rule 3 that "the requirement for competent independent advice is of particular importance in cases where the offer is a management buy-out or similar transaction". The independent adviser is therefore referred to as the 'Rule 3 adviser'.

In determining whether an adviser is independent, the Takeover Panel has noted (in Practice Statement 21) that it will examine the strength of the overall relationship between the target and the Rule 3 adviser. The Takeover Panel also noted that it will be more flexible in its approach in determining the independence of a Rule 3 adviser, but it would be prudent to consider this at an early stage in any transaction. If there is any doubt about the independence of an adviser, the Takeover Panel should be consulted.

When the independent advice and the views of the board conflict, or it is impossible to express a view on the merits of an offer or to give a firm recommendation, the Takeover Panel should be consulted in advance of any communication with the target's shareholders.

5.2 Independent board

The majority of private equity bids will involve some form of management buy-out. In these circumstances the private equity house will want (if not need) to involve at least some of the target's existing directors in the ongoing management of the target's business. These directors will often be invited to roll over their shareholdings in the target and become directors of the bidding vehicle ('Bidco'). This leads to an inevitable conflict of interest for those directors as they potentially straddle the offer process, acting for both the target and the bidder.

The third general principle, described above, makes clear that the target's board must act in the best interests of the target. This is expanded by Rule 25.2 (Note 4) of the City Code, which requires that directors with a conflict of interest should "not normally be joined with the remainder of the board" when the board circulates its views on the offer. Therefore, one of the first steps in any management buy-out is for the target board to constitute an independent committee of directors, comprising those directors who have no conflict of interest. The independent committee is simply an independent board for the purpose of considering, and potentially recommending, the offer as being in the best interests of the shareholders. It is the public face of the target insofar as the offer is concerned.

It is the independent committee with which the bidder or potential bidder will negotiate, from which the target's advisers will receive instructions and which will control the due diligence exercise. The independent committee will also consider requests from the target's directors who are involved with the bidder – including, for example, requests to spend time working for the bidder and/or to obtain any necessary waivers from their service contracts. If the independent committee is to approve such requests, it must be satisfied that they are in the best interests of the target and its shareholders.

The independent committee will be more favourably viewed if there are some members who have been directors of the target "for some time".[1] However, if there are not any continuing independent directors, it is possible that an entirely new independent committee may be formed. Participants in management buyouts will be viewed as having a conflict of interest and therefore, in line with Note 4 to Rule 25.2 of the City Code, should stand aside and not serve on the independent committee. Similarly, a non-executive director who would be continuing with the target should also cease to participate in an independent committee. Indeed, any director (executive or non-executive) with a continuing interest in the target or the bidder after a successful offer is likely to be considered to be conflicted. Finally, although conflicted directors need not necessarily resign from the board of the target, they will need to have regard to their fiduciary duties.

It is possible that all directors of the target may be conflicted, but this will not necessarily prevent the offer from progressing. In the 1998 offer for John Haggis Plc by Predictory Limited, all of the directors of John Haggis Plc were conflicted and so the independent advice was given by the Rule 3 adviser.

---

[1] Guidance on management buyouts issued by the Institutional Shareholders Committee in December 1989 and reissued in August 1993.

5.3   **Controlling information flow and undertaking due diligence**

Due diligence will be important to private equity houses and banks involved in a public-to-private, particularly as the transaction will not give them the benefit of warranties from target shareholders (other than perhaps the limited comfort available from management shareholders under the terms of any irrevocable undertakings or investment arrangements entered into with them). While there will be a certain amount of information about the target publicly available to the bidder (and often considerably more than in a private transaction), any further due diligence is somewhat more complex than in a normal management buyout. Regard will need to be had to the following issues.

(a)   *Independent committee and management directors' duties*

As described above, as a result of the inherent conflict of interest in a management buyout, confusion will ensue unless, at a very early stage of the transaction, it is clear to all parties exactly who is speaking for the target and who for the management team or bidco. Great care needs to be taken to avoid a member of the management team emerging as the spokesman, negotiator or conduit of information for the target.

As mentioned, the directors must comply with their fiduciary duties to the target, although this does not necessarily mean that they have to resign. It may, in fact, be in the best interests of the target that they remain on its board. They will nonetheless always need to remember their fiduciary duties to act in the best interests of the target (which may diverge from those of the conflicted management team and the bidder). For example, information relating to the target may be confidential to the target and its disclosure to the bidder may be a breach of the directors' duties to the target.

To prevent the independent committee from being kept in the dark as to the information that has been shared, there is a duty to disclose relevant information concerning the target (eg, a competing bid) to the independent committee. These duties are specifically referred to in the City Code – for example, Note 3 to Rule 20.2 states that the management team must cooperate with the independent committee and Rule 20.3 requires that the directors furnish the independent committee with all information provided to external providers of finance (debt or equity).

Proper housekeeping (as described below) can help to minimise the scope for management directors to breach their duties to the target.

(b)   *Information to competing bidders and potential financiers: Rules 20.2 and 20.3*

While not a formal general principle, one of the underlying principles applied by the Takeover Panel is to ensure the equality of treatment of bidders.

Under Rule 20.2 of the City Code, any non-public information generated by the target and provided to the management team/bidco/private equity house must, on request, be provided by the target to other *bona fide* competing bidders. A later bidder cannot simply ask for all information provided to earlier bidders, and must make specific requests – accordingly, it is likely that a very long due diligence checklist will be submitted to ensure that all potential previous questions are covered and all

Public-to-privates

information obtained. In practice, it should be assumed that information obtained by one bidder will be disclosable to another.

Therefore, even in a recommended offer, the amount of information that is requested and that is shared should be considered in the light of this rule – since an unwelcome offer could be made and the unwelcome bidder would be entitled to receive all the information previously obtained.

In the view of the Takeover Panel, Rule 20.2 extends to site visits and meetings with management, in addition to information disclosed by other means. Accordingly, if one bidder or potential bidder has been afforded a site visit or granted access to management with a view to discussing the target's business, an equivalent site visit or meeting with management must be granted to another bidder or *bona fide* potential bidder if it so requests. The Takeover Panel recognises that it may not be possible to replicate exactly the same site visit or management access for a subsequent bidder as was given to the first bidder, but considers the target and its financial adviser responsible for ensuring, as far as practicable, that the subsequent bidder is given equivalent access and equality of treatment.

Rule 20.3 of the City Code is in a similar vein – any information generated by the management team (or bidco) and provided to potential financiers must be provided to the independent committee if they so request.

Much responsibility for the application of these rules lies with the Rule 3 adviser, to whom the Takeover Panel would look to ensure fairness. In addition, it is critical for bidders to ensure that Rule 20.2 information can be easily distinguished from Rule 20.3 information. To do this, a bidder should manage the information flow, due diligence process and preparation of the target management business plan carefully. Unless the management team is kept away from the production of materials, such as the due diligence report and the business plan, they will be caught by a Rule 20.3 request. It is therefore good discipline for the private equity house's model, business plans and projections to be prepared by the financial advisers to the private equity house on its behalf. The underlying data from the target and target's management will obviously be available to all *bona fide* bidders, but the actual model will not.

(c) *Housekeeping*

In public-to-private transactions, information typically flows to the bidding team from a wide range of sources – after all, the key members of the bidding team are usually on the target's board. It is important, if at all possible, to ensure that all information is passed through the target's lawyers or financial advisers. As discussed above, great care needs to be taken to control strictly the dissemination of information and to ensure that at no time can the management team be accused of disclosing confidential information without authority.

(d) *Websites and electronic information*

The City Code requires both the bidder and the target to maintain a website as a point of reference for all documents, announcements and other information published by them in relation to an offer. This requirement may create some additional housekeeping work for some private equity firms that do not generally use publicly facing websites or release information to the wider market as part of their day-to-day operations.

At the same time that this change was brought in, the City Code was amended to permit electronic communication of most documents, including offer and scheme documents; although hard copies of certain documents, such as proxy cards and forms of acceptance, must still be sent. Of course, a target will need the standard electronic communication provisions to have been incorporated into its articles of association to take advantage of this change, but it can be expected that over time, the amount of physical documentation will decrease significantly for both the bidder and the target.

(e) ***Special deals***

The first general principle states that "all holders of the securities of an offeree company of the same class must be afforded equivalent treatment". This is reinforced by Rules 14 to 16 inclusive. Rule 16 is likely to be the most relevant to public-to-private transactions, as it prohibits special deals with favourable conditions being offered to some but not all of the target shareholders. Management buyouts and public-to-privates may give rise to special deals if the bidder wishes to incentivise and involve members of the target's management by rolling over their target shares, but wishes to pay cash to all other shareholders. Alternatively, there may be existing institutional or other large shareholders that wish to participate in the bidding consortium.

The Rule 16 prohibition has long been interpreted to cover both the quantum and the form of any consideration. It applies to arrangements made from the time that an offer is "reasonably in contemplation" to the time of the offer period. This period may be extended in certain circumstances under Rule 35.3, which states that a person (or persons acting in concert) owning more than 50% of the target may not enter into special deals within six months of the closure of an offer. Accordingly, if a bidder wishes to give equity in Bidco to large or management shareholders, but not to all target shareholders, it must fall within one of the exemptions to Rule 16.

There are two principal exemptions that apply in these circumstances:

- Just as the requirement for equal treatment within Rule 16 would not apply to a single bidder that already holds shares in the target, the provisions do not apply to parties that are *bona fide* 'joint bidders'. If a consortium member can be classed as a joint bidder, it may be able to receive what would otherwise be a prohibited special deal.
- An exemption is specifically mentioned in the City Code for special deals for management where certain criteria are met.

These criteria are considered below. There is an informal exemption from the requirements of Rule 16 for minimal holdings. If a significant member of a consortium happens to have a nominal shareholding in the target (eg, for informational purposes), the Takeover Panel may be prepared to waive the application of Rule 16.

(f) Joint bidder

Definition: The Takeover Panel has stated that a genuine bidder is a person that, alone or with others, seeks to obtain control of the target and that, following the acquisition of control, can expect to exert a significant influence over the target, to participate in distributions of profits and surplus capital and to benefit from any increase in the value of the target, while at the same time bearing the risk of a fall in its value resulting from the poor performance of the target's business or adverse market conditions.

The City Code does not define 'joint offeror' (to use its terminology), but the Takeover Panel has formed a list of non-exhaustive criteria that it uses to determine whether a party falls into this category. These criteria were finally set out publicly in Panel Statement 2003/25. In this context, they were used to consider whether a member of one of the competing consortia bidding for Canary Wharf Group Plc was correctly categorised as a joint offeror.

Test for a 'joint offeror': When considering whether a party is a joint offeror, the Takeover Panel will consider the following criteria:

- First, the Takeover Panel will look at the proportion of the equity share capital in Bidco that the party will own after completion of the proposed acquisition. As a very general rule of thumb, the Takeover Panel will expect a joint offeror to hold at least 30% of the equity share capital (or an equal share of the share capital; for example, where there are five identical holdings, a holding of 20%).
- Secondly, the Takeover Panel will look at whether a party can exert significant influence over the future management and development of Bidco, after the acquisition. Here, the Takeover Panel will look at the voting and veto rights of the relevant party. Once again, the 30% (or equal rights) rule of thumb test may be applied.
- Thirdly, the Takeover Panel will look at the contribution the relevant party is making to the consortium or to Bidco. This is a softer issue and the Takeover Panel will consider the experience, skills and knowledge that the party is contributing to the consortium. In the Canary Wharf decision, the individual concerned had a long history of investing in real estate and in the Canary Wharf project (indeed, he was one of the founding investors in the project), had a detailed knowledge of the project, had previously been a director and had a long history of actively supervising his investment.
- Fourthly, the Takeover Panel will consider whether the relevant party can influence significantly the conduct of the bid. For example, the Takeover Panel would look at the role the party has played in the due diligence exercise and its ability to control or veto increases in the bid price or changes to the consortium or bid structure.
- Finally, the Takeover Panel will consider the exit arrangements that are in place for the relevant party. It will be concerned to ensure that there is no short-term exit opportunity for that party and will wish to know whether there are any put/call or drag rights.

The above list of factors is not comprehensive; nor is it intended to be a cumulative test. The Takeover Panel has chosen to retain flexibility and certain factors may be inappropriate in certain circumstances. The Takeover Panel has specifically noted that each case will be considered on its individual merits, and has warned about over-reliance on previous rulings.

(g) *Management deals*
Even if the consortium member does not qualify as a joint offeror, it may still be possible to offer that consortium member a special arrangement if the party can be properly categorised as a member of management.

Rationale for the exemption: The management exemption exists because the Takeover Panel recognises that there is a legitimate commercial interest in permitting the management of the target to remain financially involved in the business. Without the exemption, public-to-private transactions would be far more difficult, if not impossible, to effect and this would be to the detriment of the market as a whole.

Tests for the exemption: In order to fall within this exemption to Rule 16, the following requirements must be met:
- First, the Takeover Panel must be consulted in all cases and its consent obtained.
- Secondly, the Takeover Panel is keen to ensure that any special deal does not protect management from the risks associated with their interest. Indeed, the Takeover Panel has specifically stated that the risks, as well as the rewards, associated with an equity interest should apply to management's retained interest. Therefore, option arrangements that guarantee the original offer price as a minimum would not be acceptable.
- Thirdly, the Rule 3 adviser will be required to state publicly that, in its opinion, the arrangements between the bidder and the relevant management of the target are fair and reasonable, and will write a letter to the Takeover Panel to that effect.
- Finally, to the extent that management are getting a retained interest (essentially an equity interest) in the target, approval of independent shareholders in a poll is required. There is no exemption for minimal interests.

Using the management exemption in a hostile context: The offer for Canary Wharf also provided some detail on how the exemption for management (contained in Rule 16.2) operates in a non-recommended situation. In that case, the executive chairman was a member of one of the competing consortia. His consortium was not the preferred bidder and so the issue arose as to how the need for shareholder approval would operate in a non-recommended or hostile context.

Clearly, the giving of the Rule 3 adviser's opinion and the convening of a shareholders' meeting requires the assistance of the target. Would the Takeover Panel compel the Rule 3 adviser and the target's board to take the necessary actions? The preliminary indications were that the Takeover Panel would not be prepared to insist on such assistance being given, but the matter was not pursued because the target and the Rule 3 adviser agreed to give an opinion on the matter and put it to shareholders. Indeed, while specifically not recommending the underlying offer, the target's board recommended that shareholders approve the special management deal so as to keep that underlying offer available for shareholders. What will happen if the target and the Rule 3 adviser choose not to assist remains to be seen.

6. **Management rollover**

A key aim in structuring management's rollover of target shares into bidder shares or loan notes is to ensure that the rollover obtains 'reorganisation treatment' under the UK capital gains tax legislation. This means that any latent gain on management's target shares is not realised at the time of the exchange, but is instead rolled over into the bidder shares or loan notes (avoiding an unfunded tax liability arising and deferring any tax charge until a later disposal of the bidder shares or loan notes).

As most of the target shareholders in a public-to-private will be 'cashing out', it is generally not possible to qualify for reorganisation treatment under Section 136 of the Taxation of Chargeable Gains Act 1992, so reorganisation treatment for management will be available only by structuring the transaction as an 'exchange' within Section 135 of the Taxation of Chargeable Gains Act.

Broadly, Section 135 applies where a bidder issues shares or loan notes to a person in exchange for shares in a target company where the bidder either holds, or will as a result of the exchange hold, more than 25% of the target's shares. If the target shareholder (and connected persons) holds more than 5% of any class of shares or debentures in the target, the exchange must take place for *bona fide* commercial reasons and not as part of a tax avoidance scheme in order for Section 135 to apply. This requirement should not present any problems in a public-to-private and advance clearance can be (and usually is) obtained from Her Majesty's Revenue and Customs (HMRC) in relation to the rollover.

A common way to ensure that Section 135 treatment is obtained for a management rollover is to take the acquisition of management's target shares outside the bid and to acquire their shares under a separate share purchase agreement between the bidder and management. The consideration for the purchase will be an agreed split of bidder shares, loan notes and/or cash. If the agreement covers at least 25% of the target's shares, Section 135 treatment will be obtained; however, if the figure is less than 25%, completion of the agreement will need to be conditional on the bidder being registered as the owner of the shares it is acquiring under the bid.

It is possible (although nowadays unusual) to structure management's rollover within Section 135 within the terms of a bid. Achieving Section 135 treatment for an exchange under the terms of a traditional takeover offer is straightforward (provided that at least 25% of the target is acquired pursuant to the offer); however, achieving this treatment as part of a scheme is more problematic.

As mentioned above, the most common scheme is a cancellation scheme; but it is not possible to structure a cancellation scheme within Section 135 as there is no transfer of the target shares to the bidder – the target shares are cancelled and new shares are issued to the bidder. Equally, in a typical public-to-private transaction, it is not usually possible to fall within any of the other rollover reliefs for reconstruction because bidder shares will not be issued to the other vendor shareholders.

Section 135 treatment is possible, however, with a 'transfer' scheme, under which the shares being rolled over are transferred by court order to the bidder, which will issue the consideration shares and/or loan notes to the transferors. The disadvantage of a transfer scheme is that it creates a 'sale' of the relevant shares, which gives rise to 0.5% stamp duty on the consideration provided.

Therefore, in this situation and/or when offerees under a scheme are given a loan note alternative, there is typically a 'hybrid' scheme whereby a cancellation scheme is combined with a transfer scheme. Under a hybrid scheme, immediately before the scheme becomes effective, the target shares are reclassified into two classes, so that one class of share is transferred under the transfer part of the scheme and the other class is cancelled under the cancellation part of the scheme. Shareholders may be given an option to elect for transfer treatment or cancellation treatment, and management will elect for transfer treatment. There are numerous recent examples of hybrid schemes including KKR/Stefano Pessina's bid for Alliance Boots, where both the Pessina-held shares and the loan note elected shares were transferred rather than being cancelled.

A hybrid scheme enables transferring shareholders to qualify for rollover treatment under Section 135 while avoiding stamp duty to the maximum extent possible, in respect of shareholders that opt for cash consideration. As before, if less than 25% of the target's shares are being transferred under the transfer scheme, it is necessary to make completion of the transfer scheme conditional upon the registration of the bidder as the owner of the shares issued to it under the cancellation scheme in order for Section 135 to apply.

Target shares held by, and bidder shares and loan notes issued to, management will be employment-regulated securities. However, it is usually possible to structure an exchange to avoid untoward income tax charges under Part 7 of the Income Tax (Earnings and Pensions) Act 2003.

Importantly, the Panel has clarified that such arrangements do not fall within the prohibition on offer-related arrangements contained in Rule 21.2 (more on these prohibitions and restrictions below).

7. **Certain funds**

One fundamental difference between a private deal and a public-to-private transaction is the need for certain funds.

Indeed, a key element of the Takeover Panel's purpose is to ensure certainty in the marketplace, and a prerequisite for this is that a bidder is permitted to announce an offer only after it has ensured that it can fulfil its obligations under that offer. Indeed, the fifth general principle states that before an offer is announced, the bidder must ensure that it can fulfil any cash consideration in full and has taken all reasonable measures to secure the implementation of any other type of consideration. In relation to this, Rule 2.7(d) states that where the offer is for cash or includes an element of cash, the announcement of a firm intention to make an offer (under Rule 2.7) must include a statement (usually by the financial adviser to the bidder) that there are resources in place to satisfy the terms of the offer and that, implicitly, the bidder has the cash facilities available. The giving of this statement triggers what is known as the 'certain funds period'.

The financial adviser may itself become liable to pay for acceptances under such an offer unless it can demonstrate that its statement was given responsibly and that it took all reasonable steps to assure itself that the cash would be available. Indeed, unless it can demonstrate such care, the financial adviser may also be subject to claims for negligent misstatement. With such potential liability (not to mention risk to its reputation), there will usually be a separate due diligence work-stream for the financial adviser and its lawyers reviewing the debt and equity documents so that the statement can be verified. Naturally, the financial adviser will seek to ensure that any remaining conditions are entirely within the control of the bidder and will usually request comfort letters from the bidder providing certain assurances and undertakings in connection with the financing.

Accordingly, the certain funds period will require that the debt and equity fund providers commit to their involvement with considerably less conditionality than in a typical private transaction. This commitment is also given much earlier than in a private transaction as it may be months before the offer finally closes and the funds are required. A longstop date is permitted for the lenders in this situation, but any conditions attached are severely restricted. Typically, the limited restrictions may include the withdrawal of funding if the bidder becomes subject to an insolvency procedure or such other limited event as is exclusively within the control of the bidder (breaching a conduct covenant or a negative covenant such as a negative pledge or prohibition on other borrowings).

Rule 24.8 is also derived from the third general principle. This rule requires a similar statement to be made in the offer document. This is known as 'cash confirmation'. It is not possible to provide a conditional form of cash confirmation under Rule 24.8. The Takeover Panel has received questions in relation to the conditions to which a cash offer may be subject. It would be concerned to ensure that the only conditions permitted are those required under law or regulation validly to issue the relevant securities – for example, the passing of resolutions to create or allot the securities, or the admittance of the securities to the London Stock Exchange.[2]

The implications of these requirements are also felt when drafting the documents, since the consent of the Takeover Panel is likely to be obtained only for a specific and exceptional condition.

8. Break fees

It used to be a feature of UK takeovers that the target company would agree to pay the bidder a fee if the proposed transaction did not complete due to certain factors (such as the announcement of a higher competing offer or the withdrawal of the recommendation of the target's directors).

---

[2] Practice Statement 10, "Cash offers financed by the issue of the offeror securities".

Such arrangements are now prohibited (subject to certain limited exceptions) following the changes that were made to the City Code on September 19 2011.

These arrangements had been particularly prevalent in public-to-private transactions as they provided a degree of cost protection (typically up to 1% of total deal value) to private equity bidders who would otherwise have incurred substantial expenses in conducting due diligence and structuring a bid, but then faced the risk of seeing their bid trumped by a higher subsequent offer from a third party.

It had been felt that the directors of target companies in the United Kingdom had become unable to resist requests from bidders for cost protection by way of break fees on the basis that such terms were perceived to be the market norm and that, consequently, the directors of target companies were being hindered in their ability to maximise shareholder value through the creation of competitive tension with other competing bidders.

Rule 21.2 of the City Code accordingly prohibited the entry by a target company into any "offer-related arrangement".

The prohibition is particularly broadly drafted, and in addition to banning break fees or other work fee arrangements, also banned:
- no-shop provisions;
- non-solicit provisions;
- notification undertakings on the target board in respect of any approaches by potential competing offerors; and
- matching or similar rights entitling the bidder to a set period of time within which to either match, or improve on any higher competing offer, with the understanding that the target board's recommendation would be maintained provided the bidder invoked such right and at least matched such a competing offer.

A further effect of Rule 21.2 is in preventing bidders and targets from entering into transaction or implementation agreements (as had become customarily the case in respect of takeovers by way of a scheme of arrangement and also increasingly so in the case of takeover offers).

In certain cases, these agreements have been replaced by so-called cooperation agreements, essentially much shorter agreements containing provisions that relate only to the management and administration of the offer process. To date, such agreements have been closely vetted by the Takeover Panel.

Accordingly, while transaction/implementation agreements and the practice of agreeing break fees remain common features of public merger and acquisition transactions in many jurisdictions, this is no longer the case in the United Kingdom, often a source of some surprise to international investors considering a public bid for a UK target.

The limited exceptions where a break fee arrangement will still be permissible (subject to the consent of the Takeover Panel having been obtained) are where either a hostile offer has been announced, in which case the target board may offer an inducement fee to a competing bidder (or bidders), or where a target board has announced that it is seeking bids through a formal sale process. The Takeover Panel has also indicated that in certain cases where a listed company is in financial distress it may be necessary for the directors to offer inducement or work fees to potential bidders in order to persuade them to commit the time and resources required to analyse a potential transaction.

The Takeover Panel has clarified that, while it sees no reason to prohibit a bidder from seeking some or all of the above protections from a target shareholder as part of the irrevocable undertakings obtained in connection with a bid, it considers target shareholders who also happen to be directors of the target to be bound by Rule 21.2 and therefore prohibited from entering into any form of irrevocable undertaking other than one where they simply undertake to accept the offer/vote in favour of the scheme.

Due to the subdued deal volumes experienced since all these changes came into force, it is difficult to assess definitively their impact. However, it is clear that the removal of the ability to take steps to manage exposure to deal costs and the likelihood of competing bids emerging makes public-to-privates more risky for private equity houses.

That said, there are precedents for major shareholders having agreed to pay break fees as part of the irrevocable undertakings that they have signed in connection with an offer, as well as providing other protections which would customarily have been provided by the target company or its directors (see "Irrevocable undertakings" below for further information).

9. Stake building

The questions of whether and when to buy shares in the target are often of central strategic importance to the success of a bid and, since the prohibitions on offer-related arrangements were introduced, stake building has become an increasingly important part of the bidding strategy of many offerors. However, before taking any action a number of factors need to be considered, and in any case some private equity-backed bidders will have difficulty stake building because of investment restrictions that many private equity houses are subject to in their fund documentation.

9.1 Concert parties

It is essential in any public-to-private transaction, especially those that involve a consortium, to establish who will be 'acting in concert' for the purposes of the City Code before any action is taken. The significance of acting in concert lies in the amalgamation of interests in shares and group responsibility for each other's actions. It is therefore of obvious importance to stake building (ie, buying shares) in a target.

Persons acting in concert comprise persons that, under an agreement or understanding (whether formal or informal), cooperate to obtain or consolidate control of the target.

There are some long-established relationships (group companies/companies and their directors or pension funds/fund managers) that the Takeover Panel will presume are acting in concert unless the contrary is established. In addition, 'affiliated persons' will be deemed to be acting in concert with each other. An affiliate of a person is one in respect of which that person:

- has a shareholder or voting majority;
- is a shareholder that can appoint or remove a majority of the board;
- is a shareholder that controls the shareholders' majority pursuant to an agreement; or
- can or does exercise control or dominant influence.

There is a presumption that a private equity house will be acting in concert with the management team during a management buyout. More significantly, problems can arise when private equity houses form part of a larger group of companies. In addition to affiliate companies, the Takeover Panel will presume that all group companies and associate companies (ie, those where there is ownership or control of more than 20% of a company) are acting in concert. In large consortium bids, when the private equity contributors may well be from large groups, the Takeover Panel must be consulted at the very early stages to establish how they will view certain relationships.

This can be an important issue as there are a number of consequences that arise as a result of being classified as a concert party to a bidder, especially when target shares are being (or may be) bought. The following rules and issues should be considered.

(a) **Rule 6**

Rule 6.1 provides that if purchases of target shares have been made either in the three months preceding the offer period or during the period between the commencement of the offer period and an announcement of a firm intention to make an offer, in either case by the bidder or concert parties, the offer may not be on less favourable terms. The Takeover Panel may apply this rule to purchases more than three months earlier if it thinks it necessary.

Rule 6.2 provides that after the commencement of the offer period, purchases of target securities by the bidder or concert parties above the offer price trigger a requirement to raise the offer price accordingly.

(b) **Rule 11**

This provides that if shares under offer have been purchased for cash by a bidder or concert parties during or within the 12 months preceding the offer period and those shares carry 10% or more of the voting rights of that class, or where any shares under offer are purchased by a bidder or concert parties during the offer period for cash, the offer must be in cash (or accompanied by a full cash alternative), and must be made at not less than the highest price paid by the bidder (or concert party) during the relevant period, unless the Takeover Panel permits otherwise. Certain share exchanges may be treated as cash purchases for this purpose.

(c) **Rule 8**

It is necessary to make a disclosure detailing the bidder's interest in any relevant securities in the target company (provided such interests exceed 1% of the relevant class of target securities). Such an announcement must be made within 10 days of the commencement of an offer period, or if an announcement of a firm intention to make an offer has been released by a bidder under Rule 2.7, such a disclosure must be made at the time that the announcement is released. Such opening position disclosures must include details of all holdings of concert parties to the bidder. Accordingly, the correct identification of any concert parties to the bidder and the accurate collation of a record of all holdings of any relevant securities should be a priority early housekeeping item for any bidder.

Rule 8 also requires the disclosure of all dealings in relevant securities by the bidder, the target and their associates. It also catches any other person that owns or controls 1% or more of the bidder or the target (or will do so), whether or not that person is an associate. The concept of associate can include relationships that are unrelated to the offer, but can also include certain concert parties (eg, parent or subsidiary companies). Indeed, because the concepts of associate and concert party overlap, it is important for concert parties to consider any obligations that may arise under this rule.

(d) **Rule 9**

Mandatory offers (or 'Rule 9 offers') may be triggered in a number of situations when *de facto* control is deemed to have been obtained. Crucially, in each case the interests of parties acting in concert will be amalgamated and considered together. A Rule 9 offer can also be triggered during an existing offer and care needs to be taken to ensure that all interests are taken into consideration. For example, a small shareholding in a group outside the main bidding party must not be forgotten. If a Rule 9 offer is triggered (either inadvertently or deliberately), there are a number of restrictions on the form of the offer that must be made, including that the offer will need to be in cash (or with a cash alternative) at not less than the highest price paid by the bidder or any concert party during the previous 12 months.

(e) **Financial Services and Markets Act and Criminal Justice Act**

It will also be necessary for a bidder considering stake building to have regard to the insider dealing and market abuse provisions of the Criminal Justice Act and the Financial Services and Markets Act respectively. In particular, care should be taken that the bidder does not receive price-sensitive information as part of its due diligence investigations that would prevent it from acquiring shares in the target company.

(f) **Shares to which the offer relates**

Perhaps the most important factor for the bidder, however, is that in an offer any target shares owned by the bidder before the offer is made (ie, before publication of the offer document) are excluded from the 90% threshold required for compulsory acquisition of the remaining minority shareholders. Indeed, even if the bidder initially intends to use a scheme and not utilise these 'squeeze-out' provisions, it is worth bearing this in mind because the bidder may change the structure of its offer from a scheme to a conventional offer.

In addition, in a scheme any shares owned by the bidder at the time of the court-convened meeting to approve the scheme cannot be voted at that meeting, but the scheme must still be approved by 75% of the shareholders present at the court-convened meeting.

(g) **Buying shares in the offer period**

Fighting off the competition: It may be tactically desirable for a bidder to buy shares during the offer period. The offer period is defined in the City Code as the time from the announcement of a proposed or possible offer until the first closing date (or until the offer lapses or is declared as unconditional as to acceptances).

Rule 4.2(b) makes it clear that purchases of target shares by the bidder during the offer period are permitted, provided that it can be established that the seller is not an exempt principal trader connected with the bidder. Rule 6.2 and Rule 8, outlined in the previous section, are clearly important to share buying during the offer period and a bidder should take care to ensure that all of their disclosure and other obligations are carefully adhered to – both before and during the offer period.

The main driver for buying shares during the offer period is the existence or threat of a competing offer. There are many reasons to buy or not to buy, and each situation should be analysed on its facts.

For example, buying target shares may, depending on its success, prevent a competing bidder from being able to rely on the squeeze-out provisions or, perhaps, even the 75% threshold required for a scheme. However, even if such a high percentage cannot be obtained, the potential existence of a hostile minority may put off an as-yet uncommitted second bidder. Buying shares may also offer a means of deal costs protection for a bidder if another bidder makes a higher competing offer that that bidder is unwilling or unable to match.

The availability of shares in the market will depend on the particular facts of the case in hand. Shareholders may be unwilling to sell if they consider that there is serious potential for a higher competing offer. Indeed, if this is the case it is possible that the market price would be above the offer price and therefore shares could not be purchased without the bidder raising its bid. On the other hand, the 'time value of money' may compel enough shareholders to sell at a small discount in the market rather than wait to be paid out under the offer.

US shareholders: Broadly speaking, buying shares during an offer period is prohibited under US securities law. However, provided that less than 40% of the target's shares are beneficially owned by US shareholders, there are two potential exemptions from the US takeover rules, known as the 'Tier I' and 'Tier II' exemptions. The US takeover rules may not be relevant if the bid is structured as a scheme, although they should be considered in all circumstances.

The Tier I exemption applies when 10% or less of the target's shares are beneficially owned by US shareholders. Provided that the terms of the offer in the United States are no less favourable than those made to non-US shareholders (although loan notes are not required to be replicated in the United States), this exemption will exempt the offer from most US takeover rules and certain registration requirements. The prohibitions on the bidder buying shares (contained in Rule 14e-5 of the Securities and Exchange Act 1934) also do not apply to Tier I exempted transactions.

The Tier II exemption applies when more than 10% but less than 40% of the target's shares are beneficially owned by US shareholders. In this case there is only partial relief from the US takeover rules and the bidder is not permitted to buy shares. Unsurprisingly, therefore, the SEC has been approached for specific exemptions to the prohibition on the purchasing of shares and has been persuaded on a number of occasions to issue favourable 'no action' letters to bidders. On deciding whether to agree that it will issue a 'no action' letter the SEC will consider:

- the number of US shareholders;
- whether the offer is being made on the same basis to US (as to non-US) shareholders;
- whether the consideration is cash or securities;
- the foreign regulation to which the offer will be subject; and
- whether the principal trading market for the target's shares is outside the United States.

This is not a definitive list of relevant factors and each case will be considered on its merits.

10. Employee share schemes

Where the target has granted share options or other awards under employee share schemes, the bidder will need to take into account the cost of acquiring the shares subject to such awards and determine whether there is a risk that the awards granted under the schemes could result in the existence of minority shareholders in the target following completion of the offer.

Awards under employee share schemes will typically vest in the event of a change of control. Depending on the terms of the employee share scheme, vesting may be subject to the satisfaction of performance conditions or pro-rated by reference to the proportion of the vesting period that has elapsed, in each case as determined by the target's remuneration committee.

Under Rule 15 of the City Code, the bidder is required to make an appropriate offer or proposal to the holders of any options to acquire shares in the target to ensure their interests are safeguarded. Equality of treatment is required. As a result, the proposals will typically aim to provide the option-holders with value equivalent to the difference between the exercise price of their option and the offer price. In certain circumstances they may also be offered compensation for any reduction in the value of their options to them resulting from early exercise.

Most commonly, the proposal will simply be that option-holders may exercise their options in accordance with the rules of the employee share scheme and then sell the shares they acquire on exercise of the options to the bidder in the offer. However, there are a number of alternatives that should be considered.

10.1 Cashless exercise

A cashless exercise facility provides that option-holders may exercise their options without paying the exercise price to the target up front on the basis that the exercise price will be deducted from the consideration they receive under the offer (together with any income tax and national insurance required to be deducted).

10.2 Cash cancellation

Cash cancellation gives option-holders the opportunity to cancel them in exchange for a cash payment equal in amount to the gain on their option or to exchange them for options over shares in the bidder with an equivalent value ('rollover').

Cash cancellation, although cheaper in cashflow terms (as the bidder is required to fund only the amount of the gain rather than the amount required to purchase the option shares), is less common than it used to be. This is mainly because the statutory corporation tax deduction that may arise on the exercise of employee share options does not arise when options are cancelled.

10.3 Rollover

Rollover is relatively rare in the context of public-to-private transactions. This is because one of the main reasons for offering rollover is that it may be beneficial to the holders of certain options approved by HMRC, as it may permit them to defer exercise until their options may be exercised free of income tax. In the context of a public-to-private this may not be possible, as the statutory conditions for an approved scheme may not be satisfied following the change of control. It would also be necessary to agree with HMRC a valuation of the bidder shares subject to approved options.

The City Code requires that, where practicable, the proposals to option holders are posted at the same time as the offer document. In practice, however, they are often delayed until the offer has gone unconditional. The board of the target must obtain independent advice on the proposals and communicate the substance of such advice to the option-holders, together with the board's views. A copy of the proposals must be lodged with the Takeover Panel. Under the City Code, copies of any relevant documents sent to shareholders must also be sent to the holders of options to acquire shares of the same class as those to which the offer relates.

The terms of the employee share schemes must be reviewed carefully to establish whether options may remain exercisable after the period during which the bidder may acquire shares under the statutory compulsory acquisition provisions. Typically the options will, to the extent not exercised in accordance with the bidder's proposals, lapse when the compulsory acquisition period expires. However, this is not always the case and care should be taken where the offer is structured as a scheme. Care is also needed to ensure the options are dealt with in as efficient manner as possible as, in particular, approved options may lose their beneficial tax treatment if they are exercised after the target's shares cease to be listed.

11. Documentation differences between public and private transaction

11.1 Public documents

The City Code contains various rules, contents requirements and standards of preparation for the documentation required in an offer, the details of which are beyond the scope of this chapter. Instead, there follows a brief look at the differences between what is required in an offer and what is required in a private acquisition.

The documentation for a public-to-private is very different from that used in a usual private purchase and can itself vary depending on whether the offer is hostile or recommended. Put simply, for a recommended offer the target and the bidder will work together to produce the documentation, whereas in a hostile offer both parties will produce separate documents.

Various press announcements will be required throughout the process and their timing and contents requirements (as set out in the City Code) must be strictly adhered to. Releasing announcements early can be as serious as releasing them too late, particularly in relation to announcements of a firm intention to make an offer (Rule 2.7). This is the key document that starts the offer: it sets out the key terms of the offer as well as any permitted conditions. As detailed below, once issued it is only in exceptional circumstances that a bidder is released from the obligation of proceeding with the offer.

Due to the recent changes that were introduced relating to announcement of a possible offer, together with the automatic imposition of 28-day put up or shut up deadlines, the need to maintain strict secrecy and carefully to choreograph the release of any announcements relating to a possible offer or a firm intention to make an offer is now of key importance.

The central document for a public offer is the offer document. The requirements for this are set out in Rules 24 and 25 of the City Code, and it should contain all the information required to decide whether to accept an offer. It is assembled by the bidder, the financial advisers, the lawyers and, in a recommended offer, the target.

Rule 24.3 requires that the offer document contain a detailed summary of how the offer is to be financed, including an obligation to publish details of those arrangements and to make a copy of the relevant documents available for inspection. Where debt financing for the offer is required and the facility is to be syndicated, if the facility contains market flex provisions, it has been possible under the new regime to obtain the Takeover Panel's consent to the non-disclosure of those arrangements, at least for a short period between the announcement of the offer and the publication of the offer document.

This provides for a shorter period than might otherwise be ideal for the syndication of a facility, during which commercially sensitive information on the headroom available to the syndication agent does not need to be disclosed.

In practice, on larger syndicated deals, this may simply lead to syndication agents demanding higher upfront pricing to ensure that syndication can be achieved rapidly.

Importantly for public-to-privates, the Takeover Panel has indicated that it is less focused on granular disclosure relating to a private equity-backed bidder's equity funding arrangements, and a general description of these, as opposed to detailed disclosure to the private equity house's fund investor level, will be sufficient.

Additionally, information regarding the bidder itself must be made public, including details of its financial and trading prospects and an estimate of all its all offer-related advisory fees and expenses.

The bidder must also make a statement regarding its intentions for the future of the target and its employees, in particular its intentions regarding employer contributions into the target company's pension schemes. This obligation extends to making a negative statement where the bidder has no plans in respect of employees, or considers that its offer is unlikely to have repercussions on employment or the location of the target's operations. Any statement made must be sufficiently specific; statements of a general nature will not be acceptable to the Takeover Panel. The bidder is then regarded by the Takeover Panel as being committed to its statement of intention (or negative statement) for the following 12 months.

11.2 Irrevocable undertakings

Irrevocable undertakings from existing shareholders are a key way for a bidder to achieve confidence about the potential take-up in an offer and are therefore often important documents. They have historically been either 'hard' or 'soft': a hard irrevocable being binding in all circumstances, and a soft irrevocable falling away on the announcement of a competing higher offer. However, their terms have become more sophisticated as a result of negotiation and competitive markets. It is now difficult to obtain a hard irrevocable from an institutional shareholder and so 'semi-soft' irrevocables have become more common. These are binding provided that there is not a competing offer with a price above an agreed threshold.

Perhaps unsurprisingly, since the introduction of the prohibition on offer-related arrangements, bidders have sought to regain some of the protections that they originally received from target companies through irrevocable undertakings from shareholders.

Consequently, there has been a marked increase in requests from bidders for the addition of protections such as matching or topping rights in irrevocable undertakings (indeed, approximately one-third of the takeovers announced in the first six months of 2013 contained such rights). Bidders have also been requesting that shareholders include break fees in their irrevocable undertakings.

The Takeover Panel has recently clarified that where such protections are requested in irrevocables to be provided by directors of the target company, these would be viewed as offer-related arrangements and therefore prohibited. As such, the enhanced level of protection mentioned is only available through irrevocables provided by third-party shareholders in the target company.

Of course, despite such alternatives, irrevocables are not always forthcoming and frequently the best a bidder can get is a non-binding letter of intent from shareholders.

11.3 Prospectuses

A prospectus or equivalent document is usually required when shares are being offered as consideration (or part consideration), and various circulars will also need to be prepared.

Of course, to ensure that responsibility should in fact lie with those who are responsible when the bidder is controlled directly or indirectly by another person or group, the Takeover Panel will often require additional persons (eg, the parent company's directors) to take responsibility for the production of the prospectus or prospectus equivalent. This is particularly pertinent to a public-to-private transaction in which a private equity house will need to take responsibility. Naturally, in a large investment house, it may be possible to agree with the Takeover Panel that only members of the relevant investment committee need to approve the document. In a public-to-private transaction, it would therefore be sensible for a private equity house to approach the Takeover Panel to discuss where responsibility should lie at an early stage of the process.

Each person making a statement should be made aware that he will have accepted and assumed personal liability for the parts of the document for which he is responsible.

11.4 Conditions to an offer

Offers will be subject to conditions (including the acceptance condition). These conditions should be set out in full in the Rule 2.7 announcement announcing a firm intention to make an offer. They will also be repeated in the formal offer document.

Generally speaking, there are several categories of specific conditions that appear – for example, the acceptance condition, antitrust and other regulatory clearance, offeror shareholder approval and the listing of any consideration securities. These are usually very specific in their drafting and it is clear to all parties whether they have been met. If a bidder has a specific concern, it is best practice for it to agree a specific condition addressing the point.

Rule 13 provides that conditions will not generally be permitted if they involve subjectivity. However, it is acknowledged by the Takeover Panel that there may be some need for subjectivity when considering, for example, obligations that are attached to the granting of a regulatory clearance and are proposed by the relevant authority as the price for the clearance.

In addition to the specific conditions, most offers also include fairly lengthy boilerplate conditions, which are drafted on a more generic basis. These are intended to cover changes in circumstances and unknown events that might occur after at the time the offer has been made. Unlike in the private arena, where the invocation of such conditions is a matter of contract law, in public-to-privates the Takeover Panel has made it increasingly difficult for bidders to invoke such conditions.

Rule 13.5(a) states that with the exception of the acceptance condition and any UK or EU antitrust condition, "an offeror should not invoke any condition so as to cause the offer to lapse unless the circumstances which give rise to the condition are of material significance to the offeror in the context of the offer".

The best example of the materiality threshold that will be imposed by the Takeover Panel can be found in the Takeover Panel's decision not to allow WPP to invoke a material adverse change clause following the terrorist attacks on September 11 2001.

The Takeover Panel's attitude towards the conditions WPP attempted to invoke was set out in Panel Statement 2001/15. In this the Takeover Panel stated that when considering whether a bidder can invoke a material adverse change clause "the [relevant] test requires an adverse change of very considerable significance striking at the heart of the purpose of the transaction in question, analogous ... to something that would justify frustration of a legal contract". This was particularly severe and as there was no other precedent, the Takeover Panel statement gave rise to fears that a bidder would need to demonstrate legal frustration if it were to rely on a material adverse change clause. It was therefore perhaps unsurprising that the Takeover Panel later noted (in Practice Statement 5) that the test is less than that for legal frustration. Nevertheless, bidders should be in no doubt that the material change required in order for a material adverse change clause to become enforceable remains considerable.

12. Timetable

Code bids are required to operate within a strict timeframe prescribed by the City Code. The following is a standard timetable showing the key milestones in a recommended code bid for both a traditional takeover offer and a scheme. The timetable commences from the date upon which a firm intention to make an offer is announced, but it should be noted that, due to the new put up or shut up regime there may have been an earlier period of activity and announcements.

If an offer is announced and then another offer is made, both bidders move onto the latter bidder's timetable so that they dovetail, with both reaching Day 60 (ie, the time limit by which one of them is required to hold in excess of 50% of the offeree) together.

The timetable for a scheme is different as it follows a court process and the requirements in the Companies Act.

Day (D)	Offer	Section 895 scheme of arrangement
Up to D -28	Announcement of a firm intention to make an offer by the bidder. At this point, the bidder is *de facto* bound to proceed with the offer and should have certain funds in place.	Announcement of a firm intention to make an offer by the bidder. At this point, the bidder is *de facto* bound to proceed with the offer and should have certain funds in place.
D -9		Issue claim form, and supporting witness statement, seeking an order of the court to convene shareholders' meeting.
D -2	Court hearing of the claim form, order granted to convene shareholders' meeting.	
D	Last date for posting the formal offer document.	Post scheme document and proxy forms to shareholders (including notice of meetings).

continued on next page

Public-to-privates

Day (D)	Offer	Section 895 scheme of arrangement
D + 14	Last date for the target board to post its response to the offer. If the offer is recommended, the target board will have already complied with this by recommending the offer within the offer document.	
D +21	Earliest closing date for the offer. Public announcement of the acceptance levels to date and, if applicable, an extension of the offer (note that this timeline would be extended to D +28 if the offer document is also to be sent to the United States).	
D +24		Court convened meeting and extraordinary general meeting held.
D +25		Lodge with court the documents supporting the adjourned claim form and application for directions to fix the date of the sanction hearing.
D +32		Hearing of application for directions, order granted for hearings to sanction the scheme and reduction.
D +33		Advertise notice of sanction hearing as directed by the court.
D +39	Last date for the release by the target of material new information (eg, trading results, profit forecasts).	
D +42	Date on which the target shareholders who have already accepted the offer can withdraw those acceptances if the offer has not been declared unconditional as to acceptances.	

continued on next page

Day (D)	Offer	Section 895 scheme of arrangement
D +43		Hearing to sanction the scheme and related reduction, final order granted and minute stamped.
D +44		Registration of order sanctioning the scheme of arrangement and the order confirming the reduction of capital with registrar of companies. Scheme becomes effective.
D +46	Last date for the bidder to revise its offer.	Advertise notice of reduction of capital as directed by the court.
D +60	Last date for the offer to be declared unconditional as to acceptances.	
D +74 (ie, 14 days after being declared unconditional as to acceptances)	Earliest date on which the offer can close.	
D +81 (ie, 21 days after being declared unconditional as to acceptances)	Last date for the offer to be declared wholly unconditional.	
D+ 95 (ie, 14 days after being declared unconditional in all respects)	Last date for payment of the offer consideration.	

13. **Squeeze-out and sell-out**

Minority shareholders are potential thorns in the side of a successful bidder. Not only are requisite thresholds put in jeopardy, but an awkward minority shareholder may also be able to generate bad publicity or undermine the smooth running of the target business, particularly at general meetings. Of course, it is also possible for the minority shareholders themselves to suffer, particularly in the context of a public-to-private transaction, when they may lose any market for their shares.

To provide both the bidder and the minority shareholders with a recourse against these issues, English law has long recognised 'squeeze-out' and 'sell-out' rights, for the bidder and the minority shareholders respectively, as soon as 90% of the shareholders have accepted an offer (see below for the relevant calculation). These rights are set out in Part 28 of the Companies Act.

For either the bidder or the minority shareholder to be able to benefit from the compulsory acquisitions provisions in the Companies Act, there must have been a takeover offer. Any offer that satisfies the following two conditions is a 'takeover offer':

- The offer is for all of the shares (or all shares of the same class) in the target; and
- The terms of the offer are the same.

As before, the squeeze-out and sell-out provisions are triggered under different twofold tests for the bidder and for the minority shareholder. The bidder's right to buy out the minority shares is triggered when it has acquired or unconditionally contracted to acquire both:

- 90% of the shares to which the offer relates; and
- 90% of the voting rights attaching to the shares to which the offer relates.

A minority shareholder's right to be bought out (at the offer price and on the same terms) arises when the bidder has acquired or contracted to acquire (whether unconditionally or otherwise) 90% of both the issued shares and the voting rights in the target. As this percentage may include shares that are never acquired by the offeror, since the relevant conditions for the acquisition of certain shares may not be met, Section 983(7) of the Companies Act provides that that minority shareholder will not be deemed to have served notice until the bidder has acquired or unconditionally contracted to acquire 90% of the relevant shares.

13.1 When is 90% not 90%?

Care should be taken to ensure that the correct figures are used when calculating the percentages for either the bidder or the minority shareholders.

When calculating the 90% threshold that will trigger the bidder's right to squeeze out, shares that were held (or contracted to be acquired) by the bidder or that were owned (or contracted to be acquired) by an associate of the bidder (as defined in the Companies Act) at the date that the offer was first open for acceptance are excluded entirely from the calculation. In both cases the Companies Act confirms that the relevant acquisition contract may be subject to conditions without affecting the calculation. However, shares acquired after the offer is made are included (whether or not they trigger an increased offer under Rule 6.2 of the City Code). The offer is made only when the offer document is despatched (and not, for example, when it is announced).

Shares that are subject to a contract that is intended to secure the acceptance of an offer when it is made, and that is entered into by deed, for negligible consideration or for consideration consisting of the promise of the bidder to make the offer, are not considered shares held (or contracted to be acquired) by the bidder and so can count towards the 90% figure needed for squeeze-out. This should allow shares covered by properly drafted irrevocables to count towards the requisite percentage, despite the fact that they are usually entered into before the offer is made.

For this reason, there have been occasions in the past where offers have been structured such that the announcement of an intention to make an offer and the offer document itself are released and posted on the same day, in conjunction with the signing of an agreement pursuant to which the bidder acquires shares in the target company. This structuring device enables those shares to be counted towards the 90% threshold.

On the other hand, when establishing when the right of a minority shareholder to be bought out arises, it is necessary to have regard to the entire issued share capital of the target, whether or not the offer was for all such shares. In addition, all of the shares held by the bidder before the offer as well as those acquired (or agreed to be acquired) after the offer opens are included in the calculation. In both cases shares acquired (or agreed to be acquired) by associates of the bidder are deemed to be acquired (or agreed to be acquired) by the bidder.

Therefore, it can be easier for a minority shareholder to trigger its sell-out threshold than for a bidder to trigger its squeeze-out threshold. For example, if a bidder has a 25% interest at the time that the offer is made, it will need to obtain 90% of the remaining 75% (ie, 67.5%), in addition to its existing 25%. Therefore, the bidder will have to have acquired (or agreed to acquire) 92.5% of the target before it has the requisite percentage. However, a minority will be able to force the purchase when the bidder has acquired (or agreed to acquire) 90%.

The offer must be open to all foreign shareholders. However, where an offer is not communicated to the target shareholders, this will not prevent the offer from being a takeover offer if:

- those shareholders have no registered addresses in the United Kingdom;
- the offer was not communicated to those shareholders in order not to contravene the law of a country or territory outside the United Kingdom; and
- either:
  - the offer is published in the *Official Gazette*; or
  - the offer can be inspected, or a copy of it obtained, at a place in a European Economic Area state or on a website, and a notice is published in the *Official Gazette* specifying the address of that place or website.

This notwithstanding, the shareholdings of these foreign shareholders will need to be included in the various thresholds mentioned above. Of course, it may not be possible for the offer to be on the same terms for foreign shareholders when, for example, foreign securities laws may conflict with some of the terms (eg, consideration).

Finally, if there have been any special deals with shareholders (eg, the management of the target), it will be necessary to establish whether the special deal can be considered part of the wider offer.

13.2 When is 100% not 100%?

When considering the effectiveness of any squeeze-out procedure, a bidder should have regard to the nature and number of convertible securities in the target. Having

established what convertible securities are in place, a bidder will be better placed to establish which of the following two procedures for acquiring them is most suitable:
- to treat convertible securities as any other class; or
- to wait for the securities to convert and treat their converted status as the relevant class.

Problems for ensuring that minority shareholders can be squeezed out arise under both methods, although more frequently under the second.

Treating convertible securities as one with ordinary shares under the Companies Act will allow warrants and convertible loan stock to be acquired. However, options are not 'securities' and therefore a bidder will be unable to utilise the squeeze-out procedure in respect of them. It is therefore possible that options becoming exercisable may not coincide with the compulsory acquisition procedure and that the bidder may be left with a minority shareholder.

If the offer is open for the security into which the convertible securities may be converted, it would be possible for a bidder to move below the 90% threshold, having previously passed it, as a result of the conversion of securities. If a squeeze-out notice has already been served, then it remains valid, regardless of this change in circumstance. However, a bidder may not serve any additional notices until the requisite threshold has been met again.

When considering what offer should be made, therefore, the bidder should consider any existing convertibles and to which securities it wants the offer to relate. In other words, a bidder can, by carefully defining the securities to which the offer relates, avoid a number of hazards. It is therefore essential that a bidder considers what 90% denominator should be used.

Finally, if a bidder cannot reach the 90% threshold for reasons other than dissenting shareholders, such as a considerable number of untraceable shareholders, then it is possible to use a scheme to remove the minority. Naturally, if the 90% threshold is not met because of opposition from certain shareholders, a scheme is unlikely to offer a bidder any chance of success.

13.3 Recent developments – getting to 100%

Traditionally, acquired wisdom was that those institutional shareholders that had not accepted an offer would, following the declaration of the offer becoming unconditional in all respects, be more than likely to accept the offer and push the bidder over the requisite threshold. This is often the case for passive tracker funds, for example. However, practice during the height of the recent boom years challenged that general proposition. This was no doubt due in part to the number of public-to-privates being financed by private equity houses, which have demonstrated an ability to make significant profits over short periods in buoyant markets. As shareholders have seen their previous investments re-sold, they have perhaps wondered why they sold in the first place. Indeed, trusting a bidder to bring greater returns, institutional shareholders may hold onto their shares and become, in effect, silent partners in the target who are permitted to hold unlisted stock.

For the shareholder and the bidder, what action to take will ultimately be a strategic decision. However, a bidder should bear a number of issues in mind (beyond the obvious concern of its relationship with the relevant shareholder) if it looks like reaching 100% will not be possible.

(a) **Banks and financial assistance**

For the financing banks, the certainty of being able to avoid any financial assistance issues is imperative and for this it is necessary to ensure that the company can be re-registered as a private limited company. It is therefore very rare to see leveraged buy-outs with an acceptance condition of less than 75%, unless a very careful analysis of the shareholders has been done and there can be little doubt that institutional 'tracker' shareholders will accept the offer immediately on it becoming unconditional and so virtually guarantee the threshold being met.

(b) **Shareholder decisions**

Ordinary resolutions require a 50% majority to be passed, but the majority of significant corporate decisions require a special resolution and so a 75% majority. Clearly, a minority shareholder that is acting as a silent partner in order to benefit from uplift in the share price will probably seek to cause as little trouble as possible, other than protecting its position. However, a shareholder determined to cause difficulties (which could, of course, be a previously cooperative shareholder) could use its leverage over this threshold to significant negative effect.

(c) **Statutory powers and protections of minority shareholders**

There are a number of minority rights contained in the Companies Act. An analysis of all of them is unnecessary and beyond the scope of this chapter; however, a bidder should consider the powers of a minority (and coalitions of minorities) carefully before lowering its minimum acceptance condition.

Benelux

Gaike Dalenoord
Elke Janssens
Margaretha Wilkenhuysen
NautaDutilh

The Benelux is a term that refers to the union of Belgium, the Netherlands and Luxembourg. This union was first initiated as a result of a joint customs agreement signed in 1944. With the formation of the Benelux, it was anticipated that the customs union might pave the way for wider economic cooperation between those countries. However, over time the Benelux as a union became less relevant because of the establishment and rapid growth of the much larger European Economic Community (EEC), later succeeded by the European Union (EU), of which the Benelux countries are among the original members. Still, the region continues to be well known for its international and entrepreneurial character and the name Benelux is now used in a more general way to refer to the geographic, economic and cultural grouping of the three countries.

Despite the commonalities of the Benelux countries, their private equity markets differ from each other quite significantly. Belgium has an increasingly active venture capital market, while the market in the Netherlands focuses more on traditional private equity and leveraged finance. In contrast, Luxembourg lacks a substantial domestic private equity market but is a major world centre for tax-efficient fund structuring. This chapter will discuss the main developments and trends – legal, transaction-related and/or tax-related – relevant for private equity in each of the three countries, taking into account the nature of its particular market.

1. Belgium

1.1 Development of private equity market

The year 2012 was not the best one for the Belgian private equity and venture capital market, 2013 proved to be better and 2014 promises to continue this positive trend. While Belgian gross domestic product (GDP) grew 1.9% in 2011, the National Bank of Belgium[1] reported a decrease of around 0.2% for 2012, due mainly to a fall in private consumption and building activity. Nevertheless, there are encouraging signs. Although considerably less than before the crisis, the amount of venture capital invested in Belgian companies in 2012 – €138 million – was still twice the amount invested in 2011 and better than the general trend throughout the European Union, where investments fell by 10%. In January 2013, Belgium ranked fifth overall

---

1 National Bank of Belgium, press release of May 3 2013, www.nbb.be/DOC/DQ/F/DQ3/HISTO/NFFE13I.PDF.

in the European Union, after the United Kingdom, Germany, France and the Netherlands.[2] In 2013 there was a moderate increase in deal volume. The private equity market expects activity to continue increasing and to regain the level it had at the beginning of this century.[3]

As a country with many small and medium-sized family-owned companies, Belgium has a lot of management buyout transactions. These management buyouts are sometimes backed by private equity funds, but very often the former shareholders remain involved. Since the transaction value is usually between €5 million and €50 million, most US or UK private equity funds have only a limited interest in Belgium. European or Belgian funds are the most active ones in Belgium.

1.2 Transaction trends, acquisition structures and legal pitfalls

There are two main strategies used by private equity players in Belgium. Some of them take a minority interest in the target company, teaming up with other private equity funds that also have minority interests. Others prefer to acquire 100% of the target's shares, in almost all cases through an acquisition vehicle in which they have a majority interest and in which management (or the former shareholders) are also expected to participate. Due to the financial crisis, some funds (mainly those linked to banks) changed strategy and do not take majority interests any more.

Private equity funds that acquire 100% of the target's shares usually focus on mature markets (eg, retail, infrastructure, production). Target companies in the growth sectors (eg, healthcare, biotech, cleantech) have a high cash-burn ratio and need to be refunded periodically. Private equity investment in these companies comes mainly from specialised funds that take a minority stake.

(a) *Acquisition structures in the event of a majority stake*

If 100% of the target's shares are to be acquired, a special purpose vehicle is usually set up to be the acquirer. In most cases this scenario requires fewer transaction documents with the sellers (share purchase agreement and some termination agreements), but these will be negotiated more rigorously. For example, representations and warranties will be more extensive, the limitation of liability less favourable and a larger amount in escrow or payment in more instalments will be required.

Management will be asked to participate in the acquisition vehicle and, for this purpose, to enter into the following agreements: (i) an equity term sheet describing the conditions under which management invests (at the time of the acquisition or in future), (ii) management agreements[4] (with good-leaver/bad-leaver provisions as well as put-and-call options) and (iii) a shareholders' agreement (some of whose

---

2 *De Tijd*, January 30 2013, p18.
3 For more information on the development of private equity in Belgium, please see: NautaDutilh, "2013 The Belgian private equity and venture capital market – an outlook" at bit.ly/1ePqbQk.
4 Please note that in Belgium management is usually not employed by the company but enters into a management agreement (and is thus self-employed). From a tax perspective this is advantageous for both the company and the director/manager. In addition, a management agreement is more flexible than an employment agreement (fixed duration without option to terminate, non-compete provision, good/bad leaver).

terms may be incorporated in the acquisition vehicle's articles of association). The provisions of the equity term sheet will be further elaborated in the shareholders' agreement.

Sometimes not only management but also the former shareholder(s) will be asked to participate, such as in cases where a former shareholder was also the managing director and a transition period is necessary to safeguard value. In such cases (and in the current market conditions) the former shareholder(s) will also often be obliged to enter into subordinated shareholders' loans. These loans are used as security for claims under representations and warranties or specific indemnities.

In practice, several classes of shares are generally created, with management mostly holding shares entitling them to participate in the profits but with no real decision-making power. Sometimes depositary receipts for shares are used for this purpose; they entitle management to the proceeds of the shares but not to the legal ownership.[5] Other types of securities often used to incentivise management are warrants,[6] options[7] and profit certificates not representing the company's share capital.[8]

(b)   Acquisition structures in the event of a minority stake
If the investment entails subscribing for a minority stake in the target company (usually within the framework of an investment round), a subscription and shareholders' agreement will be entered into.

Typically, the subscription and shareholders' agreement will contain transfer restrictions with respect to shares in the acquisition vehicle (lock-up, drag-along and tag-along, rights of first refusal, pre-emptive rights, good-leaver and bad-leaver provisions for the founders, put-and-call options etc). This applies both to majority and minority private equity transactions. In addition, it will contain provisions organising the target's management (share classes, majority requirements, dividend and liquidation proceeds preferences, composition of the board of directors). Finally, private equity funds will negotiate hard on clauses protecting against dilution (preferential rights, anti-dilution, ratchet).

(c)   A few legal pitfalls
Although there are obviously many legal issues that must be considered when structuring transactions and drafting the required documentation, a few common potential pitfalls are discussed below.

Article 32 of the Belgian Company Code provides that all agreements attributing the entire profit to one of the shareholders or exempting the contribution by one of

---

5   Typically, a *stichting administratiekantoor* (STAK) holds the shares (or other securities) and issues depositary receipts on such securities to management. In practice STAKs set up under Belgian or Dutch law are often used for these purposes.
6   Warrants issued by a company give their holders the right to subscribe for new shares in the company on predetermined/predeterminable conditions.
7   Options give the managers the right to acquire existing shares in the company from the option grantor on predetermined/predeterminable conditions.
8   The company's articles of association provide for the rights and obligations attached to the profit certificates, for instance preferred dividends without voting power (except where voting is mandatory under the Belgian Company Code).

them from every participation in the company's losses are void. Typically, put-and-call options should be scrutinised carefully for their compliance with the prohibition on such 'leonine' agreements. A clause whereby shareholders agree on a fixed price per share for the exercise of the put-or-call option with a duration of several years may be void if not drafted in accordance with the guidelines that have been developed in case law.

Shareholders' agreements can regulate, to a certain extent, the exercise of the voting rights at the shareholders' meeting (eg, appointment of directors, allocation of profit). Such arrangements must be limited in duration and must also be in the company's interest,[9] both at the time they are entered into and each time they are put into practice (ie, upon each vote subject to the voting arrangement). The law does not specify the maximum duration of such arrangements but, depending on the circumstances, periods of between five and (in exceptional circumstances) 10 years have been deemed acceptable in practice. Voting arrangements must therefore always be carefully drafted, taking into account the specific circumstances of the proposed transaction.

Similarly, it is generally considered that a lock-up (ie, an undertaking by a shareholder not to transfer the company's securities for a specified period of time) must also be limited in duration (eg, between five and 10 years, again depending on the circumstances) and must be in the company's interest. Transfers to affiliated companies are permitted. Sometimes, transfers between shareholders or a class of shareholders also qualify as permitted transfers.

(d) *Other transaction trends*

Since the start of the ongoing financial crisis in mid-2008, the approach taken to due diligence has shifted.

Due diligence work more often takes place in stages: first, a high-level due diligence review with a well-defined scope; second a high-level due diligence with a more broadly defined scope; and, finally, a detailed due diligence review covering a limited number of issues. Clients rarely request exhaustive reports. The factual part of the due diligence report remains important, however, as the private equity partner must provide the report to the bank in order to obtain financing, and financing remains the most critical part of the private equity investment.

Negotiations are usually conducted with only a limited number of bidders. Auction processes are rare because they are costly for both the sellers and the buyers. Since the onset of the financial crisis, there has been a gap between the price sellers expect and the price private equity funds are willing to pay. Buyers still expect to receive the same amounts as before the crisis, whereas private equity funds are unwilling to pay these amounts. Corporates buyers sometimes do, which prevents the gap from disappearing.

---

9 The following agreements are void: agreements contrary to the provisions of the Belgian Company Code or to the company's interest; agreements whereby a shareholder commits himself to vote in accordance with the instructions of the company, a subsidiary or one of the corporate bodies of such companies; agreements whereby a shareholder commits himself towards such companies or corporate bodies to approve the proposals of the company's corporate bodies.

Since the theory of hidden defects[10] incorporated in the Belgian Civil Code does not meet the needs of share purchasers, representations and warranties are by far the greatest concern when negotiating acquisition documents. Without being able to rely on the representations and warranties or a specific indemnity, it will be very difficult, if not impossible, to claim against the sellers.

Traditionally, the purchase price agreed at signing is adjusted on the completion date on the basis of completion accounts. Alternatively, buyers are also fond of deferring part of the purchase price by making a portion of it payable over time if certain financial targets are met (earn-out). An earn-out not only acts as an incentive to a seller to remain active in the company after completion, but also protects a buyer against the seller's insolvency in the event of warranty breaches, indemnity claims and the like.

Unless there are large and unusual fluctuations in the target company's working capital, the locked box (the purchase price is agreed on a cash-free, debt-free basis with anti-leakage provisions protecting the buyer) is often the preferred mechanism for private equity buyers. However, many strategic buyers, certainly those from the United States, are not fond of locked-box processes, which they consider too risky. In Belgium it is expected that the locked box will become more important as it is less administratively burdensome than the price adjustment mechanism.

Before 2008, it was often necessary to fulfil a laundry list of logistical conditions precedent before closing. Nowadays this is much less common because both sellers and buyers try to limit the chances of a deal failing after signing.[11] Consequently, there is a tendency to limit logistical conditions to a minimum (regulatory clearances and a focus, on the buyer's side, on getting the M&A deal terms synchronised with the financing terms insofar as possible).

Material adverse change clauses are common, especially when a long period between signing and closing is anticipated.

It is customary to negotiate a cap on the total claims under the representations and warranties. The cap (expressed as a percentage of the purchase price) depends on the value of the transaction.[12] It is also often agreed that the buyer cannot claim compensation if its claim does not exceed a certain (individual and/or cumulative) threshold.

The most seller-friendly features in current Belgian private equity deals are the locked box (as a purchase price mechanism) and the use of data room disclosure to create exceptions to the representations and warranties. The latter feature means that rather than requiring sellers to make specific exceptions to the representations and warranties through, for example, a disclosure letter, it is sufficient for the relevant

---

10   The theory of hidden defects applies only to the shares that form the object of the share purchase agreement. It does not apply to the company, its assets and liabilities, its subsidiaries etc.
11   Increasingly, logistical conditions become post-closing conditions and can no longer prevent a transaction from going through (eg, obtaining consent to a change of control from all clients and suppliers, as opposed to only major ones; repayment of all amounts owed to the company by affiliates, employees etc, whether or not they are already due).
12   The following caps are common: 14% for the first category (transactions with a value of up to €10 million), 20% for the second category (transactions with a value between €10 million and €100 million) and 40% for the third category (transactions with a value above €100 million). The average percentage is 25%.

documents to be included in the data room. Consequently, in such cases a buyer is left to rely only on specific indemnities with respect to issues disclosed in the data room and not on the representations and warranties.

Share purchase agreements governed by Belgian law are in many respects similar to US- or UK-style sale and purchase agreements. However, they are usually less extensive because a number of principles[13] are sufficiently described in the Belgian Civil Code.

1.3 Recent tax developments

The most important recent tax developments in Belgium that are relevant for private equity are briefly outlined below.

(a) Fairness tax

As from tax year 2014, Belgium has introduced a new and separate corporate income tax, called the 'fairness tax'. The fairness tax constitutes a non-deductible levy on companies that have distributed dividends during the taxable period and whose tax base has been offset in whole or in part against the notional interest deduction or carried-forward losses. The rate of this tax is set at 5.15%. The fairness tax will also apply to Belgian branches of foreign companies. For this purpose, the notion of 'distributed dividend' has been adapted to the situation of Belgian branches, and is defined as an amount bearing the same relationship to the gross dividend distributed by the foreign company as the (positive) accounting result of the Belgian branch bears to the global accounting result of the head office.

(b) New restrictions on the deduction of interest

On July 1 2012, a totally new treatment of qualifying non-deductible interest payments was introduced. The basic principle is that deduction of interest will be subject to more restrictions, both regarding the debtor of the interest and the actual amounts of interest paid. In brief, the most important changes are the following:

- The previously applicable 7:1 debt-equity ratio has been replaced by a 5:1 ratio;
- Qualifying interest now also includes: (i) interest on all qualifying intra-group loans and (ii) interest whose beneficial owner is not subject to income tax in Belgium or is subject to foreign tax treatment significantly more favourable than would be the case in Belgium;
- Publicly-issued bonds and similar financial instruments, as well as loans extended by banks and financial institutions covered by Article 56(2)(2) of the Income Tax Code, are not subject to the new rules;
- Loans to leasing companies (whether the property leased consists of movables or immovables) or companies active in the field of public-private partnerships do not qualify as debt, and the interest payments on those loans will be disallowed;

---

13 For example, Article 1134 of the Belgian Civil Code explicitly provides that all agreements must be performed by the parties in good faith. Consequently, the concept of good faith need not be explicitly mentioned and described in an agreement governed by Belgian law, for it to apply to such agreement.

- For treasury and cash-pooling activities in Belgium, a netting principle now applies. This means that only a positive balance between intra-group interest paid and received will be taken into account (the group company should enter into a framework agreement with its cash-pooling or treasury centre).

(c) *Modification of the general anti-abuse provision*

When structuring private equity transactions, the parties often use tax planning techniques to optimise their tax situation and minimise leakage. In this regard, a 2012 amendment to the general anti-abuse provision should be kept in mind. The new provision entitles the tax authorities to disregard a transaction (or a series of transactions) aimed at tax abuse, and to levy tax as if the abusive transaction had not taken place. 'Tax abuse' is defined as a transaction intentionally structured by the taxpayer (i) to escape an Income Tax Code provision that was specifically designed to catch it, or (ii) to qualify under an exemption that was designed to exclude it. Upon a showing by the tax authorities of tax abuse, the burden shifts to the taxpayer to show that the transaction was driven by motives other than tax avoidance, failing which the transaction (or series of transactions) can be disregarded.

(d) *Rules on notional interest deduction amended*

The notional interest deduction regime allows Belgian corporate taxpayers (and Belgian permanent establishments) to deduct from their tax base deemed interest on their adjusted net equity. The interest rate is fixed in advance, based on the average interest rate on 10-year Belgian government bonds (OLOs) over the past year. The current cap of 3%, or for small and medium-sized enterprises (SMEs)[14] 3.5%, remains unchanged. As from 2014, however, the notional interest deduction for a given tax year will be based on the OLO rate for July, August and September of the preceding tax year (rather than for the entire year). This will result in a reduction in the effective rate of deduction to 2.63%, or 3.13% for SMEs, for tax year 2015. Moreover, the notional interest deduction will be disallowed on shareholdings accounted for as monetary investments which also qualify for the dividends-received deduction. Such shareholdings will be excluded from the computation base.

Moreover, further to the Act of December 21 2013, the Belgian rules were brought in line with the judgment of the Court of Justice of the European Union in the *Argenta* case (C-350/11) of July 4 2013. As a result, qualifying assets of non-Belgian permanent establishments of Belgian companies are now also taken into account for the purpose of calculating the notional interest deduction.

(e) *Capital gains on shares: separate taxes of 25.75% and 0.412%*

The Act of March 29 2012 introduced a 25.75% capital gains tax on shares sold within a one-year holding period. Subject to that exception, Belgian resident companies are generally not taxed in Belgium on capital gains realised upon the sale

---

14 In order to be deemed an SME, a company must meet the conditions laid down in Article 15 of the Belgian Company Code (on a consolidated basis). This means that the following caps apply: (i) net turnover of €7,300,000 (excluding VAT), (ii) balance-sheet total of €3,650,000, and (iii) 50 employees (average annual workforce expressed in full time equivalents).

of shares. As from tax year 2014, however, a separate 0.412% tax on capital gains on shares will be introduced. This tax will be levied on capital gains that were previously fully exempt. It will not be possible to offset the capital gains against capital losses on shares. Nor will be it possible for the tax to be credited against corporate tax liability or deducted. Taxpayers will not be allowed to offset carried-forward losses (or other tax attributes such as the notional interest deduction or the investment deduction) against the tax base to determine the 0.412% tax. The 0.412% tax will not apply to qualifying SMEs.

(f)   *Financial transactions tax*

Based on a proposal from the European Commission, several EU member states (including Germany, France and Belgium) may introduce a financial transactions tax (FTT) in 2014. The proposed tax is separate from the bank levy introduced by some member states (including the United Kingdom and the Netherlands). Under the current FTT proposal, financial institutions would owe a tax on certain transactions in financial instruments. The proposed rate is at least 0.1% of the consideration paid, or the market value (if higher), for non-derivative instruments such as shares and bonds. For derivatives, the applicable rate would be at least 0.01% of the consideration or notional amount referred to in the derivative contract. The FTT remains controversial, and there is currently no consensus for the EU-wide application of this tax. An amended proposal was approved by the European Parliament in July 2013. On February 4 2014, the European Parliament plenary session debated the subject and both the European Commission and Council issued statements on the need for quick adoption of a broad-based FTT. However, at the time of writing no detailed legislation has been approved.

(g)   *Taxation of carried interest*

Carried interest[15] is a technique to remunerate private equity managers which has been used for many years in Belgium. Until recently, it was generally accepted that carried interest can be structured and taxed as a capital gain (which is exempt if the fund manager realises the capital gain in the normal course of business). In ruling decision 2011.535 of February 28 2012, however, the Belgian ruling service took the position that carried interest paid to managers of a private equity company should be treated as professional income and subject to tax at the normal personal income tax rate (50% plus local taxes). In the case at hand, the managers wished to receive an advance payment of carried interest, the amount thereof being determined based on the company's earnings before interest, taxes, depreciation and amortisation. This decision has been commented on extensively by tax advisers, who contend that the Belgian ruling service was influenced by the poor structuring of the carried interest payment. The discussion on this subject is far from closed, and it is unclear whether the ruling service will take the same position in future rulings.

---

15   The purpose of carried interest is to grant the managers a share of the fund's exit profits. Carried interest is interest in excess of a defined rate of return on the fund's starting value. If the fund does not perform well and is unable to obtain higher returns, the manager will not receive carried interest.

(h)   Withholding tax on liquidation proceeds
Withholding tax on liquidation proceeds has increased from 10% to 25% (as of October 1 2014). Until October 1 2014, it was still possible to apply a 10% tax rate to liquidation proceeds. Moreover, transitional rules are provided in order to allow companies to convert taxable reserves into capital by paying a 10% tax. Special rules determine how long the converted reserves should stay in the company (four years for SMEs, eight years for other companies). However, if the shareholder is a company holding more than 10% of the shares or whose shareholding has an acquisition value of at least €2.5 million, the tax is not due (based on both Belgian and EU law).

2.   Netherlands

2.1   Development of private equity market
Private equity is well established in the Netherlands and represents a sizable chunk of its economy.[16] The Netherlands was the first country in continental Europe where private equity played a significant role in corporate finance.[17] In 1981, the Dutch government introduced a scheme[18] under which it agreed to guarantee 50% of the losses incurred by private venture capital companies on investments in small growth companies. In reliance on this scheme, more than half of the private equity investments in the Netherlands from 1981 to 1996 were made in companies that needed the funds for their further growth. This was very different from the situation in the United States, where the first private equity wave was dominated by buyout funding. Buyout funding did not play a prominent role in the Dutch private equity market until 1995, when the guarantee scheme was abolished.[19]

2.2   Market trends
Although much larger private and public deals are done as well, most of the private equity deal volume in the Netherlands is in the mid-market segment (with deal values from €50 million to €350 million). This is considered to be a sweet spot by many Dutch private equity firms. It is expected that foreign private equity players (from the United Kingdom and the United States) will become more active. Together with the expectation of more club deals, this probably explains the clear shift in deal size in 2014 so far towards the upper mid-market compared to 2013.[20] Even in the crisis period since the collapse of Lehman Brothers, the mid-market has shown a remarkable robustness and a steady flow of good deals is visible each year. Mid-market companies are not as vulnerable to operational risks as smaller sized ones, whereas compared to multinationals they offer better opportunities for value

---

16   In 2011, private equity had invested a total of €3.9 billion in 1,161 companies that had combined revenues of €83 billion and accounted for 4.9 % of total employment and 16% of Dutch GDP.
17   A de Jong *et al*, *Hedgefondsen en Private Equity in Nederland (Hedge Funds and Private Equity in the Netherlands)*, a report issued by Erasmus University Rotterdam with the Dutch Ministry of Finance (2007).
18   Guarantee scheme for private venture capital companies 1981.
19   A de Jong *et al*, *Hedge Funds and Private Equity in the Netherlands*, *supra*.
20   For more information see: NautaDutilh, *2014 Outlook on the Benelux Private Equity, Venture Capital & Leverage Finance Market – An Interim Report* at www.e-nautadutilh.com/40/597/uploads/nautadutilh-private-equity-report-benelux-2014--a4-format-.pdf.

creation, through buy-and-build strategies or international expansion for instance. Moreover, the mid-market in the Netherlands still has a distinctive 'Dutch touch' to it that favours local players and serves as an (albeit limited) entry barrier to outsiders. Whereas this cultural influence may be hard to pinpoint, it is believed to result in favourable financing terms and better access to deal flow for players with local clout. The mid-market is also considered to be a sweet spot by banks with local leveraged finance teams.[21] Due to competition between these banks to obtain the lead in mid-market deals, they are occasionally willing to provide relatively large buyout loans at relatively low margins. Senior debt is expected to be made available by way of a club of Dutch and international (mainly US and UK) banks. Concerns about a 'wall of debt' – debt to be refinanced without success – appear to have dropped considerably. Other ways of financing by specialised and alternative lenders, for instance in the form of 'unitranche debt', are gradually appearing in the Dutch leveraged finance market.

In addition to (i) manufacturing, (ii) technology, IT, media, entertainment and telecommunications, and (iii) energy and utilities, the Netherlands-based corporate professional services sector is clearly considered attractive by private equity investors. This is mainly due to the high cash conversion rates typical for companies in this sector and the benefit they stand to gain from the continuing trend towards the outsourcing of corporate professional services. The healthcare sector in the Netherlands has gained considerable popularity as well. Healthcare provides the major ingredients of an appealing investment case: substantial growth prospective, the potential for efficiency improvements and a need for fresh capital.[22] Still, investors do not seem to step into mainstream healthcare.

In short, despite the financial crisis the Dutch private equity industry remains well positioned. The overall expectation in the market is that private equity deal volumes will increase in the short term.[23] This is especially so in the mid-market where value can be created even without strong economic growth and without great reliance on financial engineering.

2.3 Transaction trends

Where, in 2013, the one-on-one sale was clearly the preferred way to get to a deal, the increased optimism in 2014 has led to more controlled auctions and 'dual track' transaction processes.[24] Some even predict initial public offerings will be a popular way to exit in 2014/2015, despite the absence of a successful alternative investment capital market for SME companies in the Netherlands.

---

21   ABN Amro, Deutsche Bank, ING, NIBC and Rabobank
22   For more information see: NautaDutilh, *2014 Outlook on the Benelux Private Equity, Venture Capital & Leverage Finance Market – An Interim Report* at www.e-nautadutilh.com/40/597/uploads/nautadutilh-private-equity-report-benelux-2014--a4-format-.pdf.
23   *Ibid.*
24   *Ibid.*

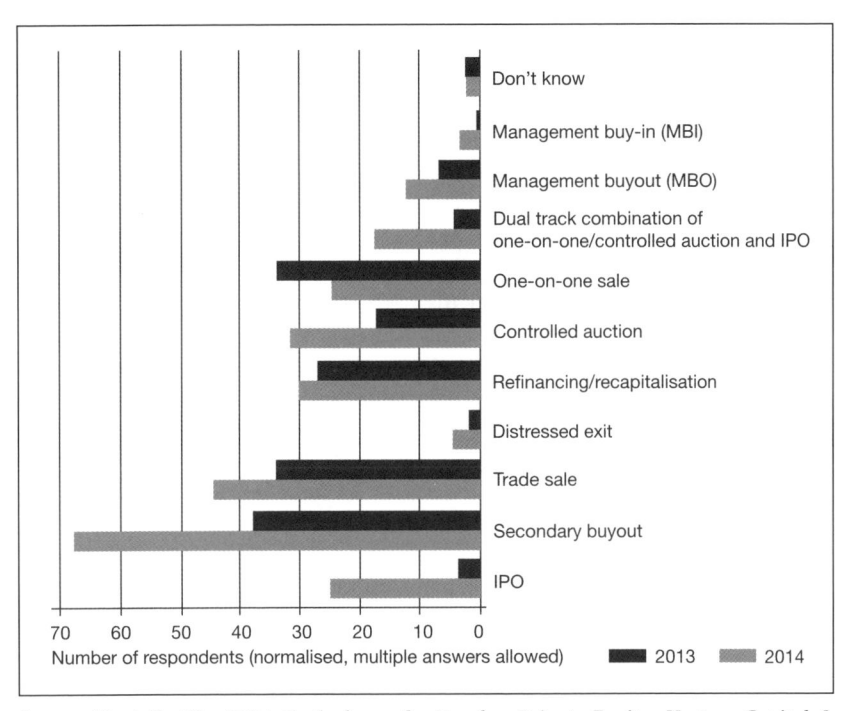

What do you think will be the preferred exit routes for sponsors over the next twelve months?

- Don't know
- Management buy-in (MBI)
- Management buyout (MBO)
- Dual track combination of one-on-one/controlled auction and IPO
- One-on-one sale
- Controlled auction
- Refinancing/recapitalisation
- Distressed exit
- Trade sale
- Secondary buyout
- IPO

Number of respondents (normalised, multiple answers allowed) ■ 2013 ▨ 2014

Source: NautaDutilh, 2014 Outlook on the Benelux Private Equity, Venture Capital & Leveraged Finance market – An Interim Report

Without a true European bond market, leveraged finance provided by banks is still the typical source of debt in the Dutch market. Despite the relatively small number of banks active in this field in the Netherlands, there is fierce competition among them, leading to prices and terms and conditions for leveraged loans often being more attractive than those seen in the UK and US markets. On the equity side, the first signs of direct co-investment by Dutch pension funds are appearing, introducing a new trend in private equity transactions.

2.4 Recent legal developments

Since October 2012, new legislation introduced in the Netherlands has also changed the transaction parameters in private equity deals. The rules applicable to Dutch private limited liability companies (BVs) have been considerably relaxed as a result of the entry into force of two new acts: the Flex BV Act (October 1 2012) and the One-Tier Board Act (January 1 2013). The new rules have:
- reduced the required formalities (eg, a BV can now be set up in one day);
- abolished many restrictions (eg, the financial assistance rules); and
- introduced many new options (eg, non-voting shares and shares without profit participation rights).

The new rules have made it possible to structure transactions more quickly, easily and flexibly. There is more room for customisation and the somewhat cumbersome constructions that were used to get around statutory restrictions – such as the financial assistance prohibition – are no longer necessary. This section will discuss the main changes that are relevant for private equity investors.[25]

(a) *Flex BV Act*
Abolition of financial assistance rules: From an acquisition financing point of view, the most important change for parties seeking to acquire a Dutch BV, or a stake in such a company, is the abolition of what were known as the financial assistance rules. Before October 1 2012, there were stringent restrictions on the provision by a BV of financial assistance for the purpose of the acquisition of shares in its own capital. Loans were permitted only up to an amount not exceeding the company's distributable reserves, and all other forms of financial assistance were prohibited. These restrictions were especially cumbersome in relation to the financing of acquisitions where the banks demanded collateral not only from the borrower but also from the target company and its subsidiaries. Whether a company may provide financial assistance must now be assessed by its management board on the same basis as any other transaction. A board not acting with due care in making its assessment may risk personal liability for the board's members. In addition, a transaction involving the provision of financial assistance may still be challenged where it is considered to be *ultra vires*.

New rules on distributions: Among the most far-reaching changes brought about by the new rules are those in relation to distributions, including dividend payments. In the new situation, retention of a 'capital cushion' consisting of the share capital is no longer required in order to make a distribution. This, in effect, increases a BV's distributable capital (provided that the articles of association allow this). The decision-making process on distributions must now fulfil stricter conditions. Above all, this process entails clearer responsibilities for management board members.

Under the old company law rules, the management board's role in relation to resolutions of the general meeting of shareholders on distributions was purely advisory. The new rules require the approval of the management board for such resolutions (this is deemed to have been granted implicitly if the management board actually makes the distribution). The management board may withhold its approval only if it knows or should reasonably foresee that the BV will be unable to discharge its due and payable debts after the distribution. If any such payment problems nonetheless occur after the distribution, the management board members and any *de facto* management board members will, in principle, be jointly and severally liable for the shortfall that has occurred as a result of the distribution. In effect, this provision on liability codifies the existing case law on management board liability in this area.

To determine whether a proposed distribution can be expected to cause financial

---

25   These changes are also summarised in chart form in Section 2.4(c).

problems for the BV, the management board must carry out a liquidity test in advance. This involves gauging the consequences of the distribution for the company's continuity based on a qualitative criterion (continuity assumption) and a quantitative criterion (determination of scope for distribution).

If the company has been profitable in recent years and there have been no indications of a possible continuity problem, the liquidity test does not require the management board to carry out a more detailed analysis of the BV's continuity. If such an analysis is necessary, all relevant circumstances must be taken into account. Examples of negative indications are the loss of an important sales market, potential claims, major corporate losses or signs that debtors cannot meet their obligations. According to the legislative history, such an analysis should cover a one-year period. If the distribution is made on the basis of the most recent annual accounts and, as is often the case, these make provision for a distribution, it may be inferred from the auditor's unqualified opinion that the continuity of the BV is guaranteed for at least a year.

The maximum scope for a distribution is determined by reference to financial indicators that can be easily generated from the accounts: the quick ratio and the operational cash flows. The precise amount is ultimately determined by the management board and the shareholders, who are required to make allowance for uncertain factors and future projections that are not apparent from the financial records. Examples are future investment commitments, claims and repayment obligations. If the liquidity test is met, a distribution can be made even if it will result in a negative (or significantly negative) equity (provided that the articles of association are, if necessary, altered to allow this). A simplified flow chart showing the steps necessary to gauge the consequences of a distribution for the company's continuity (and the necessary level of review) is set out below.

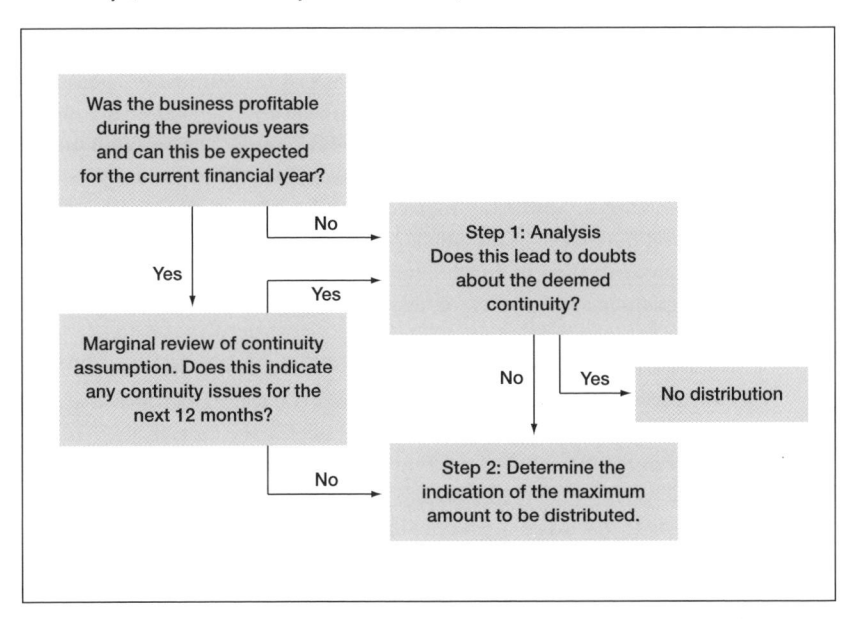

In principle, this opens up new opportunities for making distributions, although one regulatory caveat is necessary. The greater flexibility to make distributions under the new Dutch company rules has been somewhat curtailed by the anti-asset-stripping rules laid down in the Alternative Investment Fund Managers Directive, which were introduced in the Netherlands on July 22 2013. Under these rules, the manager of a 'regulated' alternative investment fund that has acquired control of a company may not, for a period of 24 months following the acquisition, facilitate, instruct, support or vote in favour of any distribution, capital reduction, share redemption and/or acquisition of own shares by the company that will cause the company's net equity to fall below the amount of the issued capital plus the non-distributable reserves. This rule is directed at fund managers instead of the BV's management board, and the power of enforcement is vested in the regulatory authorities.

The anti-asset-stripping rules based on the Alternative Investment Fund Managers Directive will probably lead to more pre-closing restructurings to facilitate distributions, as well as the use of new workarounds designed to address this regulatory obstacle. When there is doubt, especially in more aggressive financing structures, it is expected that company management boards and fund managers will engage financial and legal advisers to assist them in creating a paper trail and negotiating the appropriate allocation of liability risks, thereby introducing new dynamics to distributions made by private equity-owned companies.

Introduction of non-voting shares: Before the enactment of the Flex BV Act, it was not possible for Dutch companies to issue non-voting shares. To achieve a similar effect, a structure was developed in Dutch practice whereby the legal ownership of shares (and therefore the voting rights) is separated from their beneficial ownership (ie, the right to participate in the profits) through the use of depositary receipts. Under this structure, the shares are held by a 'friendly' trust office foundation (*stichting administratiekantoor*), which retains their legal ownership. The articles of association and the administration conditions of the foundation generally include provisions on the rights of the foundation attached to the shares administered by it, such as with respect to voting and subscription rights. The foundation then issues depositary receipts for the shares, giving the holders of such receipts a contractual right against the foundation to receive the profits distributed by the relevant company on the shares. In the Dutch private equity context, depositary receipts have traditionally been used to enable high- and low-level managers and key employees to participate in the profits of acquired companies for, among other things, alignment of interest purposes.

Under the new rules, there are two types of depositary receipts: those with meeting rights and those without meeting rights. Meeting rights consist of the right to attend and address general meetings. Depositary receipt holders only have meeting rights if the articles of association specifically so provide. Typically, depositary receipt holders in a private equity structure do not have meeting rights.

A question that arises is whether the introduction of non-voting shares will lead to the disappearance of the depositary receipts/trust office foundation mechanism in private equity transactions. On the one hand, this mechanism makes the corporate structure more complicated, can be more expensive to implement and is unknown outside the Netherlands and Belgium. On the other hand, depositary receipts without meeting rights have certain advantages over non-voting shares that will probably cause them to remain popular, especially in private equity transactions.

For one thing, under Dutch law non-voting shares always carry meeting rights, whereas it may sometimes be desirable to give fund managers and employees profit participation rights without the right to attend shareholder meetings. Additionally, the consent of all persons with meeting rights is required in order to pass resolutions without holding a meeting. The use of non-voting shares may make this practice less efficient than it would be in the case of depositary receipts without meeting rights issued by a foundation.

Another advantage of depositary receipts over non-voting shares is that the former can be transferred by a private deed (whereas the transfer of shares in a BV requires a notarial deed).

The following table shows the main differences between shares and depositary receipts.

Rights / Instruments	Voting rights	Attend general meeting	Address general meeting	Profit sharing rights
Shares	X	X	X	X
Non-voting shares		X	X	X
Depositary receipts with meeting rights		X	X	X
Depositary receipts without meeting rights				X

Share transfer restrictions: Under the old rules, specific share transfer restrictions had to be included in a BV's articles of association. Such restrictions are no longer mandatory. If the articles contain share transfer restrictions there is now more freedom to structure them as desired. For example, the statutory rules on the determination of the share price (requiring that the price be determined by one or more experts) need no longer be applied; the articles may set out different rules for this purpose. This makes it possible to include good-leaver/bad-leaver arrangements, incorporating the desired price determination mechanism, directly in the articles. A lock-up provision may now also be included in the articles and not only, as before, in a shareholder agreement. This means that any transfer of shares during the lock-up period is no longer simply a breach of contract but is invalid pursuant to statutory corporate law. By contrast, the advantage of a shareholder agreement is that it is private, whereas the company's articles of association are contained in a public document. It therefore depends on the circumstances of the case in question whether it is better to include certain provisions in the articles or a shareholder agreement.

Power to issue specific instructions: The Flex BV Act makes it possible to include a provision in a BV's articles of association requiring the management board to follow specific instructions issued by another corporate body of the company, such as the shareholders or the holder(s) of specific shares. The management board must comply with these instructions, unless this would be contrary to the company's interests. Previously, instructions could only be given regarding the company's general policy. Under the new rules, the management board can, for example, be instructed to conclude or terminate certain contracts, suspend payments, appoint or dismiss personnel, or establish or close down departments. The inclusion of such a provision in the articles of one or more subsidiary BVs can be used to give the parent company – such as a private equity fund – an additional legal tool for pursuing group policy objectives. The person or entity issuing the specific instructions risks directors' liability if he/it can be held to act as a 'quasi-director'.

Appointment and removal of management board and supervisory board members: Finally, if so provided in the articles of association, management board members can now be directly appointed and removed by a particular shareholder (although each shareholder with voting rights must be able to participate in decision-making regarding the appointment of at least one management board member). The cumbersome arrangement in which a binding nomination by a particular shareholder was combined with an agreement between the shareholders to vote in accordance with the nomination is therefore no longer necessary. As a result of its inclusion in the articles, the system of direct appointment and removal has corporate effect and is no longer merely contractual, based on the shareholders' agreement. The appointment and removal of supervisory board members can be arranged in the same way, except in companies subject to what is known as the 'structure regime',[26] a set of mandatory rules for large BVs/NVs meeting certain tests.

(b) *One-Tier Board Act*

The One-Tier Board Act, which entered into force on January 1 2013, gives Dutch companies (both BVs and NVs) greater freedom to design and configure their management and supervision model. Companies now have a statutory option to institute a single board made up of both executive and non-executive members (in contrast to the traditional two-tier system, in which a management board and supervisory board exist side-by-side). Foreign companies are often more familiar with the one-tier management model; consequently, the introduction of this model in Dutch law may make BVs more attractive for such companies.

---

26   This regime requires large companies to appoint a supervisory board or, in the case of a one-tier board, non-executives to oversee the activities of the management board/executive directors. The supervisory board/non-executives of a structure regime company has/have significant legal powers. A 'large' company is defined as one that meets certain criteria on a continuing basis as laid down in statutory law. Under certain circumstances a mitigated structure regime can be applied.

Additionally, the One-Tier Board Act provides a clearer and more specific statutory basis for a division of duties within the management board (whether or not one-tier). A division of duties between the board's executive and non-executive members must be set out in the articles of association, whereas any other division of management duties can be set out in management board bylaws for instance. Despite such a division of duties, the principle that management board members are jointly and severally liable for mismanagement will continue to apply: a management board member will be liable in full unless he can prove that the mismanagement was not attributable to him/her and that he was not negligent in acting to prevent its consequences. A division of duties may nevertheless have a bearing on whether mismanagement can be attributed to an individual board member in a specific case. From the perspective of liability risks, a good and clear division of duties within the management board can therefore be important.

Conflict of interest rules: The One-Tier Board Act also introduced new conflict of interest rules for BVs (and NVs). Under the new rules, a conflict of interest between a management board or supervisory board member and the company will only have consequences with respect to the internal decision-making. A member of either board may not participate in any deliberations or decision-making of that board if he has a direct or indirect personal interest with regard thereto that conflicts with the BV's interests. If he does participate, the decision will be voidable and he can be held liable to the BV. Unlike under the former rules, however, the transaction with the third party will remain valid. A management board member with a conflict of interest can therefore still represent the BV even if the current articles expressly prohibit this. The new rules can be set aside (if all management board members and supervisory board members have a conflict of interest and it thus becomes impossible to make a decision) by including a provision in the articles authorising management board members to participate in the decision-making in that situation despite a conflict of interest.

2.5 **Recent tax developments**
This section explains the main recent Dutch tax developments that are important to bear in mind when setting up a private equity structure in or through the Netherlands.

(a)   *Deductibility of interest*
For optimising a private equity structure, the deductibility of interest at the level of the acquisition vehicle is of major importance. As a general rule, interest payments on conventional loans by Dutch entities (ie, loans that do not qualify as equity for tax purposes) are deductible for corporate income tax purposes. Nor is such interest subject to withholding tax. There are, however, rules limiting the deductibility of interest. In this respect, two major changes to the Dutch Corporate Income Tax Act 1969 entered into force on January 1 2013. These changes are particularly relevant in the context of cross-border transactions and reorganisations, and should be taken into account when investing in or via the Netherlands.

Summary of main changes pursuant to Flex BV and One-Tier Board Acts

Subject	What has changed?	How does this affect or benefit private equity?
Capital structure	• Non-voting shares and non-profit participating shares permitted; not possible to issue shares that have neither voting rights nor profit rights • Abolition of the rules on the provision by a BV of financial assistance to third parties for the purchase of shares in the company's own capital • Abolition of various restrictions on a BV's ability to buy back its own shares • Abolition of the lengthy (used to take more than two months) procedural requirements for reduction of a BV's capital	• Increased possibilities for the structuring of participation by portfolio company's management: special profit-participating rights, special veto rights • Downside is that non-voting shares always have meeting rights in a general meeting, which may not be ideal in the event of participation by employees/management. Shareholders may not want employees/lower management to be present at shareholders' meetings (see below) • Debt push-downs and statutory mergers between bidco and target are no longer needed in order to get around the financial assistance rules • Dividend recaps and other forms of financial restructuring are facilitated by these changes
Depositary receipts (equity with only economic rights granted to persons: shares are usually held by 'friendly' foundation)	• Depositary receipts only have meeting rights if this is laid down in the articles of association (should be included in articles when they are next amended). Such rights must be recorded in the shareholders' register	• Depositary receipts without meeting rights are often used in private equity transactions in order to let management/employees participate in the profits of the company without giving them any voting/meeting rights: end of risk that holders of such depositary receipts get unwanted voting/meeting rights. This is still an advantage compared to non-voting shares, whose holders will always enjoy meeting rights • Depositary receipts can be transferred by private deed, while non-voting shares will always need to be transferred by notarial deed

continued on next page

Subject	What has changed?	How does this affect or benefit private equity?

Share transfer restrictions	- No longer mandatory
	- Determination of price up to shareholders
	- Following restrictions now allowed in articles of association:
	  - lock-up provision (usually up to five years)
	  - tag-along provisions, as well as good-leaver/bad-leaver provisions
		- A share transfer in violation of the articles of association is null and void, while a violation of a similar provision in a shareholders' agreement only leads to liability to pay damages
		- A disadvantage is that these (often very detailed and commercially sensitive) arrangements become public through inclusion in the articles

Board(s)	- One-tier board system (single board with executive and non-executive members) now provided for by statute - Amended rules on liability of board members - Appointment of board members by individual shareholders possible	- Allows for a US-/UK-style governance structure - Formal introduction of a clear division of duties between board members in articles of association or board rules may limit responsibilities/liability of individual board members (a management board member will be liable in full unless he can prove that the mismanagement was not attributable to him and that he was not negligent in acting to prevent its consequences) - A right to appoint board members directly in the articles is stronger than a combination of a right of nomination plus a voting agreement
New conflict of interest rules	- A conflict of interest has consequences only in respect of the internal decision-making. Any board member who has a personal interest that directly or indirectly conflicts with the interests of the BV may not participate in the deliberations and decision-making. If he does so, the decision will be voidable and he can be held liable to the BV	- The transaction with the third party will remain valid. A management board member with a conflict of interest can therefore still represent the BV even if the current articles of association (based on the old conflict of interest rules) expressly prohibit this

continued on next page

Subject	What has changed?	How does this affect or benefit private equity?
Specific instruction rights	• Articles of association may provide for the right of a party to give specific instructions to the management board (as opposed to only general guidelines, which was the old rule). In principle, such instructions must be followed by the management board.	• Management board members must not follow such instructions if they are contrary to the interests of the company and the enterprise connected with it. This rule can potentially create tensions between a company's management board and the shareholders • The possibility of giving specific instructions to the management board creates greater flexibility for shareholders to exert control over or direct management actions. For tax reasons – especially substance requirements – it is not advisable to give specific instructions to trust/service providers acting as 'resident directors' of a company • Extensive use of this right may result in the relevant party being considered a *de facto* management board member, thus leading to unwanted liability
Quality requirements /contractual obligations	• Requirements as to certain qualities (eg, being a party to a shareholders' agreement concerning the governance of the company and its management) on the part of shareholders may be laid down in the articles of association • Contractual obligations of shareholders (eg, additional liability up to a certain amount or an obligation to provide a loan) may be included in the articles	• See comments under "Share transfer restrictions"
Distributions	• A shareholders' resolution to make a distribution will only take effect if the management board approves the distribution • Management board to perform a liquidity test and (limited) balance-sheet test when deciding whether to grant approval (see Section 2.4(a) under "New rules on distributions" above)	

continued on next page

Subject	What has changed?	How does this affect or benefit private equity?
Balance-sheet test	• (Limited) balance sheet test: net equity may not be less than the reserves required by law or under the articles of association (issued capital may also be distributed) • Under the anti-asset-stripping rules introduced by the Alternative Investment Fund Managers Directive, the manager of an alternative investment fund that has acquired control of a company may not, for a period of 24 months following the acquisition, facilitate, instruct, support or vote in favour of any distribution, capital reduction, share redemption and/or acquisition of own shares by the company that will cause the company's net equity to fall below the amount of its issued capital plus non-distributable reserves	• Since there are usually no non-distributable reserves (ie, reserves required by law or under the articles), it has become much easier to make a distribution (provided the liquidity test is met). A company's net equity may become negative (or even significantly negative) as the result of a distribution: watch out for minimum-equity requirements in bank facility documentation • The Alternative Investment Fund Managers Directive's anti-asset-stripping rules somewhat curtail the new scope for making distributions
Liquidity test	• Management board may only refuse to grant its approval if it knows or should reasonably foresee that the company will not be able to continue to pay its due and payable debts following the distribution	• The maximum scope for a distribution is determined by reference to financial indicators that can be easily generated from the accounts: the quick ratio and the operational cash flows. Company risks such as potential litigation, termination of contracts and the like should be taken into account
Liability	• Management board members are jointly and severally liable for a deficit caused by a distribution made in conflict with the distribution rules • Shareholders are liable for a deficit if they knew or should reasonably have foreseen that the company would not be able to continue paying its due and payable debts following the distribution	• Although we believe that this is merely a codification of case law, it does increase the need for management boards to clearly set out all the considerations underlying a decision to approve a distribution

The first change is that the Dutch thin capitalisation regime has been abolished. Before 2013, the Dutch Corporate Income Tax Act 1969 contained a provision restricting the permissible maximum debt-to-equity ratio (as a rule, the maximum ratio was 3:1 for domestic corporate taxpayers). Interest payable on debt in excess of this ratio was generally not deductible for corporate income tax purposes.

At the same time, a new statutory restriction on the deductibility of interest was introduced. This new rule deviates from the general principle that in the Netherlands, interest expenses may be utilised to offset taxable profits. The new restriction is intended to further combat 'abusive' debt financing, supplementing existing measures such as the anti-base erosion rules and the other restrictions on the deduction of interest in respect of acquisition debt.

Under the new statutory restriction, interest on 'excessively' leveraged acquisitions of (Dutch and foreign) participations qualifying for the participation exemption[27] is non-deductible to the extent such interest exceeds €750,000 in any given year. Basically, a company is deemed to have made excessively leveraged acquisitions under this provision insofar as the combined acquisition price of all its participations exceeds the company's total shareholder equity according to its fiscal balance sheet. An interest deductibility restriction (for interest above €750,000 in any given year incurred on the excess leverage) is the 'penalty' for being excessively leveraged. The provision contains a formula for calculating the amount of interest that relates to the excess leverage. Under that formula, the amount of such interest in a given year is calculated by dividing the average excess leverage in that year by the average total debt level in that year, and multiplying the outcome by the total amount of interest paid in that year.

A potentially significant exception applies to interest paid to acquire (or increase) a participation intended to expand a group's operational activities. Provided that the interest has not already been deducted elsewhere within the group and that the financing is not predominantly tax driven, the deductibility of interest payments made to finance the expansion of business activities should not be limited by this new rule.

(b) *Taxation of carried interest arrangements*

There have not been any significant changes in the taxation of carried interest arrangements in the Netherlands since 2009, when rules targeting 'excessive remuneration' were introduced. However, the current political climate in the Netherlands is not altogether favourable towards perceived high-earners. That is particularly true for managers and executives of financial institutions and investment funds and others working in the sector that are commonly blamed for the current economic and financial crisis. As a result, the discussion about how their remuneration (including carried interest arrangements) should be taxed is ongoing in the

---

27 Under the Dutch participation exemption, profits derived from a qualifying participation – whether in the form of dividends or capital gains – are exempt from Dutch corporate income tax. Generally, a shareholding of 5% or more in a company's nominal paid-up share capital is regarded as a participation for purposes of the exemption. In order for the participation exemption to apply, certain other requirements must be met as well.

Netherlands, but no bills are currently pending. In this respect, close attention is being paid to the relevant developments in the United States and the United Kingdom, including the bills in the United States to treat carried interest as services income.

3. Luxembourg

3.1 Introduction

Although Luxembourg lacks a substantial domestic private equity market, its flexible legal and tax framework, efficient infrastructure, economic stability, governmental responsiveness to the needs of the financial sector and multilingual, highly-skilled workforce make it an ideal location for foreign private equity (and other) investors to set up an investment platform. With €2,498.84 billion net assets under management as at August 2013, Luxembourg is the second largest investment fund centre after the United States.

With regard to private equity, Luxembourg's legal arsenal offers a number of highly suitable investment vehicles, which may achieve tax neutrality. These include the following types of entity:

- The *société de participations financières* (SOPARFI) – a standard holding company and an unregulated entity. There are no limitations on its eligible investors or investments, making it extremely flexible. It is the vehicle most often used by private equity, although it was not introduced for this purpose.
- The *société d'investissement en capital à risque* (SICAR) – a lightly regulated vehicle specifically designed for private equity investments by 'well-informed' investors (which includes institutional investors, professional investors and certain private individuals). A SICAR may only invest in 'risk capital' (see below) but is not subject to other specific limitations on its eligible investments.
- The specialised investment fund (SIF) – a lightly regulated investment vehicle similar to a SICAR except that it may invest in any asset but is subject to risk diversification requirements.
- The undertaking for collective investment (UCI) Part II – a UCI that is open to all investors, is subject to risk diversification requirements and is not eligible for distribution in more than one EU member state. Of the four vehicles, this is one used least often by private equity investors.

In practice, SICARs, SIFs and UCIs Part II will usually qualify as alternative investment funds under the EU Alternative Investment Fund Managers Directive, which was transposed into Luxembourg law in July 2013. However, most of these vehicles are already to a large extent compliant with the directive. While in numerous other EU member states the directive will require many funds to operate for the first time in a regulated environment, SICARs, SIFs and UCIs Part II have operated in such an environment for quite some time. The infrastructure is therefore already in place and the regulators are already familiar with these types of funds. This may be expected to increase Luxembourg's attractiveness as a platform for private equity investments.

The specific tax treatment and some additional features of each of the vehicles will be outlined below.

3.2 General rules

Luxembourg tax residents benefit from 64 double tax treaties and from other taxpayer-friendly cross-border rules, including those transposing the EU Parent-Subsidiary Directive. SOPARFIs benefit from the whole network of treaties, while the other investment vehicles may benefit from only some of them on a case-by-case basis. The absence of withholding tax on interest payments or liquidation proceeds distributed to creditors makes it possible to set up a variety of tax-efficient repatriation mechanisms for foreign investors. More generally, no withholding tax will be levied on any distribution by a regulated vehicle, whether to residents or non-residents (subject to the EU Savings Directive). Furthermore, the absence of controlled foreign company rules creates flexibility and facilitates adequate responses to foreign legal or tax requirements.

As far as intra-group cross-border activities are concerned, Luxembourg law generally follows the principles laid down in the Organisation for Economic Cooperation and Development's Transfer Pricing Guidelines. Therefore, intra-group transactions must be sufficiently documented to show that they are at arm's length and that the Luxembourg entity receives an appropriate remuneration, notably with respect to the functions performed, risks assumed and assets employed.

Whether a SOPARFI, SICAR, SIF or UCI Part II is treated as transparent or opaque for tax purposes depends on the legal form chosen for the relevant investment vehicle. Income derived from a transparent investment vehicle will be subject to tax at the level of its investors. Consequently, non-resident investors will not be liable to tax in Luxembourg. Opaque investment vehicles are in principle subject to tax in Luxembourg but benefit from a wide range of exemptions, which allow for tax-neutrality. In order to give investors additional certainty regarding their tax position, agreements may be made upfront with the Luxembourg tax authorities and laid down in an advance tax agreement.

3.3 Specific vehicles

(a) SOPARFIs

The tax treatment of a SOPARFI is similar to that of all companies subject to Luxembourg tax and includes income tax and net wealth tax. A SOPARFI usually takes the form of a public limited liability company (*société anonyme*) or a private limited liability company (*société à responsabilité limitée*) and must have a minimum share capital of €31,000 or €12,500, respectively.

A SOPARFI benefits from the tax-efficient parent–subsidiary regime. Under certain conditions, dividends, liquidation proceeds and capital gains received by a SOPARFI may be exempt from Luxembourg corporate tax. Likewise, dividends distributed by a SOPARFI may be exempt from Luxembourg withholding tax, and qualifying participations held by a SOPARFI may be excluded from its unitary value for the computation of net wealth tax.

Acquisitions made by a SOPARFI may be financed through either equity or debt. Although there are no formal thin capitalisation rules, an 85:15 debt-to-equity ratio is traditionally required, except in back-to-back financing situations.

Profits can be repatriated either in an ongoing manner, for example via profit participating instruments, or upon exit, depending on the investors' needs. For this purpose, SOPARFIs often issue hybrid instruments, including convertible preferred equity certificates and preferred equity certificates, allowing for a tax-efficient repatriation of investment proceeds.

(b) **SICARs**

A SICAR's activities are restricted to direct/indirect investment in securities that represent 'risk capital', defined as high-risk investments made with a view to the launch, development or stock exchange listing of the target company. Beyond that, however, there are no restrictions on the eligible investments. Unlike the SIF and the UCI Part II, a SICAR is not subject to risk diversification requirements; it may, for example, invest solely in one or a few companies, in equity or debt, and so on. Investors are in principle limited to professional and institutional parties, but under certain conditions may also include private individuals.

A SICAR may take the form of a company or partnership and is subject to a minimum capital requirement of €1,000,000. An advantage of using a corporate SICAR (in contrast to a tax-transparent one) is that while it is subject to income tax in Luxembourg, income arising from its investments in risk capital (held for more than 12 months) is exempt. In addition, a SICAR is not subject to net wealth tax or withholding taxes. Consequently, a corporate SICAR is in principle covered by the favourable tax regimes under various EU directives and is entitled to benefit from Luxembourg's tax treaties.

(c) **SIFs**

A SIF may invest in a wide variety of asset types but, in contrast to the SICAR, is subject to risk diversification requirements (ie, a 30% maximum on securities from the same type of issuer). Its investors are subject to the same restrictions as those in a SICAR. A SIF may take the form of either a mutual fund (*fonds commun de placement*) with no legal personality, in which case it must be managed by a management company, or an investment company (*société d'investissement à capital variable* or *société d'investissement à capital fixe*). The net assets of a SIF may not be less than €1,250,000. If the SIF takes the legal form of an investment company and is incorporated as a limited liability company, a minimum capital of €12,500 (for a private limited liability company) or €31,000 (for a public limited liability company) is required upon incorporation.

A SIF is not subject to net wealth tax or, in contrast to the SICAR, income tax. It is in principle liable to subscription tax at a yearly rate of 0.01% of its net asset value but some exemptions apply.

(d) **UCIs Part II**

A UCI Part II is an undertaking for collective investment established under Part II of the

Law of December 17 2010. Although it offers greater flexibility in some respects than a SICAR or SIF, it is not eligible for distribution in more than one EU member state.

A UCI Part II may take the legal form of a mutual fund or an investment company. The minimum investment for a UCI Part II, as for a SIF, is €1,250,000.

Like a SIF, a UCI Part II is not subject to income tax or net wealth tax and is in principle subject to a subscription tax at a yearly rate of 0.05% of its net asset value. The subscription tax may be reduced to 0.01% in certain specific cases and, here again, some exemptions apply.

3.4 Company law regime

(a) *Setting up a Luxembourg company*

The incorporation of a Luxembourg company generally takes from three to five business days, depending on the legal form chosen and on how quickly (i) a bank account can be opened and – if shares issued at incorporation are to be paid up in cash – be operational, (ii) an address for a registered office can be arranged, and (iii) the composition of the company's board(s) can be finalised. Once these steps have been completed, a deed of incorporation (containing the articles of association) must be executed by a notary and the founding shareholders or their representatives.

The bank account must be opened in the company's name before its incorporation. The bank will first have to comply with its know-your-client and anti-money-laundering obligations, which entails the provision of certain information and the observation of certain formalities. The length of this process depends on the complexity of the company's shareholding structure. Once the account is operational, any cash contributions on shares must be paid into the account.

The founding shareholders (or their representatives) must then appear before a Luxembourg notary to execute the deed of incorporation. Certain additional formalities must also be performed by the notary, but these are generally of a less burdensome nature.

A particularity of Luxembourg law is that a company's incorporation is effective as from the time at which the deed of incorporation is executed. In principle, the filing of the deed with the Luxembourg Trade and Companies Register and its publication in the Luxembourg official gazette are not prerequisites for the company to have the capacity to enter into transactions.

A bank account is still required even if the shares issued at incorporation are to be paid up by means of contributions in kind rather than in cash. However, the opening of the account will not have to be verified by the notary and is therefore not a condition for the process of executing the deed of incorporation.

Finally, it should be noted that where the company will be subject to additional regulation (eg, by reason of the activities in which it will engage), the process of setting it up will be more burdensome and time-consuming.

(b) *Financial assistance*

The general rule under Luxembourg law is that a commercial company may not directly or indirectly advance funds, lend money or grant third-party security for the acquisition of its own shares by a third party. There is an ongoing debate as to whether this prohibition applies only to public limited liability companies and partnerships limited by shares (*sociétés en commandite par actions*) or also to private limited liability companies, which are frequently used in private equity deals. A bill aimed at ending this debate by providing that the financial assistance prohibition also extends to private limited liability companies is currently in the pipeline.

Because the financial assistance prohibition often proves troublesome in the context of a leveraged buyout, Luxembourg law provides for a whitewash procedure under which a company's board can request its shareholders to authorise transactions that would otherwise be contrary to the prohibition and therefore void. In such a case, the board must draw up a special report for the shareholders and the level of assistance may not exceed the company's distributable reserves.

The prohibition does not apply to transactions entered into by banks and other financial institutions in the normal course of business, or to transactions effected with a view to the acquisition of shares by or for a company's employees. In the case of private limited liability companies, at any rate until the abovementioned bill becomes law, it is generally advisable to apply a contractual whitewash procedure in the event that some form of financial assistance is envisaged.

(c) **Participation by senior management**

Senior management of a target company acquired by a private equity fund will often take minority participations in the Luxembourg main holding company, either directly or indirectly through a special purpose vehicle. Such vehicles may be set up either individually or jointly. The method chosen will depend mainly on the personal tax situation and treatment of the individual in question. The participations usually consist of shares carrying a preferential economic right, referred to as a 'promote', or the right to a ratchet dividend. These preferential economic rights may be triggered upon an exit or during the life of the investment, depending on certain financial thresholds and hurdles linked to the private equity fund's return on investment. The minority participations will usually be acquired with the individual's personal funds, but the private equity fund may also contribute indirectly by offering special favourable terms (eg, regarding financing).

The participation of senior management in a Luxembourg company does not, in principle, create any control issues as their combined voting rights usually still represent a minority. In the case of a private limited liability company, however, the number of shareholders who are senior management should be carefully monitored, as the support of a majority of the shareholders is necessary to pass a vote on amendments to the company's articles. It should be pointed out that a public limited liability company is allowed to issue non-voting shares but subject to conditions that – in practice – are usually too stringent for private equity vehicles. Luxembourg law does not provide for the issuing of non-voting shares by private limited liability companies.

(d) **Leaver provisions**

The taking of participations by senior management is usually subject to good-leaver and bad-leaver provisions (such as call options that can be exercised upon the occurrence of a good-leaver/bad-leaver event). Such provisions are generally set out in a shareholder agreement, but may also be included in the company's articles of association.

(e) ***Tag-along and drag-along rights***

Tag-along and drag-along rights are not provided for by Luxembourg law and, if they are to apply, must therefore be set out in the relevant company's articles of association or in an agreement entered into between the company's shareholders and acknowledged by the company. Consequently, any tag-along or drag-along rights or obligations have a contractual rather than a statutory character.

In the case of a private limited liability company, the exercise of any tag-along or drag-along rights may require a shareholder resolution to approve the relevant share transfer to the extent that the transferee is a new shareholder. Under Luxembourg law, any transfer of shares in a private limited liability company to a non-shareholder must be approved by existing shareholders of the company representing at least 75% of its share capital.

(f) ***Alternative Investment Fund Managers Directive and asset-stripping rules***

As stated in the section on the Netherlands, the Alternative Investment Fund Managers Directive imposes restrictions on distributions (dividends), capital reductions and share redemptions or acquisitions of own shares by controlled portfolio companies during a certain period. This has been implemented in Luxembourg law.

The asset-stripping provisions of the directive apply to both listed and unlisted portfolio companies. For unlisted companies an alternative investment fund manager will generally be deemed to have control if it holds more than 50% of the company's voting rights. For listed companies, the level of control is defined by reference to the Takeover Directive and, as it relates to Luxembourg, has been set at 33.3% or more.

However, the practical implications of the prohibitions to which qualifying alternative investment fund managers are subject are not yet entirely clear. They may have an impact on exits and deal structuring in private equity. If alphabet stock is issued to investors with the intention of redeeming or liquidating the relevant shares within a period of less than two years, that intention would potentially be thwarted. As Luxembourg law does not prevent redemptions or repayments of shareholder debt, debt structuring alternatives could be considered.

France

Maud Manon
Xavier Norlain
Jeremy Scemama
Guillaume Valois
DLA Piper

1. **Introduction**

The French private equity market has been quite erratic since the collapse of the world's debt markets in 2008.

France remains the second largest European private equity market after the United Kingdom[1] and Paris is the fourth city in the world for private equity with 43 active private equity firms and $22 billion under management.[2]

But each quarter does not look the same compared to the previous one in terms of value and volume of leveraged buyout transactions: 82 leveraged buyout transactions closed in France during the first quarter of 2013 – a 15% increase compared to 2012 first quarter[3] – but leveraged buyout transactions during the second quarter of 2013 dropped by 63% in terms of volume and by 82% in terms of value compared to the first quarter.[4]

The current economic crisis in most countries of the Eurozone combined with the slowdown of Chinese growth does not augur well for a bright future in the medium term, but it is also true that private equity funds have purchased a large number of portfolio companies since 2007 and they must exit from them soon, and that 24,000 French small and medium-size companies are expected to need a change in shareholdings in the next 10 years.[5]

In this environment, purchasers want to be protected more and more by specific legal mechanisms such as price adjustment at closing or thereafter and full representations and warranties from sellers. Debt providers want the same (and covenant-light credit agreements have disappeared completely), even though distress situations in France have proven that a long list of contractual covenants and representations and warranties from borrowers do not help with repayment of debt.

At the same time, earn-out mechanisms help purchasers and sellers to find an agreement on the purchase price, and have become common.

In general, the principles, structure and documentation applicable to a leveraged buyout transaction in France are similar to those in other countries for major leveraged buyout transactions such as the United States and the United Kingdom. However, there are some issues and constraints specific to France which must be

---

1 Boston Consulting Group/IESE Business School.
2 Preqin.
3 Capital Finance.
4 Epsilon Research
5 Les Échos/Association Française des Investisseurs pour la Croissance (Afic).

borne in mind by private equity funds when contemplating completion of a leveraged buyout transaction in France, and which are not always easily understood by foreign market players.

This chapter sets out the main issues and constraints to be taken into account by private equity investors, in particular with respect to:
- the financing structure of a transaction;
- the involvement of the target company's management team; and
- the tax structure.

It also examines the main issues that may arise in connection with a public-to-private transaction with respect to a French listed company, which is governed by particular regulations.

2. Debt finance in France

This section explains the key French constraints that must be borne in mind when contemplating the structure of a debt package in France (including the security package). In particular, it considers financial assistance, corporate benefit and banking monopoly rules, and some specifics in terms of security interests governed by French law (particularly in light of French tax and insolvency rules) that have a key impact. Finally, it describes briefly some market trends in France over the last couple of years.

2.1 Financial assistance and corporate benefit

The Commercial Code prohibits the grant by a limited company (a *société anonyme* or a *société par actions simplifiée*) of financial assistance regarding the acquisition or the subscription of its own shares by a third party.[6] A loan, guarantee, other security interest or other type of financial assistance granted in breach of such statutory provisions will be void.

This rule prohibits the granting of upstream guarantees by a French target company and target group members for the acquisition loan; there is no way to avoid this prohibition (France has no equivalent to the former UK whitewash procedure). This means that should lenders wish to have direct security over the shares or other assets of a French group member that is part of the acquired group, the French group member should be made a borrower under, for example, a revolving facility, a refinancing facility or an acquisition/capex facility; or it should be made a guarantor, provided that the guarantee does not contravene the French corporate benefit requirements.

Regarding the guaranteeing of third-party obligations by a French company, the following conditions must be met:
- It must be part of the corporate purposes of the guarantor as provided for in its bylaws. It should be noted this condition is met when the bylaws specify (as is most frequently the case) that the corporate purpose includes entering into all financial transactions directly or indirectly related to the stated main corporate purpose;

---

6   Article L 225-116 of the French Commercial Code.

- The guarantor must derive an actual benefit, consideration or advantage from the transaction involving the granting by it of the guarantee, taken as a whole. The following must be borne in mind:
- The grant of a downstream guarantee is usually in the corporate interest of a company. Where the guarantee is cross-stream or upstream (or indeed where the companies are not part of the same group), the grant of the guarantee should be directly or indirectly linked to, and of benefit to, the activity of the guarantor;
- This is primarily a matter for the guarantor and its officers since they may be exposed personally to civil and – in extreme cases – criminal liability if they act in breach of their fiduciary duties to the company in this respect;
- In practice, a French guarantor usually guarantees the obligations of its direct and indirect subsidiaries without any limitation, and the obligations of other members of the group up to the amounts borrowed (directly or indirectly) by the guarantor by way of intra-group loans (with the proceeds of these intra-group loans coming from facilities excluding the acquisition facilities made available to the acquisition vehicle);
- The security interests must secure amounts that are commensurate with the financial capabilities of the guarantor company and the amount of its assets. Typically (except in the case of downstream guarantees, where there would be no such limit), reference is made in practice to the liability taken on by the guarantor not exceeding a percentage of the value of its net assets at a particular time (eg, the time when the guarantee was granted).

2.2 Banking monopoly rules

The French banking monopoly rules, set out in the French Monetary and Financial Code, prohibit entities other than authorised institutions from carrying out credit operations in France on a regular basis.

As a consequence, the granting of loans to a borrower located in France (ie, a French entity or the French branch of a foreign entity) and the purchase of non-matured loans from an entity located in France (ie, a French entity or the French branch of a foreign entity) constitute credit operations that fall within the scope of the banking monopoly rules.

Although there are some exceptions to these rules, it is vital when structuring a financing package in France to check that no member of the lender pool is in breach of the French banking monopoly rules. Although the Supreme Court ruled that a loan made available in breach of the French banking monopoly rules was not automatically void, it failed to give clear guidance regarding the applicable criteria for potential voidance and there is still a risk of imprisonment and/or a fine.

It should be noted that some modifications of the French banking monopoly rules have been recently adopted (June 2013) and became applicable in most respects from January 1 2014 (while further proposed changes have not yet been adopted).

The banking monopoly rules have always had a key impact in France in situations such as structuring a mezzanine/unitranche financing package for a French acquisition vehicle. If the mezzanine/unitranche lenders (at the time of funding the acquisition) are not authorised credit institutions under the relevant French or European regulations, it is not possible to structure the mezzanine/unitranche financing in the form of a credit facility. This is the key reason mezzanine/unitranche financings in France are structured as warranted or warrantless mezzanine bonds (ie, bonds issued by the French acquisition vehicle and subscribed for by the mezzanine/unitranche debt providers).

Because bonds issued by a French company are securities governed by certain French corporate law rules, the process of obtaining, for example, a waiver from the bondholders will differ from the process that applies to the senior pool of lenders. Approval of the waiver request is obtained by decision of a bondholders' meeting specifically convened for the purpose. In practice, for the waiver request to be approved by the debt providers, it is insufficient simply to obtain countersignature of the waiver request by the bondholders' representative after obtaining the relevant majority from the syndicate members, as is the case for the senior agent. In relation to bonds issued by a French company, the majority required for any changes to the terms and conditions of such bonds is, under the law and with very few exceptions, set at two-thirds.

2.3 Security interests

Although reforms have been put in place with a view to simplifying the granting and the enforcement of security interests (the first key reform was enacted by Ordinance 2006-346 of March 23 2006 relating to security interests), the system is still more complicated in comparison to the UK and US security interests regimes.

Types of French security interest include:
- pledges over shares, bank accounts, receivables and intellectual property rights;
- an efficient receivables security assignment mechanism that may secure only the own borrowing obligations of the assigner with a European-regulated banking institution which is acting in France under the European passport for the provision of financial services;
- pledges over movable property, which may now be constituted without physical dispossession of the pledger subject to registration on a special public register; and
- pledges over companies' business (ie, aggregation of the company and business names, leasehold interests, goodwill, business furnishings, tools and equipment and intellectual property rights) – although this type of security interest is generally inappropriate for large entities of the type involved in leveraged buyout transactions and should not be confused with a floating charge or a debenture over all of the company's assets.

No omnibus security interest is available.

A pledge over shares and other kinds of securities is construed as a pledge over a financial instruments account, with the relevant financial instruments being credited to a special dedicated shareholders' account opened in the pledger's name. French law also requires that a specific bank account be designated as part of the pledge in order to receive the 'fruits and produce' arising from the pledged financial instruments (eg, dividends if the pledged financial instruments are shares). In practice, this bank account must be opened in the name of the pledger at a French credit institution. In addition, for a pledge over shares issued by a French entity to be valid and enforceable, the pledge must be one over a financial instruments account under French law, to the exclusion of any pledge governed by a foreign law.

Another crucial detail of French law is that a security interest may be enforced only if the secured obligations are due and payable, meaning that a provision stating that the agent may enforce the security interest in the case of the occurrence of an event of default where the debt is not due and payable is invalid under French law. The trigger event for enforcement of any kind of French law security interest, usually defined as an 'enforcement event', is generally written as follows:

'Enforcement event' means any failure to pay on its due date any secured obligations or the service of any notice of acceleration in accordance with [clause X (acceleration and cancellation) of the [credit agreement]].

Since there is no concept of partial enforcement in France, the beneficiaries of a French pledge generally have no real economic interest in enforcing the French law security interest in the event of the occurrence of just an interest payment default; indeed, if they decide to enforce the security interest, the enforcement proceeds to which they will be entitled will be limited to the amount of the unpaid interest, so they will have no more security interest securing the principal amount of the secured obligations if the latter has not previously been declared immediately due and payable through the acceleration process provided for in the facilities agreement.

It should also be noted that security packages in France cannot be properly determined without taking into account some specific French tax rules; indeed depending on who is the granter of security interests (related party or not) and the type of guarantee/security interests granted, part of the secured debt could fall within certain limitations on deductibility of debt at the level of the French borrower.

2.4 French insolvency rules

Under Article L632-1 of the French Commercial Code, security granted by a French company during the hardening period will be considered void if it secures debt previously incurred. The hardening period may be determined by the insolvency court to have commenced a maximum of 18 months before the date of the judgment declaring the relevant debtor insolvent. Therefore, this rule must be kept in mind when contemplating, for example, additional security interest to be granted post-closing by a French entity if it is not to secure a specific new drawing under a given facility.

In addition to this specific rule, some important issues are worth consideration in cases where French insolvency proceedings concern a French entity and where lenders have provided debt financing to that entity.

In this chapter the term 'insolvency proceedings' refers to proceedings that affect creditors' rights in a French debtor company by virtue solely of being started without the creditors' consent. Three types of proceedings are currently available in France: safeguard (and accelerated financial safeguard) proceedings, reorganisation proceedings and liquidation proceedings.

The safeguard (and accelerated financial safeguard) proceedings are one of the major changes to the rules concerning insolvency proceedings against French companies. They can be used only if the French company is not insolvent and may be opened only at the request of the company itself. The trigger event for opening safeguard (and accelerated financial safeguard) proceedings is for the company to have difficulties and not be in a position to overcome them.

Since March 1 2011, the accelerated financial safeguard proceeding has been made available to French debtors. This new procedure enables debtors to negotiate a restructuring plan with their financial creditors, without their trade creditors being involved in the process.

In contrast to the simple safeguard proceedings, the accelerated financial safeguard proceeding is available to operating and holding companies already engaged in a conciliation process when a restructuring plan is expected to be approved by the creditors by a two-thirds majority. It benefits from a shorter process period than the one applicable to the simple safeguard proceedings and is available as long as the following thresholds are reached:

- operating companies will be able to have access to the procedure as long as their turnover exceeds €20 million and they have more than 150 employees; and
- holding companies will be able to have access to the procedure as long as:
- their balance sheet exceeds €25 million; or
- their balance sheet exceeds €10 million and they control a company whose turnover exceeds €20 million and which has more than 150 employees; or
- their balance sheet exceeds €10 million and they control a company whose balance sheet exceeds €25 million.

It should be noted though that safeguard and accelerated financial safeguard proceedings should be carefully monitored because the opening of any such proceeding has other consequences that could in some respects be prejudicial to the debtor's business and relationships with other lenders and suppliers.

From the opening of bankruptcy proceedings by the court, the debtor is prohibited from paying debts incurred before the date of the court order. Conversely, creditors (whether secured or not) may not pursue any legal action against the debtor with respect to any debt incurred before the court order if the purpose of such legal action is to:

- obtain the payment of such debts;
- terminate any agreement with the debtor for non-payment of amounts owed by it; or
- enforce the creditors' rights against any asset of the debtor.

The prohibition on legal action to enforce creditors' rights prohibits the enforcement of a security interest that requires some form of legal action. The only French security interests that do not require legal action for enforcement are those in respect which it is legally possible to organise in advance and contractually (a 'forfeiture clause') to carry out the enforcement process out of court, such as a pledge of shares. Without going into details, the idea of a forfeiture clause is to provide for the process of conventional appropriation of the shares by the pledge's beneficiaries should the latter decide to enforce the pledge (French law requires that an expert valuation of the relevant shares be obtained).

To understand this issue, two rules must be considered:
- The opening of insolvency proceedings against a French company prohibits creditors from terminating any agreement with that company for non-payment of amounts owed by it (ie, any acceleration of loans will not be possible after the opening of bankruptcy proceedings, despite the fact that such an event is usually treated as an event of default in most loan documentation); and
- To enforce a French law pledge the secured obligations must be immediately due and payable (it is therefore crucial that the acceleration decision be made before the opening of bankruptcy proceedings).

If the French company is a direct borrower, declaring acceleration of the loan in order to be able at the same time to enforce pledges of shares (through provisions of a forfeiture clause) issued by subsidiaries of the company will usually result in the company becoming insolvent immediately. In that situation, it is no longer possible to open safeguard proceedings and there is a maximum period of 45 days before the company is placed in reorganisation proceedings or, as the case may be, liquidation proceedings.

2.5 Current trends in the French market

The credit crunch in 2008/2009 has had a dramatic impact on the French market in terms of the ability of borrowers and sponsors to find new money from their usual banks. But over the last three years, even though the volume of senior debt is far from that seen during the golden age, senior lenders have demonstrated they are still there (despite a more and more competitive market both in terms of variety of debt providers and in terms of pricing).

During the last two years there has also been a real development of alternative forms of financing by debt providers other than banks; this type of financing is often designated as 'unitranche' or 'unirate' financing. In practice such financing consists of one or several issues of bonds (with or without attached warrants) by the French debtor(s), usually arranged by a single entity.

More and more leveraged buyout restructurings have been seen over the last few years, and it is not unusual to see mezzanine debt providers (and more rarely senior lenders) taking the keys of the group, the sponsor having sometimes no choice but to exit completely or in part, subject to certain (theoretical) return mechanisms dealt with in the waterfall clause of an amended intercreditor agreement.

It is also worth mentioning that France has entered into a period of leveraged buyout debt refinancing. Indeed within the €550 billion of leveraged buyout debt in Europe whose maturity falls between 2012 and 2016, more than €86 billion relates to France (being just behind the United Kingdom).[7]

---

7   Dealogic.

3. Involvement of target company managers

More than ever, a key factor in successful leveraged buyouts is the involvement of the managers of the target group in the planned transaction. Managerial involvement is even more important given that the period within which financial sponsors must reach a satisfactory return on their investment is limited, which can mean that major restructurings of the target may be required and new, more rigorous business practices – in particular in the areas of cash management and financial reporting – must be implemented.

The best way to secure management involvement in the efforts of financial sponsors is to arrange for them to invest alongside the sponsors in the newly created company to purchase the target group.

Management packages in the French market are quite similar to those existing in other markets. However, because of some specific rules, the French packages have developed their own particularities and are now mainly driven by negotiations between the financial sponsors and the management and by French market practice.

This section describes the main options for structuring managers' investments and the main rules that govern relations between the financial sponsors and the managers as shareholders of the acquisition vehicle. It also considers how the early departure of a manager from the target group is dealt with in respect of that manager's shareholding in the acquisition vehicle.

3.1 Investments by the managers in the acquisition vehicle

In France, several options are possible for investment by managers in the acquisition vehicle. These may be used alone or in combination. The right option will depend on the level of financial involvement that each manager can afford, with the current norm being equivalent to between six and 12 months' salary if the target group has not already been acquired under a leveraged buyout and the manager has not invested in a previous transaction.

The managers' level of financial investment is key to ensuring their involvement in the development of the target group. It is also important to minimise the taxes to be paid by managers on the sale of their interest in the acquisition vehicle. A high level of investment will help to demonstrate that the managers should be regarded as investors rather than mere employees, and therefore that the proceeds from the sale of their interests should benefit from the more favourable capital gains tax regime rather than being considered as income.

However, some managers do not always have enough assets to invest such a significant amount alongside the financial investors. In such cases their investments may be financed by a third party (a bank or the financial sponsors), but the acquisition vehicle cannot grant a loan to these managers to finance the acquisition of its own shares as financial assistance of this sort is strictly prohibited by French corporate law (see section 2.1 above).

French law also provides for stock option plans or similar free shares mechanisms, but the legal and tax constraints of these are not always compatible with the constraints and needs of the financial sponsors (eg, an employee cannot transfer his or her options during an initial two-year period, which is problematic if the sponsors wish to sell the acquisition vehicle or the target quickly). In addition, the tax regime applying to these incentive mechanisms became less attractive recently.

Once the managers' level of financial involvement is determined, they may be offered the same return on investment as the financial sponsors, whereby they invest with the sponsors on the basis of equal treatment and are then invited to spread the investment over each part of the sponsors' interest (ie, shares, loans or other financial instruments). In this situation the return on the managers' investment will depend only on how much each manager initially invests. However, in order to reinforce their involvement in the planned transaction, managers could be offered an additional return on investment higher than that of the financial sponsors.

A first option to achieve this goal is to invite managers to invest solely in the share capital, rather than to spread their investment in the same manner as the financial sponsors (ie, not only in shares, but also in loans or other financial instruments). By investing in share capital only, the managers' return on their investments will be higher than that of the sponsors, since the return on investment for loans or other financial instruments is limited to the interest rates on these loans or instruments.

Another option to offer managers a higher additional return on investment is to transfer to them part of the financial sponsors' capital gains on exit, if the latter reach certain predefined levels based on the target group's projected operational results as provided in the business plan, and on the sale price of the target group.

These projected returns on investment are generally calculated on the basis of specific investment multiples and/or internal rates of return that the financial sponsors seek to achieve on sale of the target group. In France, the average internal rate of return expected by sponsors in the mid-cap market has fallen since 2007 and is now between 15% and 20% rather than higher.

Therefore, if at the time of the sale of the acquisition vehicle or target, the financial sponsors have made an internal rate of return or money multiple that is higher than projected, they will transfer a share of their capital gains to the managers. The share to be transferred depends on how much higher the rate of return or money multiple is compared to the projected targets.

From a French legal perspective, although there are various ways to set up this transfer of the additional share in returns, in practice the trend is towards issuing preferred shares giving access to additional economic rights on the share capital at the time of exit. These preferred shares will be issued at the time of the original investment.

The advantage of this option is that this share of investment by the managers is restricted to the subscription price of the preferred shares, which will obviously be lower than their final value. However, the greatest care must be taken in setting the subscription price of these preferred shares, which should be at market value at the time of subscription, in order for managers to benefit from the favourable tax regime for capital gains.

The share capital of the acquisition vehicle could also be allocated by issuing certain instruments to the financial sponsors, which will enable them to dilute the managers' shareholding should the sponsors' projected internal rate of return or money multiple not materialise at the time of sale of the acquisition vehicle or target. Financial sponsors are likely to approach this option with caution due to past experience where the dilution mechanism has proven particularly difficult to implement from a technical point of view, as managers have strongly resisted the conversion of such instruments into share capital.

Since the beginning of the credit crunch and the onset of the economic crisis, the management incentivisation packages put in place when the French leveraged buyout market was at its peak (between 2005 and 2007) have become problematic. Such packages were based on business plans anticipating significant growth of the target groups' activities over the next five years and on expectations of high internal rates of return for financial investors on exit. The contemplated returns for managers on their own investment were also very high.

The economic slowdown has changed everything. The high internal rates of return expected for financial sponsors are difficult to achieve in the medium term and the high returns for managers then also become unrealistic. Managers must then find the incentive to tackle operational difficulties knowing that their initial investments will not bear the fruit originally expected.

Even worse, for those managers who have not invested alongside the financial sponsors on the basis of equal treatment and whose group faces significant operational difficulties, the investment returns will be lower than those of the financial sponsors, as the losses of the latter will be limited by the interest on shareholder loans or other financial instruments issued by the acquisition vehicle and not subscribed to by the managers.

This situation discourages managers and can be the source of strained relationships within the target group and with the financial sponsors. As such, many financial packages put in place several years ago have been renegotiated during the last few years by swapping the original securities issued to management when the target group was originally acquired for new share or option plans offering a less favourable but more realistic return to the management which is still sufficient to motivate them in this period of difficulty.

In addition, managers now often require as part of a new management incentivisation package an equal return with financial sponsors in the event of poor economic circumstances, even if they have not invested in the same instruments as the sponsors.

3.2 Main rules between the shareholders of the acquisition vehicle

On completion of the acquisition of the target, the financial investors and managers, together with any other minority investors and the mezzanine lender, if the latter has been issued shares or other securities by the acquisition vehicle, must determine the rules that will apply to them in their capacity as joint investors in and shareholders of the acquisition vehicle.

In France, these rules mainly relate to corporate governance matters and the transfer of securities issued by the acquisition vehicle, and are set out in a shareholders' agreement. The shareholders' agreement may also set out rules relating to investments by managers, but in practice these rules tend to be set out in separate agreements and/or in the terms and conditions of the securities subscribed by them.

With regard to the corporate governance rules, the financial investors' involvement in the management of the new group is usually considered to be of a restrictive nature; that is, their involvement is limited to extraordinary decisions, with the day-to-day management left to the management team. This approach gives the management free rein to implement the business plan agreed with the financial investors and limits to a certain extent the financial investors' legal liability with regard to the management of the group. This limitation has become a more sensitive matter in light of the economic crisis and recent case law where some financial sponsors have been regarded as in fact being managers of their portfolio companies because of a broad and/or undefined involvement in the day-to-day management.

Accordingly, financial investors are often represented through a corporate body, as required by law or implemented in the bylaws of the acquisition vehicle, which has no general management powers but does have supervisory powers, such as acting as a supervisory board. They have majority control of that corporate body. As such, certain extraordinary management decisions that are listed in the shareholders' agreement (eg, obtaining new bank financing or selling subsidiaries) are subject to the prior consent of the supervisory board.

However, the financial investors do not completely abandon control of the management, as reporting requirements that are often binding on the management provide them with detailed information. In addition, in almost all situations the financial investors have the power to dismiss, whether directly or indirectly, the members of the group's management bodies, including the managers.

The rules regarding the transfer of securities issued by the acquisition vehicle are now well established and generally include the following:

- an undertaking from the managers not to transfer their securities for a certain period of time;
- a pre-emption right allowing a security holder to acquire the securities of another security holder if the former receives a good-faith offer from a security holder or a third party (the management only rarely has such a pre-emption right);
- a tag-along right in favour of all security holders when one security holder transfers its securities to another security holder or a third party, including the right of a security holder to sell all of its securities if there is a change of control of the acquisition vehicle as a result of such a sale; and
- the right of the financial investors that hold the majority of the share capital of the acquisition vehicle to force all the other security holders to sell their securities if they wish to sell the group and thus realise the capital gains made on their initial investment.

In connection with these well-established principles, discussions often relate to the terms and conditions of such transfers, for example:

- there will be negotiations regarding the representations and warranties that will be given by the security holders at the time of the transfer and the allocation of any resulting liability;

- the financial investor often includes a provision that if it gives representation and warranties on a sale they will be given by all sellers on a *pro rata* basis; and
- there will be negotiations as to the price at which the securities must be transferred, particularly if that price is constituted by some form of consideration other than cash.

Furthermore, increasingly managers try to be closely involved in any sale of the group which may give rise to the exercise of the drag-along rights mentioned above. This has the disadvantage of giving them even more power in the event of discussions with several potential purchasers during a sale by auction.

Some or all of the rules referred to above can also be set down in the acquisition vehicle's bylaws if it is incorporated in France, particularly if the acquisition vehicle is in the form of a *société par actions simplifiée* (simplified joint stock company). The main advantage of such a duplication of the rules lies in the fact that a breach by a shareholder of certain such rules can result in the compulsory enforcement of that shareholder's obligations, while the breach of an obligation set out in a shareholders' agreement will generally only entitle the other parties to claim damages.

However, since the bylaws of any company must be filed with the Commercial Court Register, such duplication has the disadvantage of making public the various agreements between the shareholders. Accordingly, in practice, shareholders generally decide to reproduce in the bylaws only certain rules provided in the shareholders' agreement which they do not consider to be confidential.

3.3 Early departure of managers

Having taken a share interest in the acquisition vehicle, managers become co-investors with the financial sponsors, and as such should transfer their share interest in the company – at the same time as the financial sponsors and on the same terms and conditions – on the sale of the acquisition vehicle or the target to an industrial entity, or in the context of a secondary leveraged buyout or public listing.

There are, of course, unknowns, and it is critical that guidelines be agreed concerning how situations in which a manager leaves office before the financial sponsors exit the acquisition vehicle or target should be managed.

In France, managers generally grant financial sponsors a call option on their interest in the acquisition vehicle, which the sponsors can exercise should the relevant manager leave the target before the former exit the acquisition vehicle or target.

Regarding the purchase price to be paid by the financial sponsors on exercising a call option, a distinction is generally made between a manager who leaves office for reasons other than personal choice or reasons that are acceptable to the financial sponsors (eg, death or discharge without wrongdoing), in which case he or she is known as a 'good leaver', and a manager who voluntarily leaves office or leaves for reasons that are unacceptable to the financial sponsors (eg, discharge for serious or gross misconduct), in which case the manager is known as a 'bad leaver'. Some situations, such as discharge without serious or gross misconduct, can be classified as 'intermediate leaver' situations.

In bad leaver situations, the purchase price paid is often equal to the amount initially invested by the manager, unless his or her interest in the acquisition vehicle is worth less at the time of departure.

In intermediate leaver situations, several options for the purchase price can be considered, one of them being the a mechanism providing that over time an increasing proportion of the manager's shares will be valued at the good leaver price and the rest at the bad leaver price.

Where a manager is a good leaver, the purchase price is often equal to the actual value of his interest in the acquisition vehicle, and financial sponsors may choose not to exercise the call option, instead allowing the manager to keep his interest in the acquisition vehicle and to make the same return on investment as other managers on the sale of the acquisition vehicle or target.

Financial sponsors therefore have two options where a manager is a good leaver: the first raises the problem of having to finance the purchase price for the call option, while the second leaves the sponsors with a minority shareholder who no longer has a particular interest in the management of the target.

Whatever the circumstances surrounding the departure of a manager from office, the fact is that whether a departing manager is a good leaver or bad leaver is often not clear-cut, and some scenarios should be considered in advance. For example, what is the best approach in negotiating the termination of a manager who disagrees with the strategy that the financial sponsors want the target to implement? How should the retirement of a longstanding and loyal manager be handled?

Each situation should be analysed on its own merits and, in most cases, parties negotiate terms on the basis of situations that are not as well defined as the scenarios described above. One option is to include vesting mechanisms on the shares held by the managers, thus ensuring that a manager always retains a fixed return on shares once he or she has acquired an interest in the acquisition vehicle.

Some financial sponsors also grant managers a put option that can be exercised on leaving office, particularly where the manager is a good leaver. For the sponsors, this raises the issue of having to set and finance the price for purchasing the departing manager's interest in the target.

However, there is no obligation to grant such put options and most financial sponsors are disinclined to do so since they may be considered to represent a leaving bonus paid to the manager on termination of his contract. As such, where put options are agreed, the purchase price tends not to be based on the actual value of the shares subject to the put option, but rather on the subscription price of the shares plus an agreed rate of interest.

It is also common for financial sponsors to decide not to exercise the call option granted by a manager at the time of departure, thus effectively giving him the same return on investment as the sponsors at the time of exit. For the same reason the manager is unlikely to exercise any put option unless he needs to recover the initial investment immediately for financial reasons, since by doing so he could lose out on a significant return on the investment.

As a result of the credit crunch and the economic crisis, the actual value of the interest of the financial sponsors and the managers in the acquisition vehicle is sometimes less than the subscription price that they initially invested. This creates some issues in good leaver situations where a manager may leave the group and have his interest in the acquisition vehicle purchased at the subscription price, which means that he suffers no loss from the investment, although other managers will have to wait for the exit of the financial sponsors and may lose part or all of their investment unless the target group improves its operational results significantly. In this particular situation, financial investors will choose not to exercise the call option granted to them, but as mentioned above, it means that the manager remains a shareholder in the acquisition vehicle and some put options in favour of the managers may exist.

4. Specific French tax concerns

This section explains some of the French tax issues that must be considered when contemplating the structure of a private equity transaction, in particular with respect to matters concerning tax consolidation, deductibility of interest and withholding tax.

4.1 Tax consolidation and alternative solutions

Tax leverage in French leveraged buyout structures is typically achieved by implementing a tax consolidation between the acquisition vehicle and the French companies of the target group, which enables the financial charges and acquisition costs to be offset against the operating profits of the target group and thus dramatically reduces the amount of corporate income tax to be paid by the French group during the fiscal years following the acquisition.

However, forming a French tax consolidation with the companies of the target group is only possible between entities subject to French corporate income tax (no tax consolidation with non-French-resident entities is possible) and to the extent that the acquisition vehicle owns, directly or indirectly, at least 95% of the share capital (financial and voting rights) of the target companies (exceptions to the 95% condition apply in some limited cases involving share incentives to employees).

French tax rules are such that there is a first period when the tax-consolidated entities continue to pay taxes as if they were not members of a tax consolidation, with the tax authorities repaying those excess payments at a later stage. These cash outflows and the corresponding treasury costs must be taken into account in the business model and debt covenants. The circulation of cash within a French tax consolidation in the context of a leveraged buyout is generally structured in such a way that the cash effect of the tax leverage appears in the hands of the acquisition vehicle, which can use this cash to service its debt. Additional cash can also be upstreamed to the acquisition vehicle from the target group companies through dividend distributions, with either a minimal 1.72% tax or even no tax leakage.

Alternative solutions may also be envisaged to ensure the tax deductibility of at least part of the interest on the acquisition debt, such as a push-down of part of the debt to the level of the profit-making target operating companies if a tax-consolidated group cannot be implemented (see section 5.3 below with respect to public-to-private transactions), or when a significant portion of the taxable profit of the target group is derived from foreign companies. These alternative techniques must be carefully structured.

4.2 Rules of deductibility of interest

The tax leverage in leveraged buyout financing in France will be optimal where the transaction costs and interest on the acquisition debt can be fully deducted for French tax purposes. However, certain rules may limit this deduction.

As a general rule, interest on third-party loans (eg, from banks) is deductible to the extent that the debt has been subscribed for sound business reasons, on arm's length conditions, and the borrower can demonstrate that it can service the debt. However, if the third-party loan is provided by a related party, subject to certain exceptions it will be treated as a related-party loan within the scope of the specific limitations described below.

There is a general limitation on the deduction of the net financial expenses incurred by companies subject to income tax.[8] Under this rule, 15% of the net financial expenses of the company should be added back to its taxable income for the fiscal year ending on December 31 2013. This percentage is increased to 25% for fiscal years starting from January 1 2014. The limitation does not apply to companies whose net financial expenses do not exceed €3 million; this amount being a threshold and not an exemption. This general limitation does not include the expenses that are non-deductible under any other limitation rules (as described below).

There is a specific limitation on the deduction of interest on loans granted by minority direct shareholders: interest on direct non-controlling shareholders' loans is only deductible to the extent of a maximum interest rate published from time to time by the French tax authorities.[9]

There is also a specific limitation on the deduction of interest on loans granted or secured by a related party. The deduction of interest on loans granted or secured by a related party (a parent or an affiliate that directly or indirectly controls the borrowing company or which is under common control with the borrowing company, with the issue of control being assessed from a legal and factual standpoint) is subject to

- the same interest rate limitation as mentioned above, although the maximum deductible interest rate can be exceeded if the borrowing entity can prove that the market rate is higher; and
- alternative thin capitalisation tests.

According to this last rule, the portion of interest accruing on the annual average amount of related-party loans which exceed the highest of the three following thresholds will not be deductible from the borrower's taxable income:

- 1.5:1 debt-to-equity ratio;
- 25% interest coverage ratio;
- The amount of interest received by the borrowing entity from related parties.

Certain exceptions apply to the above limitations.

In addition, the 2014 Finance Law introduced a new restriction on the deduction

---

8 Article 212 *bis* of the French Tax Code, introduced by the 2013 Finance Law.
9 Article 39-1-3° of the French Tax Code.

of interest on related-party loans. Under this rule, interest on related-party loans is no longer tax-deductible unless the borrower can prove that the interest is subject to income tax in the hands of the lender at a rate at least equal to 25% of the standard French income tax rate.

There is a specific limitation on the deduction of interest on loans subscribed for the acquisition of shares qualifying for the French participation exemption regime. Subject to certain exceptions, this mechanism disallows the deductibility of interest on acquisition-related expenses when the shareholding is not actually managed (and controlled if it is a controlling participation) by the French acquirer.

There is a further specific limitation on the deduction of interest in the case of tax consolidation. When the acquisition vehicle is controlled by re-investing shareholders of the target group and the companies of the target group become members of the same tax consolidation as the acquisition vehicle, complex French tax provisions may prevent the deductibility of the part of the interest accrued on the debt incurred by the companies forming this tax consolidation. This issue must be carefully monitored, particularly in the context of an owners' buyout, secondary leveraged buyout transactions involving re-investing managers, or when a post-closing restructuring is implemented.

Finally, there is a specific limitation on the deduction of interest paid in non-cooperative jurisdictions. Subject to certain exceptions, interest is non-deductible if paid to a recipient incorporated, domiciled, established or acting through an office located in a non-cooperative jurisdiction (a list of such jurisdictions is published each year by the French tax authorities) or if paid on a bank account opened in a financial institution located in a non-cooperative jurisdiction regardless of the tax residence of the bank account owner.

4.3 Withholding tax on interest paid to foreign lenders

As a general rule, no withholding tax applies on interest paid by a French debtor to a non-French creditor as long as it does not qualify as being non-deductible and is therefore deemed to be a dividend distribution (and so subject to dividend withholding tax).

Subject to certain exceptions, interest paid by a French debtor can, however, be subject to a 75% withholding tax where paid in a non-cooperative jurisdiction (a list of such jurisdictions is published each year by the French tax authorities).

4.4 Specific contribution on dividend distributions

Subject to certain exceptions, a 3% specific contribution applies on amounts treated as dividends distributed by companies or entities liable to corporate income tax in France.

The main exceptions are for small and medium-sized enterprises (as defined by EU law) and distributions within a tax consolidated group.

5. Public-to-private transactions

The term 'public-to-private transaction' usually refers to a situation where one or more private equity firms acquire, with leveraged financing, a listed company in conjunction with a management team and with a view to delisting the target company.

The constraints set forth by the French laws and regulations, notably with respect to the ability to delist a target company and to create a tax consolidation group (as mentioned in section 4.3 above), have restrained the development of public-to-privates in France.

However, the year 2013 and the first quarter of 2014 have seen a marked increase in this kind of transaction in France. The decrease in the market value of shares in listed companies, notwithstanding good financial performance from certain companies, has made them more attractive for private equity investors. This could lead to the development of public-to-private transactions in France specifically targeting small and medium-sized companies where external financing from banks for a lesser amount may be required.

Typically, a public-to-private transaction in France consists of the acquisition by private equity firms of one or more blocks of shares from the target company's significant shareholders, followed by the filing of a cash public tender offer with the French Financial Markets Authority over the remaining shares of the target company.

This section sets out the main issues that may arise during a public-to-private transaction in relation to private equity funds.

5.1 Main issues that may arise during the preliminary steps of a public-to-private transaction

(a) *Due diligence process*

One of the issues raised in France is whether, and to what extent, a potential purchaser of listed securities is legally entitled to carry out due diligence before the contemplated acquisition. The purpose of such due diligence is to increase its understanding of the target listed company.

In this respect, the view is generally taken that conducting due diligence on a French listed company is allowed provided that:

- the due diligence process complies with certain guidelines published by the Financial Markets Authority;
- the target company's directors are not in breach of their duties; and
- the confidentiality of discussions is preserved.

Guidelines: In order to prevent the disclosure of price-sensitive information and insider dealing, the Financial Markets Authority has recommended that:

- data rooms be organised only for the sale of significant shareholdings;
- access be limited to committed buyers that have shown a serious interest and have signed a letter of intent and a confidentiality agreement; and
- equal access be granted to all bidders in the event of competing offers.

In addition, since a due diligence process also raises the issue of equal access to information regarding the listed company, the Financial Markets Authority has recommended that any price-sensitive information disclosed in the data room be disclosed to the market following completion of the acquisition or failing such completion.

Furthermore, the purchase of securities on the market prior to the launch of the contemplated offer is prohibited if price-sensitive information has been obtained by the potential buyer within the framework of the due diligence process.

Directors' duties: Under French law, directors of a French company (whether listed or unlisted) have a duty to keep strictly confidential all information that they receive by reason of their position. Therefore, a director is not entitled to contact potential purchasers to provide them with confidential information without the board of directors' agreement. Consequently, any bidding process to be implemented by a listed company must be approved by the board of directors before launch.

Confidentiality requirements: A potential purchaser, the selling shareholders and the target listed company must try to maintain the confidentiality of discussions. Indeed, as soon as the confidentiality of discussions is breached, French regulations require that the market be informed immediately through publication of a press release. However, any such public announcement is likely to have a strong adverse impact on the shares' market price.

In addition, if the confidentiality of discussions is breached, the Financial Markets Authority, on the basis of the Takeover Bids Law of March 31 2006 (directly inspired by the 'put up or shut up' rule adopted by the Takeover Panel), may require that the potential purchaser announce its intentions to the market, and if the potential purchaser declares that it does not intend to launch a tender offer, in principle it will be prevented from doing so for six months.

(b) *Securing acquisition of block of shares*

In practice, a private investment firm eager to complete a public-to-private transaction in France will usually, before the launch of a tender offer, try to secure the acquisition of a block of shares from the main existing shareholders.

In this respect, the two principal methods are:
- to purchase a block of shares in a private transaction; or
- to obtain irrevocable undertakings from the main shareholders to contribute their shares to the public tender offer.

However, with respect to the second of these methods, the French courts consider that in the event of a counter-offer, the shareholders of the target company remain free to accept the best offer, notwithstanding any irrevocable undertakings that they may have previously given to a bidder. Therefore, it has become common for potential bidders, while negotiating such an undertaking, to seek an agreement with the concerned shareholders under which the latter would pay an indemnity should the undertaking be withdrawn in the event of a competing offer.

Consequently, to avoid this issue and to limit the risk of any counter-offer, potential bidders prefer to purchase a block of shares from significant shareholders in a private transaction.

In practice, with a view to completing a public-to-private transaction, it is common that the bidder will acquire at least 30%[10] of the share capital or voting rights of the target company in this initial block of shares, thus triggering an obligation on the purchaser to launch a tender offer for the remaining shares of the target company.

5.2   **Main issues that may arise during tender offer to be launched following acquisition of block of shares**
When contemplating a public-to-private transaction in France, private equity investors should keep in mind the following principles which apply to a tender offer to be launched following the acquisition of an initial block of listed shares.

(a)   Minimum level of acceptances
A compulsory tender offer may not contain a clause requiring a minimum number of securities to be tendered in order for the offer to be fulfilled. In addition, even with respect to voluntary tender offers, the Financial Markets Authority has always adopted a restrictive approach thereto on the basis that such a clause would create too much uncertainty in the market. Consequently, it has generally vetoed any acceptance condition higher than 66.67% of the share capital or voting rights.

(b)   Tender offer price
Under French laws and regulations, when a person, acting alone or in concert, comes to hold more than 30%[11] of a listed company's equity securities or voting rights, that person must file a draft offer for all the company's equity securities, as well as any securities giving access to its capital and voting rights, on terms that can be declared compliant by the Financial Markets Authority.

In such a case the proposed offer price must be at least equivalent to the highest price paid by the bidder, acting alone or in concert, in the 12-month period before the mandatory tender offer's threshold was crossed. However, the Financial Markets Authority may request or authorise a price modification if this is warranted by a manifest change in the characteristics of the target company or in the market for its securities, particularly in the following cases:
- if events liable materially to alter the value of the securities concerned occurred in the 12-month period before the draft offer was filed;
- if the target company is recognised as being in financial difficulty; or
- if the price mentioned above results from a transaction that includes related items involving the bidder, acting alone or in concert, and the seller of the securities acquired by the bidder over the last 12 months.

---

10   The 30% threshold of the share capital and voting rights is applicable to companies listed on a regulated market (eg, Euronext Paris). With respect to companies listed on a controlled market (eg, Alternext of Euronext Paris) the threshold of the share capital and voting rights is set at 50%.
11   Please refer to the previous footnote.

(c) Equal treatment of shareholders – involvement of existing shareholders and managers

When assessing the compliance of the contemplated tender offer to be launched following the acquisition of an initial block of shares, the Financial Markets Authority will check that all shareholders are treated equally by the bidder.

Consequently, the Financial Markets Authority will specifically address cases where certain existing shareholders, founders or managers are given the opportunity to roll over all or part of their existing shareholdings in the acquisition vehicle and agree different terms such as a management incentivisation package.

Indeed, in such cases one may argue that these shareholders and managers are offered a better deal than other shareholders who are not given this opportunity, and that therefore the bidder does not ensure equal treatment among the shareholders. As a result, minority shareholders might also require the right to roll over into the acquisition vehicle or, more realistically, to be offered a better price for their securities in order to take into account the economic value of the roll-over opportunity given to the management.

However, the Financial Markets Authority is keen to agree to such roll-overs and management packages because it recognises that there is a legitimate commercial interest in permitting the management of the target company to remain financially involved in the business. Indeed, without this exemption, public-to-private transactions would be far harder to effect, to the detriment of the market as a whole. In such cases the Financial Markets Authority will make sure that any deal entered into with the management does not protect the latter from the risks associated with its interest. In this respect, any option arrangements that guarantee an exit to the management at a price at least equal to the original offer price would be unacceptable.

In addition, under French laws and regulations the target company is required to appoint an independent appraiser to prepare a report on the financial terms of the offer, which will take the form of an opinion on the fairness of the offered price, since this kind of agreement between the bidder and the management

- is likely to cause conflicts of interest within the management or supervisory body that could impair the objectivity of the reasoned opinion to be issued by the latter regarding the benefits or consequences of the offer for the target company, its shareholders and its employees; and
- may jeopardise the fair treatment of shareholders.

5.3 Main issues with respect to delisting the target company

A public-to-private transaction is made with a view to delisting the company. However, French law compares unfavourably to UK law in terms of a bidder's ability to delist a target company and to create a tax consolidation group. Indeed, under French laws and regulations, the delisting of the target company is possible through a squeeze-out procedure only if the bidder holds 95% of the voting rights and the share capital of the target company, unlike the situation in the United Kingdom, where the bidder's right to squeeze out will be triggered as soon as a lower threshold (90%) is reached. Following the passing of the EU Takeover Directive in 2004, a committee established by the Financial Markets Authority issued a report recommending that the 95% threshold be lowered to 90%. However, this recommendation has not yet been implemented by Parliament.

Consequently, in order to try to secure the squeeze-out threshold, an alternative solution is to provide shareholders with price incentives in the form of a price supplement once the 95% threshold is reached.

Failure to reach the 95% threshold also prevents the bidder from obtaining tax consolidation with the target company and its 95%-held French subsidiaries, thereby making the interest charge incurred at the bidder's level tax-deductible from the profits made at the target's level. Indeed, under French laws and regulations, tax consolidation is available only to the extent that the bidder owns 95% of the share capital and voting rights of the target company (in contrast to the 75% threshold applicable in the United Kingdom). In this case, one alternative solution to ensure the tax deductibility of the interest on the acquisition debt may be a push-down of part of the debt to profit-making operating companies in the group (see section 4.1 above).

Furthermore, the fact of being unable to delist the target company will have, among other things, the following detrimental consequences:
- The target company will remain subject to oversight from the Financial Markets Authority and, in particular, the disclosure obligations and standards of the French public market, which may significantly increase functioning costs compared to a non-listed company; and
- Minority shareholders in the target company can complain about high dividend payments if it can be demonstrated that these high dividends were exclusively decided because of the bidder's need to service its debt, and are in excess of the target's financial abilities (although in practice, such a complaint would likely occur only in the event of the target's bankruptcy).

Germany

Georg Schneider
Noerr LLP

1. **Introduction**

The German private equity market and its legal practice have evolved from the growth of private equity driven by players from the United States and the United Kingdom. German private equity fund and deal structures essentially follow established structures common in the United States and the United Kingdom. This analysis is true irrespective of the fundamental changes that the industry faced when the venture capital boom ended in 2000 or when the credit crunch hit in 2007.

Differences that arise in German private equity transactions largely result from two areas.

First, tax considerations must be taken into account from the perspective of:
- German investors investing in German or non-German fund vehicles;
- non-German investors investing in, or in parallel to, German fund vehicles;
- German fund managers as carry-holders in a German or non-German private equity fund; and
- the need for a tax-efficient investment or de-investment structure.

Secondly, the German industrial environment demonstrates certain peculiarities, in that it:
- sees private equity as a still-maturing industry, which is consequently confronted by entrepreneurs, employees and tax authorities that are sceptical as regards the largely unfamiliar private equity investment model;
- lacks transparency regarding the players in the market and investment or refinancing opportunities; and
- remains characterised by family-owned small and medium-sized enterprises (95% of all companies in Germany).

While German private equity practice aims to follow international standards, this chapter focuses on German legal and tax issues that have a significant impact on the structuring of private equity fund formations or equity investments involving Germany.

2. **German private equity market**

2.1 Development of private equity in Germany

Investment companies providing equity financing to unquoted companies have been recognised in Germany since the 1960s. The development of private equity in

Germany as an acknowledged concept of equity financing, based on established investment structures and financially engineered investment methods, had its breakthrough in the late 1990s. It was driven mainly by US venture capital funds and by the initial success of the German tech market on the Frankfurt Stock Exchange. Irrespective of the collapse of the venture capital hype that resulted in the closure of the German tech market as a segment of the Frankfurt Stock Exchange on June 5 2003, the venture capital boom was essential for the sustainable development of the German private equity industry. In a short period a fair number of domestic players, including entrepreneurs, corporate finance advisers, lawyers and bankers became familiar with the rationale of private equity funds and their investment model. In addition to the creation of a sizeable class of private equity professionals, another feature for the growth of private equity was the introduction of German corporate tax reform in 2000. Not only did the tax reform reduce the corporate income tax rate from between 30% and 40% to 25% for retained distributed profits, it also introduced an extended tax exemption for capital gains realised by German corporations. This change in tax law was a key driver in the unwinding of the so-called Deutschland AG, a situation characterised by cross-shareholdings between banks and insurance companies and banks holding a vast portfolio of controlling stakes in major clients. In addition, it encouraged German corporations to divest their non-core businesses. To a large extent, private equity houses initiated and benefited from the merger and acquisition activities created by such opportunities.

Traditionally, Germany has developed more as a private equity in-bound market for the execution of private equity-backed investment, and less as a country of origin of capital. According to statistics published by the European Private Equity and Venture Capital Association for 2013, 0.215% of German gross domestic product (GDP) was invested in private equity, compared to the European average of 0.267% and the UK figure of 0.842%. A substantial contributing factor in this deviation is the different structure of the pension system. The German pension system is based on statutory and contractual claims against the employer and does not require funding. As a result, German pension funds do not invest in private equity in a similar manner to such funds in, for example, the United States and the United Kingdom.

However, the success of private equity as an additional finance stream for business growth and the concerns caused by private equity funds appearing on the German market with non-German investment vehicles and professionals operating mainly from outside Germany led to scepticism and fear. Finally, in 2005 these reservations resulted in the characterisation of private equity funds by the then chairman of the Social Democratic Party, Franz Müntefering, as "swarms of locusts" landing on a company, feasting on its assets, generating profits through job cuts or asset-stripping and then flying away, leaving only a husk. For a long time this figurative comparison dominated an animated debate, involving the political blacklisting of large buyout houses. Since then, public discussion has changed and the language used has evolved to a more factual and rational discussion. As a counterpoint to public critics, the private equity industry has increased its lobbying, and attempted to influence public opinion by disclosing the unknown elements of private equity, its measures and success.

2.2 Recent market trends

Today, the German private equity industry is characterised by an increased maturity, which has established private equity as an accepted investment activity. The recorded transaction volume grew from €500 million in the mid-1990s to €7.1 billion in 2008, reduced to €4.47 billion in 2011, but recovered to €6.46 billion in 2013; today, there are 5,000 private equity-backed companies in Germany, representing 8.5% of German GDP and employing a million people. Furthermore, Germany has developed a new generation of established domestic private equity providers, as well as family offices and dedicated funds pooling commitments of wealthy German families, which serve the private equity market as local players. Some 200 private equity houses are recognised in Germany.

Since mid-2007 Germany has seen a massive drop in private equity investments due to the lack of large buyouts and the effect of the credit crunch. However, this has not brought German private equity business to a standstill, merely led to a slowdown. The mistrust of German banks, which hindered the syndication of leverage, still reduces the availability of leverage. In addition, highly leveraged buyout investments have sometimes become distressed assets, and secondary portfolio transactions as well as minority investments have risen substantially.

The challenges of the actual market environment have a two-sided effect on the general partners or fund advisors operating in Germany. Due to the slowdown of fundraising, a number of German private equity teams have substantially reduced their headcount, have asked members of the team to move in particular to London, or have closed down German offices. At the same time, private equity houses have changed the emphasis of value creation in their portfolio companies from sophisticated financial engineering to implementing growth strategies such as an internationalisation strategy, extension of product facilities and buy-and-build strategies. The new focus on value creation is these days one driver for a number of funds from other jurisdictions branching out into Germany in order to be closer to their investment base as part of their value-creation strategy.

3. Fund formation

3.1 Objectives

The legal form, the terms and conditions and the corporate governance of private equity investment structures are determined by reconciling the requirements of different categories of investor, the priorities of the fund management team and the possible impact of the investment strategy. On the other hand, a regional focus on carrying out investments in Germany, or in any other specific jurisdiction, is not in itself decisive for the determination of fund structures. Such aspects must be considered by a fund during the course of the acquisition planning, while fund formation predominantly focuses on the legal and tax requirements of investors or members of the management team.

The general objectives of German investors (eg, a tax-efficient structure, limited liability and corporate governance procedures that are tested and easy to operate) and the terms and conditions that German investors expect to be reflected in the

documentation of a private equity fund are, broadly speaking, similar to those offered to investors in UK limited partnerships. These aspects are not, therefore, discussed here in detail. The differences that have an impact on the determination of a suitable structure from the German perspective mainly result from:
- marketing considerations;
- tax considerations of German or non-German investors;
- tax consideration of German management;
- statutory provisions limiting, for example, German public saving banks;
- restrictions binding German insurance companies under the Restricted Assets Directive and
- the requirements of the new Capital Investment Code (*Kapitalanlagengesetzbuch*).

From the German tax perspective, fund formation in the case of common partnership structures is largely influenced by the German concept of funds qualifying as 'business-active' (*gewerblich*) or 'non-business-active' (*vermögensverwaltend*) – an unusual concept compared to international fund formation standards. This might affect the tax transparency of any fund formation, with an impact on investors and carryholders investing in a German fund, or German investors or carryholders investing in a non-German fund (see section 3.4 below).

There are various other considerations apart from legal and tax aspects to be taken into account when structuring a private equity fund as, for example, a main fund, special fund, feeder fund, parallel fund, dedicated fund or fund of funds in Germany for German investors or, conversely, for non-German investors to reflect their specific needs relating to, for example, regulatory requirements, different fee structures, intended distribution policies or reporting requirements. Therefore, the establishment of a German fund is determined by two perspectives:
- German investors might want to invest in a German fund vehicle that invests as a feeder fund into, or in parallel with, an international fund scheme;
- non-German investors may have requirements that should be reflected in a separate German fund vehicle investing in parallel to a main fund established in Germany.

It has become common that the specific needs of different categories of investor may be unable to be reflected in the structure of a single fund entity, but instead may require the establishment of a multinational fund scheme with a number of investment vehicles, which might be set up in different jurisdictions investing in parallel.

3.2 Non-German fund structures

The vast majority of German investors do not face substantially different legal or tax obstacles to direct investment in non-German private equity fund structures rather than a German fund vehicle. German investors considering direct investment into a non-German private equity fund are likely to focus on the following objectives:
- clarity of fund documentation, limited liability and the enforceability of investor rights;

- tax transparency of the non-German fund under German tax law;
- whether the vehicle will actually qualify as a 'fund' (*Investmentfonds*) or as a 'partnership-investment-company' (*Personen-Investitionsgesellschaft*) under the German Investment Tax Act;
- lack of creation of a foreign permanent establishment;
- application of double tax treaties;
- passing on of tax credits and minimisation of withholding taxes on foreign dividends and interest; and
- ability to fulfil German tax filing requirements under applicable German tax provisions based on information to be provided by the fund (eg, determination of the nature of income under German tax law principles).

In the case of an investment by a German investor in a non-German partnership, the nature of the income generated by the fund and allocated to the German investor is determined for German taxpayers according to the same principles as those that apply to income from German funds. Therefore, if a German investor intends to invest in a fund that is tax-transparent and considered to be non-business-active for the purposes of German tax law, the non-German partnership must be structured and must perform its activity in such a manner that it is not considered to be 'in business' under the German tax law principles (see section 3.4 below).

For example, while it might be possible to avoid a deemed business qualification under German tax law by a very standard amendment to a limited partnership agreement which is governed by German law, under foreign jurisdictions the necessary allocation of management authority to a limited partner might:
- conflict with the limited liability status of a limited partner;
- create value added tax (VAT) issues; or
- infringe statutory provisions.

In addition, it will be important to understand whether the fund managers of a non-German private equity fund are prepared to perform the activities of a fund in such a way as to achieve non-business-active tax treatment under German tax law, or to provide German investors with the necessary information to fulfil German tax-filing requirements.

Such aspects will be taken into account when considering whether to establish a German parallel fund for German investors which invests alongside a non-German private equity main fund.

3.3 German structures under the new Capital Investment Code

On July 22 2013, the act implementing the EU Directive on Alternative Investment Fund Managers (AIFMD) in Germany entered into force. As its centrepiece, it introduced a new Capital Investment Code, which superseded in particular the Investment Act (*Investmentgesetz*) that had been previously in effect and also set out fund formation requirements for closed-ended funds, which had essentially been unregulated in Germany before.

The Capital Investment Code covers both undertakings for collective investments in transferable securities (UCITS) and alternative investment funds (AIFs). Whereas the Investment Act was based on a formal concept of investment fund, in that a fund was subject to the act only if it satisfied the act's requirements, the Capital Investment Code is based on a material concept of investment fund. This means that investment funds (as defined by the fulfilment of certain criteria) fall within the scope of the Capital Investment Code in any event, either as a UCITS or as an alternative investment fund, unless one of the narrow exceptions in the Capital Investment Code applies.

The Capital Investment Code distinguishes between open-ended and closed-ended funds. An alternative investment fund manager of an open-ended alternative investment fund is one that manages an alternative investment fund the shares or units of which are, at the request of any of its shareholders or unitholders, repurchased or redeemed prior to the commencement of its liquidation phase or wind-down, directly or indirectly, out of the assets of the fund and in accordance with the procedures and frequency set out in its rules or instruments of incorporation, prospectus or offering documents. All other funds are closed-ended funds.

Open-ended funds are divided into UCITS (for which the corresponding provisions of the Investment Act were taken over practically unchanged) and open-ended alternative investment funds. Closed-ended funds always qualify as (closed-ended) alternative investment funds.

(a) *Open-ended and closed-ended alternative investment funds*

Alternative investment funds, both open-ended and closed-ended, can be public alternative investment funds in which retail investors may (also) invest or special alternative investment funds in which only professional investors or semi-professional investors may invest. The term 'professional investors' is to be understood in the sense of the term 'professional client' within the meaning of the EU Market in Financial Instruments Directive (MIFID). The term 'semi-professional investors' includes the management team of a fund, investors committing to invest at least €200,000 subject to various checks regarding the investor's being sufficiently sophisticated, and investors committing to invest at least €10 million (in this case without the need for any investor checks).

Open-ended public alternative investment funds: Open-ended public alternative investment funds include the following types of funds deriving from the Investment Act: mixed funds (*Gemischte Sondervermögen*), other funds (*Sonstige Sondervermögen*), funds of hedge funds (*Dach-Hedgefonds*) and real-estate funds (*Immobilien-Sondervermögen*). However, compared to the Investment Act, the Capital Investment Code introduced the following modifications.

Mixed funds are no longer permitted to invest in real-estate funds. This is intended to combat the problem that had arisen in the (quite recent) past that mixed funds had to suspend the redemption of units because the real-estate fund in which they were invested had suspended the redemption of units. In addition, mixed funds are no longer permitted to invest in hedge funds.

Like mixed funds, other funds are no longer permitted to invest in real-estate and hedge funds. In addition, other funds are now entirely forbidden from investing (directly) in company shares, due to the illiquidity of these shares.

Infrastructure funds, which were a separate type of fund under the Investment Act are, because of the illiquidity of their investments, now only permissible as closed-ended funds.

The provisions of the Investment Act on funds of hedge funds have been transferred into the Capital Investment Code with editorial amendments only. Authorised asset management companies are permitted to launch both single hedge funds and funds of hedge funds. However, units in single hedge funds, which under the old law could not be marketed to retail investors publicly except by way of private placement, are now prohibited for such investors (see also below). Regulations in respect of funds of hedge funds include that no more than 20% of a fund of hedge funds may be invested in a single target fund, leverage is prohibited and short selling may not be carried out. In addition, before investing, the asset management companies must ensure that they have access to all the information on the target fund in which they wish to invest that is necessary for their investment decision.

Open-ended special alternative investment funds: First, open-ended special alternative investment funds include 'general' open-ended special alternative investment funds. They are entitled to invest in all assets the market value of which can be determined.

Secondly, special funds (*Spezialfonds*) within the meaning of the Investment Act continue to exist as open-ended special alternative investment funds with fixed investment rules in order to take account of the requirement of the investment fund industry for the maintenance of established product rules and the statutory framework conditions for accountancy and tax treatment. For these funds the provisions relating to open-ended public alternative investment funds generally apply with regard to fund assets and investment limits, although the relevant rules can be deviated from subject to compliance with certain minimum requirements.

Finally, units in single hedge funds must now be held exclusively by professional and semi-professional investors.

Closed-ended public alternative investment funds: Closed-ended alternative investment funds include closed-ended public alternative investment funds, in which retail investors may (also) invest. In the Capital Investment Code they are treated almost in the same manner as open-ended funds.

First, there is a definitive list of assets in which closed-ended public alternative investment funds may invest (which includes, in particular, direct or indirect investments in real estate including forest and farm land, ships, aircraft, power generation plants from renewable energy and interests in public-private partnership companies, participations in non-listed companies and units in other closed-ended funds). Secondly, debt financing is restricted at fund level to 60% of the value of the fund. In addition, the transparency of blind pool concepts is intended to be increased by the requirement to describe specifically the investment strategy. The

Capital Investment Code contains provisions on fund rules, sales prospectuses and key investor information which replace the corresponding provisions of the Capital Investments Act (*Vermögensanlagengesetz*) that had only come into force on June 1 2012. The restriction of currency risks to assets making up a maximum of 30% of the value of the fund is also worthy of mention.

Units in closed-ended public alternative investment funds that are only invested in one or two single assets may only be held by investors committing to invest at least €20,000 and fulfilling the other criteria of the semi-professional investor and provided these funds do not invest in private equity.

Closed-ended special alternative investment funds: Closed-ended special alternative investment funds form a second group of closed-ended alternative investment funds accessible only to professional and semi-professional investors. They are entitled to invest in all assets the market value of which can be determined.

In addition, the Capital Investment Code implements the special provisions of the Directive on Alternative Investment Fund Managers for private equity funds. Thus, it sets out special information obligations on nonlisted companies and relating to the employees of such companies, control of which the alternative investment fund acquires, and measures to prevent asset-stripping with regard to these companies.

(b) *German fund vehicles*
Following the concepts that were used in the Investment Act, the Capital Investment Code provides for 'funds' (*Sondervermögen*) and investment stock corporations with variable capital as possible fund vehicles for investment funds within the meaning of the UCITS Directive as well as for open-ended (German) public alternative investment funds. For open-ended (German) special alternative investment funds, the Capital Investment Code further provides for the legal form of an open investment limited partnership with variable capital. With the latter, the legislature intended to create a tax-transparent vehicle to be used for pension asset-pooling in Germany in order to keep the assets of pension funds of major German corporate groups in Germany and possibly to also attract assets from their foreign subsidiaries to Germany.

For closed-ended funds, the Capital Investment Code mandates (ie, without any further choice) the use of investment stock corporations with fixed capital (*Investment-AG*) or closed investment limited partnerships (*Investment-KG*) as fund vehicles.

3.4 German limited partnership funds

(a) *Legal structure*
The German limited partnership (*Kommanditgesellschaft* or *KG*) which may be used under the Capital Investment Code as a legal form for a closed-ended alternative investment fund – called under the code an 'investment-limited-partnership' (*Investmentkommanditgesellschaft*) – has become the most common vehicle for private

equity funds established in Germany. If it is carefully structured and managed by the fund managers, it fulfils the requirements of the majority of German or non-German investors in private equity funds. In particular, German limited partnership law allows funds subject to the US Employee Retirement Income Security Act of 1974 to fulfil US tax and legal requirements.

The concept of a German limited partnership is similar to a Scottish limited partnership, which is treated under German commercial law as a deemed legal entity. As with the UK vehicle, a German limited partnership provides for limitation of liability by having two types of partner: the general partner, which is subject to unlimited liability for all debts and obligations of the partnership extending to its personal assets; and the investors as limited partners, whose liability to creditors of the German limited partnership is limited to the amount of their unpaid capital commitment or the amount that is registered in the Commercial Register as the liability amount.

The commonly used form 'GmbH & Co KG' usually has a limited liability company (GmbH) as general partner. To avoid a deemed business qualification under German tax law, it is common to allocate management authority to a limited partner under the provisions of the partnership agreement (see below).

(b) *Tax considerations*

The partnership in form of a closed-ended fund is now, under the Investment Tax Act, treated as a 'partnership-investment-company' (*Personen-Investitionsgesellschaft*). However, in contrast to investment funds (*Investmentfonds*), which are subject to their own tax-transparent tax regime and require certain structuring elements – such as redemption once a year, a risk-diversified asset portfolio and limitations with respect to the (percentage of) holding assets and leverage – a partnership-investment-company is subject to the general tax principles applicable to partnerships.

Tax transparency and non-business-active status: A German limited partnership is not subject to corporate or income tax at partnership level as it is fiscally transparent. Therefore, for German tax purposes, the income of the partnership is directly allocated to its partners in the amount of their respective profit share, and taxed at the partners' level subject to the individual tax position of the respective partner. In particular, withholding tax on dividends will not apply at fund level, but may accrue at portfolio level.

However, if under German tax law the fund qualifies as 'business-active', the partnership will be subject to trade tax. Trade tax is levied by the local municipality with varying tax rates to be assessed on the basis of the taxable income for trade tax purposes, which usually results in an overall trade tax burden at partnership level of between 7% and 17.15%. Trade tax can be credited against the investors' income tax liabilities at investor level, but this is subject to a specific procedure and tax leakage might occur.

A German partnership is fiscally transparent for trade tax if the fund qualifies as being 'non-business-active'. Non-business-active status permits a partnership to achieve the following objectives in the interests of both German and non-German investors:

- tax transparency for German income tax, corporate tax and trade tax;
- privileged carry taxation for German-resident carryholders in the fund (the partial income tax system, comprising a 40% tax exemption);
- avoiding the creation of a permanent establishment for non-German investors in the German private equity fund; and
- suitability for tax-exempt investors (eg, pension funds and charitable trusts).

The tax treatment of a German private equity fund as business-active or non-business-active results in different taxation for German and non-German investors. Non-German investors might become subject to limited tax liability under German tax law to the extent that the German tax authorities treat the partnership interest in a business-active partnership as deriving from a permanent establishment, provided that the business income is connected with a German permanent establishment or a permanent agent. In order to avoid the creation of a permanent establishment or the classification of representatives as permanent agents of an investor in Germany, among other things, any contractual or non-contractual relationship between German advisers and non-German fund vehicles or investors must be structured and monitored carefully.

Up to the end of 2008, German private investors were able to generate fully tax-exempt capital gains if the following conditions were met:
- the capital was invested in a non-business-active partnership;
- the investor indirectly held an interest in the underlying assets of the partnership that was below 1%; and
- a minimum holding period of one year was satisfied.

From January 1 2009, this advantageous tax regime applying to German investors was abolished where the shares were (directly or indirectly) acquired after December 31 2008.

Under the German tax law applicable to investments of resident private investors made as of 2009, any income (capital gains, dividends, interest) is subject to a flat tax rate of 25% (*Abgeltungssteuer*), plus a solidarity surcharge of 5.5% thereon and church tax, if applicable. If the threshold of an (indirect) shareholding of 1% is exceeded, capital gains are subject to the partial income tax system providing for a 40% tax exemption (with a tax burden of up to 28.485% plus church tax, if applicable).

Requirements of non-business-active status: The status of a German or non-German private equity fund as non-business-active requires that:
- the fund does not qualify as business-active by virtue of its legal structure;
- the fund does not invest in other German or non-German partnerships that qualify as business-active, causing the fund's entire income to be treated as business income (so-called 'business infection'); and
- the fund does not carry out activities beyond those qualifying as administration of assets or asset management (*private Vermögensverwaltung*).

A German partnership is deemed to be business-active, irrespective of the categorisation of its activities as business-active or non-business active, if the partnership has only corporations as general partners and the partnership agreement entitles only such general partners, or persons not being partners in the partnership, to execute management authorities. Categorisation as business-active can be avoided if the partnership agreement allocates management authority not solely to the general partner, but also to a limited partner (a managing limited partner). According to the Income Tax Guidelines (*Einkommensteuerrichtlinie*), a limited partner that is a corporation is a suitable legal form to serve as managing limited partner, thus avoiding the categorisation as business-active. It should be noted, though, that some tax commentators take the view, with reference to the relevant provisions of the Income Tax Act (*Einkommensteuer*), that allocating management authority to a managing limited partner that is a corporation will not avoid the business-active categorisation.

In case of a business infection, a partnership will be treated as generating business income from all its sources of income. Therefore, income generated from non-business activities, such as investments in another German or non-German partnership, will be treated generally as business income. To prevent this, it is common to invest through a German or non-German corporation (a 'blocker' company). This results in the re-categorisation of income as, for example, capital gains realised by the blocker to be distributed by the intermediate corporation as dividends. By taking this approach, investors in the partnership will receive proceeds from the disposal of an underlying asset as an allocation of dividend income instead of capital gains. However, the tax exemption for dividends requires a shareholding of at least 10% by each investor in the respective blocker corporation. Furthermore, any tax exemption for capital gains or dividends will not be granted to the investor if the blocker corporation itself is subject to tax within the European Economic Area and is not tax-exempt, or if it is not subject to taxation of at least 15% outside the European Economic Area.

The nature of the activities on which the tax treatment of a private equity fund is based must be determined by taking into account all the circumstances. On December 16 2003 the Federal Ministry of Finance issued a decree on the tax treatment of venture capital and private equity funds. Under the decree, the ministry summarised a number of criteria which, if fulfilled in whole or in part, will result in a categorisation of a fund as business-active (the negative test). In addition, a number of fiscal authorities have issued explanatory notes to provide further guidance for the interpretation of the decree or the Income Tax Act regarding its application to private equity funds. The criteria of the negative test to avoid a categorisation as business-active include:

- no involvement on the part of the private equity fund or a related person (including related advisers) in the management of portfolio companies;
- no debt financing or collateral at fund level;
- no re-investment of capital gains or other income;
- no short-term holding periods (three to five years on a weighted average based on the holding period and the respective investment amount);
- no exploitation of a market based on professional experience; and

- no carrying out of business or maintaining offices which goes beyond what is required for the private administration of assets or asset management.

These criteria should be fulfilled not just when the partnership is originally formed or when it performs its activities. Adherence to these requirements must be monitored during the entire lifetime of the partnership. In particular, due to the impact of the credit crunch on portfolio companies, the involvement of fund managers or related persons in supporting portfolio companies must be carefully handled and monitored to ensure it stays within the limits of the decree of December 16 2003. For example, hands-on management, the provision of security for the liabilities of a portfolio company, or the grant of guarantees for debt financing of portfolio companies might conflict with the intended categorisation of a fund as non-business-active.

In general, a tax ruling by the German tax authorities can be obtained with respect to the fund structure, but this does not cover the treatment of facts and circumstances arising during the course of the management of the fund.

VAT: A German private equity fund established in a common GmbH & Co KG structure is not considered to have an entrepreneurial function according to the European Court of Justice. Therefore, such a fund is unable to recover VAT.

Under a decree of the Federal Ministry of Finance of May 31 2007, management charges payable to a fund manager with its business seat in Germany are subject to VAT at a current tax rate of 19%, even when the management fee is structured as a preferred profit share. This decree became effective as of January 1 2008 for partnerships established in Germany. As VAT is not recoverable by the fund, additional costs at fund level are created. In order to avoid the payment of VAT on management fees, German private equity funds must be managed, if possible, by fund managers acting outside Germany.

(c) *Carried interest and co-investment schemes for fund managers*

German executives entitled to carried interest should receive it as an interest in the profits of a non-business-active partnership based on the provisions of the limited partnership agreement. To the extent that a private equity fund qualifies as a non-business-active partnership, German resident carry-holders can benefit from favourable carried interest taxation under Section 18(1)(4) of the Income Tax Act. Instead of a full taxation of the carried interest, the so-called partial income tax system limits the tax assessment to 60% of the income from the fund being subject to the individual progressive income tax rate. This preferential tax treatment requires that the German executives – irrespective of whether the carry derives from a German or non-German partnership – receive the income from a private equity fund that qualifies as non-business-active under German income tax principles. Therefore, in determining the taxable income of German fund managers holding a carried interest in a non-German partnership, the German tax authorities will assess the nature of the tax categorisation of a non-German fund according to German tax law principles even where a fund manager receives its carry from a non-German fund.

Furthermore, the favourable taxation of carried interest is not available if the private equity fund is not structured as a partnership.

This notwithstanding, German executives investing side by side in a private equity fund holding shareholdings in corporations and target companies will also realise capital gains and dividends, liable to the flat tax rate of 25% or falling under the partial income tax system providing for a 40% tax exemption (a tax burden of up to 28.485% plus church tax, if applicable).

4. Private equity investments

Country-specific issues arising in a private equity deal result less from its general terms, mechanism or structure and more from the applicable legal and tax framework. The legal and tax issues to be observed are generally the same as in any private merger and acquisition transaction. The involvement of management central to any private equity transaction requires careful legal and tax structuring, as do reorganisations or acquisitions following insolvency (which have become more common in the current market environment).

Against this background, this section focuses on:
- acquisition structuring;
- takeover regulation;
- merger control;
- regulatory issues relating to foreign investments in Germany;
- transaction structuring issues determined by the execution of a share or asset deal;
- management issues; and
- distressed mergers and acquisitions.

4.1 Acquisition structuring

(a) Withholding taxes

The structure of a deal is influenced by the private equity fund's tax structure and the investors' tax requirements. Private equity funds aim to avoid the application of withholding tax on dividends or interest (which is charged at a rate of 26.375%, including solidarity surcharge) at the level of German portfolio companies. Withholding tax may arise to the extent that a double tax treaty or the EU Parent-Subsidiary Directive, as transposed into the German Income Tax Act, do not apply. Predominantly to serve the tax requirements of non-EU fund investors, the interposition of a Luxembourg or Netherlands holding company has become common, since these jurisdictions offer flexible corporate structures to distribute proceeds by way of a partial liquidation, or the avoidance of withholding taxes based on an extended double tax treaty network.

From a German perspective, it is important to examine whether a foreign holding company can fulfil the substance rules, which are tight. If the shareholders of the foreign holding company are not entitled to a withholding tax relief on a direct participation and the foreign holding company does not generate its gross income from its own business activities, the foreign holding company must prove:

- that there are economic or other significant reasons for its interposition; and
- that it has a business establishment that is appropriate for its business purpose (qualified staff, offices, premises and technical services) through which it participates in the market.

Furthermore, it must be checked that typical structures to avoid withholding tax at the level of the interposed foreign holding company (eg, hybrid structures such as preferred equity certificates) do not conflict with the intended tax treatment of German-resident investors or German carry-holders.

(b) *Transfer pricing*

Given the cross-border nature of private equity acquisition structures, transfer pricing issues cannot be disregarded. Therefore, cross-border intergroup charges for services, interest on loans and royalty payments must be at arm's length in order to avoid any adverse tax impacts. Transfer pricing documentation rules are applicable.

4.2 Takeover regulation

The Takeover Act (*Wertpapiererwerbs- und Übernahmegesetz*) applies to takeovers of all publicly held companies in Germany that are listed on a regulated market. Where a bidder, by itself or together with joint bidders, acquires 30% or more of the voting rights of such a German publicly listed company, it is obliged to launch a mandatory bid for all the remaining shares of the company. An exemption may be granted by the German Federal Financial Supervisory Authority (BaFin) in certain limited circumstances, such as a group restructuring or a crisis in the target company. If the bidder holds less than 30% of the target company's shares he may decide to launch a voluntary bid that may either be targeted towards acquiring less than 30% (ie, a non-controlling stake), or towards acquiring a controlling stake of 30% or more. The offer document for each public bid (be it mandatory or voluntary) must be filed with BaFin prior to its publication. The acceptance period generally lasts between four and 12 weeks. A squeeze-out is possible if the bidder acquires at least 95% of the shares. The squeeze-out can be implemented in two ways, either under the German Stock Corporation Act (*Aktiengesetz*) or under the Takeover Act. A third squeeze-out option requiring a shareholding of at least 90% has been introduced very recently in the Corporate Reorganisation Act. All three squeeze-out options provide different features in terms of transaction certainty and timing. The most common one is currently still the squeeze-out under the Stock Corporation Act.

4.3 Merger control

The German merger control regime applies to all mergers provided the European Commission does not have exclusive jurisdiction under the EU Merger Regulation. Mergers requiring notification may not be implemented prior to clearance by the Federal Cartel Office (FCO). Notification is mandatory if:
- the transaction is a concentration within the meaning of the German Act Against Restraints of Competition (*Gesetz gegen Wettbewerbsbeschränkungen*);
- the combined aggregate worldwide turnover of all participating undertakings

(comprising the buyer and the target company) was more than €500 million during the last business year preceding the merger; and
- the domestic turnover of at least one of the participating undertakings was more than €25 million and another participating undertaking had a domestic turnover of over €5 million.

Exemptions may apply. The FCO must prohibit mergers if the transaction will significantly impede effective competition, in particular if it creates or strengthens a dominant market position. Exemptions apply for:
- outweighing improvements of the conditions of competition;
- failing firms in the press industry; and
- minor markets.

The federal minister of economic affairs and technology may grant an exemption from the prohibition on anti-competitive transactions on grounds of prevailing benefits for the economy as a whole or for the common good.

4.4 Regulation of foreign investments in Germany

Investments by non-EU member states or non-European Free Trade Agreement (EFTA) members (Iceland, Liechtenstein, Norway and Switzerland) may be prohibited if public security and order is at risk, in particular with respect to services for the public. The Foreign Trade Act 2009 entitles the Federal Ministry of Economic Affairs to prevent transactions involving non-EU or non-EFTA investors with voting rights exceeding 25%. Investments in companies that produce certain military equipment (eg, weapons and encryption technology) must be notified, and may be restricted or prohibited. Transactions that have already been executed and completed can be unwound.

Further regulation may be applicable in respect of banking, media and financial services investments.

There are no exchange control or currency regulations, except those relating to money laundering. The transfer of money into Germany must be notified to the Federal State Bank if the amount exceeds €12,500.

4.5 Transaction structure: share deals and asset deals

(a) Tax considerations

In general, German corporate sellers prefer to sell shares rather than business assets, particularly because 95% of the capital gains realised by corporate sellers arising from the disposal of shares in corporate entities are exempt from German tax (ie, only 5% of such capital gains will be subject to German corporate income tax, at a rate of 15.825% including solidarity surcharge and trade tax). If business assets are sold, capital gains are fully subject to German corporate tax and trade tax.

In contrast to the position of a German corporate seller, a German purchaser of shares will generally prefer to acquire business assets rather than shares, because the assets are capitalised in the accounts at acquisition cost and, therefore, depreciation related to the assets will typically be higher than in the case of a share deal. In view of the increased depreciation, a corresponding part of the acquisition cost may be tax deductible.

Where German real estate is acquired, real-estate transfer tax at a rate between 3.5% and 6.5% of the purchase price, depending on the federal state in which the real estate is located, will be payable. In addition, if 95% or more of the participation in an entity owning German real estate is transferred, German real-estate transfer tax of 3.5% to 6.5% of the real estate value of the real-estate owned by the entity will be payable.

(b) *Employment*

In principle, a share deal has no impact on employment agreements. If established, an employee works council need not be involved in a proposed sale of shares by the seller unless collective agreements are in force. However, the target's management is required to inform such a council (or its economic committee) of the intended transaction, if there is to be a change of control, and of any possible consequences in connection with it.

In the case of an asset or business sale, the legal provisions of Section 613a of the Civil Code apply. Under these provisions, all employees of the transferred business are automatically transferred to the purchaser which, in principle, must continue the employment on the same terms and conditions (including pension obligations) as agreed with the seller. Some collective agreements may be displaced by collective agreements applicable to the purchaser. Any termination based on the transfer of business is invalid, but in certain circumstances employees may be dismissed for operational reasons. In executing an asset deal, the obligation of the selling employer to inform employees affected by the transfer of their employment relationship under Section 613a of the Civil Code must be observed carefully. Each employee is entitled to object to the transfer within one month of receiving valid notice. As a consequence of such objection, the employee remains employed with the original employer. Difficult situations might occur if more employees than expected object to the transfer of their employment relationships, or object long after a merger if it turns out that they were not properly informed.

If a transaction comprises a restructuring or carve-out of part of the business to be transferred (or of that to be retained), which qualifies as a change of business, the works council may be entitled to file for an interim injunction to postpone a restructuring for as long as no agreement on the reconciliation of interests (*Interessenausgleich*) for the benefit of affected employees is achieved. The possible impact of time-consuming negotiation with the works council must be considered at an early stage of the transaction.

(c) *Pensions*

The sale of shares in a share deal does not affect any pension scheme operated by the target company.

If the whole (or part of the) business is sold in an asset deal, the purchaser must continue employment on the same terms and conditions as agreed with the seller.

This also applies with respect to pension schemes for active employees. Any claims of pensioners and retired employees remain with the seller and are generally not transferred to the purchaser.

4.6 Debt financing

(a) ***Interest barrier rules***
To achieve a tax-efficient deductibility of interest at the level of a German portfolio company, different mechanisms such as a debt pushdown, a merger of the acquisition vehicle with a portfolio company or the creation of a fiscal unit between these entities might be evaluated. Furthermore, the deductibility of interest is limited under the principles of the thin capitalisation rules, which were replaced and further tightened at the beginning of 2008 through the introduction of interest barrier rules. In principle, the interest barrier rules apply to all kinds of debt and are not limited to shareholder or related-party loans. According to the interest barrier rules, tax-effective interest deduction is limited to the amount of 30% of the business's earnings before interest, taxes, depreciation and amortisation in the relevant fiscal year. However, the deduction of interest is unlimited if the taxpayer can demonstrate that the interest is less than €3 million, or the equity ratio of the business is more than two percentage points below the equity ratio of the entire consolidated group (basically determined under international financial reporting standards (IFRS)) provided that not more than 10% of the annual interest expenses exceeding interest income of a business belonging to the group are paid on shareholder loans or loans treated like shareholder loans. For that purpose, shareholder and inter-company loans, liabilities and securities will be relevant only if provided by shareholders or related parties outside the consolidated group. Any interest not deductible in the relevant fiscal year can be carried forward.

(b) ***Capital maintenance rules applying to upstream loans, collateral and cash pools***
Any financial assistance of a target company is subject to strict capital maintenance protection provisions. In particular, a stock corporation is prohibited from providing any loans or security to assist in the purchase of its own shares.

The capital maintenance provisions applicable to limited liability companies (GmbHs) are now governed by a reform of 2008. The law now makes clear that the granting of loans or collateral by a limited liability company to one of its shareholders and the extent to which it might participate in a cash pool do not constitute prohibited payments of capital if either the company receives full consideration or the payment is fully balanced by a claim for (re)payment reflected in the balance sheet applying generally accepted accounting principles. Upstream payments are also permissible if made while an agreement of domination or a profit-transfer agreement exists. Unforeseeable future events (eg, deterioration in the shareholder's financial position leading to a write-off) should not have retrospective effect, and therefore do not turn a once-admissible payment into a forbidden distribution of capital. This new concept obviously hinges on the full collectability of the company's claim against its shareholder. The difference between equity-like shareholder loans and regular shareholder loans has been abolished. Loans received by a limited liability company from a shareholder are no longer classified as equity, even if they are granted during a financial crisis, but will be treated as debt from a corporate law perspective. However, this improvement comes at a price: the shareholder's position under insolvency law has changed for the worse. Although the limited liability company may lawfully make repayments on account of shareholder loans prior to its insolvency, any such repayment is liable to be challenged by the insolvency administrator if it is made in the year before, or in the course of, the insolvency. The administrator's right to challenge extends to a period of no less than 10 years prior to the insolvency when it comes to security granted by the company in favour of a shareholder. Non-repaid (or successfully challenged) shareholder loans rank behind the claims of all other creditors (see below).

The new law on limited liability companies has extended liabilities, and has therefore created liability risks for managing directors; for example, if a limited liability company participates in a cash pool and that company's resulting claim against its ultimate parent company turns out not to be fully collectable, contrary to an earlier assessment by the managing director. In such and similar cases, the managing director risks being held personally liable if the parent company does not have the liquidity to honour the subsidiary's claim. The liability position of managing directors should be carefully reviewed in advance to avoid difficulties occurring during the course of completion if managing directors question their authority to bind the portfolio company under the finance documentation.

4.7 **Management**

Management plays a significant role in the acquisition of an investment, in regard to both achievement of the business plan and execution of a successful exit. At the start of the 21st century it was still hard for private equity houses to find suitable German management teams willing and able to develop financially engineered business models. Entrepreneurs and key managers saw employment with a company as a relationship that would last their whole working life and, to a lesser extent, saw their task as expanding the business model by committing their specific skills to a company during a particular business cycle. This section looks at key requirements under German corporate governance rules and tax law provisions that affect management incentives, and at the organisation of the relationship between the portfolio company managers and the private equity fund.

(a) *Role of management from German corporate governance perspective*

Private equity fund managers aim to control the management of portfolio companies. If the target company is a limited liability company, shareholders can give instructions to the managing director of the company. Liability issues or negative tax effects that will arise from a structure that will be categorised as non-business-active must be considered. By contrast, the management of a stock corporation is controlled by the supervisory board, but cannot be bound by instructions of the shareholders' meeting or the supervisory board.

Management duties in a buyout transaction: Under German corporate governance

rules, the management of portfolio companies must exercise management authority generally in the sole interest of the company and not that of its shareholders. Even if participation in a management incentive programme is offered to management during the course of the negotiations, and implemented, management must always act in such a way as to give priority to the interests of the company. Therefore, management must disclose to the supervisory board of a stock corporation or the advisory board of a limited liability company any approach by a private equity investor to take part in a management buyout or any other kind of conflict of interest that might occur during the course of the transaction. In addition, management must:
- maintain confidentiality and observe non-compete obligations;
- comply with stock exchange regulations (if applicable); and
- avoid insider trading (if applicable).

Management is obliged to secure a shareholders' resolution before it can grant a potential buyer or investor access to the company's books and records.

If any kind of bonus compensation, equity participation or option with respect to any involvement in a transaction is offered to the management of a public company, such compensation must be approved by the supervisory board and must not exceed a reasonable level, which is measured by the interests of the company and not the interests of an investor or existing shareholder (a well-known example is the criminal lawsuit that arose from the takeover of Mannesmann AG by Vodafone in 2004).

(b) *Management participation schemes*
Civil law aspects/effectiveness: The granting of management participation requires careful compliance with consumer protection law aspects, including fulfilment of the obligation to provide detailed information to the management, observance of revocation rights and other civil law provisions. It might be seen as unusual to treat a manager who takes part in a management buyout as a consumer. However, non-observance of these rules might result in a manager who falls under the category of a bad leaver being able to reclaim his acquisition costs at any point on the grounds that the service or shareholders' agreement setting out the management participation scheme has not become effective.

Specific legal clauses that have become standard in management participation documentation, such as put and call options and drag-along or tag-along provisions, require compliance with the German law principles of clarity and certainty to ensure that they are enforceable. Provisions such as the authority of a general partner or senior manager to allocate carry individually on a case-by-case basis, or to determine the compensation applicable in a leaver situation at the sole discretion of the general partner might be null and void if the determination is seen as arbitrary. From a labour law perspective, the principle of equal treatment might need to be respected. Leaver or vesting provisions require careful drafting. In particular, the effectiveness of compensation provisions to apply to a good leaver or bad leaver scenario can be challenged under German civil law if a court determines that a substantial disparity exists between the fair market value of a management participation that is subject to a call option under a leaver provision and the amount of compensation otherwise offered to a leaving manager under the management participation scheme. The German courts have specified the circumstances in which an investor's call option to acquire the management participation in the case of a dismissal by the employer, or the issuance of a notice of termination by the employee, might be null and void. To minimise legal risks, the management participation scheme should set out in writing the purpose of the scheme, and should describe the different economic positions and interests of the parties involved. Setting out the rationale in the documents to be signed by a manager proves that the manager was fully aware of and agreed to the mechanism of the management participation programme. Such a precaution would strengthen an argument, if there were litigation or arbitration, that the programme is not to be seen as discriminatory or arbitrary. In addition, management should receive independent advice on the mechanics of the management participation programme and its tax impact.

Tax considerations: Under German tax law, management participation schemes are typically designed as direct or indirect shareholdings in a portfolio company, which (with careful structuring) offer management the ability to realise capital gains or dividends derived from the management participation at the flat tax rate of 25% plus solidarity surcharge of 5.5% and church tax, if applicable, or under the partial-income tax scheme with a 40% tax exemption (a tax burden of up to 28.485% plus church tax, if applicable). This is instead of the full taxation which would apply to bonus payments or any consideration treated as a benefit in kind if linked to employment, irrespective of the nature of such income as capital gains, dividend, interest or other income, and irrespective of whether received from the employer or a third party (such as an investor).

Any advantage that a manager might be offered in acquiring a direct or indirect participation in portfolio companies compared to the fair market value of such a participation (in particular compared to the terms and conditions accepted by an investor) is treated as a benefit in kind. Such a benefit is subject to the full income tax rate to be paid at the time of granting of the benefit. Sweet equity investment structures, the postponement of the due date to pay the investment amount, or a dispensation from making shareholder loans or other supplemental payments might be treated as benefits in kind.

To avoid a taxation event at the time of the investment when the manager does not receive any related income resulting from proceeds derived from management participation (so-called dry income charges), it has become common for the investor to make available a loan to the manager to facilitate and ensure that he is investing on similar commercial terms as the investor. A loan provided to a manager, and in particular one that is characterised as a non-recourse loan (that is repayable by the manager only out of, and to the extent of, proceeds related to the management participation), might give rise to a taxable event as a benefit in kind subject to the full tax rate, if certain events, such as waiver of some or all of the loan, occur.

4.8 Distressed mergers and acquisitions

Private equity houses increasingly specialise in the acquisition of distressed assets with a specific focus, for example, on mergers and acquisitions of distressed undertakings or on the acquisition of a debt portfolio with a strategy to become the owner of the debtor (so-called debt-to-own).

The acquisition of an undertaking in an economic crisis is governed by a specific legal framework. The timing and procedural aspects vary depending on whether a business is acquired by way of an asset or a share deal prior to or after filing for insolvency, as do the role, economic interests and the economic situation of the different participants involved as shareholders, creditors (ie, banks or suppliers), management, employees and, in an insolvency, the insolvency administrator and the creditors' committee. The risk and opportunity profile differs if the purchaser acquires a business prior to an insolvency (eg, to execute a reorganisation, which is quite often combined with a creditors' agreement), or if the purchaser acquires the business from an insolvency administrator, thereby being able to try to negotiate with an insolvency administrator as to which specific assets, employees or contractual relationships should be transferred to the purchaser. A variety of legal aspects to be considered when determining whether to acquire a distressed business prior to or after insolvency are outlined below.

(a) Acquisition of a distressed business prior to insolvency

The acquisition of a distressed business prior to insolvency is often seen as a less attractive opportunity. However, it is in general a process that is easier to control, and can avoid some of the negative implications of an insolvency proceeding.

When filing for insolvency, the shareholders typically lose any control and value of their equity investment. Shareholder loans are classified as subordinated loans by law, and the shareholders' rights to control or to give instructions to the management of a portfolio company (including the ability to negotiate a divestment with a potential purchaser) are basically exercised by the management authorities of an insolvency administrator. In addition, the impact of an insolvency on the reputation of a business, its brand and the quality of the business relationships with customers or suppliers should not be underestimated.

Prior to insolvency, a controlled acquisition negotiated and discussed with the shareholders, creditors and the existing management can only be achieved if the transaction can be completed before the economic situation requires the management to file for insolvency. Acquisitions of shares or assets that take place in a situation where the target faces a crisis must avoid the risk that the transaction might be challenged in whole or in part at a later stage by an insolvency administrator if insolvency becomes inevitable after completion of the transaction. An insolvency administrator has the authority, among other things, to decide whether unperformed contracts (eg, share or asset purchase agreements, licence or lease agreements) shall be fulfilled by either or both of the parties. In addition, the insolvency administrator may contest the validity of contracts or other transactions that are executed within a three-month period before the opening of insolvency proceedings where they are disadvantageous to creditors of the insolvent company.

If such contracts have been agreed without consideration, or without full consideration, the right of the administrator to contest those contracts is extended to four years, or 10 years in the case of wilful discrimination against creditors. Therefore, any acquisition should be carefully structured and based on a reliable assessment that the target business will be stable in the short and medium term.

Double-sided trust agreements: A model frequently used in the market is to sell a distressed business by establishing a so-called 'double-sided trust agreement'. It is a disposal process driven by creditors (in particular banks). The trustee enters into an agreement with the shareholders on the one side and creditors on the other side. In these situations creditors agree to a standstill and require shareholders to transfer their shareholding to a trustee together with a power of attorney to sell the entire shareholding upon instruction from the creditors if defined terms and conditions are fulfilled. A shareholder will only agree to the creditors' request to hand over its shareholding to a trustee in circumstances where it has lost any remaining equity value in the business or has no willingness or resources to avoid management or a creditor filing for insolvency. Such double-sided trust arrangements typically enable the sale of a distressed business by selling the shares together with the existing debt at a price of €1.00 for the equity with the purchase price for the debt being at a discount that reflects the value of the business. Creditors initiating a double-sided trust agreement try to achieve a purchase price for their debt position that is higher than the insolvency dividend a creditor might expect to realise after the end of a time-consuming and costly insolvency proceeding.

(b) *Acquisition of a distressed business in insolvency*

German insolvency proceedings serve the purpose of collective satisfaction of a debtor's creditors by liquidation of the debtor's assets and by distribution of the proceeds, or by reaching an arrangement in an insolvency plan, particularly in order to maintain the debtor's business (Section 1 of the Insolvency Code).

If the business still has a viable core, the insolvency administrator may sell the business as a whole, or significant parts of it, to an investor (known as a 'reorganisation by way of transfer'), or asset by asset.

The acquisition of an insolvent business is based on the idea of a separation of assets and liabilities. Taking into account the right of the insolvency administrator to decide whether to continue unfulfilled contracts, it is typical for a potential purchaser to try to negotiate with an insolvency administrator the new organisation of the business to be taken over by jointly determining the assets and contractual relationships that form the transferred business. In addition, the transaction can be negotiated and executed without any involvement of the previous shareholders.

So far as employees of the distressed business are concerned, Section 613a of the Civil Code applies. This means that, if a business or part of a business passes to another owner by a legal transaction, the latter succeeds to the rights and duties under the employment relationships existing at the time of transfer. If these rights and duties are governed by the legal provisions of a collective agreement or by a works agreement, they become part of the employment relationship between the new owner and the employee and may not be changed to the disadvantage of the employee before the end of one year after the date of transfer. In principle, this provision applies as well to an acquisition during insolvency. Unlike in normal acquisitions, however, the purchaser is not liable for all existing debts to employees, but only for those that arise after the opening of the insolvency proceedings. Nevertheless, in specific cases, a purchaser might be able, in cooperation with the insolvency administrator, to prevent a transfer of the entire undertaking and to take over merely some of the employees. A well-known but cost-intensive and challenging way to achieve this goal is the formation of a transfer company (*Beschäftigungs- und Qualifizierungsgesellschaft*) funded by the insolvency administrator, the purchaser and government aid. The employees then are asked to transfer on a voluntary basis to the transfer company, which will employ them for a certain period (usually a minimum of between 12 and 18 months, depending on the funding and the notice period under the employment contracts to provide an acceptable offer to employees). Under the deal that is then concluded with the purchaser, only certain employees are offered new employment contracts with the acquiring company. In addition, it can also be agreed with the insolvency administrator that he exercise special termination rights (a short notice period of three months); this, however, can only be exercised by an insolvency administrator based on a social selection process.

While a purchaser typically acquires the assets of the insolvent company by way of an asset deal, the liabilities remain with the insolvent company. In addition, various statutory provisions providing for a mandatory transfer of liabilities do not apply if a business is acquired from an insolvency administrator.

If a company or a business managed separately within the organisation of a company is transferred in its entirety, the purchaser is liable under Section 75 of the Tax Code for taxes or tax liabilities based on the business of the company, provided that the taxes or tax liabilities accrued since the beginning of the last calendar year preceding the sale are not assessed or declared until the expiry of one year after acquisition of the business by the purchaser. However, this does not apply to purchases of an insolvent company's assets. The same applies with respect to Section 25 of the Commercial Code. Under this provision, a party that continues a trading business after acquiring it under the same name, with or without including a provision indicating the succession of ownership, is liable for all liabilities of the previous owner arising in the operation of the business. Such liability does not arise if a company and its name are acquired during insolvency.

Usually, much of the stock in the case of manufacturing or processing businesses serves as security for creditors. If any security, such as pledges or transfers by way of security, gives the creditor the right to separate satisfaction, the insolvency administrator may pass ownership free of burdens to the purchaser irrespective of good faith. However, exceptions exist, the most important being that goods supplied under retention of title must be returned to the owner if the insolvency administrator does not compensate the holder of the right of retention.

Approval of the creditors' committee is necessary and is usually provided in the transaction documents as a condition precedent. The absence of such approval does not lead to the invalidity of an asset purchase agreement, but may lead to personal liability on the part of the insolvency administrator, which is why he might want to insist on such a condition.

In negotiations with an insolvency administrator, it must be borne in mind that the insolvency administrator will exclude statutory warranties as far as legally permissible and will also not give contractual representations or warranties in respect of the transferred business at all, or will limit them to title warranties only. In some cases, complex purchase price adjustment mechanisms are negotiated with the administrator, in particular in relation to the absence of or damage to certain assets, the existence of a certain amount of inventory, fixed or current assets or third-party rights to assets. The reason for this sort of deal structuring is in many cases the personal liability of the insolvency administrator with his limited knowledge about the distressed business. Irrespective of this approach, it has become increasingly common for an insolvency administrator to organise a sales process including a virtual data room and vendor reports.

Insolvency plan: Instead of an acquisition by way of an asset deal, the Insolvency Code allows the preservation of an insolvent business as a legal entity and an acquisition by way of a share deal on the basis of an insolvency plan.

Both the debtor and the administrator may submit an insolvency plan to the insolvency court. Such a plan may regulate satisfaction of creditors, the realisation and the distribution of the insolvency estate and the debtor's continuing responsibility for some liabilities, or discharge of them following completion of the insolvency proceedings. The particular purpose of an insolvency plan is to preserve and reorganise the debtor's enterprise. Unlike reorganisation by way of sale (see above), the rules regarding the insolvency plan are designed to keep the business and the entity together. This may be preferable if, for instance, an asset sale would trigger the extinction of valuable tax loss carry-forward, the loss of a (contractual or governmental) licence or supplier, customers or other contractual partners who might not be willing to consent to an assumption of the relevant contracts by the purchaser, in particular without renegotiating their terms and conditions.

Following recent amendments to the Insolvency Code an insolvency plan may include all measures allowed under corporate law, meaning that the creditors and shareholders may be asked to vote on a recapitalisation of the company as part of the insolvency plan. Even if the shareholders do not consent to the recapitalisation provided for in the insolvency plan, their consent may be deemed to be granted in most cases, thus effectively allowing for a shareholders' 'cram down'. These amendments, introduced in 2012, substantially reduce any holdout power on the part of shareholders, which had hindered the recapitalisation of distressed companies in the past.

An insolvency plan may also provide for a debt-for-equity swap. In addition to the shareholders' cram down, the swapping creditors will be protected from liability that otherwise could arise under corporate law. Outside insolvency proceedings such liability could arise if claims contributed to the corporation in return for new shares turn out to have less than the nominal value of the new shares. The recently amended Insolvency Code overrides this corporate law rule in order to facilitate debt-for-equity swaps.

The code also makes contractual change-of-control clauses triggered by changes in the shareholder structure ineffective in the event of a debt-for-equity swap under the plan. This ensures that important supply, licence and distribution agreements to which the debtor is party may not be terminated unilaterally by the other party.

In the absence of provisions to the contrary in the insolvency plan, the debtor is released from its remaining liabilities if it satisfies creditors in accordance with the insolvency plan.

Confirmation of the insolvency plan by the court may be dependent on certain conditions. For example, a condition may be that a capital increase be implemented prior to confirmation and that the shares in the debtor be transferred to an investor. However, the shareholders of the debtor cannot be forced to transfer their shares to a third party.

Italy

Raimondo Premonte
Donato Romano
Gianni Origoni Grippo Cappelli & Partners

1. Historical trend of the Italian market

The Italian private equity market has experienced a steady growth in the past 20 years, triggered by certain legal reforms enacted starting from the late 1980s.

Following the reforms, the banking system began to participate in the private equity business: at first with specialised companies and subsequently through internal divisions of larger banks.

From the mid-1990s, an increasing number of international closed-end fund managers, along with the first Italian closed-end funds, began to invest in Italy.

In the early 2000s, the Italian private equity market began to align itself with more sophisticated foreign markets. Consequently Italy began to occupy a more prominent position in the global private equity market. By way of example, between 2002 and 2006, Italian private equity experienced a 35% increase in the number of investors, which resulted in solid growth lasting until 2006, when the value of investments reached approximately €3.4 billion.

The Italian private equity market was not spared by the recent economic crisis; however, today, data analysis reveals a recovery in private equity. According to the data released by the Italian Private Equity and Venture Capital Association, in the last year (2013) fundraising activity was above €4 billion, the value of investment activity was higher than €3.4 billion and the value of divestment transactions was higher than €1.9 billion. More importantly, as this data might suggest, the Italian private equity market has historically been more profitable than other European markets. As a matter of fact, returns relating to Italian private equity transactions, calculated on the basis of the net pooled internal rate of return, are historically 2% higher than the European average.

2. Regulatory framework

There are five main categories of professional investors in the Italian private equity market:

- investment banks and commercial banks;
- international closed-end funds;
- regional closed-end funds (local funds);
- industrial financial companies; and, finally
- funds set up and owned, directly or indirectly, by the Italian government (the most important of these funds is the F2i, whose main shareholder is, through Cassa Depositi e Prestiti, the Ministry of Economy and Finance).

The typical legal structure for the private equity industry in Italy is the closed-end fund, which means that the redemption of the units may only occur on specific redemption dates. Closed-end investment funds best adapt to the processes of selection, management, monitoring, and divestment of investments in private equity.

This is mainly due to the following three features. First, there is an inherent separation between the fund and its management. This allows for a swift and autonomous choice of investments by the management team. Secondly, the fund has an expiry date. This is important as the investors in the fund units can therefore achieve the results of their investments within an established period of time. Finally, as anticipated, due to the fact that the fund is closed-end fund investors can only exit at predefined and specified dates. This results in a stable level of capital.

The applicable regulatory framework is mainly constituted by (i) Legislative Decree 58 of February 24 1998 as amended (the Italian Consolidated Financial Act); (ii) Ministerial Decree 228 of May 24 1999 as amended; and (iii) the Bank of Italy Resolution on collective portfolio management adopted on May 8 2012.

The regime is expected to be significantly amended as a result of the implementation in Italy of the Alternative Investment Fund Managers Directive. See Section 6 for additional information.

2.1 The structure of closed-end funds

The structure of closed-end funds in Italy typically includes a management company (*società di gestione del risparmio* or SGR), a custodian bank and the investors. SGRs are financial intermediaries, regulated by Bank of Italy and the Italian Securities Regulator (Consob, the Italian government authority responsible for regulating the Italian securities market) and authorised to provide services of collective portfolio management. The collective portfolio management service includes the following activities:

- promotion, establishment and organisation of funds and administration of relationships with the investors;
- management of assets of collective investment undertakings through investments in financial instruments, receivables, securities and other assets; and
- marketing of funds' units.

More precisely, SGRs can manage both funds that they have set up themselves or those set up by others, and market their own funds.

SGRs are allowed to delegate the performance and management of one or more of the investment phases provided that they retain full responsibility for the delegated functions. The delegation is usually employed if the SGR does not possess the internal capability and the resources to perform these activities.

With reference to the corporate requirements, an SGR requires a minimum share capital of €1 million and must be incorporated as a joint stock company (*società per azioni*).

The custodian bank plays an important role in a fund's structure. In light of the significance of such a role, custodian banks must satisfy particular requirements (including a minimum regulatory capital) as set forth by the Resolution.

In particular, the custodian bank is, among other things, required:
- to keep custody of the fund's investments;
- to verify the legitimacy of the operations;
- to verify and/or perform the calculation of the net asset value of the relevant fund(s); and
- to execute the instructions given by the SGRs provided that they do not breach any applicable laws, regulations or directions by the competent authorities.

Finally, the custodian bank is liable to relevant investors and the SGR for any losses suffered as a consequence of its failure to perform.

(a) *The investors*

The investors in the funds' units supply the capital and provide the financial resources.

The relevant Italian regulatory framework is not strictly structured around the distinction between retail and qualified investors. On the contrary, the rules primarily distinguish between different types of funds (eg, EU-harmonised, EU non-harmonised, hedge funds, etc.). These rules, in turn, regulate what types of investors are eligible to invest in each fund.

The rules surrounding reserved funds (ie, reserved to qualified investors) tend to be less strict than those applicable to retail funds. This is due to the fact that professional investors have a detailed knowledge of the market and therefore have less need for protection.

According to the applicable provisions of the Italian Consolidated Financial Act, any changes to be made regarding the appointed SGR or changes to the investment policy, are required to be approved by investors. For a resolution to be adopted, the Italian Consolidated Financial Act requires the favourable vote by investors representing more than 50% of the units represented in the meeting and at least 30% of the value of units outstanding and in circulation.

(b) *The shareholdings and assets*

All instruments, cash and other assets related to private equity closed-end funds constitute an independent pool of assets segregated from the assets of, or managed by, the SGR and from those of the investors. As such, these assets are protected from legal actions brought by creditors of the SGR or the custodian bank. The SGR cannot use assets pertaining to the private equity closed-end fund in its own interest or in the interest of other third parties.

3. **Legal framework relating to leverage buyout transactions**

Private equity deals may be structured in the form of leveraged buyout transactions. From an economic perspective, such transactions involve the purchase of a target company through debt finance as well as equity. Once the deal is completed, the indebtedness accrued by the buyer for the purpose of the acquisition is then transferred to the target (or the new entity resulting from the merger, in case of a merger leveraged buyout). The relevant indebtedness will then be repaid using the funds of the target company, typically by using the target's cashflow or selling certain of the target's assets.

In such respect, Italian law used to provide some obstacles for the carrying out of these leveraged buyout and merger leveraged buyout transactions, in the form of restrictions in relation to financial assistance. Such transactions were therefore challenged on the basis of being in breach of the financial assistance restrictions, set out in Section 2358 of the Italian Civil Code.

However, the legal framework has changed in recent years, in part thanks to the increased number of private equity deals in Italy. In 2003 a new Section 2501-*bis* was introduced in the Italian Civil Code, in relation to merger leveraged buyouts. Such buyouts were expressly recognised and accepted under Italian law, thus marking an end to all debate as to whether they were in violation of the rules prohibiting financial assistance.

More specifically, merger leveraged buyout transactions have been officially recognised in Italy by having more stringent information requirements imposed in relation to them as compared to the information required in relation to ordinary mergers. In particular:

- the relevant merger plan must set out the financial resources available to repay the company's financial indebtedness following the merger;
- a report by the boards of directors of each of the companies involved in the merger must set out the reasons that justify the merger from an economic and legal standpoint, and contain an economic and financial plan demonstrating the source of the financial resources and the aims of the companies following the merger;
- a report by the independent auditor of one of the companies involved in the merger must certify that the accounting figures contained in the merger plan are reasonable and correct; and
- a report by the company's independent auditor must attest that the relevant boards of directors' sustainability analysis is reasonable.

More recently, Legislative Decree 142 of August 4 2008 implemented EU Directive 2006/68/CE and amended Section 2358 of the Italian Civil Code (relating to financial assistance provided by a company to third parties for the acquisition or subscription of such company's shares). Consequently, Italian law now enables a joint stock company (*società per azioni*) to provide loans or guarantees to third parties for the acquisition or subscription of that company's shares, provided that certain conditions are satisfied and a procedure (the so-called 'whitewash procedure') is followed (ie, the transaction has to be approved by the shareholders by the special majority required in relation to extraordinary shareholders' meetings). However, companies continue to be prohibited from accepting their own shares as a form of security. The new Section 2358 of the Italian Civil Code does not affect the provisions in the Italian Civil Code in relation to merger leveraged buyouts.

This new framework could provide greater flexibility to leveraged buyout transactions, thus boosting the number of private equity transactions in Italy.

4. Legal aspects relating to the structure of transactions and negotiation of legal documents relating to private equity deals

4.1 Structure of the acquisition

Private equity transactions in Italy are carried out either through the purchase of shares or quotas of companies or by purchasing assets or businesses.

The choice between asset or business deals as opposed to share deals depends on the specific transactions. Share deals are generally more common for larger transactions. Asset or business deals provide the following advantages for the parties:
- in general terms, the parties may choose which assets and liabilities will be included in the business to be transferred, provided, however, that the assets and liabilities to be transferred maintain an autonomous capacity for the carrying out of business activity;
- the sale of the assets or business can be completed within a short time frame, since, generally, the only corporate action to be taken is a resolution of the board of directors of the relevant companies. However, where the transfer involves the transfer of the entire business of one company, a resolution of the shareholders' meeting will be required.

Moreover, under Section 2112 of the Italian Civil Code, where a business is transferred, the employment relationships of all people employed in that business will be transferred to the purchaser; the employees will maintain all the rights granted to them in relation to their former employment relationships. Finally, in the case of a transfer of a business, the parties have the obligation to inform the relevant trade unions, by written notice to be delivered to the unions at least 25 days before completion of the transfer.

In a business acquisition, the buyer will be jointly liable with the seller to third parties for liabilities recorded in the target's book records, even if liabilities have not been specifically transferred by the seller to the buyer. However, parties may agree that liabilities arising from the conduct of the business before completion are either to be paid by the buyer or by the seller. It should be noted that such limitations will not be effective as regards third parties.

With reference to private equity transactions involving an acquisition of assets instead of shares, it is worth mentioning that the Italian tax authorities have recently challenged commonly used structures (that provided certain tax benefits) involving the contribution of a going concern into a newco and the subsequent sale of newco shares.

Share sales bring the transfer to the buyer group of all the contractual relationships and receivables of the target, and the law does not grant the counterparties to such contractual relationships any withdrawal right. There is therefore no risk that contractual relationships and receivables are not transferred to the buyer group. A sale of shares is the approach generally preferred by the seller (assuming it is a corporate entity), since it allows, if all the requirements for the application of the participation exemption regime are met, an exemption in respect of 95% of the capital gains. Capital gains arising from the sale of assets (business concern) are subject to 27.5% corporate tax (an election can be made to pay the tax in five instalments over five tax periods). However, starting from March 1 2013, all share transfers relating to Italian joint stock companies are subject to a tax (the so called 'Tobin tax') for an amount equal to 0.1% of the overall value of the transfer, if this transfer takes place on a regulated market, or 0.2% in relation to transfers that are not carried out on regulated markets.

4.2 Shareholders' agreements

Shareholders' agreements are widely used in private equity transactions, both where the private equity investors acquire a minority participation in the corporate capital of the target and where they acquire a majority participation, in order to regulate the strategy, conduct and governance of the target. The private equity investors are also interested in setting out rights in relation to the possible exit strategy from the target company. It is therefore very common in private equity deals to enter into shareholders' agreements with exit solutions, such as an initial public offer, a sale process, or drag-along clauses, tag-along clauses, put-and-call options and pre-emption rights.

Under tag-along clauses where one or more of the shareholders (generally the majority shareholders) intend to transfer their shares to a third-party purchaser, the other shareholders (typically minority shareholders) will be entitled to transfer their own shares to the same purchaser, at the same price, pro quota, offered in relation to the transferring shareholders' stake. It is usually provided that, where the third-party purchaser does not intend to purchase the shares of the other shareholders, either (i) the transferring shareholders will have to reduce the number of shares they intend to transfer, so that the other shareholders would be able to transfer their own shares to the same purchaser, or (ii) the transferring shareholders will be required to purchase themselves the shares from the other shareholders.

Drag-along clauses grant one or more shareholders, typically majority ones, the right to negotiate with a potential third-party purchaser the transfer of their shares along with the shares of the other shareholders, who will be obliged to transfer their shares to the third-party purchaser, at the same price per share agreed in relation to the transferring shareholders' shares.

These clauses aim to help private equity investors achieve better results in negotiating the exit from their investments and to enable the third-party purchaser to avoid possible issues connected with the presence in the company of minority shareholders.

It should be noted that the validity under Italian law of these type of clauses has been questioned by certain scholars. However, recent case law has held that these types of clauses are valid provided that the purchase price for shares that are to be transferred following the exercise of the tag-along or drag-along rights is equal to their fair value. According to case law, fair value of the shares corresponds to the value that would be determined for these shares in the case of withdrawal from the company by the same shareholders (ie, the value *pro quota* of the net assets of the company, taking into account its forecasted earnings as well as the possible market value of such shares, or the average closing prices of the shares during the previous six months, if they are traded on a regulated market).

Finally, in private equity transactions, it is customary to provide in the relevant shareholders' agreements put-and-call option clauses, whereby one of the parties will have the right, but not the obligation, to sell (put option) or to buy (call option) a specified portion of shares to or from the other shareholders, at a specified price, within a specified period of time. It should be noted that according to some cases and several scholars, options that provide a fixed price for the exercise of such options might be void under Italian law, as they may be in breach of the general principle prohibiting 'leonine' partnerships. In this respect, under Italian law, 'leonine' partnerships are defined in Section 2265 of the Italian Civil Code as agreements providing for the exclusion of one or more shareholders from participation in the profits and/or the losses of their companies. Therefore, if options clauses are structured in a manner that provides a total exclusion for one or more shareholders from the risk of losses or the right to receive profits, they would be deemed void under Italian law (see the decision of the Court of Milan dated December 30 2011).

There are certain other rules that have to be taken into account before entering into a shareholders' agreement under Italian law. According to Italian law:
- shareholders' agreements concerning non-listed companies cannot have a term longer than five years (three years in relation to listed companies);
- if the parties have agreed on a longer term, the agreements are deemed to have a term of five years (three years in relation to listed companies) in any case;
- the agreements may be renewed upon expiry;
- if the agreements do not provide for any term, any party is entitled to withdraw from the agreements, with prior notice of at least six months.

However, these provisions do not apply to agreements that are entered into for the purpose of joint ventures concerning the production or exchange of goods or services and relating to companies that are wholly owned by the parties to the agreement (Section 2341-*bis* of the Italian Civil Code). It should also be noted that shareholders' agreements under Italian law are binding only on the parties thereto; in the case of breach of one of the provisions of the agreements by one of the parties, the other parties can seek to terminate the agreement and claim damages.

With specific reference to listed companies, under Section 122 of the Italian Consolidated Financial Act, shareholders' agreements are to be:
- notified to Consob;
- published in the daily press (in a summarised form);
- filed with the Register of Companies; and
- communicated to the listed companies within five days from the date when they are entered into.

In the event of non-compliance with the above rules, the shareholders' agreements will be void and the relevant shareholders will not be entitled to exercise their voting rights. In the case of a takeover bid, the parties to a shareholders' agreement that intend to accept the offer will be entitled to withdraw from the agreement, without giving any prior notice.

In light of these limitations, it is quite common to introduce the provisions described above concerning exit solutions and corporate governance rights in the target's bylaws. In this way, the parties would not be subject to the above limitations; moreover, the provisions of the shareholders' agreement, as replicated in the bylaws, would be binding on any possible future shareholders of the target company, whether or not they become a party to the shareholders' agreement.

4.3 Share purchase agreements

(a) Conditions precedent

Usually, the completion of an acquisition is subject to the satisfaction (or non-occurrence, depending on the case) of one or more conditions precedent. One of the most common conditions precedent provided in Italian sale and purchase agreements concerns the approval of the transaction by either the Italian Antitrust Authority or the European Commission. Other typical conditions precedent concern approval by the Bank of Italy, whenever the target company is a bank, an SGR, or an intermediary company *(società di intermediazione mobiliare* or *società di investimento a capitale variabile)*, or by the Italian Insurance Authority (IVASS) when the target operates in the insurance sector. Moreover, specific conditions precedent will be required in agreements involving target companies that have governmental authorisations or licences. In such cases, the acquisition would be conditional on approval by the government or competent governmental entity that granted such authorisations or licences. If that target company is a party to key agreements that have 'no change of control' clauses, the relevant acquisition might be conditional on the approval of the transaction by the contractual counterparty to these significant agreements. Finally, the closing of certain private equity deals may be conditional on obtaining the necessary financing for the relevant transaction; however, this type of condition precedent is not widely used in Italian private equity deals.

(b) Representations and warranties

Representations and warranties are key aspects of share purchase agreements relating to private equity transactions.

It is important to point out the main differences between the Italian experience in the drafting and negotiation of these clauses as compared to that in other jurisdictions. Certain representations and warranties that are widely used in international agreements are also used in Italian share purchase agreements, such as representations concerning compliance with law, financial statements and the like. However, in Italian agreements, sellers typically give only 'true and fair view' representations on accounts and not a 'no undisclosed liabilities' catch-all clause, as it is considered too broad and risky. Moreover, any representation relating to no materially misleading or omitted information is rarely accepted by the sellers and, if accepted, it is qualified (ie, by stating that no misleading information has been disclosed nor information omitted which, if known, would have made a diligent potential buyer decide not to buy). Sellers aim at associating this with a general disclosure of due diligence material and vendor due diligence reports. It should also be noted that the goals of this clause are also usually addressed by the general principles of Italian law according to which the parties to a contract are bound to act in good faith during its negotiation and execution.

In recent years it has become more common to include specific disclosures as exceptions to specific warranties. Sometimes disclosure of the data room is accepted but, in such cases, the downside for the buyer can be tempered by:
- including the data room index, by way of an annex to the share purchase agreement; or
- obtaining a representation from the seller that
  - the information provided in the data room is complete, true and accurate; and/or
  - the seller has not withheld information where that information has or would reasonably be expected to have a (material) adverse effect on the target; or
- specifying that knowledge derives from the 'face value' of the documentation and not from implied information or other information that would be available only with additional investigation.

Certain case law relating to breaches of representations and warranties stated that Section 1495 of the Italian Civil Code, according to which buyers would forfeit their indemnity right after a one-year term following the completion of the purchase, prevailed notwithstanding a different term provided in the relevant share purchase agreement. However, a recent decision of the Court of Milan, dated August 26 2011, overturned the precedent case law and stated that the debarment set out in Section 1495 of the Italian Civil Code does not apply to indemnity clauses in agreements negotiated between the parties, provided that these agreements specifically set out the manner for exercise of the rights deriving from the breach of representations and warranties as well as the term for the indemnity procedure.

Italian share purchase agreements usually provide a cap on liabilities deriving from breach of representations and warranties in the region of between 10% and 35% of the purchase price. However, it is important to mention that, under Italian law, any agreement concerning a cap on liability is void in the case of liability deriving from wilful conduct or gross negligence. Certain representations and warranties as to legality (ie, as to authorisation, status, organisation, title to shares, capitalisation) and as to breach of environmental and tax requirements are generally provided without a cap or with a higher cap than the general ones. Provisions requiring that a certain threshold be exceeded for liability to be incurred are market standard in Italian transactions.

Finally, while Italian law provides an obligation on the parties to mitigate damages, this principle is usually also provided in contractual provisions. Italian law provides that damages for breach of representations and warranties cover direct damages and loss of profits to the extent they are a direct consequence of the breach.

(c) **Price and price adjustment**

The definition of the price is clearly one of the most delicate matters to be dealt with in negotiating share purchase agreements in the context of private equity transactions. In the Italian experience, the purchase price and adjustment mechanism usually take into account net asset value and earnings before interest, taxation, depreciation and amortisation and/or working capital and/or net financial indebtedness of the target at completion. Depending on the business, inventory-based adjustment may also apply. The parties usually agree in advance the definition of the accounting principles to be used in the determination of the balance sheet at completion (or after completion in case of a price adjustment mechanism). It is therefore essential to ensure that the preparation of the closing balance sheet follows the same standards as the preparation of the balance sheet that produced the working capital target amount. The closing balance sheet is generally prepared by the buyer/buyer's auditors and verified by the seller. It is quite common to have a cap on the adjustment.

It is worth noting that the 'locked box' system, common in transactions in the United Kingdom, is becoming slightly more common in Italian merger and acquisition transactions and especially in private equity deals.

(d) **Other common covenants**

Other standard covenants provided in Italian share purchase agreements include:
- non-compete;
- restricted actions; and
- notification of breaches.

In particular, under Italian law, for non-compete covenants to be enforceable they should be limited in time and to a certain territory and/or a specific activity. In any event, they cannot last more than:
- five years with respect to the seller of the business as a going concern;
- five years with respect to executives; and
- three years with respect to employees.

In transactions to be authorised by the Italian Antitrust Authority, non-competition clauses are justified for periods of up to three years when the transfer of the undertaking includes the transfer of customer loyalty in the form of both goodwill and know-how; when only goodwill is included, they are justified for periods of up to two years.

However, it should be pointed out that the above rules are only Italian rules, without prejudice to the EU rules and regulations governing non-compete covenants as well as other covenants restricting competition, with reference to both horizontal agreements and vertical agreements (defined under the Commission Regulation (EU) 330/2010 as agreements or concerted practices entered into between two or more undertakings each of which operates, for the purposes of the agreements or the concerted practices, at a different level of the production or distribution chain, and relating to the conditions under which the parties may purchase, sell or resell certain goods or services). In such respect, by way of example, at European level, Commission Regulation (EU) 330/2010 provides that the term for non-compete obligations contained in vertical agreements cannot exceed five years.

It is also common to provide a list of restricted actions: actions that cannot be carried out by the seller between signing and completion without the consent of the buyer. Sellers usually accept the obligation to notify any breaches of representations that occurred during the period between signing and completion. It is not common for the buyer to obtain the right to terminate the share purchase agreement in the event of a breach, save in the case of the occurrence of an event causing material adverse change. Notifications made by the seller do not normally provide relief from indemnification obligations in favour of the buyer.

(e) *Remedies*

It is uncommon for parties in a private equity deal concerning Italian entities to choose a foreign law as the governing law of the relevant agreements relating to the deal. In the vast majority of cases, private equity deals concerning Italian targets are governed by Italian law. Moreover, Italian law is generally chosen in share deals relating to a non-Italian target if the buyer and the seller are both Italian entities.

As to the jurisdiction, the duration of judicial proceedings in Italy is very long and therefore arbitration is usually preferred to ordinary jurisdiction of local courts, notwithstanding the higher costs implied. In addition to timing reasons, arbitration is also preferred for the specific expertise of the panel as opposed to the general – and not specialised – knowledge of ordinary judges.

5. Taxation

A new tax regime for investment funds (other than real estate funds) was enacted in Italy with effect from July 1 2011, aiming at (i) aligning the tax treatment of Italian investment funds with that of foreign 'harmonised' funds and (ii) removing tax discrimination between investments in Italian funds and investments in certain types of foreign funds.

Under the new regime, Italian investment funds are no longer subject to 12.5% tax on the management results and the taxation has been shifted to the investors' level, where they are generally taxed on a cash basis (ie, on proceeds' distributions by the fund).

The new tax regime applies to both open-ended and closed-end investment funds, including certain open-ended funds based in Luxembourg, proportionally to their units placed in Italy (so-called 'Luxembourg historical funds').

Italian corporate income taxes do not apply to Italian investment funds – though they have been included, together with Luxembourg historical funds placed in Italy, in the list of entities liable to corporate income tax. Italian investment funds are not subject to regional tax on productive activities either.

Furthermore, ordinary Italian withholding taxes do not apply to the main categories of income realised by Italian investment funds. In particular, Italian withholding taxes do not apply to the following categories of income:

- dividends and capital gains from shareholdings;

- interest and similar proceeds from government bonds and bonds issued by banks and listed companies;
- interest and similar proceeds from current bank accounts (provided that the amount deposited is not higher than 5% of the average value of the investments of the fund);
- income from repo and stock landing transactions; and
- income from participations in other Italian investment funds (including real estate funds) and from foreign investment funds.

It should be noted that under Italian law when withholding taxes are payable, they are applied either as advance payment (thus giving rise to a tax credit towards the Italian Tax Authority) or as a final payment (thus not creating any tax credit in favour of the taxed entity towards the Italian Tax Authority). When applicable, withholding taxes are levied on the funds as a final payment and therefore no tax credit is granted to the relevant funds.

5.1 Italian taxation levied at the level of the investors in real estate investment funds

As explained, with effect from July 1 2011, taxation no longer applies at the fund's level, being instead levied directly on the investors.

In particular, according to the new rules a 20% withholding tax will apply to:
- periodic distributions received by investors (the taxable base consisting in the proceeds actually distributed);
- the redemption, liquidation or sale of units – in this case the taxable base is equal to the difference between the value of the redemption, liquidation or sale of the units and the weighted average cost of subscription or acquisition of the units (these items to be determined on the basis of the net asset value provided by the management company).

The withholding tax is applied as final payment or an advance payment depending on the category of investor and, in particular:
- as a final payment in the case of individuals who are Italian tax residents not holding the fund units in connection with a business activity;
- as an advance payment, in the case of:
  - Italian tax resident individuals who hold the fund units in connection with a business activity;
  - commercial entities (eg, limited liability companies, joint stock companies); and
  - a permanent establishment in Italy of non-resident entities, if the units are attributable to that permanent establishment.

In these cases, the relevant proceeds are included in the taxable basis for personal and income tax purposes (personal income tax is levied at progressive rates up to 43% plus local surcharges, while corporate income tax is generally levied at a rate of 27.5%), depending on the type of investor. Moreover, certain types of investors (eg, banks and insurance companies) may also be subject to regional tax on productive activities, at rates that vary in each region (eg, 4.25% is the standard rate for banks and insurance companies).

The withholding tax is also charged as a final payment in the case of non-resident investors with no Italian permanent establishment to which the units are attributable.

However, a withholding tax exemption is granted to certain non-resident investors (so-called 'qualified investors'):

- investors resident in countries that allow an adequate exchange of information with the Italian tax authorities (so-called 'white-list' countries), as currently listed under Ministerial Decree of September 4 1996;
- institutional investors established in white-list countries, even if not subject to taxation there; and
- international bodies and organisations established in accordance with international agreements ratified by Italy, as well as central banks or other organisations managing the official reserves of the state.

In addition, the 20% withholding tax is not levied with respect to proceeds from the funds realised by Italian real estate funds, certain pension schemes, Italian investment funds and Luxembourg historical funds placed in Italy.

From a procedural perspective, the withholding tax has to be applied:

- by the management company (for Luxembourg historical funds placed in Italy, the withholding tax has to be applied by the Italian intermediaries in charge of the placement);
- in the case of units traded on regulated markets, by the Italian intermediaries in charge of the trading of the fund units; and
- in the case of fund units held in a centralised depositary system, by the Italian intermediaries with which the units are deposited, adhering (directly or indirectly) to a centralised depositary system managed by authorised companies, or by non-resident intermediaries adhering to the same system or to foreign centralised depositary systems that participate in the above system.

The reform mentioned above substantially aligned, in the hands of Italian investors, the tax treatment of investments in foreign funds with that of investments in Italian funds. In particular, proceeds arising from foreign investment funds investing in transferable securities are subject to the same tax regime outlined above in respect of proceeds arising from Italian investment funds (ie, ordinarily, the application of the 20% withholding tax), provided that such foreign funds qualify:

- either as 'harmonised' funds (ie, compliant with the Undertakings for Collective Investment in Transferable Securities Directive) and are established in an EU or EEA white-list country; or
- as non-harmonised funds (ie, not compliant with the Undertakings for Collective Investment in Transferable Securities Directive) established in an EU or EEA white-list country and subject in that country to regulatory supervision.

Proceeds arising from foreign investment funds investing in transferable securities other than those listed above will not be subject to the ordinary 20% withholding tax.

The reform also addresses, although only partially, the applicability of tax treaty benefits to funds. In particular, it expressly states that foreign investments falling within either of the above bullet points may benefit from relevant double taxation conventions in respect of Italian-source income, but (i) only for that part of the income proportionally referable to fund units held by persons resident in the other tax treaty country, and (ii) provided that the country of residence of the foreign fund grants, on a reciprocal basis, similar treaty benefits to Italian investment funds.

5.2 Taxation of the management company

Finally, it should be noted that Italian management companies are subject to corporate income tax according to ordinary rules. The management fees charged by the SGR to the fund are VAT-exempt.

It is necessary to point out that Italian tax law does not provide any special tax treatment in relation to the shares held by executives running companies backed by private equity funds or in relation to any carried interest. In this respect, capital gains and dividends are subject to a 26% tax as from July 1 2014 (previously it was 20%). However, the individual profits deriving from dividends or capital gains are not subject to social security contributions.

Finally, private equity investors are also usually managers or employees of the companies backed by the private equity fund. The remuneration received by these executives in their capacity as employees or directors of the relevant companies is subject to an income tax of up to 43% plus local surcharges.

6. The potential impact of the Alternative Investment Fund Managers Directive on the private equity industry in Europe and Italy

The implementation in Italy of the Alternative Investment Fund Managers Directive is likely to entail significant changes to the legal framework for alternative investment funds (including private equity funds).

On March 25 2014, by means of Legislative Decree 44 of March 4 2014, the Alternative Investment Fund Managers Directive was implemented in Italy, with effect from April 9 2014.

However, it is not yet possible to provide a thorough assessment of the impact of the directive on the Italian alternative investment funds industry.

Nevertheless, according to the position of certain market operators, the directive is expected to provide a boost to the marketing of alternative investment funds in Italy. This will be mainly due to the introduction of new marketing rules, including the introduction of a 'European marketing and management passport' for EU and non-EU alternative fund managers.

However, European associations representing the private equity industry have expressed their concern regarding the costs and complexities that will result from the full transposition of the European legislation at a domestic level. In particular, several requirements will have to be implemented in the day-to-day running of operations (eg, risk management tools, mandatory depository requirements, etc.).

In conclusion, the full effects are yet to be seen, but the directive may have a significant effect on the growth of the Italian private equity industry.

Spain

Fernando de las Cuevas
Pío García-Escudero
Gomez-Acebo & Pombo

Venture capital in Spain was at first a little-known form of corporate finance, used mainly by public investors to help deprived areas. In the 1970s, small public entities invested in companies in their initial phase of development with the purpose of developing underprivileged regions. Between 1987 and 1991 there was a growth period for what is now known as private equity caused in part by the entry of Spain into the European Union, which attracted international operators.

The second phase of expansion began in 1997. The approval in 1999 of the first law that regulated private equity funds and their management companies was a determining factor in the growth of the sector, and there was a significant quantitative leap forward in 2000, when investment passed the €1 billion mark for the first time. In the following years, the Spanish private equity market underwent a profound transformation and became a realistic investment option for small and medium-sized entities.

But after some years of registering record growth, the sector was severely affected by the financial crisis, with the immediate result of much reduced access to debt. Although the total value of investment by private equity fund managers is still higher than 10 years ago, there has been a sharp decrease in the number of investments, which reached their lowest point in 2009 without a clear recovery afterwards.

1. Market overview

1.1 Type of investors

The main investors in private equity in Spain, in order of the size of investment, are financial institutions, private investors, funds of funds, pension funds and public investors. Investments made by financial institutions during the last few years have represented a major part of the total investment made in private equity funds in Spain. Recently, the concentration of the banking sector has led to risk concentration issues that have resulted in secondary sales.

1.2 Types of investments

Leveraged buyouts, which were frequent in Spain for years, have been affected by the current economic climate which is characterised by difficulties in obtaining outside sources of finance, and by the tight credit policy. In spite of this, as the financial markets continue to recover commentators expect to see an increase in the number of these types of transactions, albeit using less leverage than at the onset of the economic crisis.

The Spanish market has, though, seen a growing number of investments in companies in the expansion phase of their development, given the excellent investment opportunities the market is offering (especially in sectors where there has been a significant lowering of prices) and due to the potential return offered by certain companies affected by the economic crisis. The tight credit policy has also encouraged other business development transactions, for example in companies starting up and in the initial phase of development. The restrictions of Spanish insolvency law, however, have not facilitated the carrying out of turnaround transactions.

From a sectorial point of view, investments in industrial products and services, financial services, computer-related services, other services (such as business process outsourcing, customer relationship management, environmental and energy-efficiency services, and building and facility maintenance), and the healthcare and consumer-related products sectors have been the most common during the last few years.

2. Funds

2.1 Fund structures

The legal structures used in Spain as a vehicle for private equity investments are venture capital companies and private equity funds, regulated by Law 25/2005, of November 24 2005, Regulating Private Equity Entitles and Their Management Companies (the 'PEEL'). The PEEL differentiates for the first time between common regime and simplified regime private equity entities (that is those in which a strictly private offer is made, with a minimum investment commitment of €500,000 required from each investor and with 20 or fewer shareholders or participants), the latter benefiting from faster processing of the authorisation required to operate in the market and the advantage of not having to produce a prospectus.

Venture capital companies must be a public limited company (*sociedad anónima* or 'SA'). Their way of operating does not differ greatly from any other type of trading company, but they must have the particular characteristics stipulated in the PEEL (as regards minimum capital, corporate purpose, etc).

In contrast to venture capital companies, private equity funds are non-legal entities, involve a large number of investors and are based on Anglo-Saxon limited partnership structures. The management and representation of private equity funds corresponds to management companies whose operating rules and codes of conduct are also set out in the PEEL and who play a role similar to that of general partners in limited partnerships.

Before being allowed to start operations, venture capital companies must obtain authorisation for their incorporation from the Spanish Securities and Exchange Commission (the 'CNMV'), have the incorporation of the company recorded in a public deed that has to be registered at the Commercial Registry (these are optional requirements in the case of private equity funds), and be registered in the relevant CNMV register.

Both venture capital companies and private equity funds benefit from advantageous tax regimes, as explained in paragraph 7.1. below.

2.2. Regulation of fund raising and fund managers

The regulation of capital contributions in venture capital companies and private equity funds is set out in the PEEL. The law includes requirements for a minimum capital that must be invested in venture capital companies (€1,200,000) and in private equity funds (€1,650,000), the minimum amount which must be paid up initially (50% in venture capital companies, while in private equity funds the minimum initial equity must be fully paid up) and the nature of the contributions (which cannot consist of fixed assets in the case of private equity funds).

The codes of conduct and operating rules of private equity management companies are also contained in the PEEL and require, in the first place, prior authorisation from the CNMV. The law stipulates a minimum initial share capital for management companies of €300,000, which must be fully paid up. Management companies are also required to be properly organised and have sufficient resources to perform their corporate purpose, meaning that they must have adequate administrative, accounting, human and technical resources for their business and turnover. Management companies must also prepare binding internal rules of conduct to govern the actions of their administrative bodies, managers and employees.

Management companies are obliged to provide the CNMV with any and all information required of them, and must provide information relating to the history of the funds they manage and the level of compliance with the various legal requirements (including the ratios of asset investments, liquidity, positions in the management company's group, list of purchase and sale transactions, etc).

2.3. Customary or common terms of funds

Management regulations, which stipulate how the funds operate, contain the routine requirements included in limited partnership agreements: duration of the fund, conditions for subscription and redemption of the shares, regularity with which valuations of the shares have to be made, rules for administering, managing and representing the fund, the way in which profit and loss is determined and allocated, rules for the winding up and liquidation of the fund, the form in which the management company is remunerated (basically, by means of a placement, management, investment or success fee), investment policy, disinvestment formulas, types of financing granted to subsidiaries and formulas that allow the management companies to participate in investee companies and in their administration bodies.

In general, the way in which these matters are dealt with is similar to those of other European countries. The management rules usually establish a limited duration for the fund (normally between seven and 10 years), a placement fee (around 2.5% of the value of each subscribed share), a management fee (approximately an annual 2.5% of the subscribed equity) or a success fee (which is usually established at 20% of the profit obtained by the fund), as well as minimum guaranteed return for the participants, which generally fluctuates between 6% and 8% of the participants' contributions. It is usual for an investment committee and a supervisory board to be established, made up of representatives from among the participants in the private equity fund and independent professionals, if applicable.

3. Debt finance

3.1 Restrictions on granting security

The financial assistance regime in Spain is more restrictive than in other European countries. Without exception, no company may advance funds, grant loans, give guarantees or provide any type of financial security to enable a third party to acquire its shares or shares in its controlling company. For this reason, with leveraged buyouts it is necessary to design structures that do not violate the prohibition on granting financial security. In this respect, both the legislation and the few existing court rulings on matters of this nature (specifically, Madrid Provincial Court Decision of January 9 2007) provide that a merger of the newco and the target, after the acquisition and prior to commencing repayment of the existing debt, is the appropriate procedure to avoid the application of the rules on financial assistance, on the understanding that a merger sufficiently protects the interests of the parties that could be affected by these transactions (mainly shareholders and creditors). For this reason, forward and reverse merger leveraged buyouts have been used almost exclusively in Spain as the mechanisms for carrying out these transactions.

In this respect, Law 3/2009 governs mergers carried out within the framework of a leveraged buyout, specifying the information requirements and calling for a report from an independent expert, so that duly informed creditors and minority shareholders can exercise their rights in the merger process according to the law. In the opinion of most lawyers, Law 3/2009 should be interpreted to mean that a merger precludes the applicability of the Spanish regulations prohibiting the granting of financial assistance.

3.2 Inter-creditor issues

The fact that a number of different financing parties often participate in private equity transactions creates the need for an agreement governing the relationship between all such financing parties and establishing the debt hierarchy. From a legal point of view, it is a question of including mechanisms in the agreements to guarantee that the financing party assuming less risk will receive a lower return than the financing party assuming a higher risk in the transaction. This is not always as simple as it appears, as there are different cases, particularly those related to Spanish insolvency law, in which there can be variations and changes in the hierarchy agreed and accepted by the parties. Consequently, the issues to be considered when recording the debt hierarchy should focus on maintaining the agreed risk–return model. To do this it is common practice to negotiate standstill, cross-default or step-up clauses. In the case of leveraged buyouts, it is usual to add equal ranking, negative pledge or material adverse change clauses or financial convenants to these clauses.

In addition to the issues mentioned above, the provisions of the Insolvency Law (Law 22/2003) need to be taken into account, since the order of payments foreseen in the Insolvency Law may differ from the order stipulated in the agreement between the financing parties to the transaction. To protect the economic model, the order recorded in the agreement must first be made consistent with the legal order and thereafter mechanisms provided to effect an eventual variation. For example, the Insolvency Law considers as subordinate loans those loans made by those related to the debtor, group companies of the debtor and their shareholders being in this category. It is therefore important for the financing parties to look through their portfolios and rule out the risk of becoming subordinate creditors.

3.3 **Syndication**

In transactions that require a large investment it is usual for the debt financing parties to syndicate their loans. To ensure the success of syndicated loans it is essential to guarantee that the system for notifying and adopting resolutions between the agent bank and the rest of the financing parties is appropriate, to avoid undue inefficiency or delays in decision-taking. In this respect, a system requiring majorities for the adoption of specific resolutions that affect all the members of the syndicate of financing parties is in force in Spain. The relatively recent introduction of the majority rule has proven to be more satisfactory than the unanimity rule that prevailed previously and which frequently led to consortiums with a large number of participants being unable to operate. Along with the majority rule, it is crucial that the agent bank should diligently fulfil its duties, in particular, its duty as notification agent.

In addition to the aspects mentioned above, gross-up clauses, clauses relating to the fixing of commissions, unexpected cost increases, supervening illegality, financial covenants and early maturity clauses in the event of a decrease in guarantees, deterioration of the borrower's solvency or cases of cross-default are extremely important.

3.4 **Alternative means of financing**

In addition to the traditional forms of financing for private equity transactions (mainly, either external debt funding by obtaining loans and/or bank credits, which in the larger transactions are structured as senior and mezzanine, or funding contributed by the shareholders of the newco), funding can be obtained in Spain through the issuance of high-yield bonds. They are not very frequent in private equity transactions, partly because the issuance of bonds in Spain is subject to considerable restrictions such as the limitation established by the Spanish Company Law, prohibiting the issuance of bonds for an amount higher than the issuing company's capital plus its reserves. Funding by means of the issuance of high-yield bonds usually delays completion of the funded transaction by several months, although the problem of delays involved in the issuance of bonds is usually solved by a bridging loan from the bank that subsequently handles the issuance and placement of the bonds.

Another form of financing used in Spain is equity loans, which are usually granted by the venture capital companies to their subsidiaries for periods that vary between three and five years. This type of loan is regulated in Royal Decree-Law

7/1996 and is characterised by having a variable interest rate linked to different factors that indicate the company's economic situation (net profit, business turnover or the company's total assets, for example), although it is also customary to establish a fixed interest rate which is generally small. Equity loans are considered by company law to be net assets for the purposes of share capital reductions and liquidations, and in the order of loan priority place the parties making them behind common creditors (ie, as subordinate creditors).

4. Equity structures

4.1 Role of management

Senior members of the management team of the acquired company participate in the target company usually by continuing in a management capacity as members of the board of directors or of the executive committee, as applicable. The managers usually also participate in the company's capital by becoming shareholders, and participate in the taking of decisions by attending the general shareholders' meeting.

Without prejudice to all those clauses common to senior executive contracts, the main contractual clauses relating to the management team are those that impose a non-compete obligation, which may not exceed two years, and a continuance obligation in the event of sale to a third party.

The managers receive a participation in the share capital of the company in exchange for their tangible or intangible contribution. This participation is in excess of their cash contribution because it also includes the managers' know-how, and consists of the acquisition of privileged shares and the granting of either the right to subscribe without a premium at face value, or with a lower premium, or the granting of qualified voting rights for specific matters in the administrative bodies.

Management may also benefit from equity ratchets, vesting systems or stock option plans. The structure of these incentive arrangements will depend in particular on tax issues.

4.2 Common protection for investors

Before a deal is entered into, investors will undertake due diligence. This will help establish the correct price, and once it has been established, the sale and purchase agreement is likely to contain clauses related to financial representations and price adjustment mechanics.

During the life of an investment, the private equity fund investment is protected by specific clauses in shareholders' agreements and the bylaws of the investee company. The main clauses in this respect are: those protecting confidentiality, requiring the consent of the investor before any actions can be taken, setting out pre-emption rights and mechanisms aimed at ensuring their validity (eg, a requirement for a qualified majority for the exclusion of pre-emption rights, the fixing of the price by a third party in the case of disagreement, etc), restrictions imposed on the managers in relation to the free transfer of shares and participations, and pre-emption rights with respect to the distribution of dividends.

When investors exit the company, investor protection is assured by means of several clauses. It is frequent to see preference clauses in a liquidation that operate by creating preferred shares or participations, paid up out of a special reserve, an undertaking to vote in favour of distributing the special reserve following the sale and, in the event of the sale of 100% of the company, an agreement that grants the investor a pre-emption right over the shares being sold. If the sale is to a third party then tag-along and drag-along clauses are usual. If the sale is to the rest of the shareholders, then re-purchase or buy-back clauses are commonplace. Finally, if the exit is by way of an initial public offering then pre-emption rights in the listing, registration rights, temporary restrictions (usually from three to six months) on a future sale of shares, the elimination of restrictions on free transfer and reinforced voting majorities, and the automatic conversion of the preferred shares to common shares are all very common.

4.3 **Common protection for managers**

As protection mechanisms in favour of managers, common clauses are those that establish issues that are confidential or subject to a qualified majority, and the adoption of anti-dilution protections (for example, by granting the managers vetoes or by including qualified majority clauses for decisions on share increases).

With respect to the possibility of an unexpected need for further funding, clauses could be included relating to the issuance of promoted stock, without a premium and on favourable conditions, to the managers. Likewise, preference clauses are usually included with regard to the distribution of dividends, especially if the company's profits exceed certain thresholds. With respect to the managers' exit from the company, there are typically tag-along clauses – although the issues of whether they should be registered and their non-applicability to third parties may raise problems under Spanish law – lock-out clauses and clauses that accelerate vesting if the liquidity event occurs prior to the vesting dates.

4.4 **Management warranties**

The warranties that will be required from the management team by the private equity house when it invests (which will usually appear in the shareholders' agreement) are those necessary to cover any and all risks arising from an incorrect valuation of the company and from any potential contingencies. Consequently, the required warranties are the same as those that are usually included in sale and purchase agreements (covering administrative, labour, tax, environmental, intellectual property, real-estate, contractual and corporate risks, etc). Therefore, the managers will not only be liable for the management of the target company, but also for the management of the acquired company, insofar as it has led to a change in the sale price.

In this respect, in Spain the liability of the management team generally extends for a period of between one and two years after the transaction has been completed, except when liability arises from obligations that are subject to a statute of limitations, in which case the limitation will usually be longer. In any event, the established liability caps are usually standard for this type of transaction.

4.5 Good leaver/bad leaver provisions

Clauses that link the managers' participation in the company's capital to their continuance in the company are usually present in Spanish equity-based incentive schemes. If a manager holding shares leaves the company before the investor has exited, this will give rise to a buy-back right in favour of the company or other shareholders. Voluntary resignation breaching a continuity obligation, fair dismissal and breaches of contract are normally considered bad leaver scenarios, whereas unfair dismissal and leaving because of permanent disability or severe disability will fall within good leaver scenarios. Managers are required to undertake more severe commitments (generally non-compete obligations) in bad leaver scenarios.

4.6 Public-to-private transactions

In Spain it is not usual for private equity funds to make offers for listed companies. In fact, public-to-private transactions were not included in the corporate purposes of venture capital companies until the PEEL. Even though some public-to-private transactions have taken place since the PEEL came into force, such as those involving the companies Recoletos, Amadeus and Cortefiel, these were specific cases, and such transactions are not frequent in Spain, where the natural private equity market is the middle market.

The main aspect to be considered when carrying out a public-to-private transaction is that, under Spanish law, when a company decides to delist its shares, it must launch a buyout bid for the remaining shares within 12 months following the acquisition of the participation unless the bidder owns 90% of the voting rights as a consequence of a previous public offer. This generates the need for a greater degree of transparency and information with respect to the shareholders and competent authorities (in Spain, the CNMV). It is important to include in the purchase agreement clauses relating to break fees, undertakings to launch a takeover bid or non-acceptance of competing takeover bids and, if applicable, clauses that allow the acceptance of a competing bid if it improves on the price of the original bid by an agreed minimum amount, after paying the original bidder a corresponding fee.

5. Exits

Selling to a third party is the most common disinvestment mechanism in Spain, while initial public offerings continue to be a seldom-used exit mechanism. There are basically two reasons: the complexity of and the costs associated with an initial public offering and the difficulties of ensuring a successful exit in an uncertain, immature secondary market. Having said that, where initial public offerings do occur in Spain, the clauses common to this type of process elsewhere are typically used (lock-ups of around six months' duration, elimination of restrictions on majorities and voting rights, conversion of preferred shares into common shares, registration rights, etc).

It was precisely the abovementioned lack of maturity of the secondary market, the regulatory obstacles and, in general, the difficulties of carrying out an initial public offering that were the main reasons that led to the rise of secondary buyouts as an exit mechanism used by market operators with high liquidity and few good investment opportunities. In secondary buyouts the negotiation process and the agreements (between parties with common interests and concerns) are usually simpler and do not contain warranties and representations, or only with regard to strictly delimited and clear areas of responsibility for the seller. The most common exit mechanism continues to be trade sales. The purchaser's knowledge and his capacity to identify risks in the target company and reflect this in the price, result in the fact that the relevant sale and purchase agreements usually also have limited warranties and representations, consistent with the fund's interest in limiting eventual liabilities to the period of its duration.

Finally, even when turnaround transactions should be commonplace in an economic environment such as that prevailing at present, the truth is that the risks arising from the Insolvency Law (principally revocatory actions and the possibility of liability if the judge hearing the insolvency proceedings considers that the transaction is detrimental) result in such transactions seldom being carried out in Spain.

6. Tax

6.1 Taxation of fund structure

Venture capital companies and private equity funds are subject to taxation in accordance with the general corporation tax regime with the special feature that the proceeds generated by the sale of shares/participations in companies in which such private equity entities invest (provided that the transfer is carried out after the commencement of the second year from the moment of acquisition or delisting, up to the 15th year, inclusive), benefit from a partial exemption of 99%. However, the exemption is not applicable when, among other things, the acquiring entity is linked to the venture capital company or is resident in a tax haven.

Transactions to incorporate companies and increase the share capital of those private equity entities that fulfil the criteria in the PEEL are exempt from stamp and transfer tax.

Dividends or any participation in profit received by residents in Spain from promoting companies, irrespective of the size of their shareholding in such companies and the length of time they have possessed such shares, will be subject to a 100% deduction to offset internal double taxation of dividends, or total exemption.

For individuals who are shareholders or entities subject to non-resident income tax without a permanent establishment in Spain, dividends and any participation in profit received from a venture capital company are treated as not obtained in Spain and consequently will not be subject to taxation in Spain (this will not be applicable if the income is received through a country or territory classed as a tax haven).

6.2 Carried interest

A carried interest consists of a share of any profits that the managers of private equity funds receive as compensation, motivating them to work towards improving the fund's performance. If the carried interest consists of remuneration or salary, the person receiving it would be subject to personal income tax. However, if this income (a bonus for example) has been generated over more than two years, only 60% of it is taxable (subject to an overall limit of €300,000 per year), as it would be classed as irregular income.

In contrast, if it is in fact profit on a real investment made by the executive, then a capital gain is generated and is subject to taxation at a maximum rate of 27%.

6.3 Management equity

In the specific case of a free distribution of shares to executives, the distribution will be exempt from tax up to an annual share value of €12,000, provided that the shares are held by the executives for no less than three years, and provided that the offer is made on the same conditions to all employees and the employees, together with their relatives, do not own more than 5% of the share capital of the company or of another related company.

Granting share or stock options to the directors or other employees (including managers as long as they are considered employees) is a more commonly used alternative that could offer certain tax advantages if certain criteria are met. The main tax advantage, in addition to the one explained above, is that the income derived from the exercise of the share options held by the directors or other employees benefits from a reduction of 40% (subject to certain restrictions), making only 60% of it taxable.

6.4 Loan interest

If interest on loans is paid to a credit entity in Spain, it will not be subject to withholding tax. However, if the interest is paid to a non-bank financial institution it will be subject to a withholding tax, subject to what is said below.

If the interest is paid to a non-resident other than a company resident in another member state of the European Union, it will be subject to taxation in accordance with the non-resident income tax regime, at the general rate of 19% (for the tax year 2014, the withholding tax rate is increased to 21%), and tax agreements entered into by Spain with other countries will be applicable, avoiding double taxation.

Interest paid by a company resident in Spanish territory to a company resident in any other member state of the European Union (except Cyprus) will not be subject to withholding tax in Spain.

6.5 Transaction taxes

Acquisition of shares by venture capital companies will be exempt from value added tax (VAT) or transfer tax. However, if the acquired shares are of companies principally linked to real estate, the acquisition could be subject to capital transfer tax (generally at the fixed rate of 7%) or VAT (at the rate of 21%) on the value of the property owned by the target company — depending on the type of the real-estate transaction behind the acquisition of the shares.

If the acquisition relates to a company's assets rather than shares, the transaction would be subject to VAT (at the rate of 21%). If the acquired assets constitute a branch establishment (tangible and intangible assets that constitute an independent economic unit capable of developing a business or professional activity on its own), the transaction would not be subject to VAT.

In any case, if the transaction is subject to VAT, the input VAT paid in the acquisition could be deductible (against output VAT) or refundable (where input VAT exceeds output VAT at the end of the tax period) for the acquirer, if they are an entrepreneur or professional established in Spain for VAT purposes and the acquisition is related to their economic activity. On the other hand, the transfer tax is never deductible for the taxpayer.

7. Current topical issues and trends

According to reports from the Spanish Association of Capital-Risk Entities, 2013 was one of the most difficult years for Spanish venture capital and private equity since the beginning of the economic and financial crisis, even worse than 2009, with a low volume of overall activity in the first half of the year. The situation, though, changed dramatically at the end of the summer.

Investment volume fell by 7.5% in comparison with the previous year, slightly surpassing €2,357 million in 543 transactions. However, 80% of the total investment volume occurred in the second half of the year, highlighting the change in trend. As many as 91% of the transactions were in start-up and growth companies and involved less than €5 million in equity, thereby contributing to the creation of new companies and to the development of small and medium-sized enterprises. It is worth noting that international funds accounted for 70% of the amount invested, and for five major transactions closed during the year in four companies.

With regard to the midmarket, 19 transactions closed throughout 2013 (compared to 28 in 2012 and 42 in 2011), of which 17 were carried out by Spanish operators. Only two international firms carried out transactions in the midmarket. Midmarket transactions accounted for 20% of total investments in 2013. There was a drop in the number of leveraged transactions (from 32 in 2011 to 15 in 2012, and to only 12 transactions in 2013), which reveals that difficulties in securing financing persist.

Growth capital represented 62% of transactions in 2013, and 33% of the total volume. Although investment levels in venture capital remained within the same range as in past years (€208 million invested in 377 transactions), Spanish start-ups are attracting more international venture capital funds and numerous divestments are being carried out by foreign investors.

Fundraising for investments continues to be a priority. Many Spanish investors have disappeared or reduced their contributions, while others now concentrate their contributions abroad, such as pension funds and insurance companies. The total volume of new fund raising in 2013 was €2,274 million, which represents an increase of 11% compared to 2012. Only €633 million was raised nationally, and the remainder (€1,641 million) was raised internationally. Of these €633 million, €155 million came from national public entities, and €478 million was raised from national private investors. This situation will radically change throughout 2014 due to the contribution of a public fund of funds (FOND-ICO Global).

The number of operators in venture capital and private equity having branches and investing in Spain went from 196 registered firms at the beginning of 2013 to 201 by year-end. During these months, 15 firms terminated their operations in Spain and approximately 21 new operators (20 international and one national) entered the market.

Divestments performed well in 2013, reaching a value of €1,564 million in 342 transactions, which represents a 20% increase in value despite a fall of 20% in the number of transactions. The most-used divestment mechanisms were trade sale (38.7% of the total volume), followed by management buy-back (20.5%).

The number of portfolio companies of the 201 operators rose to 2,502, (1,201 without syndicated transactions). The price of these investments at cost is €21,799 million, with an estimated 502,222 jobs created in these companies.

Finally, a bill is currently being passed in the Spanish Parliament to transpose European Parliament and Council Directive 2011/61/EU of June 8 2011 on alternative investment fund managers into Spanish law. This bill will change the current legal framework of the private equity sector. Among other things, it regulates, for the first time, the requirements for marketing shares in private equity funds or other foreign closely-held collective investment schemes in Spain.

Sweden

Jens Bengtsson
Malin Leffler
Roschier

1. Introduction to the Swedish private equity market

1.1 General

The Swedish private equity industry was established more than 30 years ago, influenced by the US and the UK markets, and is today well-developed and mature. It has grown to become of major importance for Swedish society, as the industry represents a significant part of the Swedish economy in terms of contribution to gross domestic product (GDP) and employment. In 1985, Swedish private equity funds managed funds of SKr 1.5 billion in total. In 2013, the number was estimated to have increased to SKr 500 billion (approximately €57 billion), a more than 300-fold increase. Out of the current funds under management, approximately 50% remains to be invested.[1]

In 2013, Swedish private equity funds held investments in more than 850 companies worldwide and out of these, 700 are Swedish.[2] The turnover of Swedish private equity owned portfolio companies amounted to SKr 311 billion in 2011, corresponding to approximately 8.8% of Swedish GDP.[3] Out of the overall contribution to 2011 GDP, buyout-backed portfolio companies contributed the major part – SKr 296 billion (8.4% of GDP) – while venture capital-backed portfolio companies contributed SKr 15 billion in revenue (0.4% of GDP).

Investments made by private equity funds with offices in Sweden remain, in terms of contribution to GDP, well above the European average. In 2012, investments made by Swedish private equity funds represented about 4.82% of GDP, while the average in European countries was 2.64%.[4] When looking at the portfolio companies located in Sweden during the same period, the contribution to Swedish GDP was approximately 6% of GDP, which put Sweden top of European countries in 2012.[5]

---

1   Swedish Private Equity and Venture Capital Association (SVCA), www.svca.se/sv/Om-riskkapital/Om-riskkapital/Fragor-och-svar/.
2   SVCA, www.svca.se/sv/Om-riskkapital/Om-riskkapital/Riskkapital-i-siffror/.
3   SVCA, *Private Equity Performance Study 2012*, 3teb2c1lwdxt239e7o8ayp21cy2.wpengine.netdna-cdn.com/wp-content/uploads/2014/04/PS-2012_FINAL.pdf
4   European Private Equity and Venture Capital Association (EVCA), *2012 Pan-European Private Equity and Venture Capital Activity, Activity Data on Fundraising, Investments and Divestments*, www.evca.eu/media/12067/2012_Pan-European_PEVC_ Activity.pdf.
5   *Ibid*.

1.2 Private equity funds active in Sweden

Some of the largest private equity managers in Europe and some of the most successful private equity managers in the world have their origin in Sweden and/or invest in the Nordic market through investment teams based in Sweden and elsewhere. Among the well-known private equity investors with their origins in Sweden are EQT, Nordic Capital, IK Investment Partners, Altor and Triton.

Some of the well-known international private equity funds with investment teams based in Stockholm are CVC, Permira, Bridgepoint and 3i. Others like KKR, Advent, Cinven and BC Partners cover Sweden and the Nordic region mainly out of London.

(a) EQT Partners

In 1994, EQT Partners was established by Investor AB, AEA Investors, SEB and the senior members of the initial investment team.[6] Today, EQT has 18 offices in 14 countries on three continents. EQT has raised 17 funds in total. At present, EQT owns about 50 companies in a variety of industries with more than 550,000 employees and revenues of approximately €25 billion.[7]

Whereas EQT started off with a focus on buyout investments alone, EQT has since (unlike the other Swedish private equity managers) followed the same route as Blackstone, KKR and a handful of other mainly US private equity managers in branching out its investment operations to include funds targeted at distressed investments, infrastructure investments and mezzanine investments alongside its buyout funds. EQT closed its latest infrastructure vehicle on €1.9 billion.

(b) Nordic Capital

Nordic Capital was founded 1989 in Stockholm when Skandia Life Insurance, the largest insurance company in the Nordic region, and Svenska Handelsbanken, a major Nordic bank, established a joint venture to pursue buyouts.[8] Nordic Capital is at present registered in Jersey but still has an advisory company located in Stockholm, Sweden (among other places).[9]

Currently, Nordic Capital has three funds under management which manage more than €7 million in total, and which have stakes in 26 portfolio companies. Since the establishment of Nordic Capital, eight funds have been raised.

(c) IK Investment Partners

IK Investment Partners (IK) was established in London in 1989 (as Scandinavian Acquisition Capital) by SEB and the senior members of the initial investment team (with a number of other Nordic institutional investors as co-investors). The fund was separated from SEB in 1993 and the investment team has since continued to raise six additional funds backed by Nordic and international institutional investors.[10] IK

---

6 www.eqt.se/Organization/History/.
7 www.eqt.se/About-EQT/Fast-facts/.
8 www.nordiccapital.com/about-us/history.aspx.
9 www.nordiccapital.com/funds/fund-overview.aspx.
10 www.ikinvest.com/ABOUT-IK/HISTORY/.

currently has offices in London, Hamburg, Paris and Stockholm. Currently, IK has €7 billion in fund commitments and has since 1989 acquired 80 companies.[11]

(d) *Altor Equity Partners*

Altor Equity Partners, which formed its first fund in 2003, focuses on Nordic mid-market buyout investments.[12] Today (2014), Altor's three funds have completed investments in over 30 companies and another 30 add-on acquisitions.[13] Altor has offices in Stockholm, Oslo, Helsinki, Copenhagen and Jersey.

(e) *Triton*

Triton was established in 1997 and since then has completed 41 investments. At present, Triton is actively involved in 24 portfolio companies. Triton has offices in Stockholm, London, Jersey, Frankfurt, Luxembourg and Shanghai.[14]

(f) *Other funds with investment teams in Stockholm*

In addition, several international private equity houses, such as CVC Capital Partners, Permira, 3i Group Plc, Bridgepoint, Vitruvian Partners and Axcel have chosen to have local offices in Stockholm. Currently there are similar plans at other large international private equity players.

1.3 Sweden as part of the Nordic market

The Nordic countries (Sweden, Finland, Norway, Denmark, and Iceland) are historically closely related, culturally as well as economically, which has caused the respective legal systems to have many similarities. Within the civil law and the commercial law areas, the countries have had a longstanding tradition of cooperation regarding legislative matters. However, the cooperation was formally terminated when Denmark entered into the European Union in 1973, where it was later joined by Sweden and Finland in 1995. Despite the formal termination of legislative cooperation in these areas, the close relationship between the Nordic countries still remains. This especially applies to Sweden and Finland, which share a 600-year history as one country (they were separated in 1809) and still have very close links. Sweden and Norway were separated in 1905 after a much shorter joint history. The close relationship between the Nordic countries also applies to the Nordic private equity market.

From a global and a European macroeconomic perspective, the Nordic market is generally seen as strong and stable. Sweden in general, and Stockholm in particular, has historically been seen as the economic centre of the region. The largest market within the Nordic region is by far the Swedish market. In terms of deal value, the Swedish market represents approximately half of the total amount of deal volume in the Nordic countries.[15]

---

11 www.ikinvest.com/ABOUT-IK/.
12 www.altor.com/wp-content/uploads/2013/05/Background_to_Altor_Equity_Partners.pdf.
13 www.altor.com/.
14 www.triton-partners.com/about-us/.
15 www.unquote.com/digital_assets/6659/Nordic_Report_2013_lo.pdf.

With the oil and offshore industry booming, however, Norway has during the last few decades also developed into a Nordic economic power centre.

Due to the establishment in Stockholm of the Nordic private equity pioneers, Stockholm has developed into the capital of the Nordic private equity industry. However, domestic private equity funds investing across the Nordic region have developed also in many of the other Nordic countries – CapMan originated in Finland, Herkules and FERD in Norway, and Axcel and Polaris in Denmark.

1.4 General outlook

The availability of bank finance has traditionally been one of the strengths of the Nordic market, which is also true for the Swedish market. The turmoil in the global economy has been challenging for all European countries. However, the Nordic region has been less affected when compared with many other European countries. The financial system in most of the Nordic countries, Iceland excluded, has remained relatively stable and among the Swedish banks there were no failures. Even during the peak of the financial crisis in 2009, at least two of the major banks remained open for business.[16] While, as a result of this, Swedish private equity investments never fully came to a halt,[17] investment activity went into a sharp decline in 2008 and 2009, and after a brief period of recovery in 2010, declined again in 2011. During 2013, the number of Nordic private equity deals amounted to just 61, which shows the slow pace in the market.[18] Nevertheless, there have been a number of high profile private equity transactions in both Sweden and the Nordic region during this period. For instance, in 2011 Nordic Capital announced the €9.6 billion sale of Nycomed,[19] the largest private equity trade sale in Europe and the third largest ever globally.[20]

In 2012, CVC Capital Partners bought Ahlsell for approximately €1.8 billion, the largest Nordic private equity investment that year and one of the largest in Europe. The same year, the largest exit recorded in the Nordic region was EQT's and Investor AB's sale of the remaining division of Swedish healthcare business Gambro Group to Baxter International for SKr 26.5 billion (approximately €3 billion).[21]

One notable divestment during 2013 was Nordic Capital's sale of Permobil for €655 million to Investor AB. In April 2013, Nordic Capital acquired the Danish logistics company Unifeeder from Montagu Private Equity for €400m.

Two notable Nordic deals in the first half of 2014 were CVC Capital Partners' acquisition of the optical chain Synsam Nordic A/S and Volkswagen AG's €6.7 billion public cash offer for Scania AB.

There are again signs of a slow recovery, although the market outlook is still uncertain. There have never been more funds available in private equity funds for investment in the Nordic region and the very large number of private equity

---

16 www.unquote.com/digital_assets/6659/Nordic_Report_2013_lo.pdf.
17 Nyman, Lundgren and Rösiö, *Riskkapital: Private Equity- och venture capital investeringar* (2012), p11.
18 www.unquote.com/digital_assets/7788/Nordic_Report_2014_lo.pdf, p3.
19 www.unquote.com/nordics/official-record/2172262/nordic-capital-et-al-sell-nycomed-spinoff-fougera-usd15bn.
20 www.nordiccapital.com/news/news-listing/nordic-capital-announces-closing-of-the-%E2%82%AC96bn-sale-of-nycomed.aspx.
21 www.unquote.com/digital_assets/6659/Nordic_Report_2013_lo.pdf.

investments made during the period between 2005 and 2008 eventually need to be exited. The stock market has also recovered with a very strong market for initial public offerings (as of mid-2014). Furthermore, the Nordic debt market is open for mergers and acquisitions deals. Since 2012, all the banks in the Nordic countries have been offering finance for private equity investments. Nordic banks continue to be willing to lend very large amounts for individual transactions.

2. Doing private equity deals in Sweden

The Nordic countries are economically and politically one of the world's most stable regions. The workforce is highly educated, most inhabitants speak English fluently and both Sweden and the Nordics have an historical strength in a number of technology-heavy areas, contributing to a steady stream of growth companies reaching the market. This forms an advantageous basis for private equity deals in the region. For Sweden specifically, doing a private equity deal is in general terms not very different from doing a private equity deal in most other mature private equity markets. The same types of structured processes are used, in many cases handled by international investment banks (or domestic banks applying similar standards). Swedish industry and culture is in many ways international and, as with the Nordic region in general, most people are used to and handle the English language well. The transaction documentation generally used is influenced by the documentation used in a UK context. However, there are differences, of which some of the most important are highlighted below.

2.1 A common law model in a civil law country

Documentation used for private equity investments in Sweden is generally influenced by corresponding documentation used in the United Kingdom and the United States, but adjusted to fit the Swedish legal system.

The Swedish legal system is a civil law system. The civil law system has its origin in Roman law and was codified in the Corpus Juris Civilis of Justinian and thereafter developed in continental Europe and throughout other parts of the world. The civil law system was eventually divided into two streams: codified Roman law (for example the French Civil Code of 1804, and its progeny and imitators) and uncodified Roman law (as seen in, for example, Scotland).

In comparison with common law systems, some distinguishing features can be found in civil law systems. Civil law systems are highly systemised and structured, and rely on declarations of broad, general principles.[22] Another distinguishing feature is the existence of comprehensive legislation, often codifying the general principles. Furthermore, the rules of evidence tend to allow for a more contextual and teleological interpretation of the general legislation and of contracts in particular. Naturally, this is reflected in Swedish legal contracts. The contracts are generally shorter and less detailed than the contracts found in common law systems, such as in the United States and the United Kingdom.

Additionally, unlike under the parole evidence rules that apply in most common

---

22   www.mcgill.ca/files/maritimelaw/mixedjur.pdf, p5.

law systems, where it is assumed that the contracting parties have reduced their agreement to the written contract, Swedish legislation provides complementary rules that apply if something is not clear from the agreement. When interpreting the agreement, the parties' intention is of crucial importance. The contract is also interpreted in the light of reasonableness, good faith and good practice.

This means that a UK or US-style document will in most cases and by most Swedish or Nordic parties be found unnecessarily 'heavy', and some of the concepts used under English or US law have no meaning or a different meaning under Swedish law – such as the concept of 'consideration', or the meaning of 'representations' or the use of deeds. Nevertheless, the fact that the transaction documentation is influenced by international markets means that UK and US market participants will recognise the style and terminology of Swedish legal contracts, which makes co-operation and negotiations easier in cross-border transactions.

2.2 Transparency and a cooperative climate

The Swedish business climate is cooperative and consensus-driven. This may partly be explained by the fact that the Swedish market is a relatively small business community where almost everyone knows everyone.

Transparency is strongly promoted in the Swedish legal system and in Swedish society generally. This is shown in a variety of ways. For instance, Swedish companies – irrespective of how they are owned or operated – are required to file annual reports (including their annual accounts) with the authorities, and the annual reports become publicly available. Information about the shareholders of limited companies cannot be kept confidential. Employees of limited liability companies with more than 25 employees are entitled to board representation, and employee representatives on the board have the same rights and obligations as any other director on the board.[23] Many corporate governance experts in Sweden consider this right for employees to board representation as one factor contributing to the success of Swedish industry as, for example, the employees are able to give the board a unique perspective on the operations of the business and since, with full information about the company's financial situation, the employee representatives can take a realistic approach in negotiations between the unions and the company. Transparency is likely to be one of the key factors that has led Swedish unions to have been fairly supportive of the private equity model, at least historically.

Recently, public opinion in Sweden has been less in favour of private equity. The reason mainly lies in public debate over, and criticism levelled against, "taking profits from the welfare system" due to investments in private suppliers of publicly funded welfare services, such as healthcare and education.

---

23 See Act (1987:1245) on Representation on the board for private sector employees (Sw: Lag (1987:1245 om styrelsrepresentation för privatanställda.

2.3 Some practical differences

(a) Disclosure schedules

While disclosure schedules are sometimes used in Swedish mergers and acquisitions transactions, the market practice is that the entire data room (whatever is fairly disclosed therein) is disclosed against the warranties in the sale and purchase agreement.

(b) Tax deeds

So-called tax deeds – a legal document setting out indemnities relating to tax liabilities – are generally not used in Swedish mergers and acquisitions transactions. Instead, tax liabilities will be covered by warranties and indemnities in the sale and purchase agreement and would have to be valid for a claim made within a period of six years in order to fully cover any tax liability. However, that is often difficult to get where the seller is a private equity fund.

(c) Management warranties and questionnaires

The use of management warranties and questionnaires in relation to shareholders' agreements is less common in Swedish transactions as compared with UK practice. If used at all, they are typically 'light'. For example, a commonly applied management warranty in Swedish transactions, if used at all, is that the management warrant that to their knowledge the facts in the due diligence reports produced in connection with the relevant transaction are accurate. When they are used, breach of management warranties and questionnaires are normally linked to a bad leaver provision in the shareholders' agreement.

(d) Taxation of management shareholders

If the management acquires shares on terms more favourable than market value, the benefit will be taxed as employment income in the tax year in which the acquisition takes place. The benefit is calculated as the difference between the fair market value and the purchase price at the acquisition date. The difference will be considered as employment income. The marginal tax rate on employment income amounts to approximately 57%. The benefit is also subject to social security charges of up to 31.42%. A subsequent disposal of the shares is taxed as capital income at a tax rate of 25%. In case of an initial public offering, the capital gain will be taxed with a tax rate of 30%. It should be noted that if the company qualifies as a closely held company the capital gain may be taxed as employment income.

(e) Taxation of leavers and other restrictions

A few years ago, the taxation of leavers was a well-discussed topic within the Swedish private equity industry. The Swedish Tax Authority took the position that a management team member subject to good/bad leaver provisions or transfer restrictions should pay taxes based on the value of the shares at the time of the lifting of restrictions or disposal instead of the value at the time of the acquisition. This meant that the increase in value between the time of the acquisition and the time of the lifting of restrictions/disposal was taxed as employment income, which in conjunction with employee benefits, resulted in a taxation of 86%. However, later court rulings have made it clear that although certain restrictions in shareholders' agreements, such as a prohibition on exercising the shares' voting rights, can have negative tax consequences, leaver and transfer restrictions in line with Swedish market practice have been accepted as not affecting the tax status of the relevant instruments.

3. Some recent market trends

3.1 Few controlled auctions and an increased number of initial public offerings

The financial crisis has resulted in a patchy, two-tier mergers and acquisitions market with an often messy price structure, an uneven path for new controlled auctions, a valuation gap between buyers and sellers, and with few deals leaving the drawing board. Thus, with uncertainty about how successful a broad auction might be and with a risk of getting stuck with a failed deal, the preferred exit route is still (even in 2014) on many occasions a bilateral deal or a limited auction. It is considered by many uncertain whether the mergers and acquisitions market of 2007 with its many controlled auctions with high competitive pressure will ever come back, or if the norm is going to be a more cautious market and approach.

The market for initial public offerings has been slow in Sweden for several years, and the private equity industry has, with very few exceptions, not viewed it as a viable exit route for some time. Although it still remains to be seen whether any initial public offerings will actually result from it, the market sentiment with regard to initial public offerings was clearly more positive during 2013, and during the first half of 2014 the market has picked up speed drastically. However it remains to be seen how long this upturn in the market for initial public offerings will last. One fairly common topic of discussion has been the possibility of including a new long-term anchor investor prior to an initial public offering in order to improve the market's perception of the quality of the asset and the credibility of pricing in the offering, as well as to increase the scope of the private equity investor sell down in the initial public offering.

3.2 Representation and warranties insurance

Partly due to the difficulties and costs involved for private equity funds in giving post-completion protection when selling portfolio companies, the use of representation and warranties insurance has increased significantly in the Nordic markets. Today, many of the insurance brokers active in the field consider Sweden as one of the most developed countries in this area (together with the United Kingdom and Australia).

While representation and warranties insurance has been available for many years, the use of it has only picked up during the last 10 years. The very active mergers and acquisitions market during the boom years and more insurers entering the market have caused pricing to come down, the underwriting process to become better aligned with the mergers and acquisitions process, and terms to become more beneficial to the policyholders, with wider coverage, longer terms and a lower retention.

A normal representation and warranties insurance policy can, in a well-structured setting, be put in place in a week. Very high insurance coverage (up to $1 billion coverage is potentially available) may take considerably longer to arrange.

3.3 Infrastructure investments

The Nordic countries have large energy companies such as E.ON, Fortum and Vattenfall, some of which have been very active in divesting assets. The same applies to other infrastructure-related assets such as gas, trains and harbours. The Nordic infrastructure sector has therefore attracted interest from many Swedish and international private equity funds.

In July 2012, EQT raised more than €1.2 billion for its second infrastructure fund. EQT's first infrastructure fund, backed by limited partnerships such as Pantheon and Skandia, holds a substantial infrastructure portfolio.

4. Taxation of carried interest

During the last few years, tax issues related to the private equity industry have been putting the Swedish private equity market in the limelight in a rather undesirable way. The key issue in terms of taxation is the taxation of carried interest. In tax audits covering almost all of the private equity funds with Swedish offices, the Swedish Tax Authority has reclassified carried interest in traditional private equity structures with a general partner and a separate advisory/management company. The Swedish Tax Authority claims that carried interest is, in substance, a performance-based form of compensation, and has deemed the carried interest to be received by the ultimate beneficiaries (key executives and other employees) after having been routed through the advisory/management company. The advisory/management company is, therefore, according to the Swedish Tax Authority, liable to employer's social security charges on the carried interest. In line with this approach, the Swedish Tax Authority decided that the ultimate beneficiaries (key executives and other employees) were liable to employment tax on the carried interest. The Swedish Tax Authority's reassessments cover several years and tax surcharges are levied on top of the additional taxes/social security charges. The reassessments have been appealed and the parties involved are vigorously contesting this new approach from the Swedish Tax Authority in relation to an industry that has been active in Sweden using the same structures for almost 30 years. In December 2013, the Administrative Court of Appeal in Stockholm overruled the Administrative Court in Stockholm and ruled in favour of the private equity parties. The judgment has, however, been appealed to the Supreme Administrative Court by the Swedish Tax Authority. No leave to appeal has yet been granted. While the final outcome of the tax litigation may not be known for many years yet, the ruling from the Administrative Court of Appeal has brought some cautious optimism to the market. Until the matter is finally settled, there will be a degree of uncertainty in the Swedish private equity market and the long-term effects on the market remain unclear.[24]

In March 2012, the Swedish Ministry of Finance published a policy note,

---

24 www.unquote.com/nordics/analysis/2290402/eqt-tax-ruling-sends-shivers-through-swedish-pe-industry.

suggesting a hybrid taxation model for carried interest where the first SKr 5 million would be taxed as earned income at 57% (excluding social charges), while any excess would be taxed at 30%. The note also commented on the current uncertainty when it comes to the taxation of carried interest. In April 2012 the Ministry of Finance moved to drop the proposal due to massive criticism from the respondents and lack of support from the Parliament on the matter. Depending on the outcome of the court process, new legislative proposals may come in the future with respect to the taxation of carried interest.

5. Fund structuring in Sweden

Most large private equity funds originating in Sweden have adopted commonly used offshore structures, such as Jersey or Guernsey-based limited partnership structures. However, lately there has been a move among private equity funds to go 'onshore' when they set up new funds. This is driven in part by the above-mentioned tax processes relating to carried interest, but also because it is perceived to be beneficial from a media perspective. In practice, however, most large funds in the end still opt for a standard international structure – mainly because that will make it easier to attract international investors.

Sweden has two main legal structures that can be used for establishing domestic private equity funds: Swedish limited liability companies (*aktiebolag*) and Swedish limited partnerships (*kommanditbolag*). Historically, most Swedish private equity funds have been set up in the form of limited liability companies. For such funds, the terms and conditions that are typically found in the limited partnership agreement are instead found in a shareholders' agreement.

Investors in Swedish partnerships and foreign limited partnerships (if regarded as legal persons for Swedish tax purposes and not subject to income tax in their state of residence) can benefit from the Swedish tax participation exemption. Capital gains on interest in partnerships within the European Economic Area (EEA) are exempt from tax if received by a qualifying investor. Dividends on shares held by partnerships are also exempted from tax to the extent that the dividends would have been tax-exempt if received directly by the investor in the partnership.

Normally, this also applies to EEA companies, provided the company has its permanent establishment in Sweden and the company's shares are, for tax purposes, considered as assets in that permanent establishment. Unlisted shares are considered business-related and therefore qualify for the tax exemption. Listed shares are also considered to be business-related, if the company holds (ie, owns) at least 10% of the voting rights or if the shares are held for organisational purposes in the course of business. No minimum holding period is required on sales of unlisted shares, but a one-year holding period is required to qualify for tax exemption of listed shares.

6. The Alternative Investment Funds Managers Directive

In 2009, the European Commission presented the Directive on Alternative Investment Fund Managers (AIFM), with the aim of establishing a common regulatory and supervisory framework for all investment managers of alternative investment funds promoted to investors in the European Union. The directive was implemented in Swedish law in July 2013 through the Alternative Investment Funds Managers Act 2013.[25] This is the first comprehensive regulatory framework covering private equity in Sweden. However, the private equity industry in Sweden has used a variety of domestic and foreign structures and is also involved in a process of reassessment of historical structures, partly for reasons unrelated to the current reforms. This makes it difficult to assess the real impact of the reforms on the industry. Many observers expect that the structures actually employed in future will minimise the practical implications of the reforms on the private equity industry in Sweden.

---

25 Swedish: Lag (2013:561) om förvaltare av alternativa investeringsfonder.

Private equity deals in the United States: separated from the United Kingdom by a common language?

Lillian Lardy
Howard Sobel
Huw Thomas
David J Walker
Latham & Watkins

The modern private equity industry began in the United States during the early 1980s, fuelled by the widespread availability of high-yield financing. The private equity market in the United Kingdom grew rapidly at the same time, helped in part by changes introduced by the Companies Act 1981, which established a 'whitewash procedure' and made it possible (subject to tight controls) for a target company to give security over its assets for the purchase of its shares. It was this change that made leveraged buyouts easier to execute in the United Kingdom (before then, most private equity transactions took the form of equity-only development capital deals). Today, the United States remains the world's largest market for private equity transactions, with the United Kingdom second only to the United States in size. The US and UK private equity markets are becoming increasingly connected, particularly as US private equity sponsors are focused on buyouts of European targets and as some US private equity sponsors have raised European funds. In addition, in the wake of the financial crisis and the collapse of the European collateralised loan obligation market, we have seen increasing use of US bank financing and the US high-yield bond market in European leveraged buyouts. Against the backdrop of this increasing interplay between the US and UK markets, it is important to understand some of the differences and not so obvious similarities between private equity deal terms in the United States and the United Kingdom.

1. **Deal certainty**

Deal certainty (in particular, financing certainty) has historically been one area where US and UK market practice has differed significantly in leveraged acquisition transactions. However, the US market has now arrived at much the same point as the UK market with respect to deal certainty, albeit by a different route. The US position is, in terms of practical effect, very similar to that of the United Kingdom, though it remains quite different contractually.

1.1 Historical evolution of deal protection measures

Whereas UK market practice might once have allowed a sponsor contemplating an acquisition not governed by the Takeover Code to get away with a 'trust us' approach to deal protections and deal certainty, that position was long ago undermined as sellers sought the protections embodied in the Takeover Code for private transactions. The Takeover Code has a requirement for 'certain funds': an offeror may announce a bid only after ensuring that it can fulfil any cash consideration in full. As discussed below, the Takeover Code also generally prohibits many of the deal protection measures that are common in the United States in the context of public acquisitions and, again, sellers have sought to use this certainty on public company deals to their advantage in private transactions. As a consequence, deal protection measures do not have the same relevance in UK deals as they do in the United States. Typically, a purchase agreement in the United Kingdom has required regulatory consents as the only conditions precedent to closing.

The US market, on the other hand, has taken a different and slightly longer course, without the regulatory imperative of the Takeover Code requirement for certain funds. Before 2005 and the beginning of a notable boom cycle in US merger and acquisition activity, neither sellers nor buyers devoted much energy to protecting themselves from the potential for failure to complete a transaction. In the standard deal structure, a private equity buyer created a shell company to contract with the seller, allowing no recourse to the private equity sponsor (there being no third-party beneficiary rights or separate guarantees to support the equity commitment letter delivered by the buyer's shell company). The consequence of this model, in addition to the prevalence of express financing conditions (which make a buyer's obligation to consummate a leveraged acquisition conditional on the receipt of financing), was that all financing risk was assumed by sellers, who accepted such a model because (i) the incidence of failure was extremely low, and (ii) the perception in the seller community was that the lasting reputational risk to a private equity sponsor and/or a bank for failing to close a transaction provided sufficient assurance to a seller that a given transaction would be consummated. So, this resulted in a similar situation to the bygone 'trust us' approach in the United Kingdom, described above.

As the frenzied boom cycle emerged in the United States between 2005 and 2007, sellers found themselves with enhanced bargaining power, given the amount of competition in the marketplace, and began to demand greater contractual protections, including requiring limited guarantees and enforceable equity commitment letters from private equity sponsors, and resisting the inclusion of financing conditions in purchase agreements. To balance the private equity sponsor's need to remain competitive in the marketplace with its desire to cap its exposure for a failed deal, the reverse break-up fee emerged in the United States as the private equity sponsor's primary contractual tool to mitigate deal failure.

In the wake of the 2007–2008 financial crisis (which saw nearly $170 billion in aggregate enterprise value of bidder-initiated deal terminations), a new paradigm evolved in the United States that has further reduced financing conditionality and left private equity sponsors and banks with much less room to terminate transactions due to a financing failure; namely, detailed commitment letters from banks, the absence of financing conditions, a significant reverse break-up fee (payable by a buyer and supported by a sponsor guarantee) for transaction failure due to failure to obtain financing, rigorous obligations on the part of the buyer to obtain debt financing, and 'SunGard' provisions limiting a bank's conditions to funding and specific performance rights. Taken together, these measures make it very painful indeed for a buyer to abandon a deal, and result in a very pronounced level of deal certainty.

1.2 Deal protection measures

(a) Absence of financing conditions

In the United Kingdom, the certain funds concept means that it is very rare for a purchase agreement to include any financing conditions. A UK buyer must, therefore, obtain a binding commitment from a lender for the debt component of the purchase price before signing the purchase agreement, which can take the form either of an interim facility agreement or of a fully formed facility agreement. An equity commitment letter from the private equity sponsor then covers the remainder of the purchase price.

In the United States, while it took longer to arrive at the same point, market pressure to reduce closing conditionality during the 2005–2007 period, followed by an enhanced concern that private equity sponsors would terminate transactions during and after the recent financial collapse, has led to the near extinction of financing conditions in purchase agreements, even in mid-market transactions. Unlike in the United Kingdom, however, definitive debt financing documentation is entered into after the execution of the purchase agreement. As a result, the US market has developed a number of deal protection devices not seen in the United Kingdom.

(b) Debt commitment letters

In the United States, in order to mitigate the additional risk resulting from the fact that definitive debt financing documentation is not executed before the execution of the purchase agreement, private equity buyers will typically negotiate and execute extremely detailed financial commitment letters with lenders, which are delivered to sellers before signing. In addition to setting out all the material terms of the debt financing, the commitment letters frequently refer to precedent debt financing documentation for all other terms that are not specifically included in the commitment letters, which further reduces the uncertainty regarding whether the debt financing documentation will be successfully negotiated during the period between the signing and closing of the purchase agreement.

The language of the conditions in such commitment letters, if drafted skilfully, mirrors that of the underlying purchase agreement completely, meaning that there are no circumstances in which the private equity sponsor is required to close the purchase agreement while the lenders have a condition precedent under the commitment letters enabling them to withhold funding. It is common, for example, for the material adverse change condition in the debt financing commitment to conform virtually word for word to the material adverse change condition in the purchase agreement. This limits the conditions to a lender's funding under the commitment letters and essentially requires the financing sources to take on a level of risk similar to that of the private equity sponsor. Further, the inclusion of a SunGard provision, which limits the representations and warranties to be made by the buyer to the lender under the commitment letter to those that are made by the seller under the purchase agreement (along with limited specified representations that relate only to the buyer), is now widespread in private equity transactions.

The result of the emergence of extremely detailed financing commitments, matching conditionality in purchase agreements and commitment letters and SunGard provisions, is that the US model has come to more closely resemble the UK certain funds approach to financing conditionality.

(c) *Financing covenants*

Private equity buyers in the United States are typically required to give strict and extensive covenants requiring them to use reasonable best efforts, commercially reasonable efforts or some similar variation thereof to satisfy the conditions to the debt commitment letter and to cause the lenders to provide funding under the commitment letters or to sue the lenders if they refuse (and, if necessary, to pursue alternative sources of financing). The seller typically also agrees to cooperate with the buyer's efforts to obtain the financing, including through participating in roadshows and lender meetings, providing information and necessary documents, making available personnel and obtaining legal opinions.

(d) *Reverse break-up fees*

In the absence of financing conditions, US purchase agreements almost universally contain a provision allowing the buyer to pay a fee (known as a reverse break-up fee or a reverse termination fee) to the seller as the seller's or the target company's sole monetary remedy against the buyer in the event that all of the conditions to closing are satisfied or capable of being satisfied, but the buyer is unable to obtain the necessary financing to consummate the transaction. Generally, the private equity sponsor provides a limited guarantee of the shell buyer entity's obligation to pay the reverse break-up fee.

When reverse break-up fees first appeared, they generally mirrored the standard termination fee that was payable by a seller if the seller terminated a purchase agreement to pursue a better proposal (in the range of between approximately 3% and 4% of the equity value of a transaction). Since sponsors resisted the remedy of specific performance, the reverse break-up fee operated as an absolute cap on damages for the buyer. However, as buyers demonstrated their willingness to abandon transactions during the financial crisis and actually to pay the reverse break-up fees, sellers no longer felt that the reverse break-up fee created the proper incentive for a buyer to consummate a transaction. As a result, reverse break-up fees since the financial crisis have been set significantly higher (in the range of between approximately 5% and 7%[1] of transaction value), making it far less likely that a buyer would willingly pay the fee to abandon a transaction.

In recent years, a number of nuanced reverse break-up fee structures have emerged, including the two-tier fee (with a higher fee paid in the event of a wilful breach by the buyer, as opposed to a financing failure) and the hybrid fee (payable for specific situations, such as a financing failure or failure to obtain antitrust approval, otherwise leaving specific performance as an available remedy). As discussed below, it is now common to see a reverse break-up fee coupled with a limited specific performance remedy.

The ubiquity of reverse break-up fees has also led to the emergence of so-called 'Xerox provisions' as a feature of US purchase agreements. Named for their use in the 2009 agreement governing Xerox Corporation's acquisition of Affiliated Computer Services, these provisions are included at the request of the lender and aim to make clear that the buyer's payment of a reverse break-up fee limits any remedies the seller might otherwise have against the lender. Xerox provisions, which are now prevalent in private equity transactions in the United States, are a result of the litigation that many lenders became entangled in following the financial collapse, and lenders' desire to limit future exposure stemming from failed transactions. Xerox provisions refer collectively to the following contractual terms, some or all of which are commonly included in leveraged private equity transactions in the United States: (i) provisions establishing exclusive jurisdiction in New York courts (in lieu of potentially more plaintiff-friendly jurisdictions) and the waiver of the right to jury trial; (ii) provisions specifying that the reverse break-up fee is the seller's sole and exclusive remedy against the lenders (so that lenders do not, counter-intuitively, have greater liability than buyers); and (iii) provisions forbidding the parties from amending such Xerox provisions in a manner adverse to the lenders without their consent, along with a statement that the lenders are express third-party beneficiaries of such provisions.

In the United Kingdom, of course, reverse break-up fees are virtually non-existent, for the simple reason that the certain funds model means that lenders are fully committed at the point at which the purchase agreement is signed and, therefore, there should be no circumstances in which a reverse break-up fee would be payable. At the same time, private equity buyers need to give equity commitment letters covering 100% of the required equity for a deal. This might lead one to believe that private equity buyers in the United Kingdom have more at risk than in the United States, which would be true were it not for the prevalence of specific performance remedies in the United States.

(e) *Specific performance*

In the United States, purchase agreements entered into by private equity buyers before the financial crisis of 2007–2008 typically did not allow the seller to sue the buyer to complete the acquisition (a remedy known as specific performance). Rather, as noted above, the buyer could walk away from a deal by paying a relatively low

---

1   According to Houlihan Lokey's 2012 Transaction Termination Fee Study, published in June 2013, the median reverse break-up fee in 2012 for deals involving financial buyers of public US target companies was 6.1% of transaction value.

reverse break-up fee. Today, however, sellers are not content to rely on a reverse break-up fee and the threat of reputational harm alone to ensure deal completion and commonly require a specific performance provision that allows the seller to sue to force the buyer to complete the transaction (ie, to draw down the equity) if all of the conditions to closing have been satisfied, the debt financing is available and the seller is ready, willing and able to close the transaction. When read in connection with a reverse break-up fee provision, the effect is to ensure that a reverse break-up fee is not a pure option held by the buyer, but is only available to share completion risk in cases where the financing is not available due to the failure of the lender to perform its obligations under the debt commitment letters. To ensure the reverse break-up fee will be paid, the private equity fund will be required to provide a direct guarantee to the buyer. Of course, specific performance is generally available to force the buyer to comply with its other obligations in the agreement, such as to file for regulatory approvals and to use its best efforts to obtain the required financing.

Today, the combination of a reverse termination fee and a limited specific performance construct is the predominant mechanism for allocating risk for financing failures in leveraged acquisitions in the United States. It is critical, however, that the reverse break-up fee and specific performance provisions are drafted unambiguously. Courts in the United States will tend to honour the express intentions of the parties if clearly stated, but a specific performance remedy may not be granted if there is ambiguity in its application or if the provision conflicts with other terms of the acquisition agreement.

In the United Kingdom, equity commitment letters will either expressly permit specific performance or at least not exclude it (although, of course, the remedy of specific performance remains at the court's discretion). Ultimately, these provisions in equity commitment letters and purchase agreements are of little consequence in the UK construct: as stated above, if the debt is available (and a seller will have been shown the certain funds bank commitments), then the private equity sponsor is committed to fund 100% of the required equity commitment and complete the acquisition. Typically, the equity commitment letter will be addressed to the seller or at least give it express third-party rights.

1.3 Go shop and break-up fees

Thus far, we have focused on how the development of US deal certainty measures has brought the US market to much the same position (at least, in terms of practical effect) as the UK market. However, one area where major differences persist is with respect to 'go shop' provisions and break-up fees, which are common in public acquisitions in the United States. The persistence of this particular divergence stems from differences in US and UK corporate law.

Under US corporate law, the directors of a target company have a fiduciary duty to shareholders (often referred to as the board's 'Revlon duties', after a landmark Delaware Supreme Court decision) when selling a company to seek the highest price reasonably available. Although a board is not required to conduct an auction in order to satisfy its Revlon duties, it needs to ensure that the suite of deal protection measures employed in a sale process does not preclude interest from other buyers.

When a board does not conduct a market check before signing a purchase agreement, including a 'go shop' provision in the purchase agreement will enhance the board's ability to satisfy its Revlon duties. A go shop provision in a public merger agreement allows a target to solicit interest from potential buyers for a limited period (usually between 30 and 60 days) after signing a purchase agreement with an initial buyer. Under a go shop provision, if a superior proposal emerges during the go shop period, the board will be entitled to terminate the purchase agreement with the initial buyer, subject to the payment of a reasonable break-up fee. A purchase agreement will contain detailed provisions defining what constitutes a 'superior proposal' and what rights the initial buyer has during the go shop period, including the right to obtain information regarding any superior proposal and the right to match a superior proposal within a set number of days after it is received. Go shop provisions are generally favoured by private equity buyers, who prefer that the target not conduct an auction before they negotiate an agreement. Although fiduciary duties also apply in the private company context, go shop provisions are not used in the United States where the target is a private company.

The amount of the break-up fee payable to the initial buyer (commonly referred to as a 'stalking horse') if the purchase agreement is terminated due to a superior proposal varies. In essence, break-up fees in the United States increase the cost to subsequent buyers of submitting topping bids, because any such bid must exceed the purchase price of the first buyer by at least the amount of the break-up fee. Some agreements employ a two-tier break-up fee, whereby the target company pays one break-up fee if the board approves a superior proposal during the go shop window, and a higher break-up fee if the board approves a superior offer after the go shop window has closed. Courts in the United States have not provided any bright line rules regarding the acceptable size of break-up fees, but have generally stated that they cannot be so large as to preclude superior proposals. Currently, break-up fees generally fall in the range of 3% or 4% of transaction value.

In the United Kingdom, on the other hand, the Takeover Code generally prohibits break-up fees and other 'offer-related arrangements' capable of having a similar financial or economic effect, including 'no shop' provisions and notification undertakings (with limited exceptions available for minimal inducement fees offered to 'white knight' bidders in hostile bid situations or to preferred bidders in formal sale processes, at normally no more than 1% of the transaction value, and payable only if an offer becomes wholly unconditional). For more details see the chapter on public-to-privates.

In addition, public companies and their subsidiaries in the United Kingdom are subject to onerous restrictions on the giving of financial assistance for the acquisition of shares in a public company. Similar to a US board's Revlon duties, a UK target company's directors have a duty to act in a way that they consider would be most likely to promote the success of the company for the benefit of its members as a whole, but they will usually obtain comfort that they have properly discharged this duty from the facts that (i) as a further requirement of the Takeover Code, they will have obtained competent independent advice on any offer (which will usually involve an investment bank carrying out detailed valuation analysis), and (ii) once the offer has been announced, it remains open to competing bidders to make a higher offer.

1.4 Material adverse change conditions

Another key perceived difference between US and UK acquisition agreements is in the area of material adverse change conditions (sometimes referred to as material adverse event conditions), which permit a buyer to walk away from a deal without liability if something catastrophic has happened to the value of the target business between signing and closing. While these are rarely seen in the United Kingdom, purchase agreements in the United States typically include a material adverse change condition.

The definition of material adverse change in a US purchase agreement includes an overall description of forward-looking events that would constitute a material adverse change, along with numerous carve-outs for force majeure-type events, general economic or industry conditions (other than those having a disproportionate effect on the target) and many other exceptions negotiated by the parties. While there is often a longer period in the United States between signing and closing than is seen in the United Kingdom (on account of the need for a 'marketing period' for the buyer to obtain financing), the actual risk that there is a failure of a condition due to a material adverse change is extraordinarily low. Generally speaking, the event causing a material adverse change must significantly threaten the overall earnings potential of a target for a significant duration (ie, years not months). Indeed, no Delaware court has ever found a material adverse change to have occurred.

While the definition of material adverse change itself is fairly standardised, the carve-outs thereto, which explicitly exclude certain events from the definition of a material adverse change, are negotiated and often bespoke to each deal. Frequently, a definition of material adverse change can include between 10 and 15 carve-outs, including changes arising from the announcement of the deal, changes in industry conditions that do not affect the target company disproportionately, acts of terrorism or war, changes in law, changes in economic or political conditions, changes to generally accepted accounting principles, decline in the target company's stock price, failure of the target company to meet projections, actions taken with the consent of the buyer and changes arising from the performance of the purchase agreement itself. Through negotiating an increasing number of these carve-outs to the definition of a material adverse change, sellers have been able to further weaken the effect of the material adverse change condition. At best, some buyers are able to use the threat of invoking a material adverse change to renegotiate the terms of a deal upon the occurrence of certain adverse events. In essence, since there is such a high threshold for a material adverse change condition to be satisfied, the market and systemic risks in the United States are effectively borne by the buyer between signing and closing, as is the case in the United Kingdom.

1.5 Closing conditions.

In the United States, in addition to a material adverse change clause and bring-down provision (see below), there are often a number of additional closing conditions specified in the purchase agreement that one or both parties must satisfy before closing, which are generally precise and limited. Some conditions may be required by law, such as federal antitrust approval under the Hart-Scott Rodino Act. Other common closing conditions include delivery of an officer's certificate by each respective party, compliance with covenants, and receipt of certain third-party consents (if such consents are deemed material enough to the overall transaction).

In the United Kingdom, the market really only allows for mandatory regulatory authorisations to be closing conditions. This is not always the case, and sometimes a purchase agreement will be subject to other conditions, such as those relating to the solvency of the target group, breaches of covenants between signing and closing or specific commercial conditions (such as change of control consents). In general, additional closing conditions for private equity transactions in the United Kingdom are the exception rather than the rule.

2. Indemnification and limitations on liability

While there are notable differences in US and UK market practice as regards representations, warranties, indemnification and limitations of vendor liability, the resulting practical effects, as is the case with the issue of deal certainty, are quite similar.

2.1 Representations and warranties

In contrast with the position in the United Kingdom, where private equity sellers generally only give warranties as to title to the shares in the target company and capacity and authority to enter into the purchase agreement and to sell the shares, representations and warranties given by private equity sellers in the United States tend to be detailed and extensive, covering a wide variety of information about the target company and the assets and liabilities being transferred. Unlike in the United Kingdom, however, where management of the target company is often required to give a full set of warranties (albeit with their liability capped at relatively low amounts), management of the target company in the United States does not provide warranties.

Although it used to be common for buyers in the United States to insist on a so-called '10b-5 representation' (full disclosure representation, named after Rule 10b-5 under the Exchange Act), in addition to the myriad specific representations provided by the seller with respect to the target company, today it is no longer market practice in the United States for sellers to provide this type of representation. In fact, sellers may request the inclusion of an 'anti-sandbagging' provision, which provides that a buyer cannot bring an indemnification claim based on a breach that the buyer was aware of before closing. Buyers resist the anti-sandbagging provision, and it is more common for an agreement to be silent on the point as a compromise, or even include a pro-sandbagging provision (which specifically reserves the buyer's right to bring an indemnification claim for a breach even if the buyer was aware of it before closing). In this respect, the US and UK markets are fairly well aligned but see the chapter on acquisition agreements for the English law position on this subject.

However, in the United States, representations and warranties are typically given on an indemnity basis, meaning that (subject to the agreed limitations of liability, which are discussed below) the buyer may in theory seek compensation for any breach on a dollar-for-dollar basis, unconstrained by common law rules limiting recovery. This is in sharp contrast to the position in the United Kingdom, where warranties will almost never be given on an indemnity basis and are thus categorised as damages claims and subject to common law rules on remoteness of damage and mitigation of loss.

Additionally, in the United States, the representations and warranties made by the seller will typically be repeated ('brought down') at completion. As well as allocating risk and driving disclosure (the two primary functions of the representations and warranties), the representations and warranties in a US purchase agreement act as an additional condition to closing, since the agreement will typically include a condition requiring that the representations and warranties brought down remain true and correct as of closing. The bring down condition is generally made subject to a material adverse change or 'in all material respects' standard (some agreements include a stricter standard for fundamental representations, or a multi-tiered approach treating various representations to different bring down standards), which sets an exceedingly high hurdle for invoking the bring down condition (although an indemnity claim could be brought after closing in the event that a representation was breached). In the United Kingdom, on the other hand, the only warranties that are typically brought down are the fundamental warranties (usually title and capacity, sometimes solvency) and these are rarely linked to a closing condition.

2.2 Disclosure schedule

As in the United Kingdom, the representations and warranties contained in US purchase agreements are qualified by certain disclosures. These are contained in a disclosure schedule to the purchase agreement, which is akin to a disclosure letter delivered by a seller in the United Kingdom (although, unlike in the United Kingdom, a disclosure schedule in a US transaction is incorporated into the definitive purchase agreement). In the United Kingdom there are often very wide general disclosures, including of the entire data room on an auction. Such general disclosures are resisted by buyers in the United States, who insist on specific and extensive disclosures. In the United States, although representations and warranties are brought down at closing, there is not typically any additional disclosure at closing, so changes between signing and closing could give rise to claims for breach (if such changes lead to a representation or warranty no longer being correct). In the United States, in some instances sellers negotiate the right to update disclosure schedules between signing and closing. In such cases, disclosure schedules can typically only be updated to include events arising after the signing date or events of which the seller only obtained knowledge after the signing date. If updated disclosure schedules include facts that constitute a breach of a representation or warranty and such breach results in the failure of the bring-down closing condition, the buyer can choose not to close the transaction. Typically if the buyer does choose to close the transaction regardless of the new information provided in an updated disclosure schedule, it cannot make a claim for breach of a representation or warranty after closing based on the facts included in the updated disclosure schedule.

2.3 Limitations on liability (cap, basket and time)

Both US and UK private equity acquisition agreements typically include cap, 'basket' and per-claim threshold amounts, which operate to limit the seller's liability for breaches of representations and warranties (other than breaches of the fundamental representations and warranties).

There are no real differences in caps, but there are disparities in relation to the 'basket', which sets a threshold amount of losses that must be exceeded in order to seek indemnification from the seller. In the United States, this is most commonly in the form of a 'deductible' basket (whereby the seller is liable only for the excess amount above the threshold); in the United Kingdom a 'tipping' basket (whereby the seller is liable for all losses once the threshold is reached) is more common. However, in the United States, the basket threshold tends to be set at a lower level (1% or less of transaction value) than in the United Kingdom (where the starting point is 1%, but the amount commonly reaches up to 5% of transaction value).

In addition, a per-claim threshold that must be exceeded before a specific claim can be made and count towards the basket is commonly specified in both US and UK acquisition agreements. Again, in the United States this tends to be set at a much lower level (typically as a fixed dollar figure in the tens of thousands) than in the United Kingdom (typically between 0.1 and 1% of the transaction value).

In the United States, to ensure that funds are available to meet any indemnification claim, buyers will typically require a private equity seller to place an amount in escrow as the buyer's sole recourse to cover indemnity claims for the duration of the survival period. Alternatively, a US sponsor may provide a limited guarantee of the seller's indemnification obligations, as the seller entity is typically a shell entity and not independently creditworthy. However, in robust, competitive auctions involving private equity sellers, it is not uncommon for buyers to have no recourse after closing other than for a separate tax indemnity (in this case, sellers still give representations and warranties, which function as closing conditions and for diligence but are not given on an indemnity basis). In the United Kingdom, the refusal of private equity sellers to give anything other than the fundamental warranties means that the availability of funds for indemnification is effectively a non-issue and escrow and guarantee arrangements are extremely rare.

In the United States representations and warranties typically survive for an audit cycle (between 12 and 18 months), but fundamental warranties (title, authorisation, capitalisation) and tax warranties usually have a longer survival period. In the United Kingdom, the position is similar; it would not be unusual for fundamental warranties to be unlimited in time and, for tax, a period of six years is a common starting position.

2.4 Conclusion

In practice, as a result of qualified representations, scheduled disclosures and other limitations on liability, sellers do not face a significantly greater threat of liability in the United States than under UK purchase agreements, where representations and warranties tend to be more limited. Again, while the scope of representations provided in US purchase agreements is broader and the inclusion of a representation bring-down does in theory lead to increased conditionality and less deal certainty, given the qualifiers typically included in seller representations and the difficulty (if not virtual impossibility) of invoking a bring-down clause qualified by an material adverse event standard, there is little practical difference in sellers' exposure to indemnification liability compared to private equity transactions in the United Kingdom.

3. Purchase price adjustments and locked box

The approach to the issue of purchase price adjustments remains a notable difference in UK and US practice in private equity transactions. Whereas there is a preference in UK private equity deals for a 'locked box' mechanism, it is much more common in the United States for a purchase agreement to provide for a purchase price adjustment after closing based on a set of completion accounts and a target level of working capital.

The fundamental difference between these two approaches is the date on which economic risk is transferred from the seller to the buyer. With a locked box mechanism, economic risk is transferred with effect from the locked box date, which offers price certainty before closing and can avoid the expense of calculating adjustments after closing (and any accompanying disputes). Under a completion accounts model, the economic risk is transferred on the closing date. The advantage of the completion accounts model is that the price paid by the buyer, in theory, more accurately captures the value of the business on the closing date. Locked box deals give more certainty to sellers, and it is in part because of the number of private equity secondary sales that locked box pricing mechanisms have taken hold in the UK market.

4. Management equity compensation

As in the United Kingdom, key managers of the target company in US private equity transactions typically receive some form of equity interest in the target company. While the structure of management equity differs between the United States and the United Kingdom, the terms and conditions applicable thereto overlap in most respects. In the United Kingdom, a typical suite of core equity documents would include: an investment or shareholders' agreement, articles of association and employment contracts. In the United States the typical core equity documents would include an equity incentive plan, option agreements (or profits interest agreements), a management shareholders agreement (or management-specific provisions in an limited liability company or partnership agreement) and employment contracts.

4.1 Structure of equity compensation

Management equity in the United States takes two forms. First, key managers will typically be issued 'incentive equity' in the form of stock options in a corporation or profit interests in a limited liability company or limited partnership. The pool of incentive equity reserved for employees is normally granted at the discretion of the target company's board of directors and, generally, the unallocated portion of the pool is not required to be distributed before exit. These incentive equity awards are customarily subject to distinct rights and obligations (as described below) under an equity compensation plan, award agreement, security-holders or similar agreement and/or a limited liability company or partnership agreement, as applicable.

Incentive equity in the United States might be thought of as analogous to the 'sweet equity' that would be allotted to key managers in a UK private equity transaction. The difference is that the UK model relies on managers subscribing a (usually) relatively small amount of cash for shares that have the benefit of the leverage created by the private equity sponsor's subscription for loan notes or preference shares, and any gain realised on those shares on an exit will generally fall within the capital gains tax regime. In addition, UK management is quite often further incentivised by a performance ratchet, which would grant them a greater percentage of the ordinary equity if the private equity sponsor achieves a certain internal rate of return and/or money multiple. This ratchet structure is not employed under the US model. In the United States, managers will usually not pay anything for the stock options or profit interests awarded to them, and any gain realised on options or profits interests may fall within the income or capital gains tax regime depending on, among other things, the classification of the options or profits interests and whether or not certain tax elections (such as a Section 83(b) election) are made. Although incentive equity in the United States may be structured in a myriad of ways with varying tax results to both the managers and the equity issuer, in the most typical structures, recipients of profits interests make Section 83(b) elections more frequently than recipients of options (due to the existence of a safe harbour relating to the tax treatment of certain profits interests), with the result that the eventual gain realised by a manager on options is more often taxed as ordinary income and gain on profits interests is more often taxed as capital gains (subject to certain limits under current US tax law).

The second form of management equity in the United States is 'co-investment equity', which key managers will often be required to purchase (via a rollover of existing target company equity or otherwise). The aggregate amount of such co-investment equity varies from transaction to transaction. It regularly takes the form of post-closing equity in the target company (or a holding company thereof) and consists of shares of stock in a corporation or capital and profits interests in a limited liability company or limited partnership. Such equity typically has rights upon a liquidity event similar to those of the equity owned by the private equity sponsor, but is also subject to distinct rights and obligations (as described below) under a subscription agreement, security-holders and/or limited liability company or partnership agreement, as applicable. Such co-investment equity is very similar to the UK concept of the 'institutional strip' or 'strip', whereby key managers will be required to subscribe for equity and loan notes or preferred shares (in an equivalent strip to the private equity investor) through a rollover of a portion of their gains on any existing target company equity held by them. This highlights the key difference between co-investment equity in the United States and the UK strip, in that, in the United States, the co-investment equity is acquired as ordinary equity only. The private equity investor in the United States would typically not acquire preferred shares or loan notes, as in the United Kingdom.

4.2 Rights and restrictions on equity compensation

(a) *Vesting*

In the United States, incentive equity (which is typically granted for no consideration) only vests upon the achievement of certain conditions, which may include (1) continued employment, (2) annual company performance goals (eg, earnings before interest, taxes, depreciation and amortisation) and (3) private equity sponsor return on exit (eg, multiple of money and/or internal rate of return of investment). Awards that have not vested upon termination of an employee's employment are typically forfeited without consideration. Awards that have vested upon termination are typically retained by the former employee, but remain subject to company and/or sponsor repurchase rights set out in any applicable equity compensation plan, award agreement, security-holders or similar agreement and/or limited liability company or partnership agreement. Accelerated vesting may occur in certain circumstances, such as a change of control, termination by the company without cause within a certain period following a change in control, or death or disability. Again, this contrasts with the position in the United Kingdom, where the concept of vesting is less common. Management's sweet equity is typically subject to a good leaver/bad leaver regime (described below) and sweet equity held by a third class of intermediate leavers will often be subject to a form of time-based value vesting such that a portion of that sweet equity will receive good leaver treatment and a portion will receive bad leaver treatment, depending upon how long the manager has remained with the target company. Further, US style performance vesting is generally not seen in UK private equity transactions.

The second type of management equity in the United States, co-investment equity (which will have been paid for at fair market value, either by rollover or actual cash outlay), is generally not subject to any vesting. Accordingly, it will normally be retained upon termination of employment, but often remain subject to company and/or sponsor repurchase rights set out in the applicable subscription agreement, security-holders or similar agreement and/or limited liability company or partnership agreement. This largely mirrors the UK position for strip in that, historically, strip has been treated differently from sweet equity and not subject to the good leaver/bad leaver regime. There are signs that is changing, however, and compulsory transfer provisions upon cessation of employment (including time-based value vesting for intermediate leavers) are now sometimes being applied to the strip as well as to sweet equity.

(b) *Call rights*

In the United States, both vested incentive equity and co-investment equity are generally subject to call rights upon certain events, including termination of employment, non-permitted transfer and breach of restrictive covenants. Such call rights customarily can be exercised for up to a year or longer by the company or, if not exercised by the company, by the private equity sponsor or other owners of the company. These call rights allow the private equity sponsor to prevent an employee from sharing in the appreciation of the company's equity value following the time when he is no longer involved in the company's success (or has actively engaged in limiting the company's success). As with the UK good leaver/bad leaver regime, the repurchase price often depends on the nature of the triggering event. If termination of employment by the company is without cause (or, in some cases, by the employee for good reason), the repurchase price is typically the fair market value of the repurchased equity. In the event of a termination of employment by the company for cause (or, in many cases, by the employee without good reason or due to any voluntary resignation), non-permitted transfer or breach of restrictive covenants, the repurchase price is typically the lesser of fair market value and original cost.

Call rights in the United Kingdom are substantially similar, save that, as noted above, the compulsory transfer provisions in the United Kingdom have historically not applied to the strip (although this appears to be changing) and these rights are typically only exercisable by the sponsor when an employee leaves the employment of the target company (and for between six and 12 months thereafter). UK investment and shareholders agreements will often include a cross-default provision, which entitles the target company to terminate the manager's employment immediately if he commits (and fails to remedy within a reasonable period, if remediable) any breach of the terms of that agreement or of the target company's articles of association. This has the effect of bringing the circumstances in which a call right can be exercised closer to the practice in the United States.

(c) *Put rights*

While put rights are virtually unheard of in the United Kingdom, key employees in some US private equity transactions may obtain put rights, whereby they are entitled to force the repurchase of their equity awards upon termination of employment or other triggering events. However, put rights are rare and, if contemplated, generally only relate to founders or other senior executives who are significant equity-holders with respect to their co-investment equity.

(d) *Tag-along rights, drag-along rights and exit provisions*

A key concern for managers in both the United Kingdom and the United States relates to their ability to obtain liquidity upon a change in control or other significant disposition of equity by the private equity sponsor. Further, sponsors must have the ability to deliver the equity of a portfolio company (including management equity) to a buyer effectively in connection with a change in control or other significant equity sale. As a result, management equity in both the United Kingdom and the United States is typically subject to tag-along and drag-along rights.

One difference in the United Kingdom is that a UK investment agreement will typically require quite extensive cooperation from a management team to effect any exit proposed by the sponsor.

(e) *Registration rights*

In the United States, management's concerns regarding the liquidity of their equity can also arise in connection with an initial public offering, particularly since there is no requirement under US law for the target company to list the whole class of shares if it undertakes an initial public offering.

As a result, management equity (in particular, co-investment equity) in the United States may have 'piggyback' registration rights in connection with an initial public offering, whereby, to the extent permitted by the underwriters, management is entitled to sell all or a portion of its management equity in the initial public offering (or secondary offerings thereafter). The terms of such registration rights vary greatly, but are customarily limited by any cutback required by the underwriters and a management lock-up, rarely allow management to demand the registration of target company equity, and typically allow a maximum sale equal to the *pro rata* percentage sold by the private equity sponsor in an offering. In some cases, the registration rights are limited to secondary offerings following the initial public offering.

In the United Kingdom, the requirement for the company to list the whole class of shares if it undertakes an initial public offering means that, if there are no contractual restrictions and subject to statutory dealing restrictions, the managers will have complete liquidity following an initial public offering and demand or piggyback rights are simply not required. However, in addition to customary provisions requiring the managers to assist in getting the target company ready for an initial public offering, private equity sponsors will typically seek undertakings from the managers that they will give reasonable lock-up covenants following any initial public offering.

(f) *Transfer restrictions*
Except as described above, managers in the United States are typically only permitted to transfer their management equity to family members and family trusts, and then often only with the consent of the target company's board or similar governing body. Similarly, though it used to be standard in the United Kingdom for managers to be permitted to transfer their equity to family members and family trusts for tax planning purposes, it is now often the case that such transfers are prohibited without the private equity sponsor's consent.

(g) *Restrictive covenants*
In the United Kingdom, it is usually a condition to receiving management equity (specifically, incentive equity) that the manager agrees to restrictive covenants, including non-competition, non-solicitation of employees and customers, and non-disparagement provisions, typically for a duration of one to two years. In the United States, non-competition and non-solicitation restrictions of one to two years are also often implemented. However, in the United States, non-compete and similar restrictions are subject to state law, under which the enforceability of such restrictions varies greatly (and in some states, such as California, non-compete restrictions entered into in connection with management equity awards will generally not be enforceable at all). Accordingly, any provisions implementing such restrictions in the United States must be carefully drafted based on the location of the company's employees and business, choice-of-law considerations and other factors tailored to the particular investment.

5. Conclusion

While there are readily apparent differences in the overall structure and standard contractual terms of private equity transactions in the United Kingdom and the United States, a closer examination reveals that the practical effects on these transactions in the United Kingdom and the United States are nevertheless remarkably similar. A slate of deal protection measures common in the US market ensures that deal certainty there is at comparable levels to the United Kingdom and its certain funds model. Moreover, the potential liability for sellers in the United States remains comparable to that of sellers in the United Kingdom (despite US sellers providing more extensive representations) on account of contractual limitations on liability, qualified representations and reliance on disclosure schedules. Similarly, while management equity granted in the United Kingdom and the United States differs in structure, the terms and conditions thereof largely mirror one another. To be sure, meaningful differences do persist in the UK and US markets, including with respect to purchase price adjustments and break-up fees, and dealmakers and their lawyers must be able to navigate around them. An intricate understating of the structures needed to accomplish the private equity house's commercial objectives is imperative, particularly as the markets continue to evolve.

About the authors

Jens Bengtsson
Partner, Roschier
jens.bengtsson@roschier.com

Jens Bengtsson heads Roschier's Stockholm office, as well as its internationally recognised private equity practice. He specialises in complex cross-border M&A transactions and has extensive experience of leading negotiations and projects for major international private equity sponsors and corporate investors. He joined Roschier as a partner in 2006. He is recognised as one of the leading experts in his field in Sweden by *Chambers Europe*, *Chambers Global*, *Legal 500*, *IFLR1000* and *Who's Who Legal*.

Justin Bickle
Managing director, Oaktree
jbickle@oaktreecapital.com

Justin Bickle is a managing director in the European control investing team at Oaktree in London and a member of that strategy's investment committee. Oaktree currently manages around $93 billion worldwide and is listed on the New York Stock Exchange.

Before joining Oaktree nine years ago, Mr Bickle was a partner in the financial restructuring department of US law firm Cadwalader, Wickersham & Taft LLP, where he specialised in European debt restructurings.

Mr Bickle is a board member of various Oaktree portfolio companies and has responsibility for structuring and executing Oaktree's principal investments across Europe, including those in Ireland.

Mr Bickle is a guest lecturer in distressed investing at London Business School, is chairman of English National Ballet and a trustee and founder supporter of the Creative Industries Federation.

Mr Bickle is a UK solicitor and a law graduate from the University of Exeter.

Jonathan Blake
Head of international funds group, King & Wood Mallesons LLP (formerly SJ Berwin LLP)
jonathan.blake@eu.kwm.com

Jonathan Blake is head of King & Wood Mallesons LLP's (formerly SJ Berwin LLP) international funds group and until May 2012 served for two consecutive three- year terms as the firm's senior partner. He was responsible for negotiating with the (then) Inland Revenue and Department of Trade and Industry the agreed statement and guidelines on the use of limited partnerships as venture capital investment funds. He is a former council member of the British Venture Capital Association (BVCA) and a former chairman for 15 years of the Tax and Legal Committee of the European Venture Capital Association. In 2004 Mr Blake was admitted to the BVCA Hall of Fame in recognition of his contribution to the private equity industry over the past two decades. In 2005 he was named global lawyer of the year for private funds by *The International Who's Who of Business Lawyers*. In 2007 he was admitted to *The Lawyer's Hall of Fame*. In 2011 Mr Blake was named as one of the 100 most influential people in private equity over the last decade by *Private Equity International*.

About the authors

Helen Croke
Partner, Travers Smith
helen.croke@traverssmith.com

Helen Croke trained at Travers Smith, qualified in 2001 and became a partner in 2008. A member of the firm's corporate department, she specialises in UK and international private equity, including acting for institutional investors, investee companies and management.

Gaike Dalenoord
Partner, NautaDutilh
gaike.dalenoord@nautadutilh.com

Gaike Dalenoord specialises in corporate and securities law, with a particular focus on domestic and international private equity. He has broad experience in cross-border mergers, acquisitions and capital markets transactions, acting for private equity firms, banks and corporate clients.

Mr Dalenoord graduated from Groningen University in 1995, joined NautaDutilh in the same year and became a partner in January 2003. He has completed post-doctorates in corporate law and securities law (*cum laude*). He practised at NautaDutilh's offices in Amsterdam and Rotterdam, spent nearly three years at the firm's former offices in Southeast Asia and was managing partner of NautaDutilh's London office for almost five years. At present, Mr Dalenoord leads NautaDutilh's private equity team in Amsterdam and chairs the firm's international strategy committee.

Fernando de las Cuevas
Partner, Gómez-Acebo & Pombo
fcuevas@gomezacebo-pombo.com

Fernando de las Cuevas is a partner in the corporate department and head of mergers and acquisitions at Gómez-Acebo & Pombo, Madrid. He holds an LLM, a bachelor of business science and a diploma in European studies, all from the University of Deusto (1981), a diploma in higher European studies from the College of Europe, Bruges (1982) a research scholarship from the European Free Trade Association, Geneva (1982-1983) and a PIL from Harvard Law School (1990).

He specialises in banking law, securities market law, collective investment institutions, mergers and acquisitions, and family and private equity businesses.

He has led Gómez-Acebo & Pombo teams in a number of corporate transactions, including private and public companies.

Tom Evans
Partner, Latham & Watkins
tom.evans@lw.com

Tom Evans is a partner in the London office of Latham & Watkins. Mr Evans specialises in advising on cross-border mergers and acquisitions, equity financing, arrangements between private equity houses and management teams and joint ventures. He contributed to the previous edition of *Private Equity: A Transactional Analysis* and to *Private Equity Exits: A Practical Analysis* (both published by Globe Law and Business).

Pío García-Escudero
Junior associate, Gómez-Acebo & Pombo
pgarciaescudero@gomezacebo-pombo.com

Pío García-Escudero is a junior associate in the corporate department at Gómez-Acebo & Pombo, Madrid. He holds a law degree and a business administration degree from the *Universidad Pontificia de Comillas* ICADE (2007 and 2008), and took part in an ERASMUS student exchange programme at *Université Paris Dauphine* (2007-2008).

Graham Gibb
Partner, Macfarlanes LLP
graham.gibb@macfarlanes.com

Graham Gibb qualified as a lawyer in 1997 and joined Macfarlanes in 2003 from another major City firm. He became a partner in 2006.

He is a member of the firm's corporate department and has been active in all fields of company and commercial law, including private acquisitions and disposals, public takeovers, joint ventures and public equity offerings.

Barry Griffiths
Partner and head of quantitative research,
Landmark Partners LLC
barry.griffiths@landmarkpartners.com

Barry Griffiths is the partner in charge of quantitative research at Landmark Partners LLC, a private equity secondary group. He is responsible for quantitative analysis for Landmark's private equity and real estate areas, including customer-oriented research, performance analysis, and risk management activities.

Before joining Landmark, Dr Griffiths was head of quantitative research at Goldman Sachs private equity group. Previously he was an aerospace engineer specialising in guidance, navigation and control problems. Dr Griffiths is a chartered financial analyst and holds a PhD from Case Western Reserve University and an MSc and a BSc from Michigan State University.

Chris Hale
Senior partner, Travers Smith
chris.hale@traverssmith.com

Chris Hale is senior partner of Travers Smith and the founding partner of its private equity transactional practice. For the past 20 years he has specialised in UK and international buy-out work, acting for both institutional investors and management teams on investments and divestments, as well as private equity-backed companies on mergers and acquisitions and other corporate matters. He is rated in various legal directories, such as *Chambers Global* and the *Legal 500*, as among the world's leading lawyers in private equity.

Kirstie Hutchinson
Senior counsel, Macfarlanes LLP
kirstie.hutchinson@macfarlanes.com

Kirstie Hutchinson is senior counsel in the banking and finance practice at Macfarlanes LLP, London. She acts for private equity sponsors, corporate borrowers and issuers, senior, subordinated and alternative lenders, lead arrangers, investment funds and distressed debt investors on a range of financing transactions, with an emphasis on all aspects of acquisition and leveraged financing including super senior, bank-bond, high-yield and bridge financing structures.

Ms Hutchinson has more than 10 years' experience of UK, European and global cross-border financings. Her international experience includes working at a leading German law firm in Frankfurt on a number of European market-leading deals.

Elke Janssens
Partner, NautaDutilh
elke.janssens@nautadutilh.com

Elke Janssens focuses on corporate law, public and private M&A and corporate governance issues. Her background in both law and economics is highly valuable in M&A transactions. She advises both listed and unlisted companies and is regularly involved in restructuring transactions.

Ms Janssens received her law degree from the *Vrije Universiteit van Brussel* (VUB) in 1996. In 1998 she obtained an LLM in business law from the *Université Libre de Bruxelles*, followed by a master's in management from VUB in 2001. She also completed coursework in the Solvay Business School's MBA programme in 2006-2007. Ms Janssens was admitted to the Brussels Bar in 1997 and joined NautaDutilh in 1999.

Ms Janssens is the author of numerous publications in the fields of corporate and financial law. She is also a member of the editorial board of various law journals (*T Fin R, RABG, TVS, NV in de praktijk*) and regularly speaks at seminars.

About the authors

Lillian Lardy
Associate, Latham & Watkins
lillian.lardy@lw.com

Lillian Lardy is an associate in Latham & Watkins' New York office. She has a broad practice, representing public and private companies, including private equity firms and strategic investors, in connection with mergers and acquisitions, dispositions, joint ventures, reorganisations and other general corporate matters. She has represented numerous public and private companies and private equity firms in transactions involving a wide range of industries, including telecommunications, pharmaceuticals and energy.

Christopher Lawrence
Partner, Macfarlanes
christopher.lawrence@macfarlanes.com

Christopher Lawrence is a partner in the finance group at Macfarlanes, advising on a broad range of banking transactions.

He leads the firm's acquisition finance practice and advises private equity sponsors, corporate borrowers and mezzanine lenders on acquisition finance transactions, investment grade loan facilities, guarantee and security issues, mezzanine debt and intercreditor issues.

He also advises debtor and creditor stakeholders on restructuring and insolvency transactions and hedge funds and managed account platforms on their derivative, trading and prime brokerage needs.

Malin Leffler
Partner, Roschier
malin.leffler@roschier.com

Malin Leffler heads Roschier's private M&A practice in Sweden. She specialises in complex cross-border M&A transactions and private equity. She has extensive experience in leading negotiations and projects for major domestic and international private equity sponsors and corporate investors. In addition, she also specialises in fund structuring and representing sponsors and institutional investors in connection with fundraisings as well as investments in private equity funds. Ms Leffler is recognised as one of the leading experts in corporate/mergers and acquisitions and private equity in Sweden by *Chambers Europe, Chambers Global, Legal 500, IFLR 1000* and *Who's Who Legal*.

Richard Lever
Partner, King & Wood Mallesons LLP
(formerly SJ Berwin LLP)
richard.lever@eu.kwm.com

Richard Lever has extensive experience in all areas of corporate finance and focuses on advising private equity sponsors, public and private companies, financial institutions in the private equity, consumer and business sectors.

Amy Mahon
Partner, Clifford Chance LLP
amy.mahon@cliffordchance.com

Amy Mahon is a partner in the corporate practice of Clifford Chance and specialises in private equity transactions. She has advised on a range of transactions, including domestic and international leveraged buy-outs, divestments, consortium transactions and minority investments, and has acted for financial sponsors, including private equity houses, infrastructure funds and investment banks. She is a member of the BVCA Legal and Technical Committee.

Maud Manon
Partner, DLA Piper
maud.manon@dlapiper.com

A graduate of the HEC Paris School of Management, Maud Manon also holds a postgraduate degree in business law from the University of Paris XI Sceaux.

Her practice focuses primarily on leverage

acquisition finance, representing financial institutions (senior (banks or debt funds) and/or mezzanine lenders) as well as sponsors.

Ms Manon began her career in 1998 at White & Case in Paris, before joining the finance team of Ashurst Morris Crisp. In 2001 she joined Linklaters, where she spent five years in the finance team, before becoming counsel at Latham & Watkins in 2006. She joined Frieh & Associés as a partner in September 2009. Ms Manon joined DLA Piper in October 2012.

Her expertise covers the financing of the acquisition of listed companies and corporate syndicated loans. She also advises debtors, creditors and/or sponsors in the context of debt restructuring operations.

Charles Martin
Partner, Macfarlanes LLP
charles.martin@macfarlanes.com

Charles Martin joined the firm in 1983, and became a partner in 1990 and senior partner in 2008. He works principally in mergers and acquisitions and private equity, acting for sponsors and corporates. Much of his work is cross-border in nature.

Mr Martin is rated in the top tiers of the most highly recommended M&A and private equity lawyers in the United Kingdom by the leading directories, including Chambers. Clients look to him particularly for strategic counsel and tactical input on a wide variety of legal matters, including M&A negotiations and litigation.

Recent highlights include advising Verizon Communications Inc on its acquisition of Vodafone's interest in Verizon Wireless for $130 billion, Brit Insurance NV on a recommended $1.3 billion cash offer by Apollo and CVC, and the independent directors of TNK-bp in relation to a proposed transaction with Rosneft.

He was named Law Firm Leader of the Year at the *Legal Week* British Legal Awards 2013.

Xavier Norlain
Partner, DLA Piper
xavier.norlain@dlapiper.com

Xavier Norlain leads the corporate practice group of DLA Piper in Paris. Specialising in mergers and acquisitions, he advises numerous investment funds on leveraged buy-outs, venture capital and development capital transactions, as well as industrial or service groups on their equity finance operations, restructuring and external growth transactions. He also advises managers on the definition of their status and their remuneration, as well as in the context of operations associating them with investment funds.

Before joining DLA Piper, Mr Norlain was an associate in the Paris and New York offices of Willkie Farr & Gallagher, counsel at Latham & Watkins and then a partner at Frieh Bouhénic.

Before becoming a lawyer, Mr Norlain worked as a market analyser at Aerospatiale and as a consultant with KPMG Peat Marwick, a strategy and organisation consultancy firm.

Benedict Nwaeke
Senior associate, Latham & Watkins
benedict.nwaeke@lw.com

Benedict Nwaeke is a senior associate at Latham & Watkins and specialises in advising on cross-border mergers and acquisitions and private equity transactions, as well as restructurings and general corporate matters.

Raimondo Premonte
Partner, Gianni Origoni Grippo Cappelli & Partners
rpremonte@gop.it

Raimondo Premonte specialises in M&A, private equity and corporate law, being involved in some of the major transactions concerning Italian and foreign listed companies in the last years. He joined Gianni, Origoni, Grippo, Cappelli & Partners in 1995, becoming partner in 2005. From 2000 to

About the authors

2003 Mr Premonte was a senior associate in the New York office of Linklaters, and also a sessional lecturer in corporate law, New York University Faculty of Law. Mr Premonte is currently resident partner in the London office and head of the corporate finance and private equity team.

After graduating in law from the University of Rome in 1992, he attended the visiting scholar and research fellow programme at Columbia University Law School. Mr Premonte is recognised as leading lawyer by Chambers.

Lorraine Robinson
Consultant solicitor, King & Wood Mallesons LLP (formerly SJ Berwin LLP)
Lorraine.robinson@eu.kwm.com

Lorraine Robinson joined King & Wood Mallesons LLP (formerly SJ Berwin LLP) in 1996 and qualified into the firm's international funds group in 1998 after completing her training contract. She has been involved in venture capital and development capital investments, management buy-outs and general M&A work, as well as working on the structuring and establishment of numerous private equity investment funds. She also acts for investors on their investment into private equity funds. She is now a consultant solicitor to the international funds group.

Donato Romano
Senior associate, Gianni Origoni Grippo Cappelli & Partners
dromano@gop.it

After graduating in law *maxima cum laude* from the University *La Sapienza*, Rome in 2004, Donato Romano obtained a JD *maxima cum laude* from the same university in 2006. He obtained an LLM in international business law from University College, University of London in 2008.

Before joining Gianni, Origoni, Grippo, Cappelli & Partners in 2009 Mr Romano worked for a leading international law firm. He speaks Italian, English, French and Spanish.

Kathleen Russ
Partner, Travers Smith
kathleen.russ@traverssmith.com

Kathleen Russ is head of the tax department and has been a partner since 2001. She specialises in private equity transactions, regularly acting for founders, management teams and institutional investors.

Ms Russ has been a member of the BVCA Tax Committee since 2002 and is regularly involved in discussions with Her Majesty's Revenue and Customs on the BVCA's behalf. She is also a frequent speaker at conferences.

Jeremy Scemama
Partner, DLA Piper
jeremy.scemama@dlapiper.com

Jeremy Scemama holds a postgraduate degree in international law – international commerce from the University of Paris II Panthéon-Assas.

From 2000 to 2008 he practised law in the Paris and New York offices of Willkie Farr & Gallagher, where he mainly specialised in public M&A transactions. He joined Frieh & Associés as a partner in April 2008 and DLA Piper in October 2012.

Mr Scemama has advised industrial groups and investment funds on a large number of transfers, acquisitions and mergers of listed companies (by means of cash tender offers, exchange tender offers, buy-out offers, squeeze outs or standing market offers) or minority interest acquisitions.

He has also acted as adviser on numerous initial public offerings and issuance of financial instruments through a public offering or private placement, either for the issuer or for the bank underwriter. Mr Scemama is also active in private equity transactions.

Georg Schneider
Partner, Noerr LLP
georg.schneider@noerr.com

Georg Schneider is a partner at continental European law firm Noerr LLP. He heads the firm's private equity group. Mr Schneider advises German and foreign clients with respect to private equity/venture capital investments, the legal and tax structuring of private equity funds, management compensation systems and M&A transactions. In addition, he is a member of numerous supervisory boards. He joined Noerr in 1996 and became a partner in 2002, having spent 2000 in London working on leveraged buy-out transactions and fund formation.

He is recognised by various directories such as *Chambers Europe*, *JuVe*, *Legal 500* and *Practical Law Company* as a leading lawyer for private equity, and was ranked by *Best Lawyers* as a Best Lawyer Germany 2014 for private equity.

Howard Sobel
Partner, Latham & Watkins
howard.sobel@lw.com

Howard Sobel is a partner in the New York office of Latham & Watkins. Mr Sobel's practice focuses primarily on the representation of private equity firms in leveraged acquisitions of privately held and public companies, including going private transactions, co-investment opportunities and acquisitions and reorganisations in bankruptcy proceedings. Mr Sobel has also represented major public corporations and investment banking firms in a spectrum of transactions that includes numerous mergers and acquisitions (including highly structured leveraged buy-outs), international joint ventures, equity offerings, Section 144A offerings of high-yield securities and general corporate matters. He also advises officers and directors with respect to fiduciary matters.

Rüdiger Stucke
Director and head of quantitative research, Warburg Pincus LLC
ruediger.stucke@warburgpincus.com

Rüdiger Stucke is a director and head of quantitative research at Warburg Pincus in New York. Before joining Warburg Pincus, Dr Stucke was a quantitative researcher on private equity for almost 10 years, the last seven of which were at Oxford University's Saïd Business School. Dr Stucke holds a PhD in finance (*summa cum laude*) from Paderborn University, where he previously received an MSc and a BSc (*summa cum laude*) in economics, business administration and computer science.

Huw Thomas
Associate, Latham & Watkins
huw.thomas@lw.com

Huw Thomas is an associate in Latham & Watkins' London office and focuses on mergers and acquisitions, private equity, joint ventures, corporate restructurings and general corporate matters. Mr Thomas has provided legal advice to financial institutions and corporates across a wide range of industry sectors and has particular experience in the energy, infrastructure and financial services sectors.

Guillaume Valois
Partner, DLA Piper
guillaume.valois@dlapiper.com

Guillaume Valois holds postgraduate degrees in tax law and European tax law from the University of Burgundy.

He began his career in 1998 at Clifford Chance, where he practised in Paris and London, before joining the Paris office of Weil Gotshal & Manges in 2005. He joined Frieh Bouhenic in July 2012 and DLA Piper in October 2012.

Mr Valois has strong expertise in domestic and cross-border M&A transactions and group reorganisations (in particular, acquisitions, mergers, leveraged buy-outs and joint ventures). He advises investment funds and companies, as well as managers and individuals.

He also has expertise on the tax structuring of real estate investments and serves French real estate investment trusts and management companies of real estate investment funds. He deals with dispute resolutions, tax structuring of distressed M&A transactions (debt and equity restructuring), and complex individual matters.

David Walker
Partner, Latham & Watkins
david.walker@lw.com

David Walker is a partner at Latham & Watkins, and co-chair of the global private equity practice. He has more than 20 years' experience acting on all forms of private equity transaction, from venture and development capital to large UK and international leveraged buy-outs, infrastructure investments, equity raisings and divestments. He is the editor of *Private Equity Exits: A Practical Analysis* (Globe Law and Business).

Margaretha Wilkenhuysen
Partner, NautaDutilh
greet.wilkenhuysen@nautadutilh.com

Margaretha Wilkenhuysen is a partner in our Luxembourg corporate practice. She specialises in cross-border transactions. She holds a law degree from the University of Leuven (1991), a master's in business and tax law from the *Université Libre de Bruxelles* (1993) and an LLM from Duke Law School (1996).

Ms Wilkenhuysen has published various books and articles. She contributed to the Luxembourg sections of *Capital Directive* (Cambridge University Press, 2014) and *Corporate Governance Review* (Law Business Research, 2013).

For four consecutive years (2011-2014) Ms Wilkenhuysen has been nominated as a Leading Lawyer by *IFLR 1000*, and was recommended by *Legal 500* in its 2013 edition. She is admitted to the Brussels Bar and the Luxembourg Bar.